An Abstract of

North Carolina Wills

FROM ABOUT 1760 TO ABOUT 1800.

SUPPLEMENTING GRIMES' ABSTRACT OF NORTH CAROLINA WILLS 1663 TO 1760.

————:.:————

Prepared from the originals and other data by

FRED A. OLDS

CLEARFIELD

Originally published
Oxford, 1925

Reprinted
Southern Book Company
Baltimore, Maryland
1954

Reissued
Genealogical Publishing Co., Inc.
Baltimore, Maryland
1965, 1968, 1972, 1978, 1983

Reprinted for
Clearfield Company, Inc. by
Genealogical Publishing Co., Inc.
Baltimore, Maryland
1994, 1996, 1998, 2001

Library of Congress Catalogue Card Number 65-20634
International Standard Book Number: 0-8063-0268-2

Made in the United States of America

Publisher's Note

This is a reprint of a copy of the original edition of 1925, which was kindly loaned to us by the National Society, Daughters of the American Revolution. Manuscript corrections were made in this copy from time to time by various people. We cannot, however, vouch for the validity of these corrections.

INDEX TO COUNTIES

THE NORTH CAROLINA WILLS

In 1906 the late Secretary of State J. Bryan Grimes published a very valuable book containing abstracts of the "State Wills," as they are called; that is to say the wills during the period between 1663 and 1760, when it was required that all should be filed in the office of the secretary of the Province of North Carolina. After 1760 it was permitted to have the wills in the counties.

A request has arisen for a book covering abstracts of wills to 1800, from 1760, and this volume is the answer to it; an answer made under innumerable difficulties. This 40-year period covers the last 15 years of the Provincial Period, the 8 years of the war of the Revolution, 1775-1783, and the 17 years after the Revolution. A good many wills of date prior to 1760 will be found in the book, there having been failure to send these to the secretary of the Province.

The losses of original wills have been great. It was said in 1752 that many court documents had then been lost. Frequent changes in the location of the seat of government contributed to those losses, but fires caused a great percentage.

Of the present 100 counties 32 existed in 1775, when British rule and the Provincial or Colonial system ended with the flight in June of Governor Josiah Martin. Between 1775 and 1800 there were formed 28 counties, three of these in the closing days of 1799, namely Ashe, Greene and Washington. Thus the total number when 1800 began was 60, as follows:

Anson, 1749, Ashe, 1799, Beaufort, 1705, Bertie, 1722, Bladen, 1735, Brunswick, 1764, Buncombe, 1792, Burke, 1777, Cabarrus, 1792, Camden, 1777, Carteret, 1722, Caswell. 1777, Chatham, 1771, Chowan, 1672, Craven, 1712, Cumberland, 1754, Currituck, 1672, Duplin, 1749, Edgecombe, 1741, Franklin, 1778, Gates, 1778, Granville, 1746, Greene 1799, Guilford, 1771, Halifax, 1758, Hertford, 1759, Hyde, 1705, Iredell, 1788, Johnston, 1746, Jones, 1778, Lenoir, 1791, Lincoln, 1779, Martin, 1774, Mecklenburg, 1762, Montgomery, 1779, Moore, 1784, Nash, 1777, New Hanover, 1729, Northampton, 1741, Onslow, 1734, Orange, 1752, Pasquotank, 1672, Perquimans, 1672, Person, 1791, Pitt, 1760, Randolph, 1779, Richmond, 1779, Robeson, 1787, Rockingham, 1785, Rowan, 1753, Rutherford, 1779, Sampson, 1784, Stokes, 1789, Surry, 1771, Tyrrell, 1729, Wake, 1771, Warren, 1779, Washington, 1799, Wayne, 1779, Wilkes, 1777.

The courthouses of the following counties have been burned: Anson (1868); Bladen (1800 and 1893); Buncombe (1830 and 1835); Cabarrus (1874); Currituck (1842); Greene (1876); Guilford (1872); Hertford (1832 and 1862); Iredell (1854); Jones (1862); Lenoir (1878); Martin (1884); Montgomery (1835); Moore (1889); New Hanover (1798, 1819 and 1840); Orange (1789); Pasquotank (1862); Pitt (1857); Rockingham (1906); Rutherford (1857); Sampson (1921); Washington (1862, 1869 and 1873); a total of 29 fires.

Most wills are carried only in the will books, the originals having ceased to exist. Of the will books, many have been lost. Taking certain counties as examples, the will books begin as follows: Buncombe, 1831; Burke, 1865; Cabarrus, 1828; Camden, 1815; Chatham, 1798; Granville, 1772; Greene, 1868; Guilford, 1799; Hertford, 1830; Iredell, 1807; Lenoir, 1878; Montgomery, 1843; Moore, 1794; New Hanover, 1798; Onslow, 1784; Pitt, 1858; Rockingham, 1814.

In some cases only the year of the probate appears; in some the year and the month, and in some the year, month and day. The County Court met four times a year. In some cases there is no date of probate given in the records, and in such cases there is nothing else to do but set down the date of the will. Great carelessness occured in probating and also in recording wills. In a few cases some wills are recorded in the office of the Register of Deeds and others in the Clerk's office.

There are many errors in the spelling, not only of family but of Christian names, and so far as possible these errors have been corrected. Not a few of these errors are due to the transcribers of the wills. As far as possible, the original wills have been used in making these abstracts, but only a small portion of the originals now exist.

ANSON COUNTY—WILLS

A.

1760 ARMSTRONG, JAMES, William, Martin, James, Joseph, Benjamin, Mary and Matthew.

1780 AULD, JAMES, Rosanna (wife); John, Michael, Ann, Mary and Elizabeth.

1789 AULD, MICHAEL, Sedney (wife); John and Ann; Mary and Elizabeth (sisters); Rosanna (mother).

1802 ADCOCK, HENRY, Wife (not named); John, Thomas, Henry, James, Eleanor, Mary and Sapphira.

B.

1785 BLACKFORD, SAMUEL, Rachel (wife); Matthew, Keziah, Sarah, Ruth and Manning.

1783 BENNETT, JAMES, Wife (not named); John, James, Silas and Minard.

1790 BLEWETT, WILLIAM, Elizabeth (wife); Thomas, William, Eli, David, James and Morris.

1802 BALEY, (BAILEY), THOMAS, Jenny (wife); John, Sally, Jacob, William, Katie, Polly and James; Elizabeth Hildreth and Milly Plunkett (daughters).

1798 BUCHANAN, BENJAMIN, Judah (wife); Benjamin, William, Mary, Joseph, John, Delphia and Henry; May Chapman and Judith Pace (daughters). *Mary m. Chapman; May is son See will in File Case.*

C.

1754 COBURN, JOHN, Samuel, Jonathan, Jacob and Isaac (brothers); Jacob, Rebecca, Sarah and Mary (sisters).

1782 CLEMENTS, MATTHEW, Mary (wife).

1788 COLSON, JOSEPH, Mary (wife); Joseph, Susanna, John, Mary, Charity, Phereba, Nellie, Jacob, Thomas, Martha and Sanders.

1790 CLARK, CHRISTOPHER, Joseph and Francis; Ann Moorman, Agnes Hardon and Mary Stitt (daughters).

1791 COLSON, JOHN, Margaret (wife); Mary; Mary Colson and John Colson (grandchildren).

1792 CURTIS, FRANCES, Anna and Nathaniel; John and William Hamer (sons by a former marriage); Frances Hamer (daughter by a former marriage).

1795 CLARK, BEVERLY, Carey (wife); John, Benjamin, Lucy, Robert, and Polly; Ann Hamer (daughter).

1797 CLARK, CORNELIUS, Sarah (wife); children (not named).

1799 CORTNEY (Courtney), JOHN, Mary (wife); Sarah, Emanuel, Peggy, John and Stephen; Rebecca Pale (daughter).

D.

1786 DAVIS, CHRISTOPHER, Mary (wife); Arthur, Thomas, John, Lewis and Elizabeth; Sarah Benton, Mary Baker and Dicey Brazzill (daughters).

1790 DUNHAM, JOSEPH, Wife (not named); Lucretia Seago (daughter) and her daughter Mary.

E

1793 EDWARDS, NATHANIEL, Isaac, Joshua and Nathaniel.

1792 EDGEWORTH, RICHARD, Elizabeth (wife); Lovell and Sneyd.

1700 EDWARDS, DANIEL, Susanna (wife); Daniel, William, Nancy and Sidnett (Sidney).

F

1761 FERGUSON, DAVID, wife (not named), Mary F. Jane, Elizabeth and Sarah (sisters).

1791 FINNEY, THOMAS, Cherry (wife), John.

1791 FALKNER, BENJAMIN, Elizabeth (wife); John and Henry.

1799 FIELDS, J. SMITH, Elizabeth (wife); James, John, Micajah, Celia and Elizabeth.

1792 FLAKE, SAMUEL, Abbie (wife); Elijah, Thomas, Samuel, Jarders, Mary, Elizabeth, Jemima and Sarah.

G

1766 GILES, JOHN, Mary (wife).

1790 GALEWOOD, ROBERT, Gabriel, Thomas, Griffin, Lucy, Polly and Sally.

1802 GRANADE, MARTIN, Susanna (wife); Eliza Thurman and Nancy Thurman (daughters); Benjamin Granade (nephew).

H

1754 HOUGH, RICHARD, Martha (wife); William, Thomas and Richard; Hannah Crabbe and Elizabeth Sharpe (daughters).

1760 HICKS, JOHN, Obedience (wife); William, John, Frances, Mary and Sarah.

1774 HUSBANDS, JOHN, Tabitha (wife); Children (not named).

1793 HOGAN, JAMES, Silence (wife); David, Elijah, William, James, Griffin and Edmund; Elizabeth Pyle, Nannie Lee and Sarah Pyle (daughters).

1796 HARRINGTON, CHARLES, Bena (wife); Charles, Sukey, John, William and Whitmel; Nancy Carroll, Mary Stegall and Nelly Hudson (daughters).

1781 HAYMES, JOHN, Ruth (wife); William; Netty Hancock and Charity Thomas (daughters).

1803 HOGAN, SILENCE, Nancy.

I.

1775 INGRAM, GEORGE, John, Tabitha, Jesse and Nancy.

J.

1794 JACKSON, JOHN, Wife (not named); Rebecca, Isaac, Samuel and Jonathan; Sarah Stansill, Huldah Hill, Mary White and Elizabeth White (daughters).

1786 JOHNSON, WILLIAM, Wife (not named); Hugh, Mary Ann, William, Daniel, Malcolm and James; Katherine Kennedy (daughter).

1772 JACKSON, JOHN, Elizabeth, Mary, Sarah, Rebecca, Phoebe, Jemima and Hannah.

K.

1799 KNOTTS, JOHN, SR. Wife (not named); Ann, Absalom and Susanna.

L.

1766 LEE, ROBERT, Sarah (wife); William, Judith, Richard, James, Robert, John, Elizabeth and Millie; Mary Yarborough (daughter).

1753 LOVE, WILLIAM, Father (not named).

1793 LACY, THOMAS, Keziah (wife); Mary, Sarah, Stephen, Thomas, Elizabeth, Lucretia, Anna, Griffith and Jesse.

1794 LEWIS, JEREMIAH, Sarah (wife); Thomas, Jeremiah and Martha.

1797 LOWRY, PETER, Mary (wife); Eli and William.

1778 LEE, JOHN, Elizabeth (wife); Richard, Anthony, John and Elizabeth.

1789 LANIER, SAMPSON, Elizabeth (wife); James.

1792 LITTLE, JAMES, Nancy (wife); James, Hosea, Agnes and Sarah.

M.

1754 McDOWELL, CHARLES, Rachel (wife); John; Rachel Eagan (daughter); Joseph McDowell (brother); Ann Evans, Elizabeth Barnes, Mary McPeters and Hannah Calloe, (daughters).

1760 McCONNELL, ALEXANDER, Catherine (wife); Agnes.

1760 MOORE, JOHN, Mary (wife); Moses Moore (nephew).

1774 MEADORS, JASON, Elizabeth (wife); Lewis, Thomas, Jason, Jcb and Maria.

1773 McLEOD, JANET, Norman McLeod (brother).

1774 MORRIS, CHARLES, Elizabeth (wife).

1778 McPHERSON, PRISCILLA, Shadrach Denson (son by a former marriage).

1784 McCLENDON, JOHN, Ann, Dennis, Sarah, Rebecca and Simon.

1785 MEREDITH, JAMES, Elizabeth (wife); Sanders (son).

1787 MARTIN, JOSEPH, Catherine (wife); Jesse, Nancy and John.

1793 MARTIN, WILLIAM, Rebecca (wife); Sarah, Nancy, William, Abraham, Katherine, Lewis, Andrew and Isaac.

1794 McGREGOR, JOHN, Mary (wife); William, Elizabeth and Flowers; Sarah Williams, Frances Standifer, Cynthia Standifer and Jean Brown (daughters).

1798 MEDCALF (Metcalf), WILLIAM, Amelia (wife); William, Anne, Emanuel and Joel.

1798 MOORMAN, BENJAMIN, William, Michael and Benjamin.

O.

1792 ODUM, RICHARD, Honour (wife); William, Nancy, James, Isaac, Jacob, David and Richard; Lucy Fair and Elizabeth Franklin daughters).

P.

1777 PRESSLER, JOHN, Mary (wife); John, Elias, Anthony, Levi, Susanna and Morgan; Elizabeth Maness, Ann Nunnally and Mary Basley (daughters).

1790 PROCTOR, JOHN, Lenny (wife); William and Sterling.

1793 PURYMAN, MILTON, Mary, John, Sarah and Mumford (brothers and sisters).

1798 PICKETT, JAMES, Martha (wife); Joseph, William, Frankey, Hannah and Martin; Mary Robards (daughter).

R.

1777 RATLIFF, WILLIAM, Susan (wife); Thomas, James, John, Robert, Zachariah and William.

1777 RYLE, JOHN, Wife (not named); James, John, Elizabeth, Mary and Larkin.

1781 ROPER, JAMES, Wife (not named); Martha, Lucy, Mary, William, Susanna and Green.

1793 ROSS, HUGH, Margaret (wife); Donald Hugh, Mary, Jean and Katherine; Margaret Campbell (daughter).

1799 ROGERS, JOB, Wife (not named); Job, Thomas, Mark, Sarah and Keziah.

1797 ROBERTSON, DRURY, Amy (wife); Nathaniel and other children (not named).

S.

1751 SMITH, THOMAS, Sarah (wife); Ann, Elizabeth and Charles.

1775 SNEED, SAMUEL, Temperance (wife); Israel, David, Philip, William and Daniel; Ann Crossland and Temperance Crossland (daughters).

1781 STEPHENS, JOHN, Nancy and Sarah Stephens (sisters).

1784 SEAGO, JOHN, William, Robert, John, Ann and Elizabeth; James Seago (grandson).

1781 STEWART, JOHN, Nancy Caine and Sarah Stewart (sisters).

1798 SPARKS, CHARLES, Jane (wife); John, Nancy, James and Elizabeth; Sarah Lyons and Polly Tompkins (daughters).

1791 SMITH, FRANCIS, Frances (wife); Richard, Ann, Francis, David, Nathaniel and John; Unity Hammons, Sarah Poindexter and Elizabeth Buchanan (daughters).

T.

1775 TERRY, WILLIAM, Mary (wife); James; Martha Puckett, Mourning Coleman and Margaret Smith (daughters).

1800 TYSON, JEHU. Mildred (wife); John, Joel. Lucretia, Sukey, Jesse, William, Uriah and Mason.

V.

1762 VANHOSEN, JOHN, Wife (not named); John, Valentine, Christian, Mary, Joab, Elizabeth and Yonkey.

1785 VAUGHN, STEPHEN, Mary (wife); William and Sarah.

W.

1779 WILSON, GEORGE, Wife (not named); Robert, George, Samuel, Solomon, Anderson and John.

1786 WADE, THOMAS, Jane (wife); Thomas, Sarah, George and Holden; Mary Vining (daughter).

1785 WHITE, THOMAS, Unity Purnal (daughter).

1791 WRIGHT, STEPHEN, Henry Hardy (cousin).

1793 WADE, THOMAS, Elizabeth (wife); Thomas, William and Joseph.

1802 WISDOM, WILLIAM, Mary, Francis, John, Thomas, Martha, Eugenia, Sarah, Braddock and McGehee (children).

1802 WILLIAMS, ROLAND, Phereba (wife); Stephen, Agnes, Rowland and Thomas.

BEAUFORT—WILLS

A.

1759 ALLEN, TIMOTHY, Rebecca (wife), Ephraim, Martha, Prudence, Salathiel, Jeremiah and Elizabeth.

1797 ARCHBELL, SAMUEL, Elizabeth (wife); William, John, Martha.

1761 ALDERSON, JOHN, Ann (wife), Levi and Simeon.

1759 ADAMS, JAMES, Mary (wife), James, Dorothy and Winifred.

1760 ADAMS, ANN, Kennedy and John.

1765 ABBOTT, WM., Elizabeth (wife), James and Walter.

1763 ADAMS, JOHN, Ann (wife), Dinah.

1790 ARCHBELL, NATHAN, John, Nathan and Elizabeth.

1791 ADAMS, ABRAHAM, wife, Celia, Ephraim, Levi, Isaac, George and William.

1792 ABLE, ARTHUR, Ann (wife), John and William.

1792 ADAMS, JAMES, Sarah (wife), Henry, Sarah and Abraham.

1796 ADAMS, ISAAC, Thomas and Miles Adams (nephews).

B.

1720 BRIGHT, JOHN, (Hyde precinct) Elizabeth (wife), Henry, Richard, Simon, Lydia, Mary, William, James and John.

1731 BRIGHT, RICHARD, Wife (not named), James, Christian, Elizabeth and Simon.

1784 BREWER, WM., Mary (wife), William.

1759 BECTON, RICHARD, Elizabeth (wife); four nephews, George, Edward, Fred and Michael Becton.

1760 BUCKINGHAM, STEPHEN, Wife (not named), Solomon and Ebenezer.

1769 BOND, JAMES, Wife (not named), James, Abraham and Ezbona.

1776 BLOUNT, READING, Reading, Joseph, Nathaniel, Jesse and Bryan.

1778 BROOKS, HORATIO, Elizabeth (wife), Peggy, Lawson and John.

1779 BLOUNT, JOSEPH, Sarah (wife), Joseph, Wilson, Mary and Sally.

1779 BONNER, HENRY, Elizabeth, Mary, William, Henry, Patience, James, Ann and Edward.

1779 BOUTWELL, SAMUEL, Ann (wife), Rebecca, Jemima and Abigail.

1780 BROWN, DOROTHY, Bonner, Thomas (friend).

1781 BARROW, JOHN, Martha (wife), Samuel, Martha, Mary, Rebecca, Fanny, Ruth, Thomas, Susan, Rhoda and William.

1783 BONNER, JAMES, Anna, Sarah, James, Elizabeth, Samuel, Mary, Henry, Joseph and Willis.

1783 BLUE, PETER, Maria (a slave); Maule, Anna (a friend); Willis, Samuel (a friend).

1785 BOYD, THOMAS, Elizabeth (wife), Thomas, William and Rebecca.

1786 BURBAGE, JOHN, Mary (wife), William, John. Hugh, Mary, Thomas, Peter, George, Ephraim, Beardwin and James.

1787 BONNER, JOHN, James, Joseph and Henry (brothers); Blount, Joseph and Wilson; Foreman, James.

1787 BENNETT, LUKE, Leah (wife), Dicey, Lydia and Luke.

1790 BARROW, MARTHA, Thomas, Susanna, Rhoda. William and Fanny.

1796 BONNER, GEORGE, Richard, Nancy.

1797 BOYD, WILLIAM, Anna (wife); John.

1791 BONNER, JAMES, Ann, Sarah and Nathan.

1792 BEASLEY, THOMAS, SR., Mary (wife), Thomas, Sarah, James, Robert, Frances, Elizabeth and Mary.

1793 BLOUNT, THOMAS, Elizabeth (wife), Cornelius and Nathan.

1793 BARROW, WILLIAM, Elizabeth (wife), Penelope and Wyriot.

1795 BEANER, RICHARD, John, Richard, Mary and Winifred.

1763 BELLOTE, HILARY, Susanna (wife), Caesar, Elizabeth and Ann.

C.

1731 CONNER, PHILIP, (Hyde precinct), Catherine (wife), Ann, Margaret, Mary, Catherine, Isaac and Jacob.

1733 CANNON, SARAH, David, Edward, Margaret, Dennis, Sarah, Jean, Henry, Mary, John and Ruth.

1733 COUTANCHE, MICHAEL, (Bath county), Wife (not named), Michael, Benjamin and Susanna.

1798 CORDING, THOMAS, Ann (wife); Thomas, Jacob.

1784 CROFTON, THOMAS, Nancy.

1734 COOPER, SAMUEL, (Bath county), Elizabeth (wife), James, Jessie, Mary, William, Sarah and Edward.

1741 COYLE, CORNELIUS, Gray, Rebecca, Absalom and Cornelius (friends).

1762 COUTANCHE, MICHAEL, Sarah (wife), Susanna, Benjamin and Michael.

1762 CAMPEN, JAMES, Sarah (wife), Robert, James, Hannah, Mary and Rebecca.

1764 CHAUNCEY, WALLY, Jemima (wife), Isaac, Samuel and Nancy.

1765 CLEMENT, THOMAS, Crossley, Esther (a friend).

1771 CAMPEN, JORAM, Elizabeth, Robert and Dorothy.

1775 CAMPEN, JOSEPH, Mary (wife), Joseph, Robert and Thomas.

1779 CONGLETON, DAVID, Jane (wife), Elizabeth, Sarah and Floyd.

1779 COFFEY, WM., Mary (wife).

1780 CURTIS, ANN, Ann, John, Thomas and William.

1797 COX, ABRAHAM, Mary (wife); John, Elena.

1781 COOK, THOMAS, Sarah (wife), Charles and James.

1785 CAMPEN, ROBERT, Wife (not named), Joram and Mary; Thomas and Robert Campen (nephews).

1789 CLIFFORD, JAMES, Sarah (wife), John, Sarah and Mary.

1790 CAMPEN, ROBERT, Wife (not named), James, David and Mary.

1791 CURTIS, JOHN, Mary (wife), David and Esther.

1793 CLARK, GEORGE, Wife (not named), Polly, Susanna, James, Nancy and Louise.

1795 CAMPEN, ROBERT, Joseph (brother).

1797 CHESTON, Elizabeth and Forney (daughters).

D.

1726 DAVIS, JOHN, (Bath county), Dorothy (wife), William, John, Nathaniel, Mary, Samuel and Sarah.

1751 DOE, EDWARD, Alsey (wife), Elihu and Elisha Doe (grandsons).

1763 DUNBAR, MARY, Frances (sister).

1780 DIXON, THOMAS, Martha and Mary.

1788 DEAN, MOSES, Martha (wife), William, Abner, Anthony and Mary.

1792 DOWTY, ELISHA, Eliashe (wife), Elisha, Ludovic and Job.

1792 DAW, WILLIAM, Wife (not named), Dinah, Dorcas, William, Nathan, James, Silas and Green.

E.

1750 ECHOLS, JOHN, Wife (not named), John, James, Joses, Cobb, Ann, Mary and Elinor.

1775 EVITT, WALTER, John, Thomas, Elizabeth, Rachel, Mary, Joseph, Rebecca and Ann.

1776 ECHOLS, JAMES, Martha (wife), George, William and five other children (not named).

1779 EVITT, JOSEPH, Orrill, William (brother-in-law).

1780 EASON, REUBEN, Mary (wife), Clara, Sarah, Sybilla, Thomas and Mills.

1792 ECHOLS, JOSES, JR., William and Richard.

1797 ECHOLS, GEORGE, Wife; James, David.

F.

1764 FULINTON, ANDREW, Mary (wife), William and Andrew.

1729 FORTNER, JAMES (Hyde precinct), Stubbs, Joanna.

1784 FULCHER, MAXIMILIAN, Sebbie (wife), Jesse, Peter, Prudence and Mary.

1784 FALLIN, JOHN, Agnes (wife), Sarah and Agnes.

1752 FORMAN, WILLIS, Mary (wife), Elizabeth, Margaret, Dorcas and Anne.

1762 FLOYD, GRIFFIN, Peter and John.

1780 FATHEREE, HILLIARD, Ann (wife), Ebenezer, Hilliard, Nelly and Penny.

1787 FULLERTON, WILLIAM, Mary (wife), Peter, Polly and Nancy.

1790 FLOYD, PETER, Elizabeth (wife), Simeon, Olive, Sarah, Peter and Grissom.

1790 FLOYD, URIAH, Elizabeth (wife), Silas.
1793 FLOYD, SIMEON, Elizabeth (wife), Mary and Elizabeth.
1752 FLENNAKIN, JAMES, James.

G.

1786 GERRARD, FORBES, Benjamin, Simon, Betsy, William and Charles (brothers and sisters).
1784 GLADIN, JOHN, Elizabeth (wife), Daniel and Sally.
1789 GRIST, RICHARD, Ann (wife), Fred and Richard.
1790 GUY, WILLIAM, William, Mary and Henry.
1791 GODLEY, NATHAN, Martha, John, Elias, Nathan, Sally, Thomas and Robert.
1792 GROVES, WILLIAM, Parthenia (wife), Allen, Josiah, Nancy and William.
1793 GODLEY, JOHN, Rachel (wife), Robert, Mary, Thomas, Joseph, John and Nathan.
1793 GAINER, JOSEPH, Wife (not named), Joseph, Isabella and Drupina.
1795 GRIST, BENJAMIN, Ann (wife), Chloe, Sally, Betty and William.
1786 GRIST, JOHN, John, Mary, Sarah, Benjamin and Reading.
1798 GREER, ANDREW, Joseph, James and John (brothers).

H.

1789 HOLLINGSWORTH, CHARLES, Mary (wife), Sarah, Elizabeth, Dicey, Alsey, Mary and Rebecca.
1784 HARE, JOHN PORTER, Sharpe, Katie.
1784 HAWKINS, BENJAMIN, Abiah (wife), William, Ann, Willoughby, Benjamin, Abiah and Masour.
1785 HARDWICK, GEORGE, Ann.
1759 HARFOOT, ROBERT, Ellison, James (a friend).
1759 HERINTON, JAMES, brother (not named), John and Charles (brothers).
1772 HOLTON, JESSE, Sarah (wife), George, David, James, Barzillai, Peregrine and Pridgen.
1774 HARRISON, THOMAS, Hannah (wife), John and Samuel.
1779 HOLTON, PEREGRINE, Barzillai and David (brothers).
1781 HUDSON, JAMES, John, James, Ann, Mary and Elizabeth.
1785 HILL, JOSHUA, Wife (not named), Sarah, Joshua, Lazarus, John, Celia and Mary.
1791 HAWKINS, BENJAMIN, Mary (wife), Saumel, Nelly, Benjamin and Thomas.
1787 HARRIS, JOSIAH, Judah, William, Joseph, Lucretia, Nancy, James and Mary.
1795 HARRIS, WILLIAM, William.

J.

1728 JONES, WALTER, (Hyde precinct), Dorothy (wife), Simon, Alice, Betty, Ambrose, Walter and Liscom.
1732 JACKSON, JOHN, Ann (wife), John and Margaret.

1784 JASPER, ISRAEL, Lurana (wife), Jonathan, Celia, Richard, Susanna, James and Valentine.

1760 JASPER, JOHN, Dinah (wife), Jonathan.

1760 JONES, JOSIAS, Sarah, Francis, James, Mary, Elizabeth, Josias, William, Betty and John.

1769 JEWELL, THOMAS, Wife (not named), James and John.

1773 JOHNSON, ARTHUR, Leah (wife), William.

1773 JACKSON, DAVID, Anne (wife), Daniel, Julius, Alex., James, Sebrey, Corten and Thode.

1778 JASPER, JONATHAN, Dinah (mother), Gerrard, Charles (brother).

1774 JORDAN, JOHN, Thomas, John, Sarah, Daniel, Martin, Hosea, Margaret and Ann.

1796 JONES, JAMES, Joseph, Hannah, Mary.

1797 JONES, HOLLAND, Roger.

1781 JONES, THOMAS, Sarah (wife), William, Lettice, Polly, Elizabeth, Nancy and Sarah.

1793 JOYNER, ISRAEL, Elizabeth (wife), six children (not named).

1796 JONES, THOMAS, Jesse, Walter, John, Rachel.

K.

1783 KIRKCONNELL, JOHN, Walter and James (brothers).

1752 KELLY, MATTHEW, Dinah (wife).

1759 KEECH, JOHN, Rhoda (wife), Jasper, John and Joseph.

1791 KINNIN, ANTHONY, Hannah (wife), Anthony, Thomas and Elizabeth.

1795 KELLY, TULLY, Hannah (wife), Matthew and Mary.

1786 KIDD, JOSEPH, Elizabeth (wife).

1788 KEAIS, NATHAN, Barbara (wife), children (not named).

1796 KNOWIS, THOMAS, Jesse, Walter, John, Rachel.

L.

1733 LEWIS, GRIFFITH, (Bath county), Ann (wife).

1738 LEIGH, JAMES, (Bath county), Mary (wife), Peter, John, Mary and Levi.

1777 LOCKEY, CELIA, Celia.

1779 LEITH, CHARLES, Elizabeth (wife).

1781 LUERTON, JOHN, Worsley, Thomas (a friend).

1782 LUCAS, SAMUEL, Sarah (wife), Roxana, Abigail, Elizabeth, Rebecca, Jesse and Henry.

1782 LEIGH, JOHN, Bethiah (wife), Joseph, Abraham, Benjamin, John, Shadrack and Wm.

1787 LIND, THOMAS, Dorcas (wife).

1788 LAUGHINGHOUSE, THOMAS, Wife (not named), Thomas, Esther, Andrew, Richard, John and Young.

1793 LOOMIS, JONATHAN, Abner, Ezekiel, Jesse, and Solomon (brothers).

1794 LANIER, JOHN, Fanny (wife), children (not named).

1795 LEITH, ELIZABETH, Mary, James, Olivia and Elizabeth.

M.

1739 MILLS, JOHN, Mills, Moses, Courtney, and Tyson (grandchildren).

1752 MOORE, THOMAS, Sarah (wife), Edmund and Elizabeth.

1759 MAYO, WILLIAM, Martha (wife), William,

1761 McKEEL, THOMAS, Wife (not named), John, Elizabeth, Mary ,Martha and Thomas.

1762 McNAIR, CHARLES, Elizabeth (wife).

1799 MAULE, MOSES, Roulbac, William and Maule, John (nephews).

1770 McMATH, ROBERT, Brun, William (a friend).

1775 MILLER, NAT, Elizabeth (wife), Nat, Elizabeth, Abel, Rebecca, Ann and Worthy.

1797 MORRIS, ELISHA, Thomas, Sarah.

1779 MIXON, GEORGE, Elijah, Salathiel, Zedekiah and Martha.

1782 McKEEL, JOHN, Elizabeth, Sarah and James.

1787 McDONNACK, ANDREW, Mary (wife), John, Henry and Mary.

1788 McCABE, WLILIAM, Ann (wife), John and Bryan.

1790 McCONEY, ROBERT, William (brother).

1796 MAYO, SOLOMON, Betty (wife); John, James.

N.

1734 NEWTON, FRANCIS, (Bath county), Joseph.

1781 NEWMAN, JOHN, Ann (wife), Richard, John, Penelope and James.

O.

1759 ODEON, CHARLES, Rebecca (wife), Elizabeth, Frances and Mary.

1760 ODON, JOHN, Wife (not named), Woodward, John H. (a friend).

1770 ODEON, ELIZABETH, Whery, Anthony (brother).

1789 ODEN, RICHARD, SR., Elizabeth (wife), Anne, Richard, Elizabeth, John and Thomas.

P.

1785 PADGETT, JOHN, Bartlett, Thomas and Edward (friends).

1731 PROCTOR, JOHN, (Bath county), Elizabeth (wife), Ann, Elizabeth, Abigail and Mary.

1748 PEYTON, BRYAN, Eleanor (wife), Elizabeth, Eleanor, Grace and Henry.

1751 PEYTON, ELEANOR, William, Eleanor and Grace.

1758 PEARCE, EDWARD, Rachel (wife), Edward, Lazarus, Sarah, Jothan, Thomas, Rachel, Mary, Benjamin, Hezekiah and Joseph.

1751 PEYTON, ROBERT, Peyton, John (cousin).

1760 PERKINS, JAMES, Margaret (wife), David, James, Jonathan, Edward.

1761 PALMER, JOHN, Catherine (sister).

1769 PHILLIPS, WILLIAM, Mary (wife), Isaac, Henry, William, Elizabeth, Ann and Sarah.

1775 PINDER, WILLIAM, Ann (wife).

1772 PRITCHETT, JAMES, Wife (not named), Peter, Anne, Mary, Margaret and James.

1772 PRITCHETT, PETER, Wife (not named), Peter, Abraham, Sarah, Mary, Grace and Margaret.

1777 PEARCE, THOMAS, Elizabeth (wife), Basil, Lavinia, Winifred, Thomas, Rachel and Jemima.

1777 PRESCOTT, MILES, Wife (not named), John, William, Major, Mary, Sarah and Isabel.

1777 PRESCOTT, JOHN, Wife (not named), Matthew, Mary, Sarah, Martha, Hannah, Isabel and Susan.

1778 PEARCE, BENJAMIN, Mary (wife), Hezekiah and Joseph (brothers).

1779 PATTEN, JOHN, Ann (wife), Ann and Hans.

1782 PUTNALL, JOHN, Elizabeth (wife), John, Stephen, Mary, Elizabeth, Winifred, Pheraba and Anne.

1786 PALMER, WILLIAM, Mary (wife), Robert, Margaret, Ephraim, Helen and Alston.

1787 POYNER, JAMES, Dorcas (wife), Mercy, Rebekah, Sylvester and Margaret.

1787 POYNER, EDWARD, Elizabeth (wife).

1789 PUTNELL, JOHN, Stephen (brother).

1792 PEED, ARTHUR, Martin, William, John and Trigana.

1793 PRICE, WM., Mary (wife), Absalom, Mary, Elizabeth, William, Alice and Lucretia.

1794 PELLEY, JOHN, Elizabeth (wife).

1796 PRESCOTT, JOHN, Sarah (wife).

R.

1759 ROE, COLEMAN, Sarah (wife), Wliliam, Edward and Agnes.

1797 ROSE, JOHN, John.

1763 RIGNEY, JAMES, Rebecca, Hannah and Elizabeth.

1766 RIGNEY, HANNAH, Brooks, James (cousin).

1777 ROE, SARAH, Edward, William, Agnes and Coleman.

1739 RESPESS, THOMAS, Mary (wife).

1779 ROBINSON, JOHN, Rebecca (wife), Jacob, Hardy, Benjamin, Lydia and Elizabeth.

1789 RISTALOBERT, JOHN BAPTISTE, Louis, John (a friend).

1789 RAWLS, FRANCIS, Sarah (wife), Esther, James, Joshua, William and Jesse.

1791 ROBINSON, JACOB, Hannah (wife), Mary, Lydia and Janet.

1796 RICHARDS, RALPH, Martha (wife).

1796 ROGERS, STEPHEN, Rebecca (wife); Mary Jones (granddaughter).

S.

1720 SCOTT, JAMES, (Hyde precinct), Webster, Moses; Ann and her daughters, Ann and Yardley Thoroughgood; Welch, Eleanor and James.

1720 SQUIRE, JOHN, (Hyde precinct), Mary (wife).

1735 SILVENT, JOHN, (Bath county), Derby, George and Joseph (brothers); Elizabeth, Grace and Margaret (sisters).

1735 SMITH, CHARLES, Charles and Hendry.

1760 SLADE, JOHN, Wife (not named), Sarah, Major and Catherine; Joseph (brother).

1762 SHEETE, PHILIP, Mary (wife), Sarah, Mary, Susan and Elizabeth.
1764 SLADE, JOSEPH, Ann (wife), William, Hamon, Benjamin, Joseph and Mary.
1780 SHIVERS, SARAH, Mary, Pheraba and Elizabeth.
1782 SMAW, MARY, John, Henry, Lucretia and William.
1785 STEVENS, ROBERT N., Mary (wife), Julia, Marcus and William.
1787 SMITH, MARY, Smith, Lewis and Jemima (cousins).
1788 SHINGLETON, WILLIAM, Bethiah (wife), Elizabeth, Bethiah and Willoughby.
1789 SHEPHERD, SOLOMON, Thomas, James and Jordan.
1790 SANDERLING, JOHN, Mary (wife).
1790 SIMERALL, EDWARD, Pelly, John, (a friend).
1792 SYLVENT, LAMBERT, Richard, Mary and Sarah.
1792 SANDERLIN, MARY, Elizabeth, Sarah and Keziah.
1793 SIRMON, WM., Gerrard, Charles (brother).
1795 SAUNDERS, ANDREW, Mary (wife).
1795 SMAW, HENRY, Mary (wife).
1795 SHALLINGTON, WM., Ann (wife), William.
1795 STUBBS, WM., William, Samuel, Mary, Hannah.
1797 SIRMON, BENJAMIN, Agnes (wife).
1799 SLADE, HENRY, Mary (wife); William.
1779 WTITMEL, THOMAS, wife (not named); Molly.

T.

1783 THOMAS JAMES, Keais, Nathan (a friend).
1761 TRIPPE, JOHN, Sarah (wife), John, Dorothy, Henry, William, Nevill and Hewell.
1765 TRIPPE, NEVILL, Anne (wife).
1764 TAYLOR, SAMUEL G., Ormond, Nancy, (granddaughter); Adams, Sarah (housekeeper).
1766 TRIPPE, JOHN, Wife (not named), William, Henry, John, Sarah, Ann and Elizabeth.
1766 TINDEL, JOHN, Ebeth (wife), John, James and Ebeth.
1780 TRIPPE, WM., Sarah (wife), Harriet and Juliet.
1796 TUTEN, THOMAS, Wife; Absalom.

U.

1735 UNDERWOOD, THOMAS, (Bath county), Wife (not named), Thomas, James and Elizabeth.

V.

1784 VOSS, THOMAS, Mary, Lydia and Frances.
1779 VAIL, JEREMIAH, Christopher (brother).
1799 VINES, THOMPSON, Winifred (wife); Thomas, Samuel, John.

W.

1783 WRIGHT, JEREMIAH, Stephen (brother).
1789 WARWICK, JOHN, Brady, Mary and Joseph (friends).
1785 WOODARD, JOHN, Ann (wife), Isaiah, John and Elizabeth.
1734 WHITEHURST, JOSIAS, Mary (wife).

1781 WARNER, FRANCIS, Mary (wife), Joseph, Jeremiah and Mary.

1758 WALL, JAMES, Elizabeth (wife), James, Mary and Moses.

1783 WILSON, WINIFRED, Seth.

1759 WILLIAMS, THOMAS, Grace (wife), John (brother).

1790 WILLIAMS, SETH P., Elizabeth (wife), Susanna.

1764 WISE, JOSEPH, Matilda (wife), Johannes, Sarah and Crawford.

1767 WELCH, MATTHEW, Mary (wife), William, Elizabeth, Mary, Susanna and Irene.

1773 WALLIS, JONATHAN, Mary (wife), Thomas, Anne and Sarah.

1775 WALLIN, DOVE, Wife (not named), William, Thomas and Winifred.

1787 WILLIAMS, ROBERT, Wife (not named), Lovey, William and John (brothers).

1790 WILLIAMS, THOMAS S., Ann (wife), Daniel and John.

1791 WALLACE, JOHN, Polly (wife), Lenner.

1791 WALLS, JOSEPH, Joseph, Joel, Mary and Deborah.

1791 WILKINSON, AARON, The children of his two brothers.

1792 WILLIAMS, JAMES, Elizabeth (wife), Nancy and Thomas.

1793 WILLIAMS, THOMAS, Sarah (wife), Llewellyn and Nathaniel.

1793 WALLACE, JOHN, Harriet and Leven.

1794 WHITLEY, ARTHUR, Sarah (wife).

1794 WARDEN, JOHN, Wife (not named), Sarah.

1795 WIRDEN, SAMUEL, Howard, Sally.

1796 WILLIAMS, THOMAS, Anna (wife).

1796 WILLIAMS, JOHN, Elizabeth (wife).

1799 WORLARD, JOHN, Rebecca (wife); Absalom, Sarah, Jemima, Rebecca.

Y.

1797 YOUNG, WILLIAM, Etheridge, William (a friend).

BERTIE—WILLS

1762 ANDREWS, ABNER, wife (not named), Margaret, Stephen and John.

1762 AZWELL, THOMAS, Ann Gibbons (mother), Ann Virgin (sister).

1771 ASKEW AARON, Martha (wife), Jesse, Moses, Martha, Sarah, Pheraba and Ann.

1771 AVERETT, HENRY, Martha (wife), Julia and Martha.

1771 ABINGDON, JAMES, wife (not named), James, Hardiman, Martha, Elizabeth, William, Thomas, Henry, Littleberry, Sarah and Lydia.

1772 AVERETT, HENRY, Jesse and Charles; and the children of Henry (son).

1781 ASHBORN, THOMAS, Elizabeth, Benjamin, Thomas, William and Elisha.

1781 AVERITT, SIMON, Thomas, William and James.

1790 AVIS, SAWYER, Joseph.

1790 ASHLEY, THOMAS, Harrell, Amos.

1791 ARMISTEAD, WILLIAM, Sarah, Jordan, Starkey, John, William, Robert, Elizabeth, Sarah, Mary and Priscilla.

1797 ALLEN, JOHN, Ann (wife), John B., James B., Sarah B.; Hunter, Mildred.

1799 AVERETT, JESSE, Mary and Jesse.

1799 ALEXANDER, JOHN, Martha and Rachel.

B.

1762 BROWN, JENNY, Arthur, Mary, Elizabeth, Sarah and Priscilla.

1762 BRYON, EDWARD, Thomas, Martha (wife), Margaret, Sarah, Martha, Elizabeth, Ann, Janet, Sarah.

1762 BARBERREE, ABRAHAM, Isaac, Mary (wife).

1762 BARRADAILE, JOSEPH, Abraham, John and Mary (wife).

1762 BUTTERTON, JOSEPH, Robert, Joseph, John, James and Elizabeth; wife (not named).

1762 BROGDON, DAVID, Mary, John, Susanna and Fred.

1762 BASS, THOMAS, John, Jacob, Mary, Isabel and Thomasine (wife).

1762 BAILES, EDEN, Rebecca (wife), John.

1762 BOND, THOMAS, Thomas.

1770 BRYAN, NEEDHAM, Sarah (wife), William, Needham and Rachel.

1770 BARFIELD, THOMAS, Courtney (wife), Thomas, Mary and Elizabeth.

1771 BELLOTE, WILLIAM, Peleg, John, William, Bridget and Hannah.

1774 BURN, JOHN, Andrew.

1774 BROGDON, JOHN, John and Patterson.

1776 BARFELL, SAMUEL, Ruth (wife), Solomon, Elizabeth and William.

1775 BUNCH, HENRY, Bunch, Henry.

1775 BRYAN, JESSE, William, Catherine, Elizabeth.

1775 BONNER, WILLIAM, Ann (wife), William, John, George, Miles and Thomas.

1775 BRYAN, DAVID, John, Elizabeth, Mary, David, Joseph, Peggy and Rebecca.

1777 BRYAN, MARTHA, Martha, Elizabeth and Winifred.

1777 BROGDON, MARY, Ludovic.
1778 BARNES, JOHN, Katherine and Henry.
1781 BURN, ANDREW, John, James and Levi.
1783 BLAKE, JAMES, The youngest children of Walter (son)
1784 BARNES, JOHN, Elizabeth (wife), John, Solomon and Kader.
1785 BUTTERTON, ROBERT, Sarah (wife).
1785 BROWN, ARTHUR, Mary, Jesse and Arthur.
1785 BAKER, JONATHAN, Susanna, Laurie and John.
1785 BAYLEY, THOMAS, Sarah.
1786 BURN, ANDREW. Levi, John and James.
1789 BRYAN, THOMAS, Edward.
1789 BUNCH, EMBREY, Micajah and Elizabeth.
1790 BOYD, MARTHA, Jernigan, Lewis.
1791 BASS, CADER, wife; Bathsheba (daughter).
1791 BUTLER, TOBIAS, John and Jethro.
1793 BOND, JOHN, Thomas.
1794 BELOTE, SILAS, Millicent.
1794 BRYAN, MICHAEL, Olive and Needham.
1795 BROGDEN, JOHN, wife; William.
1795 BRYCE, WILLIAM, Judy (wife).
1795 BOND, THOMAS, John, Sarah, Mary, Elizabeth and Lewis.
1795 BARRY, THOMAS, John.
1796 BOGHART, DANIEL, Pugh, William.
1796 BELOTE, JOHN, wife; Thomas and William.
1797 BELOTE, AMELIA, Noah, Thomas, Catherine and Clarissa.
1798 BUNCH, JEREMIAH, William, Jeremiah, Nihemiah, Henry and Fred.
1798 BAKER, THOMAS, Blake.
1799 BRYAN, EDWARD, Martha (wife), Sarah, Susanna, Martha, Elizabeth and Mary.
1799 BIRAM, JOHN, James and William.
1799 BRIMAGE, WILLIAM, Thomas W.
1790 BAZEMORE, JOHN, James and Nillian.

C.

1771 COBB, HENRY, Mary and Charles.
1771 CAMPBELL, CORNELIUS, Elizabeth, James and Cornelius.
1771 CRAFT, JOHN, Sarah and Lucy.
1771 COKE, JOHN, Robert.
1771 CUNIFFE, JOHN, Malachi.
1777 CHERRY, SOLOMON, Sarah, William, Cader, Martha, Elizabeth and James.
1781 CAMPBELL, JOHN, James, Martha, John.
1782 CHARLTON, JASPER, Abigail (wife).
1784 CARTER, ROBERT, Isaac and George.
1785 CAPEHEART, MICHAEL, George, Michael, William, Frances, John and James.
1785 COOK, WILLIAM, Mary, John and Joel.
1788 CRITCHETT, JOHN, Thomas and Richard.
1789 CURETON, JOHN, Rachel.
1789 CHURCHWELL, JAMES, Ann (wife), Mary, Elizabeth, Jeremiah, Thomas, Allen, Patience, Sarah, Martha and William.
1791 COOK, CAESAR, Phillys and Caesar.
1792 COBB, JAMES, Henry, Jesse, William, James and Elizabeth.
1793 CALLUM, HEZEKIAH, Holland, Joseph.

1794 CLEMENTS, GEORGE, Elizabeth, Isaac, William and Hardy.
1796 COKE, JOHN, Mary (wife).
1797 CHARLTON, JASPER, Elizabeth (wife), Elizabeth and Frances.
1797 CALLUM, MARY, Thompson, Elizabeth.
1798 CAMPBELL, JAMES, George, James, Sarah, Elizabeth, Mary and Martha.
1798 COCHRAN, THOMAS, Elizabeth, Edward and Thomas.

D.

1770 DEMPSEY, PATIENCE, Joshua, Isaac, Mary, and Thoroughgood.
1770 DRAUGHAN, WALTER, Bridget, Thomasine, Thomas and Robert.
1772 DAVISON, JOHN, Edward, William, John and Amos.
1779 DAVIDSON, JOHN, Sarah, Elizabeth and Smithwick.
1780 DILLARD, GEORGE, Priscilla.
1782 DRURY, SAMUEL, Jenny and Milly.
1787 DWYER, MORGAN, Elizabeth(wife), Dennis and John.
1787 DARGAN, JEREMIAH, Ann (wife), William.
1790 DWYER, DENNIS, Ann (wife), Winifred.
1796 DAWSON, RICHARD, Jane, Hannah James, George, John and William.
1796 DUNNING, CHARLES, Celia, Exum and Eli.
1797 DAVIS, GEORGE, Elizabeth and Miles.

E.

1779 ELLIS, CATHERINE, Bryan, John, George and William; Gardner, Sarah.
1785 EDWARDS, TITUS, Isham and William.
1785 EDWARDS, WM., Thomas and Benjamin.
1786 EARLY, JAMES, Grace (wife), Shadrack and John.
1794 EASON, ABNER, Rachel, George, Joseph and Abner.
1796 EVANS, MICHAEL, Richard, Benjamin and Susanna C.
1798 EARLY, SHADRACK, Sally (wife), James, Thomas, John, Lavinia and Nancy.

F.

1769 FLEETWOOD, WM., Henry, William, John, James, Edward, Thomas, Hardy and Elizabeth.
1774 FLEETWOOD, HENRY, Wm. H., Sarah, Elizabeth and Sally.
1777 FILGO, ANTHONY, William.
1782 FREEMAN, WM., Tabitha (wife), John and Robert.
1785 FREEMAN, JOHN, Sarah (wife), Solomon, Elisha, Moses, Aaron, Elizabeth and John.
1788 FREEMAN, SOLOMON, Martha (wife), James
1793 FREEMAN, KING, Sarah (wife).
1793 FREEMAN, JOHN, Charles, Hardy, Jeremiah, Josiah and Sarah.
1794 FREEMAN, JOSHUA, Mary (wife), William, Joshua, Jacob and James.

1796   FARMER, JOSEPH, Luke, Joseph, James, Sarah (wife), King, Elizabeth, Sarah, Winnie, Judah and Rachel.

1799   FLEETWOOD, WM., Henry, Ashley, William, John, Elizabeth, Susanna, Mary, Ann, Elizabeth (wife) and Penelope.

G.

1762   GOUGH, JOHN, Charles and Lewis.

1762   GREEN, THOMAS, John, Elizabeth, Joseph, Hannah, Ann, Sarah and Elizabeth (wife).

1774   GRANBERRY, SAMUEL, wife (not named), son

1781   GLISTON, JAMES, Jacob.

1781   GRIMES, SAMUEL, Pheraba (wife); children (not named).

1784   GARDNER, MARTIN, John, Martin, Sarah, Bryan, James, Sarah (wife), Anna.

1790   GRIFFIN, EDWARD, William.

1790   GARDNER, JAMES, Mary (wife), Averett, William, Martin and John.

1795   GLISTON, ANN, Leah and Wright.

1796   GRAY, STEPHEN, William.

1797   GARRETT, JESSE, Rachel, James, Jesse, Penny, Mary, Timothy, John and Elizabeth.

H.

1761   HARRELL, FRANCIS, William, Shadrack, Mary and Martha.

1761   HOLLOWELL, WM., Elizabeth (wife), children (not named).

1762   HILL, MOSES, Sarah and Judith.

1762   HARRELL, EZEKIEL, Allie and Israel.

1762   HUGHES, GEORGE, George and Thomas.

1763   HILL, JOHN, Whitmel, Harry, Elizabeth (wife), Mary, Winifred and Sarah.

1764   HOBSON, FRANCIS, Elizabeth (wife).

1765   HARRELL, DAVID, Charity (wife), David, Noah, Sarah, Mildred and Chloe.

1767   HENDRICKS, DANIEL, Abraham, Sarah, Elizabeth.

1768   HURST, JOHN, Judith (wife), William.

1769   HARRELL, JOHN, Bailey, Lemuel, Solomon, Amos, Gileon.

1769   HARRELL, CHRISTOPHER, Wife (not named).

1772   HARRELL, SAMUEL, Cader, Elizabeth and Ann.

1774   HOLDER, THOMAS, Elisha, Susanna and Elizabeth.

1774   HOOKER, BENJAMIN, Ann, Hardy, John, James, Elisha, Benjamin, Freeman, David, Sarah and Cora.

1775   HOPKINS, JOHN, John, Alex., Aquilina, Daniel and Joseph.

1775   HARRELL, BENJAMIN, John.

1777   HARRELL, HENRY, Reuben, Benjamin, Henry, Whitmel, John W., David, Joseph, Rachel, Barbara and Elizabeth.

1777   HAWKINS, EDWARD, Eleanor (wife).

1777   HARRELL, JOHN, John, James.

1777   HILL, HARDY, Janet and Elizabeth.

1779   HARRELL, DAVID, Celia (wife).

1780   HOWE, ALEX., John, Sidney, Sarah, Mary and Thomas.

1781 HARRELL, JOHN, Winifred (wife).
1782 HIGGS, ABRAHAM, Sarah, John, Abraham.
1781 HARRELL, SAMUEL, Samuel and Mary.
1781 HARRELL, KADER, Samuel, Kader, Drewry
and Agnes.
Elizabeth, and Sarah (wife).
1783 HINTON, JOHN, Bond, Elizabeth.
1783 HARRELL, ISRAEL H., Owens, Patience, Esther, Edith and Keziah.
1783 HARRELL, JOSIAH, Fannie and Anna.
1784 HARDY, WM., William P., Sarah and Lamb.
1784 HOLLEY, NATHANIEL, John, Moore, Sarah
(wife), Sarah.
1784 HAYS, HARDY, Sarah, Joshua and Penelope.
1784 HALLOM, JEREMIAH, John and Judith.
1785 HARRELL, JAMES, Arthur, Joel, Grace, Sarah,
Elizabeth and Mary.
* 1786 HARE, THOMAS, Penelope (wife), Thomas E.
1786 HAYS, RICHARD, Edward, Penelope and Lavinia.
1788 HARRELL, JESSE, Pheraba, Josiah, Joshua and
Jonathan.
1789 HARRELL, JOSHUA, Jeconias, Hezekiah, Jemimah, Ann and Hodges.
1796 HUNTER, CADER, Humphrey and Hardy, Elizabeth (wife).
1791 HOLLAND, JOSEPH, Joel and Mary Magdalen.
1791 HARRELL, THOMAS, Angelica, John and Joseph.
1791 HINTON, JOHN, Noah.
1792 HAIRE, PENELOPE, Thomas E. and Janet.
1793 HAWKINS, THOMAS, John, Fred, Thomas and
Richard.
1793 HARRELL, WINIFRED, Chamberlain, Malachi,
Elizabeth, Penelope and Levi.
1794 HUNTER, HARDY, Rachel, Humphrey, Cader,
William, Timothy and Joshua.
1794 HYMAN, JOHN, Sarah (wife), Joel, Elizabeth, William, Thomas, John and Sarah.
1795 HOUSE, THOMAS; William, George and
Thomas.
1795 HOLLEY, JAMES, Josiah, Nathaniel, James,
Benjamin and Winifred.
1795 HARRELL, ELIJAH, John.
1796 HOUSE, GEORGE, John T., Elizabeth (wife).
1797 HARDY, LAMB, Winifred (wife), Thomas,
William P. and Elizabeth.
1797 HYMAN, SARAH, West, Mary, Elizabeth and
Margaret.
1798 HODGSON, CHARLES, Mary (wife), Mary and
Nancy.

J.

1776 JORDAN, JOSEPH, Isaac, William, Joseph and
Ruth.
1777 JORDAN, RUTH, Reed, John D., Christian and
Margaret.
1777 JACOCKS, CHARLES W., Charles.
1778 JERNIGAN, GEORGE, Pheraba (wife).
1779 JENKINS, JOHN, Mary, Zadok, Charles, Reddick, Irvin, Ephraim, Isaac, Winifred, Sally,
Abram and Keziah.
1784 JENKINS, EPHRAIM, Zadok and Owen.
1785 JERNIGAN, JESSE, James, Jesse, Jerusha, Sarah and Alex.

* See N. & S. Carolina Records by Clements, p. 115
which gives m. of a James Hare and Penelope
Jackson, 1779 in Chowan Co. n.c.

1786 JORDAN, JOSEPH, Mary, Isaac and William.
1786 JORDAN, WILLIAM, James and William.
1787 JACOCKS, JONATHAN, Charles, Jonathan, John, Ann (wife), Elizabeth.
1790 JORDAN, ISAAC, Joseph, Edward and Hannah.
1791 JORDAN, WILLIAM, Mary (wife), William and Joseph.
1790 JONES, WM., Wife (not named), James, William, Mary, Sarah and Rhoda.
1793 JOHNSTON, CAROLINE, John.
1796 JOHNSTON, BURWELL, Rebecca and Jonathan.
1797 JONES, JAMES, Jesse.
1791 JOHNSON, JOHN, Samuel W., John S., William W., Henry, Anne, Elizabeth and Alexander.

K.

1776 KNOTT, JOSEPH, Joseph, Thomas and James.
1778 KING, WM., Elizabeth, Henry, William, Charles and Michael.
1781 KNOTT, JOSEPH, Sarah (wife).
1781 KNOTT, WM., Mary (wife), James.
1786 KNOTT, WM., Sarah (wife), John and Charles.
1789 KENT, JOSEPH, Rachel (wife).
1790 KING, WM., Ann (wife), two daughters (not named).
1793 KITTRELL, JOHN, John, Dempsey, Willis, Stanly, Sarah, Louise and Jemima.
1797 KITTRELL, DEMPSEY, Martha (wife), children (not named).

L.

1761 LAWRENCE, THOMAS, Elizabeth (wife), Thomas, Asa, George and Elizabeth.
1762 LEGGETT, JAMES, Martha (wife), Thomas and Jeremiah.
1765 LEGGETT, TITUS, Mary and John.
1769 LAKEY, WM., Richard, Mary (wife), Thomas and Jacob.
1772 LAWRENCE, HUMPHREY, Ann (wife), Fred and Reuben.
1787 LASSITER, FRED, Sarah (wife), Fred and Wm.
1788 LAWRENCE, JOHN, Jean (wife), Abner, Robert and Obadiah.
1789 LEARY, DERBY, Susanna (wife).
1790 LAWRENCE, THOMAS, Sarah (wife), Williamson and Thomas.
1791 LAYTON, SAMUEL, James, Esther and Martha.
1791 LOCKHART, GEORGE, James, Susanna, Elizabeth and George.
1794 LANCASTER, MARY, Andrews, John and Stephen; Bryan, Elizabeth.
1796 LOCKHART, ELIZABETH, Mary (wife).
1797 LEGGETT, JAMES, John, James and Canath.
1799 LEGGETT, THOMAS, Margaret (wife), Jonathan and Thomas.

M.

1762 MEWBORN, MOSES, Thomas and Ann.
1774 MEWBORN, NICHOLAS, Thomas.
1780 MARTIN, THOMAS Elizabeth (wife); Nicholas, Elizabeth, Catherine, James and Ann.

1780 MEREDITH, ABRAHAM, Thomas and Greenberry.
1780 MOORE, BENJAMIN, Priscilla (wife), Sarah.
1783 MAER, ABRAHAM, Samuel and William.
1785 MOODY, KERVY, James and Philip.
1785 MANNING, BENJAMIN, Luke, Benjamin, Pherabe, Chloe, Elizabeth, Elijah' and Nancy.
1789 MOORE, EPAPHRAS, Winnie (wife), Aaron and Thomas.
1790 MOORE, JAMES, Titus.
1791 MEREDITH, DAVID, Sarah (wife), Lewis.
1793 MIZELL, WM., Mary (wife), Jeremiah.
1794 MIZELL, TIMOTHY, Jonas and John.
1795 MITCHELL, JOHN, Sarah (wife).
1796 MITCHELL, WM., Elizabeth (wife), Cader.
1796 MILBURN, SAMUEL, Alexander and Arnold.
1796 MEREDITH, DAVIS, Rachel (wife), James.
1796 MOORE, MALACHI, Sarah (wife).
1797 MILBURN, HENRY C., Martha (wife).
1798 MORE, JAMES, Seven sisters.

N.

1765 NICHOLS, JOHN, Sarah (wife), Margaret and Sarah.
1791 NICHOLS, HUMPHREY, Sarah (wife), Henry, Benajah, Fanny and John.
1791 NICHOLS, JOHN, John, George, Thomas, Isabella, Grisel, Anne and Peggy.
1793 NICHOLS, SARAH, Sarah.
1797 NICHOLS, SARAH, Benajah and Fanny.
1798 NORTH, JOSEPH, Richard and Ann.

O.

1770 OLIVER, THOMAS, David and John.
1772 OXLEY, JOHN, George, John and Olive.
1774 OLIVER, JOHN, Andrew.
1779 OWEN, JOHN, Elizabeth (wife), Agatha, William, John and Elizabeth.
1780 OUTLAW, JOHN, Jacob, James and Winifred.
1782 OUTLAW, RALPH, David, Edward, George, Ralph and Mary.
1782 OUTLAW, THOMAS, Thomas and Amos.
1793 OLIVER, ANDREW, John, Andrew, James and David.
1795 OUTLAW, GEORGE, Agnes (wife), George and Morgan.
1795 OUTLAW, AGNES, George.
1797 OLIVER, JOHN, Martin, Malachi, Shadrack, John, Mary, Winifred and Dicey.

P.

1762 PARKER, THOMAS, Abraham, Peter, Jacob and Elizabeth.
1771 POWERS, SAMUEL, Prudence (wife), Peggy.
1775 PRITCHARD, WILLIAM, Christian (wife), Jonathan, Christopher, Mary Ruth and Keziah.
1775 PEARCE, WILLIAM, Rebecca (wife), Jeremiah and William.
1777 PEARSON, JOHN, Margaret (wife).
1782 PERSEY, WM., Elizabeth (wife), William, Cader, Zadok, Nancy and Blake.
1783 PRICE, MICAJAH, Urquhart, Elizabeth.

1785 PEARSON, MARGARET, Pollok, Cullen; Johnston, Samuel; Dukenfield, Sir Nathaniel (son); Iredell, Mrs. James.

1785 PURVIS, JAMES, Jean, Allan, William, Cullen and Jane.

1786 PAGE, THOMAS, Solomon, Sarah (wife), Thomas, Joshua, Catherine, Ann and Mary.

1786 PRITCHARD, JAMES, Dorcas (wife), Reuben, James, Riggan, Penny, David, Lamb and Stephen.

1789 POWER, CHARLES, Susanna (wife); Charles and Thomas.

1792 PENNY, JAMES, Elizabeth (wife), Thomas.

1795 PENNY, THOMAS, Ann, Thomas and Mizell.

1799 PRITCHARD, HERBERT, Absalom, Elizabeth, Zadok, Hugh and Martha.

1799 PIERSE, JOHN, Mary (wife).

R.

1764 RICE, WM., Sarah (wife), James, William and Sarah.

1765 RUTLAND, JOHN, Drumer (wife), John, Blake, Milbay, Charity, Riddick and Penny.

1766 RABY, ADAM, Judah (wife), Adam and Luke.

1768 REASONS, THOMAS, Ann (wife), Ann, Renny and Sarah Foaks (sisters).

1769 RAY, ALEX, James, Samuel and Stephen.

1771 RHODES, JOHN, Thomas, Henry, William, Charles and John.

1772 RAWLS, WM., Levi, Josiah, Philip, Jonah and Joab.

1776 RASOR, EDWARD, Elizabeth (wife), Josiah, Mary, Elizabeth, Frances, Susanna, Martha, Sophia and Charlotte.

1777 ROGERS, MARY, Thomas, Mary, Frances and Minute.

1777 RYAN, JAMES, Thomas, wife (not named), children (not named).

1781 RUFFIN, WILLIAM, William.

1785 RAYNER, RICHARD, Zadok, Shadrack, Aaron, Elizabeth and Malachi.

1789 RABY, LUKE, Hester (wife).

1793 RHODES, HENRY, Alice (wife), Henry, Mary Clara and Alice.

1794 RAWLS, PHILIP, Henry and Philip.

1795 RHODES, JOHN, James and John; Perry, Alice.

1796 RHODES, THOMAS, Elisha, James, Elizabeth, Thomas, Jonathan and Margaret.

1796 RASCOE, ARTHUR, Elizabeth (wife), Sarah, Margaret, Mildred and Frances.

1796 RAYNER, JOHN, Joshua and Sarah.

S.

1762 SMITHWICK, JOHN, Martha, William, Luke and Joel.

1762 SAVAGE, THOMAS, Wife (not named), Thomas, Mary and Rachel.

1762 STALLINGS, ELIAS, Josiah.

1762 SPIVEY, JOHN F., Holmes, Frederick and Ann.

1769 SLATTER, OWEN, Alexander and Mary.

1771 SPIVEY, MOSES, Aaron and Moses.

1772 SUTTON, JASPER, Jordan, William, Jr.

1772 STALLINGS, JOSIAH, Mary (wife), John and Betsy.
1772 SCOLLAY, ELIZABETH, Pollock, Thomas and Cullen.
1774 SHEHAN, MILES M., Thomas and Miles.
1776 SHOLAR, WM., \Elizabeth (wife), James, Benjamin, Isaac, Jacob, Sarah, Rachel and Anna.
1777 SAWLKILL, JOHN, Perry, Thomas.
1779 SWAIN, WM, Tabitha (wife), John, Richard and James.
1779 SPIVEY, GEORGE, Esther (wife), Jonathan, George, David, William and James.
1779 SHEHAN, MILES, Mary (wife), Miles.
1779 SUTTON, THOMAS, Mary and Thomas.
1781 SKINNER, JOHN, Mary (wife), John H.
1781 SIMMONS, JOHN, Sallie and Malachi, wife (not named).
1783 SMITH, JOHN, Josiah, John, Henry, Malachi, Anna (wife).
1785 SWAIN, JOHN, Elizabeth (wife), William and Whitmel.
1785 SPARKMAN, WILLIAM, Mary (wife), William and Thomas.
1786 SEALS, WILLIAM, Thomas.
1791 SMITH, PETER, Arthur, George, John, Cicely, Turner and Rachel.
1792 SHOLAR, JOHN, David, Bryan and Edward.
1794 SHEBAN, THOMAS, Edward M.
1795 STANDLEY, DAVID, Sarah (wife), Jonathan, Sarah, William and John.
1796 SOWELL, FRANCIS, William, Joseph, James and Worley.
1796 SPEIGHT, THOMAS, Elizabeth (wife), Thomas H. and James.
1797 SLADE, JOHN G., Sarah (wife).
1797 STONE, ZEDEKIAH, David; Charlton, Elizabeth.
1797 SMITHWICK, JOHN, Martha (wife), William, Luke and Joel.
1799 SHANOCK, WM., James and Griffin.

T.

1766 THOMAS, MICHAEL, Ann (wife), Joseph, William and Lewis.
1767 TODD, WM., Katherine (wife), Thomas, Samuel and William.
1770 TURNER, WM., William and James.
1770 THOMPSON, HEZEKIAH, Noah, Reuben, Arthur, William and Mary (wife).
1770 TOOLE, EDWARD, Mary (wife), Jonathan, David and Geraldine.
1776 TURNER, THOMAS, David, Thomas, Benaiah, Amos and Abisha.
1777 TURNER, BENAIAH, Thomas, Amos and Abislea.
1780 THOMPSON, REUBEN, Noah, Arthur and William.
1780 THOMAS, JAMES, Sarah (wife), James, Ezekiel and Luke.
1783 TOOLE, JONATHAN, Mary (wife), Fred.
1791 TURNER, EDWARD, Elizabeth (wife), Turner, Mary, Rhoda and James.

1794 TURNER, MATTHEW, Elizabeth, Joseph and John,
1795 TODD, WM., John and Moses.
1795 TAYLOE, RICHARD, David.
1798 THOMPSON, JOHN, Polly (wife).
1799 THOMPSON, WM., Noah and Arthur.
1799 THOMPSON, NOAH, Catherine (wife), Reuben, William, Sarah and Charity.
1790 GLASCOCK, JOSEPH, Harman, Henry, Mary, Sa-
1799 TYLER, PERRY, Perry.

U.

1781 USHER, WM., Johnston, John.

V.

1762 VANLUVAN, HENRY, John and William.
1770 VANN, EDWARD, Mary (wife), William, Cader and King.

W.

1761 WILLIAMS, RICHARD, Mary (wife), Richard, Benjamin, George, Reuben, Simon, Martha, Elizabeth and Mary.
1761 WILLIAMS, SAMUEL, Mary (wife), Samuel, Moses and Benjamin.
1761 WARBURTON, JOHN, Jemimah (wife), James, Luke, Sarah and Penelope.
1769 WEST, PETER, Christian (wife), William, Peter, Thomas and Winnie.
1769 WEST, ROBERT, George and Robert.
1775 WILLIAMS, ARTHUR, Catherine (wife), Joab. and Arthur.
1777 WARD, PHILIP, James, Daniel, George, Michael, Mary, Sarah, Philip, Elizabeth, William, Millicent and Mary (wife).
1777 WATSON, JOHN, Ann (wife), Thomas, James, William, Winifred, Ann and Martha.
1779 WHITE, MORDECAI, King; Gaines, Rebecca and Sarah; Watson, Amos.
1780 WILLIAMS, JOSIAH, Sarah (wife).
1780 WARBURTON, JAMES, Winifred (wife), John.
1780 WARD, JAMES, Martha (wife), Winnie and Susanna.
1781 WILLIAMSON, HANNAH, Absalom and William.
1782 WILLIAMS, RICHARD, Drury and Reuben.
1782 WATSON, DAVID, Jean (wife), youngest son (not named).
1779 WHITMEL, THOMAS, wife (not named); Molly.
1784 WATFORD, HARDY, Millicent (wife).
1788 WARREN, WILLIAM, Elizabeth (wife).
1790 WARD, THOMAS, Anne (wife), George, Thomas, William and James.
1791 WILLIAMS, JOAB, Samuel, Francis and Arthur.
1795 WEST, THOMAS, Sally (wife), John.
1795 WATFORD, JOSEPH, Wife (not named), John, Joseph and William.
1795 WILLIAMS, JOHN, Anne (wife), Etheldred, Mary and Rachel.
1796 WESTON, WM., Sarah (wife), Malachi, Edmond and William.

1796   WHITE, LUKE, Mary (wife), Noah.
1796   WINANTS, WINANT, Mary (wife), Henry D.
1796   WARD, THOMAS, Pheraba (wife), Michael, William, James, Joshua, Elizabeth and Eleanor.
1797   WILLIAMS, EZEKIEL, Sarah (wife), George, Rachel and James.
1798   WILKES, JAMES, Mary (wife), James and Micajah.

Y.

1787   YEATS, JOHN, Thomas.
1789   YEATS, WM., Elizabeth (wife), David
1792   YEATS, ELIZABETH, David.
1795   YEATS, PETER, Sarah (wife), Thomas.
1795   YEATS, DAVID, Manning, Edward; Baley, William, Sarah; Kerr, Sarah.

BLADEN COUNTY—WILLS

A.

1796 ANDRES, JOHN JR. Children (not named).

1778 ADAIR, JAMES, Robert, (son); Susanna McTyer (daughter); Adair McTyer (grandson); Elizabeth H. Cade (daughter).

B.

1801 BALDWIN, WILLIAM, Penelope (wife); Sharles, David and William.

1797 BOWIN, GOODIN, Judith (wife); William F.

1797 BRIGHT, SIMON, Mary (wife); Simon, Robert, Elricha, James, Benjamin and Christian.

1804 BRADLEY, JAMES, Anna (wife); John Bradley Cowan (grandson).

1786 BRYAN, THOMAS, Sisters: not named except Kerenhappuch.

1791 BALDWIN, JOHN, John, Charles, William, Sarah, Betty, Anna and Nancy.

1774 BRYAN, JOHN, Jane (wife); John, Phillemore, Ann and James.

1787 BYRNE, ALEXANDER, Matthew (brother); Mary Wilkins (sister).

1767 BAILEY, THOMAS, Hester (wife); Thomas.

1783 BARNEY, WILLIAM H. James, William, Arthur and Samuel.

1774 BENEOW, CHARLES, Benjamin, Thomas, Ann. Mary, Sarah and Sapphira; Mary Clayton (daughter).

1774 BEATTY, JOHN, Margaret (wife); Mary Bins-Man and Flora Harris (daughters).

1782 BROWN, GEORGE, Elizabeth (wife); Thomas, John, George, Richard, Euphemia, Mary and Margaret.

1785 BARFIELD, RICHARD, Ann (wife); Elisha, Willis, Shadrach and Roderick; Unity Edwards, Uridea Hannell and Mary Flowers (daughters).

1772 BEARD, WILLIAM, Catherine (wife); James and John; Catherine Moore (daughter).

1777 BORDEN, PETER, Wife (not named).

C.

1798 CAIN, JOSEPH, John and James Cain (half-brothers); Joseph Cain (nephew).

1798 CLARK, DAVID, Silas Clark Frazier (nephew).

1799 COLEMAN, MOSES, Lurani (wife); John, Theophilus, Moses, Amos, Polly, Philip, Lucretia and Dempsey.

1776 COLVIN, MATURIN, Henry; Rev. Alexander Colvin (father).

1768 CRAWFORD, MARGARET, Mary Shaw (daughter).

1791 CULLUM, RICHARD, Elizabeth (wife).

1784 COOPER, BENJAMIN, Elizabeth Lock (sister); Benjamin, Joseph and William Cooper, (grandsons).

1778 CARVER, JAMES, Mary Simonds (friend).

1780 COLLUM, WILLIAM, Richard and Margaret.

1781 COHOON, JOHN, Jean (wife); Micajah, Elijah, Darby and Elizabeth.

1793 CLARDY, JAMES, Wife (not named); Sons (not named); Penelope Shaw (granddaughter).

1783 CLARK, BENJAMIN, Mary (wife); Elizabeth, William, Thomas and Luke.

1799 COOPER, JOSEPH, Mary (wife); William, Benjamin and Joseph.

1782 CAIN, SAMUEL, William.

D.

1783 DEDANE, JOHN, Wife (not named); Thomas, Rebecca, John, James, Tabitha, William, George, Ann and Margaret.

1797 DEWEY, HUPHEMIA, Her slaves and her white friends.

1790 DAVIS, WILLIAM, Ann, Leah, Hexaha and John.

1799 DOVE, ESTHER, James Crane (nephew); Esther Crane (niece).

1796 DUPREE, AMELIA, Susanna Moore (niece).

1770 DEACON, MARY, Daughters of Mary Curtis.

1790 DAVIS, EDWARD, Margaret (wife); Edward, William, Greenwood, John B., Mary and Margaret; Jean Blocker (daughter).

1794 DAVIS, TURNER, Susanna (wife); John, Thomas, Sarah, Ann and Elizabeth.

E.

1795 ELLIS, JOHN, Lucy (wife); children (not named).

F.

1801 FLOWERS, IGNATIUS, Uriah, Sarah, Ignatius, Richard and Morgan; Goolsbury Flowers (sister).

1801 FLOYD, NANCY, Elizabeth Ann and William Floyd (grandchildren).

1785 FLINN, DANIEL, Mary (wife); Daniel, Elizabeth and James.

G.

1771 GIBBS, JOHN, Amelia (wife); John Gibbs and other nephews (not named).

1799 GATES, JEAN, Edward and Margaret.

1791 GIBBS, JOHN, Amelia (wife); John and George Gibbs (nephew).

1788 GIBBS, GEORGE, Margaret (wife); George and Robert.

1789 GATES, PETER, Mary (wife); children (not named).

1792 GAUSE, NEEDHAM, Elizabeth (wife); Samuel (brother).

1779 GLASS, LEVI, Mary (wife); Solomon, Mary, Littleton, Levi, Thomas, Ritta and Rebecca.

1792 GREEN, MARY, James Green (brother).

H.

1768 HEGGANS, JEPTHA, Martha (wife); Anna.

1797 HODGE, ROBERT, Mary (wife); Moses Lewis (nephew).

1796 HOLMES, EDWARD, Ann (wife); Richard.
1804 HOLMES, MOSES, Mary (wife); John and Mary.
1805 MARVEY, TRAVIS, Eliza and Ann; Robert (brother).
1770 HILL, ISAAC, William, (brother); Joseph Lock (friend).
1791 HOWARD, JOHN, William, Sarah, Ameline, Mary, Jane and Primus.
1790 HUFFMAN, HUDNUT, Martha (wife); James, Solomon and Mary.
1785 HARRISON, JOHN, Margaret (wife); Edward, Susan, Ann Margaret and Elizabeth.
1778 HUDSON, WILLIAM, Lydia (wife); Josiah and William.
1794 HAYNES, JOSHUA, Rebecca and Ketturah Manly (nieces).

I.

1780 ISHAM, JAMES, James.
1774 IKNER, GEORGE, Dorothy (wife); George, Philip and Solomon.

J.

1804 JERNIGAN, WHITMEL, Richard J. (brother).
1789 JOHNSTON, LELAH, Robert.
1782 JONES, GRIFFITH, Wife (not named); Margaret McRee and Mary White (daughters); Griffith Houston (grandsons).
1783 JONES, ISAAC, Edward, Isaac and Musgrove; Joseph, William and Snowden Singletary (brothers).
1786 JESSUP, JOHN, Wife (not named).

K.

1793 KING, DUNCAN, Lydia (wife); Alexander and other children (not named).
1805 KEMP, JOSEPH, William, Daniel, Amelia and John; Elizabeth Salter and Mary Ellis (daughter).
1800 KELLY, MATTHEW, Matthew; Sarah Wingate (daughter).

L.

1805 LUCAS, THOMAS, Priscilla (wife); Mary and Sarah.
1798 LAMONT, DUNCAN, Christian (wife); Nancy and Daniel; Miriam McMillan (daughter).
1792 LUCAS, THOMAS, Priscilla (wife); Mary, Sarah, Susan and William.
1790 LLOYD, ANN, Mary McRee (daughter); William Smith (cousin).
1784 LUCAS, FRANCIS, Elizabeth (wife); Henry and other children (not named).
1779 LOWE, THOMAS, Daniel and John.
1781 LOCK, JOSEPH, Emma (wife); Isaac, Leonard and Susanna.
1769 LAMB, MARY, Jacob and Isaac.
1783 LOCK, LEONARD, Rebecca (wife); Rebecca, Elizabeth, Mary, Sallie, Leonard, John and David.

1787 LOCK, JOHN, Elizabeth (wife); Thomas, Hannah, Mary, Eliza, Susan and Rebecca; Elizabeth Elwell (daughter).

M.

1798 MULFORD, ELIZABETH, David, Ephraim, Abigail and John; Elizabeth Pemberton (daughter).

1801 McMILLAN, JOHN, John McMillan (friend).

1798 McREE, SAMUEL, Mary (wife); James, William, John, Alexander and Margaret; Sarah Gibbs (daughter).

1804 MESSENRER, JOSEPH, Mary (wife).

1804 McEWEN, ROBERT, Wife (not named); Jean.

1806 McMILLAN, DUNCAN, Effie (wife); John, Nancy and Esebet (Elizabeth).

1801 MORRISON, JOHN, Flora (wife); Marian and Kenneth.

1801 McLEAN, JOHN, Catherine Shaw (sister).

1790 McKOY, RALPH, Ann (mother); Archibald and Daniel (brothers).

1800 MAULTSBY, ANTHONY, William and Samuel.

1793 McREE, ROBERT, Jane (wife); Elizabeth and Robert; Sarah Chesten (daughter).

1793 MOORE, JAMES, Eurydice, Lydia and Hance.

1788 MESICK, JACOB, Elizabeth Barry and Lucy Streaty (friends).

1774 McNEILL, WILLIAM, John, Dugald and McDuffie.

1787 MOREHEAD, MARY, Jonathan, William and Elizabeth Robeson (her children); Bartram Morehead (son).

1789 MEEK, GEORGE, Mary (wife).

1793 McMASTER, FELIX, Wife (not named); children (not named).

1790 McCONKEY, ROBERT, Ruth (wife).

1770 MUSSELWHITE, THOMAS, Mary (wife); Jesse, Thomas, Anna, Elizabeth, Winifred, Ella, Bridget, Mary, Amelia, Patience and Sarah.

1775 MOORE, BERENGER, Mary (wife); Nathan Moore (nephew); John Davis, (friend).

1767 MOORE, WILLIAM, Wife (not named); Skinkins (son).

1778 MAXFIELD, MARY, Lettice Townsend (daughter); Robert Conkey (son).

1774 MOORE, WILLIAM, William, John, James and McTyer.

1780 McEWEN, JOHN, Robert, William and Matthew.

1785 McKAY, IVOR, Ann (wife); Ralph, John, Alexander, Archibald, Daniel, Isabel and Elizabeth.

1774 McKETHAN, HUGH, Elizabeth, (wife); Duncan; Margaret McPhatter (daughter); Elizabeth McDaniel (daughter.

1779 McDANIEL, JAMES, Agnes (wife); William, James, Absalom, David, Margaret, Mary and Agnes.

1778 McMILLAN, EDWARD, Margaret (wife); Neil, Jack, Margaret and Nancy.

1778 McNEILL, HECTOR, Margaret (wife); Duncan and "Bluff John", (sons); Lochiel Cameron (friend).

1789 McREE, WILLIAM, Margaret (wife); Griffith
J., James and John; William Singletary
(grandson).

1776 MALLINGTON, RICHARD, Silence Green (granddaughter); Richard M. Lewis (grandson).

1771 McDOUGAL, ALLEN, Mary (wife);

1777 MONROE, DUNCAN, Elizabeth (wife); Angus.

N.

1802 NANCE, DANIEL, Patience (wife); Joseph
and Wynne.

O.

1796 OWEN, THOMAS, Eleanor (wife); John, Mary
Stedman (daughter).

P.

1802 PARKER, WILLIAM, Mary (wife); children
(not named).

1773 PORTER, JOHN, Hugh and Samuel (brothers).

1779 PETMAN, JACCB, Hannah (wife); Bethany
and Sampson.

1794 POWELL, JOHN, Elizabeth (wife); Isaac and
Barnabas; Chloe Avery and Charity Wilkinson (daughters).

1794 POWELL, ZILPHA, Mary (sister); other sisters
and brothers (not named).

R.

1792 ROBINSON, PETER, Elizabeth (wife); Mary,
Thomas, Peter and William.

1804 REYNOLDS, RICHARD, Mary (wife).

1797 RUSS, JOSEPH, Wife (not named); John Wilson (friend).

1802 REGISTER, WILLIAM, Elizabeth (wife); Elizabeth and Ann Register (granddaughters).

1795 RUSS, THOMAS, Wife (not named); Hannah,
Thomas, Joseph, Ann, Susan and Sarah;
Margaret and Mary Harnch (daughters).

1779 RICHARDSON, NATHANIEL, Wife (not named).

1772 RUSS, MARY, Thomas, Eleanor and John;
Nancy Lloyd, Margaret Smith and Sarah Oliphant (daughters).

1780 RAY, ISAAC, Amelia (wife).

1791 RUSS, JOHN, James Russ, Sr. (nephew);
Eleazar (brother); Shepherd Russ (cousin);
Nancy Lloyd and Margaret Thomas (sisters).

1785 ROBESON, THOMAS, Mary (wife); Jonathan,
William and Bartram; Peter (brother).

1775 ROBESON, THOMAS, Peter and Thomas.

1792 ROWLAND, JAMES, Elizabeth (wife); John,
Thomas, Jomes, Samuel, David, Sarah, Mary
and Elizabeth.

1773 REGAN, JOSEPH, Ralph, John and Richard.

1780 ROBESON, THOMAS, Mary (wife); Jonathan,
Bartram, William, Elizabeth and Sarah.

S.

1799 SHAW, ARCHIBALD, Catherine (wife).

1799 SHIPMAN, DANIEL, Ann (wife); Rebecca and
Ann.

1798 SMITH, WILLIAM, Rose Bright (daughter);
      Alfred, Mulford and William Smith (grand-
      sons).
BANK—265
1793 May. RANDOL, WILLIAM, Ann (wife); Eliza-
      beth and John Cray (grandchildren); Wil-
      liam Randol (grandson).
1788 June. RESONOVER, CLARA, Joseph; Elizabeth
      Lipsey (daughter).

S.

1782 March. STEPHENS, JOHN, Elizabeth (wife);
      Joseph, George, Bathsheba, Mary, Nancy and
      Sophia.
1788 December. SMITH, WILLIAM, Sarah (wife).
1793 May. STANDLEY, JAMES, Winifred (wife);
      John, Olivet, Sarah, Elizabeth, Susanna,
      Mary, Winifred and Nathaniel.
1794 February. SIMMONS, GEORGE, Nancy (wife);
      Edward Debrool (Debruhl) (brother).
1797 May. SAUNDERS, LEVI, Sally (wife); Levi,
      Sally, Cinelda, Polly and William.
1796 August. SKEEN, SARAH, Alex, Issac, Celia,
      Jesse, Elizabeth and Elijah; Rebecca Cox
      (daughter).
1797 November. SKEEN, ISAAC, Children of John
      Cox, Elisha, Joseph and Sarah, (grandchild-
      ren).
1797 May. SMALL, REUBEN, Catherine (wife);
      Amos, George and Susanna.
1792 Bebruary. STEVENSION, CHARLES, Thomas,
      Stephen and Sally.
1792 February. STEEL, PETER, Wife (not named);
      Alex, Benjamin, Elijah, James, Esther, Sarah,
      Rachel, Rebecca and Mary.
1798 February. SKEEN, ALEX, Rachel (wife);
      Mary.
1799 November. STANTON, WILLIAM, Lydia (wife);
      Alice, Abigail, Borden, Enoch, William and
      Job.
1801 February. SKEEN, BETSY, Polly and Betsy
      Hawkins (nieces).
1801 May. SHINE, DANIEL, Barbara (wife); John,
      James and Frank; Polly Shackleford, Susan-
      na Wilton and Hannah Farnal (daughters).
1802 November. SIMMONS, JOHN, Elizabeth
      (wife); Sally.

T.

1799 May. TAYLOR, CORNELIUS, David Taylor
      (grandson).
1799 March. TAYLOR, ROBERT, John, Edmund and
      Philip; Elifee Roberts (daughter).

V.

1795 February. VENTRESS (Fentress) WILLIAM,
      George and James (brothers).

W.

1796 February. WARREN, JOSEPH, Mary (wife)..

1792 May. WATSON, JEREMIAH, James, Moses, Nicodemus and Rhoda; Anna Williamson and Mary Frazier (daughters); Sarah Simmons (granddaughter); Stephen Grant (grandson).

1793 February. WILLIAMSON, DAVID, Nancy (wife); James, Barry and Jeremiah.

1796 February. WILLIAMS, THOMAS, Elizabeth (wife); Sarah Orme (sister); John, Jr., Thomas, and Elizabeth Devereux.

1797 February. WEST, ELI, Keir (wife); Phoebe and Elizabeth; Vashti Ward (daughter).

1793 May. WATSON, JAMES, Sarah (wife); James, Sarah, Asa, Ernest and Ivy.

1793 November. WILLIAMS, CHOPLAN, Zilpha (wife); Lewis and Solomon.

1788 June. WEEKS, ARCHELAUS, Abigail (wife); Elizabeth.

1798 February. WOOD, GERSHAM. Sedea (wife); Peter, Mary, Nancy, Anthony, John and Darius; Mahala Amyett (daughter).

1802 February. WHITTEY, EDWARD, Dorothy (wife); Ann, Charles, Lewis, Joseph and Sally.

Y.

1803 November. YEATES, STEPHEN, Alice (wife); Bennett, Elizabeth and Daniel; Rebecca Eubanks (daughter).

BRUNSWICK—WILLS

A.

1797 ALLEN, DRURY, Margaret (wife); Eskandah; James Ranaldson, Drewy Allen Ranaldson; Mary Moore and Nancy Moore.

B.

1765 BERRY, DANIEL, Rebecca, Samuel.
1765 BRANTLEY, WILLIAM, Rachel (wife).
1767 BRADLEY, RACHEL, Hannah, Pariso and other children not named.
1789 BELL, JOHN, Phoebe (wife), Hannah, Robert; Eunice Bell; John Caine; Rebecca Gilbert.
1793 BELL, JAMES, Sarah (wife), James, Samuel, Nathaniel and Joseph; James Anderson; Sarah Galloway; Alfred, Cornelius, Mary, Amelia, Rebecca, Brevard and Mary Caines.
1800 BROWN, CHARLES, David.
1765 BOSHER, WILLIAM, Jean (wife).

C.

1771 CAINS, MARY, John, Lois, Sarah and Richard; Margaret Moore.
1775 CRANDELL, LYDIA, Rebecca (wife), and others not named.
1792 CLARK, THOMAS, Hooper and William Clark, and others not named.
1800 CREEL, MARK, Daily and Willis.
1781 CHAIRES, JOHN, James; Mary Wale; Sarah Parker; Margaret Smith.

D.

1775 DAVIS, JOHN, George and others not named.
1756 DAVIS, JOHN, Thomas, and others not named.
1763 DAVIS, JOHN, Sarah. (wife), and others not named.
1771 DANIEL, JOHN, Ann (wife), and others not named.
1771 DANIEL, JOHN, JR., Elizabeth (wife), and others not named.
1788 DANIEL, SARAH, Amelia (wife), Ann, Stephen, Robert and William.
1770 DALRYMPLE, MARTHA, Martha Lillington, and others not named.
1781 DENNING, STEPHEN, Martha (wife).
1779 DRY, WILLIAM, William, Jr., and others not named.
1781 DRY, WILLIAM, Virgil; Sarah Moore; Cornelius Harnett; Mary and Thomas Davis; Robert Ellis; Wm. Hill; Sarah Montain; Thomas McGuire; Mary Jane Dry; Sarah Smith; Wm. Dry (alias Wm. Moore); Rebecca, Jane, Sophia and Ann Davis.
1783 DAVIS, ROGER, SR., Roger.
1771 DANIEL, JOHN, Ann (wife), Albert, George, William, Stephen and Robert.

E.

1767 ESPY, USHER, William Lord.
1772 ELLERY, WILLIAM, John Sheea.

F.

1772 FOWLER, ANN, Jane (wife), Ann and Mary.

1791 FRINK, SARAH, Needham, Samuel and Elizabeth Gause; Mitchell, Elizabeth, Mary, and Sarah Bellune.

1795 FRINK, MARTHA, Samuel and Elizabeth Gause; Dennis and John Frink; Martin Hankins.

1795 FRANK, SAMUEL, Sarah (wife) Samuel; heirs of Dennis Hankins and Thomas Frink (not named).

G.

1767 GODWIN, JOSEPH, Ann (wife).

1783 GAUSE, JOHN, Charlotte (wife), Elizabeth, Benjamin, Charles, John, Hannah and Needham.

1795 GALLOWAY, JOHN, Alfred, Cornelius, Mary, Amelis and Nathaniel.

1793 GOODMAN, WILLIAM, Amy (wife), Sarah, William, Henry, Luke and Job; Catherine Bell; Martha Rutland; Sam Potter.

1800 GOODMAN, ANNE, Lydia Caines; Sarah Goodman; Mary Wingate; Robert and Samuel Potter; Amelia Russ.

1794 GAUSE, NEEDHAM, Hannah (wife), Needham, William, John, Bryan, and Elizabeth.

1791 GRANGE, JOHN, Mary, and others not named.

1788 GRANGE, JOHN, SR., John P. Grange.

H.

1772 HALL, THOMAS, Thomas, John, William, Susie, Frances and Roger.

1778 HOLDEN, BENJAMIN, Alfred, and others not named.

1780 HALL, ELIZABETH, William Watters; William Hall.

1781 HARLESTON, JOHN, Isaac Harleston, and others not named.

1793 HANKINS, DENNIS, Elizabeth (wife), Thomas, William, Mark, Samuel, and Dennis.

1794 HEWETT, JOSEPH, SR, Dorcas (wife); John, David, Joseph, Thomas and Samuel; Philip and Rachel Ivey; Ruth Standard.

1780 HALL, ELIZABETH, William, and others not named.

1768 HOWE, ROBERT, wife (not named).

1796 HOWE, SARAH, Robert; Mary Moore.

J.

1762 JENNERET, ELIAS, Margaret (wife); children (not named).

1767 JEANS, WILLIAM, John Truett; James McIlhenny; Joseph, Hester, Sarah, David, Abel, and Isaac Jeans (children).

L.

1798 LORD, WILLIAM E., Lord, William (nephew).

1769 LUDLUM, ISAAC, Nehemiah, and others not named.

1769 LORING, JOSIAH, Mary (wife).
1772 LEONARD, HENRY, Hannah (wife); Joseph
      Hewett; Crawford Ludlum; Job Holden;
      Henry and John Willitts; Abigail Holden;
      Ann Willitts, Ruth and Lydia Hewett.
1782 LEONARD, SAMUEL, Samuel and others not
      named.
1782 LUDLUM, CRAWFORD, Harriet Laspeyre, and
      others not named.
1770 LUDLUM, SARAH, Crawford.

M.

1764 MUNRO, REVELL, Rachel (wife), and others
      not named.
1763 McCORMICK, MARGARET, Peter Lord.
1789 McALISTER, ARCHIBALD, Mary (wife), and
      others not named.
1795 McALISTER, MARY, James, and others not
      named.

N.

1774 NEALE, SAMUEL, Henry, and others not named.
1777 NASH, FRANCIS, Sarah (wife), and others
      not named.
1781 NEAL, HENRY, Elizabeth (wife); Thomas
      Neal; John Swain.
1790 NEAL, THOMAS, JR., Wife, and others not
      named.
1790 NEAL, NANCY, Lucy Brown; Selena Vernon;
      John Mills; John, Nancy and Elizabeth Ver-
      non.
1796 NEAL, THOMAS, Eleanor (wife).

P.

1764 PINSON, THOMAS, Arthur and Amelia Spear.
1798 POTTER, MILES, SR., Robert, Miles, John and
      Joseph; Abraham Skipper; Margaret Mc-
      Murray.

R.

1765 ROSS, CHARLES, Hannah (wife), and others
      not named.
1795 READ, JAMES, John Haywood.
1771 ROWAN, JOHN, Ann (wife), and others not
      named.
1786 ROOTS, ROGER, Elizabeth (wife), Henry, Roger,
      Samuel, Sarah and Hannah.
1788 ROBERTS, AARON, Martha (wife), and others
      not named.

S.

1775 STANLAND, PATRICK, Thomas, and others not
      named.
1779 SIMMONS, JOHN, Sarah (wife).
1787 SMITH, HENRY, Thomas, Joseph and Alexan-
      der.
1794 SMITH, JOHN, SR; JOHN, JR., James, Mary
      and Memory; Spicy Reaves.
1787 SMITH, MARY, Sophia Grange; Thomas Smith;
      James Glass.

T.

1786 TAYLOR, THOMAS, wife (not named).
1799 TAYLOR, HENRY, Mary (wife), children (not named).

V.

1781 VERNON, JOHN, Lucy Jones; Sarah Robinson; William Jones; Henrietta White; William, and Susannah Vernon.

W.

1761 WILLITTS, HOPE, Samuel, Mary, Lydia, Amy, Joseph and Hope.
1772 WILKINSON, JOHN, Elizabeth and Thomas; Watt, Anna and John; Wood, Honora.
1776 WALKER, JOHN, devisees, Mary (wife), Ann and Jean.
1775 WALKER, JOHN, Mary (wife).
1779 WATTERS, SAMUEL, devisees, Martha (wife), and children not named.
1789 WINGATE, EDWARD, Sarah wife).

CABARRUS—WILLS

A.

1793 ABENSHINE, CHRISTIAN, Rynhold (son).

B.

1793 BARKER, GREENBERRY, Christopher.
1795 BARRINGER, ROTHIAS, John
1793 BERRY, GEORGE, Mary (wife).
1795 BOSHARD, JOHN, Jacob.

C.

1793 CORRIGIN, JAMES, Isabella (wife); James.
1793 CLAY, JOSEPH, Mary (wife).
1793 CORPEN, THEDFORD, Joseph.

D.

1793 DIETRICH, NICHOLAS, Mary (wife).

F.

1797 FREEMAN, CLAVAN, Patience (wife).
1794 FRANK, JACOB, ——————.

G.

1792 GILMORE, JOSEPH, John, Josiah, Nathaniel and William.
1797 GIBBON, HENRY, ———————
1793 GREEN, NATHAN, Elizabeth (wife).

H.

1794 HARRIS, JAMES, Elizabeth (wife); James, William, Houston and Robert.

L.

1794 LINGLE, PETER, Christina (wife).
1795 LEOPARD, CATHERINE, John.
1795 LEWIS, CHRISTOPHER, Jacob.
1794 LUDWIG, CONRAD, ——————.

N.

1795 NUSSMAN, ADOLPH, wife (not named).

R.

1794 RUSSELL, ROBERT, wife (not named).

S.

1793 SCONNELL, MIAMICA, Mary (wife).
1794 SELL, PETER, Susanna (wife), Peter.
1794 SEALS, FRANCIS, Mary, Samuel, William, John and Elizabeth.
1794 SHANNON, ROBERT, ——————.
1793 SHELBY, THOMAS, Sarah (wife).
1796 SCONNELL, JOHN, ———————.
1796 SHINN, BENJAMIN, Joseph, Silas and Samuel.

U.

1796 UTE, BERNHARD, Barbara (wife).

W.

1797 WALKER, NICHOLAS, Barbara (wife).
1795 WALLACE, JOHN, Jodaiah (wife).
1794 WEDDING, WILLIAM, ——————.
1794 WHITE, WILLIAM, William and Young.
1795 WESSNER, GEORGE, ——————.

CARTERET—WILLS

A.

1777 ARTHUR, JOHN, James, Seth.

B.

1749 BORDEN, WILLIAM, William.
1766 BRYANT, NICHOLAS, Eleanor, John.
1773 BENTHALL, JOHN, Reuben; Meadows, John.
1772 BENTHALL, REUBEN, Thomas, Jacob, Reuben, John.
1784 BELL, DAVID, David, Sarah, Elizabeth.
1785 BACKHOUSE, JOHN, Allen, John.
1785 BAGWELL, ROBERT, Keziah.
1788 BALL, NATHAN, Lee, Archie.
1782 BELL, NUELL, John, Nuell, Nathan.
1787 BREES, HENRY, Sarah, Ross, James.
1788 BROWN, JOHN, Joshua, Moses; Brock, Mary.
1789 BRION, NATHAN, Nancy, Mary, Edward.
1794 BELL, GEORGE, Hepsabeth, Fort, Stephen, Edward, Mary; Borden, Joseph.
1799 BORDEN, WM., SR., William, Benjamin; Wood Alsey, Hatch, Hopey.
1793 BELL, NUELL, Lesha.
1792 BELL, JOSEPH, James, Nathaniel, Nuell.
1799 BLOCKSON, SEVERN, Nancy, Jenny, Cassa, Hannah.
1775 BELL, JOSEPH, David, Malachi, Caleb, Joseph, Andrew.
1786 BARRINGTON, NATHAN, Isaac, John, Lawrence.
1769 BERKLEY, AYTWORTH, Abraham, Nancy.
1788 BERY, JAMES, Mary, David, James; Fields, Nancy.
1793 BREES, WM., David, William, James.
1781 BELL, SOLOMON, Owen.
1719 BRICE, WM., Ann, William, Eliza, Frances.
1753 BRICE, WM., Acton, Frances, Rigdon, William.

C.

1768 CAVENAUGH, WADE, Abram, Mary, Jacob; Ward, Enoch.
1774 CHADWICK, DAVID, Solomon.
1795 CANADAY, THOMAS, Solomon, Goffigan, Elizabeth.
1768 CAVENAUGH, ANANIAS, Mary.
1771 CHAPMAN, JOSHUA, Hester, Mary, Bridget, Sarah.
1782 CHURCH, CONSTANT, Shaw, Anthony.
1775 COALE, WM., Bell, Susanna, Elizabeth; Oglesby, Mary.

D

1792 DAVIS, JOSEPH, Thomas, Joseph, William.
1766 DUDLEY, JACOB, Fanny, Miriam.
1794 DAVIS, SOLOMON W., Logan, Samuel, Enoch, Nathan, Anthony, Allen, Clarey, Betsey; Wiley, Tamar.
1774 DUDLEY, CHRISTOPHER, Elijah, Christopher, Abraham.
1797 DILL, EDWARD, John, Benjamin, Edward.
1763 DUDLEY, ELIJAH, Thomas, Elizabeth, Mary.
1774 DUFFY, PELEG, Hannah, Sarah, Ruth, Aimme, Peleg, George, Watson, Walter.

E

1779 EAVES, RICHARD, Sarah, Isaac.

F.

1768　FULLER, EDWARD, John, Edward, Nathan, Belcher, Rebecca.

G.

1769　GARNER, FRANCIS, Jeremiah, Eleanor.
1765　GARNER, SAMUEL, Janie (wife) and children (not named).
1770　GASKILL, WM., William, Elizabeth, John, Thomas, Benjamin, Joseph, Jacob.
1778　GILLIKIN, THOMAS, Thomas, Alex., Sarah, Uner, Jane, Benjamin, Jessie, James, George.
1792　GREEN, SAMUEL, Cassandra, Esther, Zach, Archelus, Jonathan.
1794　GARNER, JOHN, Lucy (wife) and children (not named).
1793　GOULDING, THOMAS, Mary; Smith, Elizabeth.
1798　GOODWIN, LUCRETIA, Mary, Oliver; Daniels, Annis, Thomas, Lucretia.

H.

1765　HOCKER, EBENEZER, Ebenezer, Zachariah, James.
1767　HARPER, JOHN, John, Sarah, Lydia, Elizabeth.
1767　HERBERT, HILARY, Mary, Margaret, Sarah, William, Hilary.
1777　HAY, HANNAH, Hannah, Wade, Thomas.
1780　HUNTER, EZEKIEL, Cassy, Elizabeth, Ruth, Jennie, Jethro.
1782　HANCOCK, HENRY, Caswell, Susannah.
1791　HELLEN, JONATHAN, Elizabeth, Jonathan.
1791　HUFF, RICHARD, Thomas, Richard, Mary, Judy, Elizabeth.
1797　HATSELL, WM., Armistead, Willie, Harrod.
1797　HERBERT, HILARY, Jane, Elizabeth, Sarah, William.
1798　HILL, ABRAHAM, Annie.
1798　HOWLAND, SAMUEL, Matty, Mary, Bathsheba, Huldy, William, Charity.
1799　HUMPHREYS, NATHANIEL, Hill, John; Gill, Jack, George.

L.

1769　LAWRENCE, JOHN, John, Jacob, Laban.
1779　LOWELL, HANNAH, Fulford, Hannah, Alex.
1780　LONGEST, JOSHUA, James, Joshua; Yates, Sarah.
1795　LEWIS, THOMAS, Susanna, Prudence.

M.

1766　MORGAN, JOHN, Mark, William, Mary, Dorothy.
1777.　MITCHELL, ABRAHAM, wife and children (not named).
1784　MORSE, JOSEPH, Daniel, George, Mary, Elizabeth, Sarah, Ann, Susanna, Hannie, Alice, James, Theodore.
1791　MARLBONE, LEMUEL, Josephus, Peter; Howland, Christopher.
1793　MORSE, JOSHUA, Jacob, Jason, Isaac, Esther, Rebecca.

N.

1797 NELSON, ROBERT, Taylor, James; Bishop, John, Styron, Amasa, William; Austin, Thomas.
1799 NELSON, MARY, William.

O

1766 OWENS, WM., Arthur, William.
1796 OGLESBIE, THOMAS, Gideon, John, Absalom, Thomas, Levy.

P.

1762 PIGGOTT, JOHN, Oliver, John, William.
1789 PIGGOTT, ELIJAH, William, Elijah, Culpepper, Ithamor, Levi, Ralph, Jeconias.
1755 READ, GEORGE, Robert.
1761 RUSTULL, RICHARD, Elizabeth, Huggins, Sarah, Willis, John, Mary.
1766 ROBINSON, JOSEPH, Allen, Elizabeth; Gooding, Lucretia.
1787 ROBINSON, ANN, Allen; Lupton, Annis; Williston, Grace.
1799 SAMSON, SILVIA, Mary, Abraham.
1799 STIRON, SAMUEL, John, Littleton, Verty, Elizabeth, Rebecca, Abigail, Miriam, Hannah; Rose, Joseph.

S.

1799 STANTON, BENJAMIN, James, Benjamin, Joseph, Henry, David; Scott, Elizabeth; Thomas, William, Annie.
1799 SCARBOROUGH, WILLIAM, Anne, William, James, George.
1760 SHAW, JOHN, James; Waldron, Sarah, John.
1760 SIMPSON, JOSEPH, John, Edward, Joseph, Corne, Rossiter.
1760 SHACKLEFORD, KEZIAH, Freeman, Ellis, Susanna, Lydia, Sarah.
1784 SAVORY, ROBERT, Judy, Richard.
1784 SMITH, JOHN, Thomas.
1787 SMITH, THOMAS, Thomas, Mary, Sarah.
1788 STANTON, HOPE, Joseph, William, Borden, Benjamin, Ruth.
1793 STIRON, JOHN, John, Samuel, George, Mary, Elizabeth, Abigail, Joyce.
1790 SANDERS, SAMUEL, Mary, Sarah, Daniel, David, William, John, Samuel, James.
1795 SANDERS, THOMAS, Thomas.
1796 SMITH, THOMAS, John, Reuben.

T.

1796 TOLSON, WM., Ann, George.
1799 TAYLOR, SOLOMON, Elizabeth.

W.

1745 WADE, ROBERT, Abraham, Jesse, Jacob.
1771 WILLISTON, JOHN, Sabra, Daniel; Moore, Tamar; Fenters, Abigail.
1785 WILLISTON, JOHN, Harris, Mary W.; Guthrie, Sarah; Gaskins, Esther; Moore, Tamar.

1782   WEEKS, ISAAC, James, John, Abraham, Simmons, Citte, Jesse.

1788   WILLIAMS, WESTON, Daniel, Isaac, Elizabeth; Prescott, Mary, Lydia.

1785   WALLIS, SARAH, Houston, Mary, Rachel; Jacobs, Sally.

1795   WHITEHURST, JOHN, Richard, Margaret; Hall, John.

1798   WILLISTON, SAMUEL, George, Esther, Josiah, Andrew, Daniel, Abner, Abigail, Zilphia, Didina.

Y.

1795   YEATES, BAGE, Raffy, William, Hopey, Patty.

CASWELL COUNTY—WILLS

A.

1784 March. ALLEN, ROBERT, Hannah (wife); Josiah Allen (grandson).

1788 July. ANTHONY, JOHN, Ursula (wife); Jonathan, Elijah, John, William, Joseph, Elizabeth (children); Nancy Stone, Sarah Boney and Jane Carder (daughters).

1784 September. ATKINSON, ROBERT, Ransom, Patsy, Mary anad Jane.

B.

1777 June. BUMPASS, ROBERT, Sarah (wife); John, (son) Lucy Van Hook, Elizabeth Davey, and Sugreston.

1777 June. BARNETT, ROBERT, Sarah (wife); Robert and Andrew.

1777 June. BUMPASS, ROBERT, Sarah (wife); John, (son) Lucy Van Hook, Elizabeth Davey, Agnes Pratt, Winifred Cozart and Martha Williams (daughters).

1777 June. BUMPAS, SAMUEL, Mary (wife); Robert, Nathaniel, John, Samuel, Elizabeth and Mary.

1781 April. BLACK, ROBERT, Elizabeth (wife); George, Henry, John, Thomas, Elizabetn Fulkerson (daughter).

1784 March. BOWLES, SARAH, John and Mary.

1785 October. BURTON, CHARLES, Jean (wife); George, Edward, Robert, Charles, Theodorick and Dolly.

1787 January. BROWING, NICHOLAS, Sarah (wife); Jean, Sarah and Enos.

1787 April. BRADLEY, JAMES, Thomas, John, James, Edward and Mary.

1788 October. BARKER, GEORGE, John, Israel, James, George, David, William, Isabel and Susanna.

1789 January. BLACK, HENRY, Mary (wife); eight children (not named).

1790 April. BROOKS, RICHARD, Ann (wife); William, Betsy, Frances and John (children); Ann S. Graves (daughter).

1790 April. BAXTER, THOMAS, Rachel (wife); Frances, Thomas and Philip.

1791 July. BOMAN, ROYAL, Elizabeth (wife); Thomas, Josiah, Robert, Joseph, Samuel and Leonard.

1795 October. BELEW, ISAAC, Jemima, Daniel, Mary and Harvel.

1795 October. BRUCE, ROBERT, Wife (not named); Thomas, William, John, Robert and Betsey.

1799 January. BROWN, JOHN, William, Bedford, Sally, Green, John and Betty; Nancy Harper and Elizabeth Swift (daughters).

1799 January. BOYD, WILLIAM, Mary (wife); William, Stephen and Armistead.

1799 July. BALDWIN, HENRY, Elizabeth (wife); Henry, Edward, Luke, Betsy, Lazarus and Hannah.

C.

1782   March. CARTIN, RICHARD, Mary (wife); John Carter (brother).

1782   September. CORDER, WILLIAM, Phoebe (wife); children (not named).

1784   July. CUMMINS, WILLIAM, Martha (wife); children (not named).

1785   July. CATE, JOHN, Thomas (son); John Cate (grandson).

1789   July. CARNAL, PATRICK, Mary (wife); Richard, Fanny, Patrick, Hubbard, Archibald and Fleming (children); Nancy Mitchell, Mary White and Mildred Oliver (daughters).

1790   January. CURREE, JOHN, Wife (not named); James, Hugh, William, Mary, Elizabeth, Catherine, Martha and Margaret.

1796   July. CROSSET, JOHN, Wife (not named); William, Charity, Margaret, James, Jean and Elizabeth.

1799   CHARLES, NICHOLAS, Fanny (wife); Elizabeth, Nancy, William and Robert (children); Polly Dixon, Dolly Rice and Elizabeth Bowman (daughters).

D.

1777   December. DEWEESE, JONATHAN: Rachel (wife); Miriam, Ruth, Hezekiah, Samuel, Isaiah, Johnathan, Matthew and Cornelius.

1778   December. DOBBIN, ALEX.; Catherine (wife); John, Hugh, Agness and Elizabeth.

1781   September. DONALDSON, HUMPHREY; Mary (wife), Janet, Margaret, Rebecca, Willam, Andrew, Robert, Ebenezer and Humphrey (children); Mary Richards (daughter).

1781   December. DOBBIN, HUGH; John and James Dobbin (cousins); Mary Donaldson (friend).

1782   September. DIXON, HENRY, JR.; Martha (wife); Roger, Robert, Henry, Elizabeth and Wynne.

1782   September. DUTY, MATTHEW; Wife (not named); William, Solomon, Richard, Mary, Ann, Sarah and Littleton.

1790   January. DONALDSON, HANNAH; Robert and Mary (children); Rachel Dickson, Elizabeth Noell, Hannah Breese, Catherine Archdeacon and Sarah Wilkerson (daughters).

1791   October. DYER, SAMUEL; Elizabeth (wife), Thomas, Samuel, Anthony, Catherine and Mary.

1795   October. DIXON, HENRY, Elizabeth (wife), Charles and Tilman.

1798   January. DOBBIN, RACKEL; John (son); Margaret Comer and Rachel Van Hook (daughters); John Burch (grandson); Rachel Dobbin (grand-daughter).

1799   July. DAVIS, HENRY, Mary (wife).

E.

1782   September. ELLIS, WALTER; Mother (not named), brothers and sisters (not named).

1892   June. ENOCHS, BENJAMIN; Mary (wife); Benjamin, John, Samuel, Rice, Sarah, David and Mary Warren.

F.

1783   March. FARMER, SAMUEL; Cassandra (wife); Daniel, William, Stephen, Nathan, Pachel, Rachel and Susanna (children); Mary Wilson and Eleanor McMahon (daughters).

1784   March. FLYNN, PATRICK; Wife (not named), John, Mary, Patrick and Sussanna.

1786   January. FLETCHER, JAMES; Ursula (wife); William, James, Elizabeth, Mary, Sarah, Wesley and Grace.

1788   January. FERRELL, CHARLES; Mary Ann (wife), Elizabeth, Catherine, Rosey, William Charles.

1788   October. FARLEY, NATHANIEL; Sally (wife), Robert, Laban, George, Elizabeth, Polly and Nancy.

1790   July. FULLAR, HENRY, Peter, Elizabeth, Mary, George, Rankin, Abraham, Stephen, Isaac, John, Anne, Jacob and Isaiah (children); Sarah Majors and Keziah Reynolds (daughters).

1799   January. FARLEY, GEORGE, Catherine (wife), Partenia and Milly.

1799   October. FARLEY, STEWART; Mary (wife), Hezekiah and Daniel.

G.

1777   June. GALASBY (GILLESPIE) ALEXANDER; Ann (wife); Alexander and James.

1778   March. GOLD, EPHRAIM; Rachel (wife), William Gold (nephew).

1780   December. GUNN, JOHN; Wife (not named), Jesse, Sally, Gabriel and Daniel.

1781   June. GATEWOOD, AMBROSE; Martha (wife), Dudley Gatewood (nephew).

1782   September. GREYHAM, (GRAHAM) JAMES; Wife (not named), William, James, George, Thomas, Margaret and William.

1789   July. GREEN, SHADRACH; Thomas H. and Margaret; Sarah Crawford and Lucretia Albertson (daughters); Zachariah Swallow (grandson).

1790   January. GRAVES, JAMES; Ann Yancy (sister); Thomas Graves (brother).

1796   January. GILLESPIE, ANN; James (son).

H.

1777   December. HOPPER, THOMAS; Ann (wife); Benjamin McIntosh (grandson).

1779.   April. HARRELSON, EZEKIEL; Jane (wife), John, William and Hepzibah.

1781   June. HARRELSON, NATHANIEL; Dorcas (wife), Thomas, Nathan, Jeremiah and Forbes; Mary Smith (daughter).

1781   June. HARRELSON, ELKANAH; Jesse, Reuben, Elkanah and Bradley.

1781   June. HUSTON, ROBERT; Jane (wife), James, William and George; Mary Cooper (daughter).

1782   September. HARRIS, JOHN; Ann (wife).

1785   January. HOWARD, FRANCIS; Sarah (wife), Henry, Groves, William, Francis, Larkin, Johnston, Rebecca, Patty, Bettie and Ann.

1786 January. HENLEY, DARBY; Edmund, James and Darby.

1786 April. HALL, DAVID; Dorcas (wife); Franacis, Sarah, William, Dorcas, Ede, Samuel and John.

1787 January. HARRIS, TYREE; Tyree, Robert, Ede, Simpson, Christopher and Lydia; Nancy Abercrombie and Francis Dabney (daughters).

1789 January. HARRISON, SAMUEL; Wife (not named), Exbel (daughter).

1790 July. HARRISON, THOMAS; Arsay Fuqua and Magdalen McDougal (daughters).

1793 April. HOGG, GIDEON; Judith (wife); John, William, Elizabeth, Thomas, Agnes, Gideon (children); Ann Denton, Mourning Denton, Judith Gibson, Rebecca Shelton and Mary Yates (daughters).

1793 July. HIGHTOWER, CHARLES, Frances.

1793 October. HENSLEE, WILLIAM; John and David (brothers).

1794 October. HAMBLETT, RICHARD, Katie (wife); Robert, William, Sarah, Richard, Hannah, Elizabeth and Byrd.

1797 January. HIPWERTH, JOHN, Mary (wife).

1799 January. HARRISON, THOMAS, William, Andrew, Thomas, Charles, John, Robert, Elizabeth, Jean and Patsy.

1799 January. HUGHES, JOHN, Mary (wife); John, Andrew, Obedience and Gibson.

1799 January. HORNBUCKLE, THOMAS, Nancy (wife); Richard, William and George (sons); Milly Windsor, Elizabeth Harden, Sally Simpson and Frances Rogers (daughters).

I.

1791 October. INGRAM, JAMES, Mary (wife); Walter, Priscilla, Vachel, Clay, Benjamin and John.

J.

1779 June. JOUETT, MATTHEW, Sarah (wife); John, Susanna, Polly, Nancy, Matthew, Thomas, Betsey and Washington.

1780 September. JONES, JESSE, Frances (wife); Drury, Goodridge, William and Sally.

1781 June. JOHNSON, JOHN, Mary (wife); James, Daniel and Rachhel; Isabella Walker and Jane Christie (daughters).

1781 September. JESSE, HENRY, Wife (not named).

1783 September. JOHNSON, ROBERT, Frances (wife); William, John, Robert, George, Benjamin and Philip; Elizabeth Stewart and Judah Weake (daughters).

1797 July. JOHNSTON, JOHN, Hannah (wife); Thomas, John, James, Samuel, Jean and Elizabeth.

K.

1777 December. KIMBROW, THOMAS, Eleanor (wife); John, William, Robert, Thomas, Lucky and Nowell.

1786 October. KERSEY, JOHN, Ursula (wife); Drury, John and Elizabeth.

L.

1780 December. LOGUE, EPHRAIM, Mary (wife); Eleanor.

1781 September. LEA JOHN, Elliott, Edmund, Carter, Owen, Phoebe, Betty and Milly.

1784 July. LYON, JOHN, James, William, Peter and Henry; Elizabeth Farrar, Frances Bailey and Jane Anderson (daughters); Richard Tankersley (grandson).

1785 April. LEA, MARY, Children (not named); except Sarah Runnals.

1786 July. LONG, BENJAMIN, Sarah, Benjamin, Leah, Martha and Reuben; Mary Bennett (daughter).

1790 July. LEWIS, JOHN, Catherine (wife); John (son); Apphia Allen and Sarah Taylor (daughters).

1791 April. LONG, AMBROSE, Elizabeth (wife); Elizabeth, Frances, Reuben, James, John and Jesse; Ann Clift (daughter).

1792 January. LEITH, FREEMAN, Susanna (wife).

1792 January. LEA, ZACHARIAH, Ann (wife); Vincent, Henry, George, Rachel and Sarah; Mary Bangston (daughter).

1792 March. LEA, JAMES, Anne (wife); William, John and Major.

1796 July. LONG, JAMES, Priscilla (wife); Robert (son); Mary Dollarhide, Agnes Maxfield, Jane Upton and Rebecca Branham (daughters).

M.

1782 June. MAINS, MATTHEW, Sarah (wife); Joseph and Mary.

1777 June.. MOORE, JOHN, Joseph and John (sons); Sarah McGehee and Elizabeth Shoemaker (daughters).

1779 March. McDONNELL, DUCAN, Elizabeth (wife); Katherine Hemphill (daughter); David Hemphill (grandson).

1781 December. MOORE, JOHN, Wife (not named).

1780 December. McFARLAND, ROBERT, Margaret (wife); John, James, William, Walter, Joseph, Ellen, Robert; Martha Barrett (daughter).

1781 December. McNEILL, THOMAS, Ann (wife); Thomas, John, Benjamin, Patsy and Lois.

1782 June. MUIRHEAD, CLAUD, Elizabeth (wife); Nancy and Elizabeth Park (friends).

1784 July. McKEEN, HHGH, Agnes (wife); Alexander and five other sons (not named).

1785 January. MOORE, JOHN, Wife (not named); John, Patrick, William, Lucy and Mary; Elizabeth Lightfoot (daughter).

1785 April. MILES, ALEX, Lucy (wife); Thomas, Jacob, John and Elizabeth.

1785 October. MITCHELL, JOHN, Mary (wife).

1789 October. MINCEY, RICHARD, Judy (wife).

1791 October. MONTGOMERY, MARY, Michael ard James; Jane Maxwell (daughter).

1795 January. MITCHELL, WILLIAM, Sarah, Mary, Susanna, John, Cicely, William, James and Nancy; Elizabeth Cary (daughter).

N.

1783 March, NEELY, WILLIAM, Eleanor (wife); Samuel, Jacob and Joseph (sons); Mary Pryor (daughter).

P.

1783 December. PAINE, JAMES, William, Robert, James and John.

1786 October. PHELPS, JAMES, Mary (wife); Obadiah, Thomas, Larkin, Lucy, Betty, Polly, William and Ambrose.

1803 July. PATTERSON, GIDEON, Gideon.

1788 April. POGUE, JOSEPH, Sarah (wife); John and Joseph.

1788 July. POTEETE (Poteat) JOHN, Ann (wife); Elizabeth, William, Miles, James, Thomas, John and Richard; Mary Vann (daughter).

1788 October. PARR, WILLIAM, Mary (wife); John and William (sons); Elizabeth Brown and Rachel Walker (daughters).

1791 July. PALMAR, THOMAS, Susanna (wife); Joseph, John, Thomas and Philip (sons); Sarah Van Hook, Susanna Pellers, Beersheba Hall and Mary Woode (daughters).

× Oct.1791 July. PERKINS, JOHN, Rachel (wife); Martin and Jesse (sons); Ann Foster and Susanna Baker (daughters). Sarah Mattocks

1793 October. PERKINS, ABRAM, Cicely (wife); Abram, Philemon, Polly, Milly and Grimes (children); Fanny Ware and Elizabeth Middlebrooks (daughters).

1794 April. PORTER, DAVID, Alexander (son); Mary Kelly and Rebecca Johnston (daughters).

1794 April. POOL, MICAJAH, George.

1794 April. POSTON, JEREMIAH, Elizabeth (wife); William, Katie, Betsy, Henry, Polly, Anna, Richard and Francis; Priscilla Dickens (daughters).

1794 October. PARKER, PLEASANT, Sally Perkins and Dicey Coleman (sisters).

Q.

1792 March. QUINE, WILLIAM, Sarah (wife); Sarah; Elizabeth Stafford, (daughter).

R.

1780 September. ROBINSON, JACOB, Alexander, James, Samuel, Jemima, William, Jacob, John and Thomas.

1781 September. RAINEY, GEORGE, Mary (wife); William, George, John and Martha.

1783 June. ROBINSON, T. THOMAS, Penina (wife); named); Esther, Mark, Alex, Jemima and Thomas.

1783 June. ROBINSON, THOMAS, Penina (wife); Gideon, Nelly, Paty, Keziah and Rebecca.

× Certified copy of will names dau. Sarah Mattocks, also Susannah Barker not Baker. Will dated Dec 29, 1789.

1784 March. ROSEBROUGH, GEORGE, Jean (wife); Robert, William and Margaret (children); George Southard and Allen Fowler (grandsons).

1786 July. RAY, ROBERT, Anice (wife); Sarah, James and Wilson.

1787 January. RICHMOND, JOHN, Rachel (wife); Joshua, Joseph, Elizabeth, Eleanor, William, Margaret, Mary, John and Martha Jane.

1794 October. REID, JOHN, Susanna (wife).

1797 January. RICE, JOHN, Lettisha (Letitia) (wife); Ann, William, Mary and Nathaniel.

1797 October. RANDOLPH, JAMES, Mary (wife); John, Nimrod and Rebecca.

1782 January. RAINEY, JOHN, Wife (not named); William, James, Thomas, Elizabeth and Jenny.

S.

1777 December. SMITH, GEORGE, Jane (wife); Rebecca, Catherine, George, Robert and Ruth.

1778 December. STANSBERRY, SAMUEL, Mary (wife); Solomon, Luke, Benjamin, Sarah and Aquilla.

1799 June. STRINGER, EDWARD, Judah (wife); Edmond, Limeledge, Mary Ann, James and William (children); Agnes Whitlock, Fanny Sutherland, Lucy Browning, Tabitha Peed, Sarah Campbell and Frances Vier (daughters).

1779 September. SMITH, JOHN, Elizabeth (wife); Mary (daughter); Betsey Jowell (daughter).

1781 June. SARGENT, JOSEPH, Ruth (wife); Daniel and Elizabeth.

1781 September. SPENCER, THOMAS, Elizabeth (wife); John, Frances, Betty, Robert, Mary, Susanna and Benjamin.

1781 December. SCOTT, JOHN, Robert, Rebecca and John (children); Catherine McAden and Mary McFarland (daughters).

1782 March. STINSON, ALEX, Sarah (wife); Nancy.

1782 June. STOKES, MATTHEW, Sarrah (wife); Joseph and Mary.

1783 June. STEWART, JAMES, Wife (not named); William, Rachel, James, Agnes and Elizabeth.

1785 October. SHACKELFORD, FRANCIS, Eunice (wife); Rebecca, Armistead, Nancy, Henry, Abner, Absalom, Betsy and John.

1786 January. SIMPSON, RICHARD, Mary (wife); Richard, Sarah, Elizabeth, Mary Ann, Lydia, Ede and Nancy; Susanna Barton (daughter).

1792 January. SMITH, ANNE, Mason (son); Margaret Williams and Elizabeth Williams (daughters).

1792 March. STAFFORD, ADAM, John and Samuel and other children (not named).

1793 October. STEPHENS, CHARLES, Thomas, William and Benjamin (sons); Abbemar Williams and Elizabeth Lea, (daughters).

1794   October. SIMMONS, THOSMAS, Priscilla
(wife); Alexander and Thomas.

1797   October. SMITH, PETER, Elizabeth, Martha,
Jesse, Moses, Aaron, Presley, William,
George, John B., Elias and Elijah.

1790   October. SAWYER, WILLIAM, William, Stephen and Absalom.

1798   April. SLADE, THOMAS, Hannah (wife);
Thomas and William; Hannah Lee (daughter).

1798   April. SCOTT, JOHN, Mary (wife); James
(son); Jane Bell and Polly Strader (daughters).

1798   October. SIDDALL, JOHN, Esther (wife);
Job, Ira, Martin, Amy and Nancy; Betsy
Angler (daughter).

1798   October. SIMPSON, MARY, Richard (son);
Margaret Williamson, Keziah Reid, Elizabeth Oldham and Lydia Tait (daughters).

1799   October. SHELTON, BRYON, Rebecca (wife);
Leonard and Clever.

T.

1799   October. TERRY, JAMES, Rebecca (wife);
Sarah and Olive.

1781   June. TAPLEY, HOSEA, Sarah (wife).

1789   July. TATE, WADDY, Anne (wife); William
and other children (not named).

1790   April. TUNKS, THOMAS, Rachel (wife);
Frances, Thomas and Phillip.

1799   July. THOMAS, WILLIAM, Philip and Asa
(brothers).

V.

1785   January. VAN HOOK, DAVID, Lucy (wife);
Jacob, Kendall, David, Robert and Sarah.

W.

1777   October. WATERS, JOSEPH, Rebecca (wife);
Chloe, Priscilla, Harbin, James, Isaiah, Benjamin, Keziah, Josiah, Reason, Anna 'and
Lloyd; Susanna Hobbs and Lydia Brodie
daughters).

1780   December. WILLIAMS, JAMES, Mary (wife);
Daniel, Joseph, John, Elizabeth, James and
Washington.

1782   March. WILKINSON, SAMUEL, Wife (not
named); Mary, Francis, Ann, John, William, Thomas, Catherine and Elizabeth.

1786   January. WILLIAMS, HENRY, Daniel, Joseph,
Henry, Arthur, and Elizabeth; Nancy Reid
(daughter).

1790   January. WALKER, JOHN, Rachel (wife);
Thomas, Betsy, Benjamin, William, Polly and
Barbara.

1786   July. WILLIAMS, WILLIAM, Tobirs, Maty,
Agnes and Obedience.

1787   July. WILLIAMS, JAMES, Elizabeth (wife);
Benjamin, Neal, Mary, Lucy and Martha;
Elizabeth Mooi (daughter).

1798 July. WALKER, SAMUEL, Eleanor (wife);
      James (son); Jane Long and Elizabeth Long
      (daughters).

Y.

1799 June. YATES, JOHN, Sarah (wife); William,
      Thomas, John, James, Milly, Joyce, Keziah
      and Elizabeth.
1798 June. YATES, JOHN, Allen, Alfred, Betty,
      Milly, Dolly, Sally and Ann.

CHATHAM—WILLS

A.

1784 ASHFORD, WILLIAM, John and Sarah.
1786 ALLEN, WM., Mary (wife), John and Betsy.
1789 ALSTON, WM., John J., William C., Oroondates, Mary Ann and Ann.
1795 ANDERSON, JAMES, Martha, Jane, Susanna and Mary, Lewis, Lucy; Holcomb and Henrietta, (sisters).
1796 BROWN, ARCHIBALD, Agnes (wife), Andrew, Benjamin, Frank, Jenny, Anna.
1799 BOOKER, JOHN, Omai (wife), John, Sally, Nancy, Polly, Isaiah, Hardy, Jane, William, Phoebe, Susanna and James.
1790 BRAY, HENRY, Mary (wife), Edward and Henry.

B.

1785 BANKS, DAVID, Elizabeth (wife), Mary, James, Sarah and Drewry.
1784 BRASWELL, HENRY, Sarah (wife), Cynthia and William.
1784 BROWDER, EDMOND, wife (not named); John, Darius, Lois, Molly, Emma, Silvia and Deborah.
1784 BROWDER, ABNER, Wife (not named), Lucy, John, Nancy, Sally and Polly.
1792 BREWER, OLIVER, Rebecca (wife), George, Oliver, William, Henry, Christopher, Frances and Edward.
1796 BROOKS, THOMAS, Mary (wife), Stephen, Thomas, Samuel, Attie, Rebecca and Hannah.
1795 BEASLEY, HENRY, Isham, Martha, Tabitha and Betty.
1797 BROWN, ABNER, wife (not named); Lucy, Sally, John, Nancy and Polly.

C.

1796 CRUMP, JOSEPH, Patty (wife), John, William, Judith, Sally, Celia and Patty.
1787 CRUTCHFIELD, HENRY, Milly (wife), James, John, Henry and Elizabeth.
1791 COLLINS, WM., Sarah (wife), Mary and James.
1793 COPELAND, WM., wife (not named), Richard and John.
1795 CROW, JAMES, John, James, Stephen, Reuben,
1795 CLARK, WILLIAM, Frances (wife); Anne, Mary, Fanny and Winny.
Isaac, Abel, William, Hannah and Abba.

D.

1793 DENNIS, JOSEPH, Mary (wife), Anderson and Richard.
1784 DUNCAN, GEORGE, Elizabeth (mother), Peter (brother).

E.

1795 EVANS, THOMAS, Agnes (wife), John, Charles, Elizabeth, Susanna and Thomas.

1791 EKMAN, ADAM, Ann (wife), Elizabeth, Polly, Amy, Nancy, James.

1790 EDWARDS, EDWARD, Agnes (wife), Robert, Eliza, Hannah, John and Aaron.

F.

1799 FIELDS, HENRY, John, Richard, Lewis, James, David, Mary Ann, Theophilus, Sarah, Abraham and Isaac.

1796 FOREMAN, BENJAMIN, Mary (wife), Isabel, Millicent, Mary and Elizabeth.

G.

1796 GRIFFITH, ROGER, William, Sarah, Polly, Celia, John and Pleasant.

1798 GLOVER, BENJAMIN, Frankey (wife), Elizabeth, William, Williamson and Pacely.

1796 GLASS, THOMAS, Martha (wife), children (not named).

1798 GEORGE, HARRIS, Mary (wife), Pressley and Emsley.

H.

1795 HEADEN, SARAH, Andrew, William, Aaron, Susanna, John, Rachel and Sarah.

1786 HADLEY, JEREMIAH, Mary (wife), Lydia, James, John and Jeremiah.

1784 HIGHTOWER, AUSTIN, Martha (wife), William, Austin, Sterling, Amelia and Henry.

1791 HUNTER, MARGARET, James, Aaron, Andrew, Elijah and John.

1796 HEATHCOCK, NANCY, William.

J.

1794 JUSTICE, JOHN, Elizabeth, Stephen, Allen, Elizabeth, Keziah, John, David, William.

1792 JONES, AARON, Hannah (wife), Miriam, Jemima and Sarah.

1793 JONES, MATTHEW, Elizabeth (wife), Thomas, Polly, Robert, Mary and John (brother).

1796 KELLY, HENRY, Mary (wife), children (not named).

1780 KEMP, RICHARD, Susanna (wife), Joseph, Margery, Prudence, Richard and Rachel.

L.

1794 LEDLETTER, JOHN, Elizabeth (wife), James, Cine and Tase.

1784 LINDSAY, CALEB, John, Joan, Sarah, Susanna, James and William.

1784 LASATER, WM., Keziah (wife), Thomas, Mary, Abner, William, Hezekiah, Jacob, James and Hardy.

1785 LEDBETTER, JOHN, Amy (wife), John, Sarah and Chloe.

1797 LUTTERLOH, HENRY L., Elizabeth (wfe), James G., Charles and Henry.

M.

1796 MINTER, PHILIP, James, Celia, Elizabeth and Joseph.

1796 MINTER, WILLIAM, Sally (wife); Richard, Elizabeth, Polly and Sallie.

1788 MORGAN, CHARLES, Joseph, Hannah, Rachel Charles and Edward.

1794 McMASTERS, JAMES, Susanna (wife), John, Andrew, William, James, Sarah, Jonathan, Lewis, Samuel and Simon.

1785 MATTHEWS, THOMAS, Margaret wife), Sarah, William, Hannah, Thomas, Elizabeth, Ezekiel and Margaret.

1785 MILLIKIN, CHARLES, Ann (wife), Robert, James, Charles, George, Quentin, Jenny.

1787 MARSHALL, JOHN, Ruth (wife), Jacob, William, Anne, Ruth, Benjamin, Joseph, Isaac and Abram.

1799 McSWAN, JOHN, Clementine (wife), Dennis, Edmond, Martin, Clementine and Samuel.

1795 MADDOX, DAVID, Sally (wife), William, John, Michael and Talton.

1798 MURRAY, JANE, Jane, Jessie, Sarah and Ann.

O.

1798 OSRORN, STEPHEN, Mary (wife), Aaron, John, Christopher and Rebecca.

P.

1799 PEARCE, RICHARD, Martha (wife).

1784 PAYLET, ROBERT, Caroline (wife), James, William, John, Benjamin and Elizabeth.

1794 POE, SIMON, Rhoda (wife), Sarah, Mary, Jane, William, James, Frances.

1799 PEOPLES, HUGH, Abigail (wife), John, Abigail, Ruth and Anne.

Q.

1794 QUACKENBUSH, PETER, John, Peter, Sarah, Anne, Rhoda and Reache.

R.

1794 RHODES, WILLIAM, Susanna (wife), Lucy, William and Hannah.

1799 ROWE, JOHN, Mary (wife).

1788 RAGLAND, WILLIAM, Sarah (wife), Ann, John, Thomas, Fred, Elizabeth, Robert, Mary, Dinah and Bridget. *See Will in File Case*

1792 RAY, WM., Patty (wife), Nancy, Anne, Winnie, Milly and John.

1790 RICHARDS, HENRY, Robert, John, William, Henry, Thomas, Christian, Elizabeth, Sarah, Mary.

1798 ROYSTER, ELIZABETH, Bennett, Elizabeth (daughter), Petty, William, Thomas, Jean and Patsy (granddaughters).

1787 RATCLIFF, THOMAS, Hannah (wife); Amos and Abner.

S.

1789 SPURS, ROBERT, Elizabeth (wife).
1796 SHORT, WILLIAM, Merinia (wife), George, William, Nancy.
1792 SWANNER, RICHARDSON, Elida (wife), children (not named).
1784 SMITH, DAVID, Mary (wife), David.
1787 SNIPES, WILLIAM, Sarah (wife), Thomas, William, Sarah, Susanna, Rhoda, Tabitha.
1799 STINSON, AARON, Rebecca (wife); John, Aaron, Moses, Joshua, Rebecca, Hannah, Molly, James, Rachel, Alex, Ann and Susanna.
1794 STEWART, JAMES, Elizabeth (wife), Thomas, James, Jeptha.

T.

1798 TABOR, THOMAS, Amos, Philip, Delilah and Collier.
1784 TEMPLE, SAMUEL, Samuel, Martha, Ruth, Statia, Benjamin, Mary, Pheraba, Elizabeth.
1784 THOMPSON, HANNAH, John, Balaam, Susanna, Mary, Sarah, Hannah, Ann, William.
1792 TAYLOR, JOHN, James and Philip (brothers).
1799 TEAGUE, MOSES, Rachel (wife), David, Moses, ~~Isaiah~~ Isabelle* , Abraham, Isaac, Jacob, William, Elizabeth, Susanna, Hannah, Charlotte.
1795 TAYLOR, PHILIP, wife, Philip, John, James, Iphigenia, Alphea, Polly.

V.

1792 VANDERFORD, JOHN, Martha (wife), Richard, Elizabeth, Mary, Sally, Anna, Hannah, William, Eli, Susanna.

W.

1784 WELCH, MICHAEL, Eve (wife), Henry, William.
1784 WICKER, THOMAS, Mary (wife), Robert, David, Thomas, James, John, Temperance.
1787 WISE, JOHN, Mary (wife), Lucy.
1784 WILKERSON, JOHN, Margaret (wife), Solomon, Jacob.
1799 WHITE, JOHN, Wife (not named), Lucy, John.
1799 WINTER, DANIEL, Samuel, Sarah, Lydia, Ruth, Ann.
1794 WICKER, JAMES, Milly (wife), Priscilla.
1796 WILKINS, JOHN, Betty (wife), John, William, James, Jane, Sarah.
* 1796 WILLIS, JAMES, Elizabeth (wife), Suckey, Jemima, Wilson, Larkin, Molly, Nanny, Elijah, Elisha.
1798 WELCH, WALTER, Mary (wife), Matthew, Michael, Walter, James, Isaac, Mary, Alice, Catherine.

Z.

1795 ZACHARY, JONATHAN, Jane (wife), William, Betsy, Nancy, Jonathan.

*See will of Moses Teague, Chatham Co. N.C.
in D.H.R. File Case. m.J.H.

CHOWAN—WILLS

1768 ARMOUR, ROBERT, Argent, Simon, Miles, Robert, Sarah, Tamar, Polly, Rebecca; James, Elizabeth.
1782 ANDERSON, ANN, Kerp, George; Littlejohn, Wm., Blount, Jacob; Kerr, Ann.
1757 ARLINE, JOHN, Sarah; Odom, Jacob.
1762 ALPHIN, ABSALOM, Bonn, Sarah.
1763 ALLISON, BENJAMIN, six children.
1759 ASHLEY, MARGARET, Mary, Ellen.
1766 AARON, THOMAS, Elizabeth, James; Nickson, Orson.
1782 ASHLEY, WM., Hannah, Midia, Jeremiah, William, Mary, Edith, Margaret.
1764 ALLEN, ARTHUR, Sarah, Jemima, Elbertson; Lynch, Charles, Rumbough, Ann.
1796 ASBELL, JOHN, James, Cornelius, Ann, Judah, Elizabeth.

B.

1766 BERRY, CHARLES, Wife.
1766 BENBURY, SAMUEL, Father and brother.
1766 BONNER, HENRY, Elizabeth, Thomas, William, Henry, Richard.
1772 BLAIR, GEORGE, Jean, William, George, Samuel.
1790 BOYD, MARIAM, Wilkins, John; Culver, Ann; Taylor, Deborah.
1786 BUNCH, SHADRACK, William, Sarah, Cullen, Mary; Goodwin, Rachel.
1792 BARTER, ANTHONY, Dinah, Margaret (mother), Nathaniel.
1794 BUFKIN, SARAH, William, Lydia.
1785 BLACKBURN, JOHN, Mary; Rambough, Sarah; Hamilton, John.
1778 BENBURY, WM., Thomas; Bennett, Mary, John, William; Houghton, Sarah, Rachel, John, Thomas.
1768 BUSH, JOHN, Jackeber, Miriam; Rachel, Michael, Sarah.
1776 BRINN, JESSE, Joseph, Josiah.
1780 BATEMAN, WM., Mary, Sarah.
1793 BENBURY, THOMAS, Thomas, Richard; Blount, Mary.
1788 BUCKLEY, MORRIS, Martin, William.
1784 BATEMAN, NEHEMIAH, Sarah, Nehemiah, John, William, Streeter, Thomas.
1767 BODLEY, JOSHUA, Jeanne; Whateley, Wm., Charlton, Jasper.
1789 BONNER, MARY, Blount, John, Mary.
1769 BLOUNT, SARAH, Wilson, Mary; Beasley, Elizabeth, Rebecca, Martha.
1792 BLOUNT, EDMUND, Charles, William, Edward, Mary, Richard.
1790 BRINKLEY, THOMAS, Mary, Nathaniel.
1777 BENBURY, CHARLES, Joseph.
1762 BLANCHARD, BENJAMIN, Uriah, Reuben, Absalom.
1764 BLANCHARD, MICAJAH, William, Micajah, Abner, Mary, Elizabeth, Christian.
1762 BACKUS, JOHN, William, Margaret, Thomas,

Jane, Elizabeth, Lydia, John, Edah, Tamar.

1766 BRINN, JOSEPH, Nathaniel; McGuire, Philip.

1779 BOYCE, JOB, Jacob, Sarah, Mary, Leah.

1766 BEASLEY, ROBERT, John Baptist.

1789 BUNCH, JULIUS, Solomon, Malachi, Jacob, Miriam, Abigail, Sarah.

1789 BOYER, BENJAMIN, Nancy.

1785 BONNER, THOMAS, Mary.

1773 BLANCHARD, AARON, Millicent, Mary, Esther, Rachel.

1771 BUNCOMBE, EDWARD, Thomas, Elizabeth, Hester; Cain, Ann.

1792 BLOUNT, JOSEPH, Ann, John, Mary, Joseph, Frances, Sarah, Elizabeth.

1772 BOND, WM., Eleanor, Charity.

1767 BRISCOE, EDWARD, Dorcas, Edward.

1784 BATEMAN, NEHEMIAH, ——

1797 BONNER, HENRY, Nancy, John, Elizabeth, Sarah, William; Satterfield, Fanny.

1797 BURKETT, THOMAS, William, Lemuel.

1798 BLANCHETT, MICAJAH, William, Josiah.

1767 BACKUS, JOHN, SR , William, Thomas, James, Elizabeth, John, Lydia, Tamar.

1786 BARKER, THOMAS, Pénelope, Deborah, Elizabeth, Bethia; Winslow, Bethia; Baker, Abigail; Johnson, Samuel; Tunstall, Elizabeth; Pough, William, Thomas.

1772 BIRUM, BRIAND, James, Christian, Isaac, Joel, Rachel, Phebe.

1786 BARRY, JOHN, Edward.

1782 BLACK, SAMUEL, Dorothy; Clarkson, Elizabeth.

1792 BURKITT, WM., Delight.

1783 BUNCH, MICAJAH, Mary, Micajah, Joseph, Edward, Jones, Penelope, Lydia, Frances.

1781 BADHAM, WM., William, John, Miles, George, Elizabeth, Mary, Rebecca, Sarah, Ann; White, Martha.

1793 BENBURY, RUTH, Rountree, Priscilla.

1781 BONFIELD, CHARLES, John; Hurst, Penelope, Elizabeth.

1790 BEASLEY, JOHN BAPTIST, Joseph, Frederick.

1789 BUTLER, JACOB, Marshall, Sarah, John, Martha, Mary B; Swann, Rebecca.

1779 BOYCE, JACOB, James, Elizabeth.

1758 BOYCE, CHRISTOPHER, John, Jonathan, Stephen, Mary, Elizabeth, Charity, Sarah, Ann.

1777 BLOUNT, JOSEPH, Joseph, Lemuel, E.; Littlejohn, Sarah.

1785 BOYD, WM, Bennett, Lydia; Wells, Marion; Boyd, Marion.

1772 BARNES, JOHN C., George, John, Catherine.

1788 BLAIR, JEAN, William, George, Nelly, Peggy.

1771 BROWNRIGG, RICHARD, Mary, John, Jane, Thomas, Sarah; Topping, William.

1780 BOYD, WM., Bennett, Wm.,; Wells, Marian.

1774 BENBURY, JOHN, John, William, Thomas, Charles; Walton, Mary.

1788 BLACK, FRANCES, Clarkson, Elizabeth; McDonald, Dorothy.

1796 BORITZ, WM., James, John.

C.

1766 CRAVEN, JOHN, John, Margaret.
1772 CREECY, LEVI, Mary, Eleazar, William, Lemuel, Thomas, Henry; Robins, Martha.
1772 CARHAN, ROBERT, Henry; Robins, Martha.
1796 CHARLTON, JOHN, Bethia, Rachel, William.
1783 COLE, EDWARD, Read, Nicholas; Egan, Robert.
1765 CHAR, PETER, Mary, John, Peter.
1765 CHAPPELL, RICHARD, Micajah.
1768 CHARLTON, JOHN, Rachel, John, Job, William.
1774 CHANTRELL, JOHN, Charles, George, William; Hewes, Joseph, De Latun, Ann, John, William; Mulers, Tobias, Hathaway, John; Hopkins, Sarah.
1772 CHARLTON, WM., Thomas, Elizabeth.
1785 COPELAND, JESSE, David, Lydia, Willis, Esther, James, Jesse, John.
1768 COSTIN, JAMES, James, Dempsey.
1768 CHURTON, WM., John, Dorothy, Sarah; Fanning, Elizabeth; Lamb, Wm.
1773 COPELAND, JOHN, Sarah.
1768 CHARLTON, JOHN, Richard, John, Wm., Job.
1783 CARR, JAMES, Mary.
1777 CARR, ANN, James, Frances.
1771 COWAND, JOHN, James.
1767 COLLINS, NICHOLAS, Elizabeth, Thomas, Dorcas.
1778 CUNNINGHAM, JOHN, John.
1790 CHAMPION, HENRY, Solomon.
1784 CREECY, JOSEPH, Fred; Benbury, Penelope.
1799 CUNNINGHAM, JOHN, Lydia.
1796 CUMMINGS, WM., Hamilton, John.
1767 CATERAT, WM., Ruth.
1788 COFFIELD, JOHN, SR., Thomas, John, Jeremiah, Benjamin.
1794 CHEW, MARY, Haughton, William.
1786 COPELAND, CHARLES, Thomas, Joshua, Mary, Sarah, Jemima, Joseph, Charles.
1785 CANNON, JOSEPH, Jacob, Betty.
1794 CHAMPION, JOSEPH, Susanna, Noah.
1795 CHARLTON, WM., Holmes, Ann, William; Gregory, Elizabeth.
1779 CANNON, JEREMIAH, Rachel, Joseph, Jacob.
1784 CHOPLIN, GEORGE, Thomas, Nancy.

D.

1730 DURANT, GEORGE, George, Sarah, Elizabeth, Mary; Hatch, Anthony; Langston, Ann.
1772 DAVIESON, JOHN, Robert, Christiana.
1772 DOUGLAS, ALEX, Elizabeth, John.
1788 DITCHBURN, BARTHOLOMEW, Ann, Juliana.
1774 DEAL, JOSHUA, Mary, Joshua, John, Ann. Ruth
1777 DORMADY, WM., Thomas.
1764 DADKINS, GEORGE, Elizabeth.
1764 DAVIS, SARAH, Stern, Elizabeth.
1776 DUNSCOMBE, SAMUEL, James, Samuel, John, Edward, Hannah.
1762 DEAR, JOSEPH, George, Elizabeth, Sarah.
1772 DUNSCOMBE, SARAH, James; Butler, Sarah.

E.

1783 EVANS, JOSEPH, Ann (wife), Anna, John.
1764 EVANS, JOHN, Griffin, Amasiah, Hannah.
1773 ECCLESTON, THOMAS, Agnes, John, Thomas.
1785 EARL, DAVID, Charity, Ann; Johnson, Elizabeth.
1796 EGAN, ROBERT, Coates, John H., Elizabeth.
1796 EARL, ANN, Johnson, Charles Earl, Frances, Ann.
1783 EVANS, ELIAS, Crothers, Simon.
1799 ELBECK, WM., Dickinson, children of Elizabeth; Penelope.

F.

1761 FREEMAN, RICHARD, Amos, Dempsey; Rountree, Mary, Christian.
1776 ELBERT, JOHN, Richard, Catherine, Sarah, William, Jacob, John.
1762 FOY, DANIEL, Francis, John.
1760 FARMER, THOMAS, Joseph.
1799 FARROW, NATHANIEL, Rodenbaugh, William.
1798 FRASIER, JEREMIAH, Elizabeth, Penelope, Sarah, Ada, Zilla, Richard, Mary, Martha, John; Swain, Ann.
1776 FELTON, RICHARD, John, Cader, Noah, William, Elisha, Shadrack, Ann, Chloe; Ward, Sarah; Rogerson, Mary.
1772 FRASIER, THOMAS, Alexander.

G.

1764 GOULD, ELIZABETH, Brownrigg, Richard,
1783 FOSTER, NANCY, William, Ann.
1724 FORMAN, JOHN, Goundon, John.
Sarah; Butterton, Elizabeth; Campbell, James.
1782 GIBBONS, JOHN, Esther.
1761 GALE, MYLES, Christopher, Myles, John; Corbin, Francis; Little, George.
1772 GIBSON, JOHATHAN, Lemuel; Askew, Elizabeth; Coffer, George.
1761 GREGORIE, MARY, Thomas, John, James, William; Earl, Elizabeth; Granberry, Christian.
1797 GREGORY, LUKE, William, Jeremiah, Martha.
1782 GARRETT, THOMAS, Thomas; Riddick,Elizabeth, Christian; Hofler, Debobah; Outlaw, Richard; Walton, Leah.
1799 GREEN, JOHN, Sarah, Ann; Luten, James.
1779 GREGORY, BENJAMIN, Benjamin, Thomas, Sally, Samuel.
1798 GREGORY, ELINOR, Haughton, Samuel.
1774 GREGORY, SAMUEL, William, Luke, Samuel.
1770 GIBSON, ROBERT, Ann; Palmer, Thomas, Rachel; Hopkins, Mary, Joseph; Musereau, John.
1769 GREGORY, BENJAMIN, John, James, Sarah, Benjamin, Jenkins, Henry; Brickell, Ascension, Sarah; Bough, Comfort.
1785 GRAY, GEORGE, Gray, Abigail; Schermerhorn, Cornelius.
1784 GARRETT, JOHN, Frederick.
1762 GOODWIN, JOSEPH, Lewis, Exum, Joseph, Thomas, Ruth.
1762 GORDON, GEORGE, Josiah, John, George, Edith, Priscilla, Susan, Elizabeth; Hinton, Sarah.

H.

1762 HASLEY, JOHN, William, Jeremiah, Joseph, Samuel, Fred, Edmund, Mary.

1766 HARREN, LYDIA, Campbell, James; Millikin, Agnes, Ann; Benbury, John, William, Boyd, William; Brownrigg, Mary, John.

1771 HASLEY, JEREMIAH, Mary, James; Ming, Zephaniah.

1771 HOPKINS, MARY, Musereau, John, Hopkins, Mary.

1785 HALL, JOHN, Judith, Charlton, Lydia, Fred.

1785 HUNTER, JOHN, Allie, William, John, Mary.

1785 HOSKINS, JOHN, Ann, John.

1781 HOSKINS, THOMAS, Kessar, Sarah, John; Burrus, Mary; Coffield, John.

1781 HARRELL, WM., Elizabeth, Samuel.

1789 HUMPHREY, DAVID, William, John, Richard.

1789 HEWES, JOSEPH, Prudence, Josiah, Aaron, Joseph; Allen, Nathaniel; Blair, Helen, Peggy; Carew, Archibald.

1789 HOWCOTT, NATHANIEL, Sarah, Nathaniel, Mary; Hoskins, Sarah, Thomas.

1789 HOLT, THOMAS, Coffield, Edward, Mary.

1789 HARRELL, SAMUEL, William, Isaac, Abraham, Samuel, Rachel, Martha.

1789 HOPPER, JOHN, Thomas; Tanner, Mary.

1789 HUBBARD, THOMAS, Charity, Mary; Norfleet, Abraham; McGuire, Ephriam.

1789 HURDLE, THOMAS, Ann, Thomas, Hardy, Joseph, Martin.

1789 HODGSON, THOMAS, John; Blair, George, Peggy.

1789 HURST, JAMES, Ann (wife).

1789 HALSEY, SAMUEL, Miles, John, Fred, Edmund, William.

1789 HILL, GUY, Kadah, Guy, John, Sarah.

1789 HARDY, ROBERT, Agnes; Smith, Elizabeth, Francis, Margaret, Rachel, Robert.

1789 HOBBS, JOHN, Aaron, William, Isaac, Jacob, John.

1789 HILL, JOHN, Guy.

1789 HINTON, JOHN, Sarah; Thomas, Rachel.

1789 HOSKINS, THOMAS, Thomas, Mary, Keziah, John, William, Sarah, Rachel; Coffield, Elizabeth, Thomas, John.

1789 HINTON, JONAS, Kadar, James, Noah, Jonas, Seasbrook, Judith, Christian, Priscilla.

1789 HOSKINS, WM., Sarah, Mary, Ann, Thomas, Richard, William, John.

1789 HARELL, ABRAHAM, Mary, Amy, Adam, Elizabeth.

1789 HARRIS, JAMES, Joseph, Hezekiah, Sphynx, Abram; Brien, Sarah; Taylor, Jean.

1789 HAYMAN, JAMES, Harmon, Mary, Jeannette, James.

1789 HODGSON, JOHN, Barker, Penelope; Dalsack, William, John, Hodgson; Elbeck, Joseph H., Henry, John, Samuel, William; Blair, Margaret; Johnson, Samuel; Little, John.

1789 HOFLER, HANCE, Sarah, Thomas, Mary; Garrett, Edward.

1789 HURDLE, HARDY, Benjamin, William, Martin, Joseph, Henry, Harmon, Sarah, Hannah.
1789 HARRON, JOSEPH, Lydia.
1789 HINTON, ELIZABETH, William.
1760 HILL, ABRAHAM, Henry, Abraham, Theophilus, Judith.
1711 HARRIS, JOHN, Turner, Harris, William, Sarah.
1792 HICKS, PATRICK, Job, Elinda, Samuel.
1783 HOSKINS, MARY, John, Sarah, Mary; Leary, Rachel.
1791 HOMES, WM., William, Ann.
1791 HALL, JUDITH, Charlton, Thomas.
1780 HANFORD, RANDOLPH, Buckley, Morris.
1797 HUMPHREYS, RICHARD, David.
1797 HURDLE, MARTIN, Reuben, Thomas, Cicely, Matthew.
1792 HALSEY, JAMES, Dickinson, Samuel.
1796 HASSELL, JAMES, Abram, Miles, Benjamin, Elizabeth.
1800 HOSKINS, RICHARD, Samuel, Mary, Ann, Baker, Richard, Edmund, Lemuel, Martha, Sarah, Winifred, Elizabeth, Fanny.
1782 HARDY, AGNES, Francis.

I.

1794 IREDELL, JAMES, James, Ann Isabella, Helen S.
1826 IREDELL, HANNAH, James, Helen S.

J.

1768 JONES, EPAPHRODITUS, Rebecca, Millie, Arkade; Fryer, Mary.
1790 JOHNSON, JOSEPH, Bathsheba, Miles.
1790 JAMES, GEORGE, Robert, Allen, Willie; Lane, Tamar,
1790 JACKSON, MARY, Sarah.
1790 JORDON, WM., Mary, William, Joseph, Elizabeth, Harriet, Sally; Smithwick, Mary; Heraman, Margaret.
1775 JONES, THOMAS, Thomas, Sarah, Frances, Mary; Earl, Elizabeth, Ann.
1763 JONES, THOMAS, SR., Thomas, William, Marian.
1797 JONES, THOMAS, Zachariah, Levi Thomas; Beasley, Elizabeth.
1791 JENKINS, CHARITY, Copeland, Sarah.
1791 JONES, NANCY, Charlotte, Frily.
1765 JONES, JAMES, Mary (Wife).
1763 JONES, LEWIS, Lewis, Ann, James, Isaiah, Josiah.
1763 JACKSON, ANN, Francis Corbin.
1795 JORDAN, JACOB, Elizabeth, Jacob, Josiah, Joseph, Jonathan; Bonner, Leah; Elliott, Rachel, Patience: Valentine, Sarah.
1773 JORDAN, CHARLES, Jacob, Charles, John, James, Robert; Smith, Sarah, Leah; White, Rachel.

K.

1764 KELLY, JOHN, Ann, Elizabeth, Martha; Payne, John.
1777 KARR, ANN, James, Frances; Ormand, Ann.
1785 KING, THOMAS, Elizabeth, Henry, Thomas, Mary.
1776 KENNEDY, ANN, Houghton, Jeremiah.

L.

1764 LEONARD, THEOPHILUS, John, Benjamin, Phoebe, James.

1765 LEWIS, JOHN, Isaac, Elijah, Shadrack, Benjamin, Elizabeth, Ann, Mary, John, Martha, Esther, Sarah, Anne.

1769 LASITER, JOHN, Obadiah, Lemuel, Tobias, Jonas, Reuben, Sampson, Amos, Priscilla, Rebecca; Harrell, Isabel; Brown, Ruth.

1791 LUTON, HENDERSON, Sarah, Ephraim, James, Penelope.

1782 LOUTHER, WILLIAM, Barbara, Tristram, Peggy.

1776 LEWIS, JOHN, Mary, Elizabeth; Thompson, Elizabeth.

1784 LUTEN, JOHN, Mary, John.

1786 LUCAS, GEORGE D., Ready, John.

1777 LITTLE, ANDREW, Elizabeth, Archibald, John.

1766 LUTEN, JAMES, Henderson, James, Absalom, King, Solomon, Mary, Feraba.

1771 LEWIS, ANN, Floury, Margaret.

1767 LASSITER, MOSES, Fred, Jethro, Millicent, Jothan, Jeremiah; Coffield, Judith.

1780 LUCERF, HENRY, Mary Ann.

1761 LUTEN, THOMAS, William, John, Thomas; Matthias, Elizabeth.

1764 LASSITER, GABRIEL, Robert, Moses, Jeremiah, William, George, Jonathan, Aaron.

1780 LYON, AENEAS, Mary.

1762 LEARY, CORNELIUS, Job, John, Cornelius, William, Dempsey.

1795 LOWELL, MARY, Seawell, Sarah, Nanaber, Susanna.

1799 LAWRENCE, MARY, Alphonso; Payne, Peter.

1794 LILES, WM., Elizabeth, George, Thomas, William, Mary.

1798 LOUTHER, TRISTRAM, Penelope.

M.

1766 MARSHALL, DAVID, Anne, Jean; Glass, Frances; Palmer, Rebecca.

1771 MEARNES, WM., Dorothy, William; Snodgrass, McNeill.

1772 McKILDA, JOHN, Martha, Richard.

1788 McCORMICK, DUNCAN, Patrick, Robert, Butler, Richard, Mary.

1789 McGUIRE, SAMUEL, Samuel, Sarah, Philip, John; Parker, Mary; Robertson, Lydia; Hix. Deborah.

1777 McCONNELL, MARY, James; Branch, Sarah.

1791 MEREDITH, DAVID, Sarah, Lewis.

1784 MILLER, ABEL, Malachi, Nathaniel, Ephraim, Christopher, Abel, Frederick; Nicholson, Mary.

1797 MORTON, ANN, Rogerson, Sarah.

1797 MIDDLETON, JOHN, William, John, Joseph; Barket, Elizabeth.

1781 MIXSON, JEREMIAH, Jeremiah, Mary.

1778 MINSHEW, RICHARD, Maximillian, John, Bose, Richard, Dionysius.

1798 MING, THOMAS, Joseph, James, Willey, Penelope, Delilah; Gregory, Rachel; Warburton, Bartholomew; Babcock, Mary.

1780   McDONALD, WILLIAM, wife and children (not named).

N.

1769   NASH, THOMAS, Clement, Justina, Elizabeth, Henry, John; Owen, Ann; Holdcraft, Mary.

1754   NORFLEET, ABRAHAM, Abraham, Isaac, Elizabeth, Elisha, Benjamin, Sarah.

1797   NEWBY, WYKE, Martha.

1795   NORCOM, FREDERICK, Charles, Benjamin, Joseph, Frederick; Hoskins, Mary; Howcutt, Sarah; Beasley, Elizabeth.

O.

1764   ORENDELL, EDWARD, Job.

P.

1768   PALMER, BENJAMIN, Joseph, Robert, Thomas, Sarah, Mary Ann.

july 29, 1788   PRICE, JAMES, w̶f̶ Elizabeth, Thomas, John, ~~Myles~~, Noah; ~~Brinkley~~, Sarah, ~~Thompson~~. Elizabeth ~~Thompson~~

may 18, 1791   PRICE, NOAH, ~~Brinkley~~, Sarah ~~Brinkley~~ - sister

1789   POPPLESTON, SAMUEL, Esther, John, Hardy, Sarah.

1767   PETTIJOHN, THOMAS, Frances, John, Thomas, Abraham, Sarah.

1780   PERKINS, ICHABOD, Glass, Frances; Kearby, Charity and Mercer.

1783   PENRICE, SAMUEL, Elizabeth.

1778   PURSELL, WILLIAM, Catherine.

1760   PERRY, SAMUEL, Susanna, Samuel, Amos, Mordecai, Ann, Leah, Grace.

1762   PARKER, THOMAS, Thomas, Priscilla, Sarah, Aken, Absalom, Judith, Ruth, Telpah, Thomas, Margaret.

1772   PARISH, JOHN, Joseph, Edward; Backus, Elizabeth; Goodwin, Pethiah.

1760   PENRICE, FRANCIS, Sarah, Thomas, William, Sarah, Edmund, Francis, Joseph, Mary; Gardner, James.

1795   POLLOCK, CULLEN, George, Thomas, Ann, Booth.

1797   PARKER, NATHAN, Mary, Leah; Elliott, Sarah, Lydia; Wootten, Jonathan.

1768   PHELPS, JAMES, William, Abraham, Noah, Thomas, Ann, Aaron, Mary, Moses.

1786   PRICE, JAMES, Treasy, Samuel, Mills, John, James, Mary, Elizabeth.

1773   POWELL, ROBERT, Jacob, Shadrack, Daniel; Spaight, Felicia; Duke, Rachel.

1766   PENNY, WILLIAM, Zachariah.

1764   PARKER, JOSEPH, Job.

1785   PARKER, PETER, Seth.

1785   PENRICE, ELIZABETH, Morrison, Joseph; Sutton, Lemuel.

1769   PARKS, SAMUEL, Elizabeth, John, Daniel, Samuel, Mary.

* also bequests to Nancy, Sarah, Jeremiah; a Doctor, Elizabeth and Mills, John, a Price; also to Rebekah and Henry Thompson Jeremiah Fleetwood, relationship not stated. of will seen mch. 1936-00.

R.

1764 RICE, JOHN, Elizabeth, John, David, William, James.

1778 RHODA, PETER, Elizabeth, Ann, Mary.

1760 ROUNTREE, CHARLES, Thomas, Charles, Rachel, Christian, Judith.

1781 RUSSELL, GEORGE, Elizabeth; Clarkson, Thomas; Forbes, Elizabeth.

1763 RIEUSSETT, JOHN, David, John, Elizabeth; Williams, John, Mary, Nathaniel; Lewis, Ann; Campbell, John; Creighton, Margaret; Caila, Peter, Jane; Jones, John.

1766 ROBERTS, CHARLES, William, Liles, James, Willis, Elizabeth.

1756 ROBINSON, JOHN, Elizabeth, John, William.

1795 READY, JOHN, Lucas, George D.

1795 RANDAL, FRANCIS, Joseph.

1784 RUMBOUGH, JOHN, William.

1799 RAMSAY, ALLEN, John, James, William, and the children of Phyllis; Bateman, John.

1794 ROBERTS, WM., Williams, Elizabeth; Norcom, Penelope; Roberts, William; Hoskins, Elizabeth.

1798 ROGERSON, SARAH, McGuire, Sarah; Bunch Ishmael; Small, Reuben.

1787 RUMBOUGH, CATHERINE, William, Elizabeth, Ann.

1778 RUMBOUGH, JOHN, Catherine, John, Elizabeth, William, Thomas; Horniblow, John, Elizabeth.

S.

1772 SIMONS, JOHN, Jacob, Charlton, Argyle.

1772 SUTTON, BENJAMIN, Greenbury, Benjamin, Martha, Ann.

1783 SMITH, JOSEPH, Elizabeth, Robert H.

1769 SCHULZER, FRED, Charlotte.

1777 SOWARD, FRANCIS, Celia, Rosamond, Mary.

1797 SPIVEY, CHAMPION, Sarah, Dorothy, Delilah, Rachel.

1783 SPEIGHT, JOSIAH, Jeremiah.

1782 SMITH, ROBERT, Robert.

1758 SPIVEY, NATHANIEL, John, Champion, Nathaniel, Martha, Mary, Elizabeth, Sarah.

1781 STANDIN, HENDERSON, Marion, Edmond, Deborah, Lemuel, James, Elizabeth, Joseph, Henderson.

1795 SEAWELL, MARY, Sarah, Vanaver, Susanna.

1795 STALLINGS, ELIAS, Myles, Elias, Jemima, Phoebe, Henry, Nathan, William.

1793 SMITH, REBECCA, Blount, Mary.

1760 SMITH, MARTHA, Richard; Hazard, Sarah.

1773 SPIVEY, BENJAMIN, Richard, Dempsey, Sarah, Abraham; Minnard, Elizabeth; Spivey, Margaret.

1764 SIMPSON, JOHN, Mary, William, John, Dempsey; Bunch, Hannah.

1784 SMITH, JOHN, Elizabeth, John.

1766 STRECTON, THOMAS, Sarah; Edmondson, Betsey.

1755 SMALL, JOSEPH, Josiah, Jonathan, Benjamin, Joseph, Sarah, Mary; Bunch, Rachel; Jordan. Ann, Patience.

1759 SMITH, WM., Timothy.
1787 SKINNER, EVAN, Samuel, Richard, William, John; Topping, Mary.
1799 SIMPSON, WILLIAM, William, Robert, Dempsey, Sarah, Mary Ann, Evan, Frederick, John; Williams, Mazy; Parrish, Lovey.
1765 SUMNER, SAMUEL, Patty, Joseph J., Elizabeth.
1776 SPIVEY, JACOB, Thomas, William, Abram, Jesse, Jacob, Rachel, Millicent, Emily; Walton, Ann, Rachel.
1780 SAVAGE, WILLIAM, Flood, William, Nicholas, Elizabeth; Rue, Edward; Bachelor, Frances, John, Edward, Elizabeth; Traceny, Prudence; Clark, Elizabeth; O'Neill, Lucinda; Jones, Walter; Dickinson, Samuel; Draper, Polly.

T.

1771 TAYLOR, THOMAS, James; Sawyer, Lemuel; Richardson, John; Nash, Caleb.
1784 THOMPSON, DEBORAH, Thomas.
1777 THOMPSON, HENRY, James, William, Timothy, Deborah, Ann.
1773 TOPPING, WM., John, Richard, Dorothy B.
1763 TAYLOR, JOHN, Luke, John, Sarah, Martha, Elizabeth, Mary, Rebecca, Ann, Penelope.
1764 THOMPSON, JAMES, Henry, Thomas; Halsey, Elizabeth.
1764 TROTMAN, EDWARD, Dempsey.
1795 THOMPSON, WM., Lawrence.

U.

1789 UNDERHILL, JOSEPH, Sarah, Mary, Samuel, Andrew, Thomas.

V.

1766 VAIL, JOHN, Mosely, Mary, Rebecca, Elizabeth, Martha.
1778 VAIL, FRED, Susannah.
1777 VAIL, EDWARD, Susannah, Thomas, Fred, Jeremiah, Edward.

W.

1792 WALLACE, MARY, Coltrane, Jacob, William, James.
1793 WARD, THOMAS, Josiah, Lowdrick, Jeremiah, Fred, Shadrack, Ruth, Edith, Elizabeth.
1771 WILSON, WM., Sarah; Humphrey, Sarah; Egerton, Priscilla; Champion, Susanna; Baker, Elizabeth; Halsey, Lucy; Mewbern, Wilson, Mary; Wilders, Michael.
1767 WILLS, GEORGE, Marion, Richard, Thomas.
1770 WALTON, TIMOTHY, John B., Timothy, Lelah.
1776 WALTON, PALATIAH, Priscilla, Millicent, Christian, Sarah; Spivey, Zilphia.
1767 WOOD, JOHN, Elizabeth, Seth, Judith.
1773 WILKINS, WM., William, James, Anthony; Liles, Elizabeth.
1778 WILKINS, JOHN, Rachel, Samuel, Rebecca.
1771 WALTON, WM., Timothy, William.
1761 WEBB, ZACHARIAH, John, Moses, James.

1762 WOOLARD, WM., Sarah, Mary; Beasley, Thomas, Mary, George; Hopkins, John, Mary; Payne, Carrie, Willie; Blount, Wilson.

1771 WALTON, WM., John, Sarah, Mary Ann, Celia, Thomas, Isaac, James, Rachel.

1779 WILLIAMS, HATTEN, Ann, Willis, Elizabeth, Mildred, Mary, Nancy, Fanny.

1775 WORTH, JOSEPH, William, Nancy, Ruth.

1786 WHITE, THOMAS, Creecy, William, Lemuel, Nathan; Moore, Elizabeth; Leary, Job, John, William; Charlton, John, Thomas, Job, Mary. Mary.

1761 WALTON, SARAH, Richard, Sarah, Thomas, William, John; Hill, Christian.

1799 WARBURTON, WM , Suckey.

1760 WALTON, WILLIAM, Palatiah, Henry, Edmond, Mary.

1770 WHITE, LUKE, Solomon, Stephen, James, Jacob, John.

1765 WINSLOW, JOSEPH, Job, Israel, Jesse, Elizabeth.

1760 WIGGINS, THOMAS, Willis, James, Christiana.

1779 WEBB, MOSES, Zachariah, John, James.

1779 WARD, THOMAS, Mary.

1796 WHITE, SILAS, William, Silas, Jesse, Abscilla, Judah.

1785 WARD, JAMES, James, Elizabeth, Silvia, Judah.

1798 WARD, THOMAS, James, William, Ephraim, Humphrey, Deborah.

1798 WHITE, JUDAH, Person, Bathsheba; Griffin, Millicent.

1792 WILLIAMS, ANN, Fleetwood, Mary.

1798 WALTON, JOHN, Thomas.

1783 WEBB, ZACHARIAH, Mary, William, Zachariah, Rachel, John, Jesse, Richard, Elizabeth.

1768 WELCH, MICHAEL, Edward, Judah; Rountree, Sarah.

1783 WELCH, DAVID, Isaac, Dempsey, Lemuel, David, Jacob.

1788 WOOLLARD, MARY, Beasley, John; Bunch, Mary; Frazier, Jeremiah.

1771 WALLIS, JOHN, Miles, William, Elizabeth.

1792 WARD, RACHEL, Milly.

1792 WILLIAMS, JOHN, Cressy, Elizabeth; Wilson, Anna.

CRAVEN—WILLS

A.

1785 ANDERSON, CHARLES, Winifred, Elias, Henry, Jacob.
1787 ALLEN, JOHN, John, Walter, Sarah.
1791 ANDERSON, WM., Ann, Francis M., Ann G.
1795 ALLEN, JOHN, Ann G., Mary; Burton, John.
1796 ATHERTY, SARAH, Jonathan, Joseph.
1796 ANDERSON, JONAS, Sarah, Henry.
1800 ALLEN, JOSEPH, John, Shadrack, Joseph, Thomas, Martha, Benjamin.
1751 ARTER, JOHN, Matthew, William, Mary, Ann.
1752 ALLIGOOD, RICHARD, Hillary, William.

B.

1786 BIGGLESTON, JAMES, Ann Carolina.
1788 BROTHERS, JOHN, Sarah Ann (wife), Mary, Suckey.
1789 BRITTAIN, JOSEPH, Catherine, Avil, Joseph, Daniel, James; Physioc, Joseph.
1790 BROOKS, WM., William, Joseph, Rice.
1790 BELL, ANDREW, Lovit, Elizabeth.
1790 BARNARD, BIROM, Noble, Ashley, Douglas, Jesse, Mary.
1790 BRYAN, HARDY B., Mary, Green.
1791 BEASLEY, SOLOMON, Benjamin, James, Samuel, John, William.
1791 BRYAN, WM., Elmer, Hardy, Ellen, Mary, Green, Susanna, Margaret, Holland, Sarah, Ann, Elizabeth.
1791 BRIGHT, STOCKWELL, John.
1794 BURNEY, WM., Sarah, William, Patrick, Benjamin; Hall, Ann, Almond, Thomas, Elizabeth.
1790 BIGGAM, ALEX., Margaret, Ann.
1792 BIGGS, WM., Mary, William, Isaac; Boyhead, William, Mary; Carraway, Sarah, Edward.
1793 BARRY, ALBERT, Buston, Francis B., Sarah.
1794 BRITTEMAN, JAMES, Sally.
1794 BRYAN, ISAAC, Rachel, Lewis C., Hardy, Christopher, Searcs.
1795 BOND, FRANCIS, Elizabeth, Southy, William, Francis.
1795 BROOKS, JOSEPH, Martha, Spring, Joseph, Elizabeth, Patty, Nancy, Mary.
1796 BIGGLESTON, ANN C., Bryan, John C.
✗1796 ✗BRYAN, JOHN Lewis, Wm., John, Joseph, Jas. N., *Anne Elizabeth, all ch. of John*
1796 BRYAN, SARAH, Mary, Sarah.
1798 BEDSCOT, JOHN, wife, John.
1798 BRYAN, NEEDHAM, Betty, John.
1798 BISHOP, JOSEPH, Joseph; Stanton, Elizabeth, Lydia.
1798 BAKER, JOHN, Brothers, Nancy; Baker, Minerva.
1799 BARLETT, WM., Elizabeth.
1799 BALL, JAMES, Sarah, Stephen, Shadrack, James, Levi, Polly, Aaron, Whiting.
1799 BADGER, THOMAS, Lydia, George, Elizabeth, Ann, Frances L.
1750 BENDER, MARTIN, Daniel, John, Salome, Mary.
1751 BROCK, GEORGE, George, William, Eliza, Richard, Elizabeth.

✗ *From copy of will.*

1751 BROWN, WM., John, Sarah, Mary.
1752 BARLOW, ROBERT, William, Hannah.
1752 BORROW, JOSEPH, James, John, Joseph, Mary, Jane.
1752 BOND, SARAH, Francis.
1752 BRICE, WM , William, Rigdon, Action, Francis.
1753 BALCH, JOSEPH, Susanna, Phoebe, Mary, Joseph.
1753 BECTON, JOHN, Fred, George, Edmond, Michael.
1752 BUGNION, RALPH, Elizabeth.
1752 BRYAN, JOHN, Simmons, Needham.
1784 CHAPMAN, JOHN, Truelove, Jesse.

C.

1784 COOK, THOMAS, Thomas, Samuel.
1785 CLEMENT, JOHN, Mary, Thomas.
1785 COLE, THOMAS, Frankey; Smyth, William, Elizabeth, Salah.
1785 COOK, JOHN, Elizabeth.
1786 CARUTHERS, EUNICE, Rellears, Lydia.
1788 COOK, THOMAS, Thomas, Samuel; Johnston, Mary; Cummings, Elizabeth.
1789 CARRAWAY, JOHN, Thomas, John, Edward.
1787 COGDELL, RICHARD, Lydia (wife), Lydia, Margaret, Susannah, Richard.
1791 COLEMAN, THOMAS, Mary, Peter, Benjamin, Abner.
1791 COLLIER, THOMAS, Leah, Thomas, John.
1792 CARLTON, RICHARD, Mary, Samuel.
1795 CARRAWAY, NATHANIEL, Mary, Lewis, Dennis, Asa; Ballance, Joshua.
1795 CULLING, NEHMATH, Peter, Mary; Sparrow, Pheraba.
1776 CLARK, WM., Sarah, Elijah.
1795 COVINGTON, ISAAC; Fell, John; Rumley, Ridy.
1795 CLAYTON, MARY, Mary.
1796 CLEMENTS, THOMAS, Elizabeth.
1796 CARVEY, JOHN, Fred.
1796 COOR, JAMES, Wardens of Craven Poor; Wood, Sarah.
1798 COOKE, THOMAS, Sensey, Thomas, Samuel, Ann.
1799 CHARLET, JOHN, wife and children (not named).
1799 CLARK, JOSEPH, Bush, Joseph C., Sarah.
1752 COLLINS, URIAH, Henry.
1750 CALDWELL, ROBERT, Joshua, Sarah.
1750 COLLINS, JOHN, Joseph, Mary, Samuel.
1751 COURTNEY, ROBERT, Robert, Jonathan, Rowland.
1752 CARUTHERS, JOHN, William, John, Joseph; Rice. Sarah: Wetherington, R.
1751 CONNERLY, JOHN, Keziah, William, Cullen; Jones, Richard; Herring, Stephen.

D.

1785 DAVIS, JAMES, James, William, Thomas.
1786 DAUGHERTY, OWEN, Daniel.
1786 DAVIS, LITTLETON, Tolson, Mary Ann.
1787 DELAMAR, THOMAS, Ann, Francis, Smith, John, Stephen.

1788 DILLINHOUR, JOHN, Upton, F. M. B.
1791 DREW, JOHN, Stokes, Mumford.
1792 DAYVAULT, LEWIS, Maria R.; Adrain, Mary B.,
      Magdalen.
1792 DAVIS, BRISCOE, Sarah, Henry.
1794 DAUGHERTY, DANIEL, Elizabeth;   Arnold,
      James.
1796 DUBERTY, JOHN, Amabla, Sacker.
1796 DAVIS, JAMES, Isabella, Prudence, James,
      Ann B.; McClure, Joseph, Samuel.
1799 DELAMAR, FRANCIS, Hasty, Joseph,   Eliza-
      beth, Nancy, Thomas.
1751 DUNN, DEME, Robert, Samuel.
1751 DUDLEY, JOHN, John, David, William.
1747 DAVID, PHILIP, David; McKithin, Mary.
1752 DAVIS, JOHN, Samuel, John, Sarah; Ballard,
      Jr.
1752 DANIELS, ELIZABETH, John, William, Ann;
      Alexander, Enoch.

E.

1785 EGGLESTON, BENJAMIN, Elizabeth (wife),
      Elizabeth.
1785 ELIN, CHARLES, Keziah, Christopher, Eliza-
      beth.
1785 EGGLESTON, ELIZABETH, Burney, Sarah; Ad-
      ams, Nancy.
1788 EDMONSON, JOSEPH, Margaret, John, Edward,
      Simeon, Bryan.
1794 EDMONSON, BRYAN, Edward, Lemuel.
1797 EDMONSON, EDWARD, Elizabeth.
1799 ERMUL, AARON, Dunn, David D.
1751 EBURN, ELIZABETH, Littleton.
1751 ESTER, ABRAHAM, Elizabeth, John, Thomas,
      Lydia, Tames, Mary, James.
1752 ESTERS, JOHN, William, Thomas.
1751 ESTERS, MARY, John, William, Thomas.

F.

1785 FISHER, GEORGE; Hawks, John; Fisher, Mary.
1785 FONVILLE, FRED, John, Fred, Mary.
1788 FONVILLE, JOHN, John.
1790 FULSHER, SHADRACH, Mary, Wm. H., Joseph
      J., Thomas.
1793 FERGUSON, THOMAS, Hannah.
1794 FONVILLE, JOHN, Louis, John, Fred; Graves,
      Thomas.
1795 FULSHER, JESSE, Jesse, Gilly.
1796 FULSHER, JOSHUA, Shadrach, Ephraim, wife;
      Caruthers, Alex.
1798 FILLINGIN, ROBERT, Enoch, John, Benjamin.
1792 FONVILLE, FRANCIS, Sarah, John, Asa, Price,
      James, Jeremiah, Lewis.
1799 FOX, JOHN, Sukey, Peggy.
1795 FISHER, RANDOLPH, Thomas, George.
1751 FERGUSON, MARK, Adam, Slocumb, Elizabeth,
      Benjamin, John.
1751 FITZGARRELL, JOHN, Annie; Pearce, Arthur.
1751 FOSCUE, SIMON, Bell, Luke, John;   Silver-
      thorn, Mary; Sanders, Sarah.
1785 FITZPATRICK, EDWARD, wife: Micya, Peter.
1751 FOGG, MOSES, Hegg, Moses, Elijah.
1752 FOSCUE, JOHN, Moses.

G.

1785 GILL, LEVI, Catharine, John, Sarah.
1785 GUTTRY, EBENEZER; Broughton, Sarah; Hill, Ebenezer; Buck, Oliver.
1787 GREEN, JOHN, Mary, Elizabeth W.
1788 GRANGER, WM., Susanna; children of Wm. Blount.
1788 GREEN, JAMES, Furnifold, William, Leah, Joseph; Bryan, Green.
1791 GREEN, JOHN, Furnifold W.
1791 GREEN, JOSEPH, Elizabeth (wife) and children (not named).
1793 GATLIN, WM., Amy, David.
1797 GOOD, JOSEPH, Benjamin C., Joseph, John, Ann.
1796 GILSTRAP, PETER, Mary, Polly, Bright, Wealthy, Winifred.
1796 GODFREY, MATTHEW, Dinah, Sarah.
1798 GREEN, FURNIFOLD G., Mary, Sidney, Fonville.
1753 GRIST, RICHARD, John, Richard.
1752 GOODWIN, NATHAN, Mary.
1760 GREEN, FURNIFOLD, James, John, Joseph, Mary, Titus.
1760 GEORGE, PETER, William.

H.

1786 HARVEY, RICHARD, Lydia.
1786 HALL, JOSEPH, Oliver, Elizabeth.
1788 HORTON, FRANCIS, Howard.
1789 HUTSON, ELI, Sarah (wife), John, Sarah; Gilgo, Febrow.
1789 HORNLY, THOMAS, John.
1789 HOOVER, HENRY, Ann, Samuel, James, Shadrack, Elizabeth.
1789 HALL, THOMAS, Thomas, Robert, Sarah, Richard; Bowden, Isabella.
1790 HOWARD, RUTH, Horton, John, Mary.
1791 HOWARD, BARTHOLOMEW, James, Michael.
1791 HUMBLETON, JAMES, Patty, Sandy, John.
1792 HORSENDS, JAMES, Fred, Richard, Elijah, Jesse, John, Delitha.
1793 HYMAN, MICHAEL, James, Sidney.
1794 HOUSTEN, FRANCIS, James.
1795 HALLING, EUNICE, Solomon, Betsy, Thomas; Kelly, Thomas; Bryan, James.
1796 HUKINS, ANN, Stephens, Matthew.
1796 HEATH, THOMAS, Reuben, Furnifold, Thomas, Polly, Nancy, Gatsey, Elizabeth, Laney.
1796 HOLTON, GEORGE, Joseph.
1797 HASTIN, THOMAS, Margaret.
1797 HAMMONDSTREE, GRIFFIN, Susanna, Arnet, Joseph.
1797 HALLIS, WM., Sarah, Eunice, Mary.
1798 HOOVER, SAMUEL, William, Joseph S., John, Jacob.
1798 HEATH, HENRY, Samuel B., Francis, Mary, Henry, David, Bethany, William, Elizabeth, Temperance.
1798 HEATH, JEREMIAH, Zelphia.
1798 HEATH, REUBEN, Samuel S. and wife.
1798 HEATH, RIGDON, Elizabeth, Jeremiah, Helen, Winifred.

I.

1796 IVES, MARGARET; Foster, Elizabeth; Adams, Luvenia.
1752 IVES, JOHN, Job, Jonas, Esther.

J.

1788 JOHNSTON, CHARLES, Esther, Arthur; Dunn, Elizabeth.
1792 JANUS, JOSEPH, Mary, Charles, Joseph.
1792 JORDAN, WM., Silvia, Benjamin, Matthew.
1795 JOHNSON, CHARLES, Ann, Garratt, Charles, William.
1796 JORDAN, THOMAS; Sparrow, Thomas, Jr.; Harper, A.
1796 JOHNSON, RICHARD, Mary, Esther, Elizabeth.
1752 JOHNSON, THOMAS, Ann, Thomas, Benjamin, John; Powell, Sarah; Whitfield, Ann.
1753 JONES, EVAN, Evan, James, Roger, Charles, Tamar, Lovick.
1753 JENNINGS, THOMAS, Thomas.
1759 JONES, HARDING, Mary, John, Edward, Vailes.

K.

1791 KELLY, THOMAS, Eunice (wife), Thomas, Betsey, Elizabeth.
1793 KING, JEREMIAH, Mary, David, Thomas, Allen, Susannah.
1797 KING, CHARLES, Joel.
1798 KING, ARENTON, John.
1798 KING, BRITTAIN, Silah, John, William, Brittain.
1798 KING, JOEL, John, Elizabeth, Lydia, Aynus, Lucinda, Mary, Dorcas. Nancy.
1799 KEEF, EDWARD, Jamey, Fereby, Peggy, Alley, John.
1751 KIBBLER, ABRAHAM, Edith, James.
1751 KENNEDY, WALTER, Sarah, John, Mary.
1752 KINSEY, JOHN, Abraham.
1752 KILNWORTH, FRANCIS, Rebekah, Noble.
1773 *Kornegay, George - Susannah, Wid. ch Daniel, Elijah, John, Jacob. George, William, David, Abraham, M.*
1786 LENEY, EMMANUEL, Powell, James.
1794 LEWIS, MASON, Patty (wife), William, Patty, Joseph.
1794 LOFTIN, THOMAS; Langfield, Joseph.
1795 LIPSEY, FANNY, Wenstty.
1796 LEVERAGE, SARAH; Campbell, James; Bright, Mourning.
1796 LEWIS, JACOB, Saborah, James, Sarah.
1798 LANE, FRED, Ann G., John S., Henry B., Mary B.
William, Daniel, John, Thomas, Shine, John.
BANK—96 1-2
1799 LAWSON, SAMUEL, Hester.
1751 LEATH, JOHN, Thomas, Samuel, Charles, Peter.
1752 LEATH, JOHN, Sampson, Hannah.
1752 LEATH, RICHARD, William, Margaret, Webster, Amelia.
1753 LEE, THOMAS, Elizabeth, Isaac, Mary, Frances, Thomas.

M.

1785 MARTIN, JOHN, wife (not named), David, John, Joseph, Patsy, Betsy.

1786 McKEGG, JAMES, Lydia.

1788 MOORE, ANTHONY, Betty Ann (wife), and children (not named).

1788 MILLER, JOSEPH, Mary, Milton, William; Moore, Nathaniel, Martha.

1789 McCROHON, JOHN, Elsey, Catherine.

1792 MARSHALL, CHARLES, Amy, Elizabeth, Stanly, Sukey, Holland.

1792 McCOTTER, HEZEKIAH, Ann, Archibald, Jesse, Martin, John.

1793 MUSE, JOHN, Sarah, James.

1793 MORRIS, THOMAS, Mary, Jonathan, Sampson; Muse, Thomas.

1794 MURPHY, WM., Lucretia, Wm. S., Wm. B., Guilford.

1795 MURDOCK, DAVID, Mary, Nancy, Hannah, James, David, William, Elizabeth.

1796 McCAFFERTY, JAMES, Nancy; Steed, Thomas.

1796 MOORE, JESSE, Lathan; Bedscot, Bethany.

1797 MORRIS, SAMPSON, Sarah, John, Elizabeth.

1798 MURPHEY, MOSES, Price, Sidney, Minnie.

1799 MORRIS, JACOB, Susannah, Charlotte, Hannah.

1799 MERCHANT, CHRISTOPHER, Judith, Christopher; Tolson, John, Benjamin, George M., Elizabeth.

1799 MASTERS, JOSEPH, Thomas, Christopher, John, Joseph, Bellamy, Sally, Julian, Abner, Susanna.

1750 MORGAN, NATHAN, William, George, Sarah, Luke.

1752 MANDOVALL, JOHN, Samuel, John, Elizabeth.

1751 MOORE, SAMUEL, Samuel, Thomas.

1751 McCARTY, W. O.; Dennis, Elinor; Anderson, Leah.

1750 McKICCHAM, DUGALD, James, Duncan, Mary.

1752 MASON, MOSES, Moses, Joshua, John, Catharine, Mary, Ann, Agnes, Charity.

1752 MURPHY, JEREMIAH, Thomas.

1753 MARSHBURNE, JETHRO, Edward.

1751 McLEARAN, ARCHIBALD, Florence, John, Archibald.

1752 McNAUGHTEN, RONALD, Isabel, Noel, Charles.

1757 MARTIN, JOHN, Rosalanah, John, Joseph. Elizabeth.

1764 MILLS, JOHN, William, Susannah, John; Graham, Mary.

N.

1784 NEAL, CHRISTOPHER, Mary, Sallie.

1784 NELSON, ELI, Thomas T.

1786 NASH, ABNER, Abner, Margaret, Justina; wife (not named).

1788 NILAR, WM. S., Rachel, Sarah, William, Lydia, Sukie, Elizabeth.

1792 NEAL, VANE, Matthew.

1799 NILAR, WM., Sukey.

1799 NELSON, FRANCES, Polly.

1799 NIXON, RICHARD, Sarah.

1762 NORWOOD, WM., James, Sarah.

O.

1794 ODEN, LITUS, Thomas D.
1794 OLIVER, MARY, Craddock.
1797 OGLESBY, JOHN, Mary.
1798 OPRAY, MARTIN, Elizabeth.

P.

1785 PURIFOY, DAVID, Sarah, David, John.
1786 PEARCE, RACHEL, Aellen, J. P.
1789 PAK, JOSEPH, Hannah.
1790 PORTER, WM., Judy, Thomas, Mary H., Annie, Sally, Betty.
1790 POLLARD, THOMAS, Aquilla, Thomas, wife.
1792 PHILLIPS, THOMAS, Thomas, Richard, James, Nicey, Charity,· David, Keziah, Peter.
1794 POLLOCK, THOMAS, Eunice, George, Elizabeth, Francis.
1793 PHILLIPS, JOHN, Elizabeth, John, Thomas.
1792 PAUL, GEORGE, Elizabeth.
1792 PEARCE, JAMES, wife and children (not named).
1795 PARSONS, THOMAS, John, Jonah; Gilbert, William.
1795 PAGETT, THOMAS, Eliza; Gibson, Ann M., Mary, Jane, William, Ann C.
1796 PAUL, JOHN, Mary, John.
1798 PARSONS, JOHN, James, Mary.
1798 PRICE, JAMES, Sarah, James, Leigh, Mary.
1798 PRICE, THOMAS, Edward, Mary, Suth, Thomas.
1799 PRICE, THOMAS, Elizabeth, Joan.
1751 PHILLIPS, PAUL, Rebecca; Flood, Paul.
1748 POWELL, WM., Fielder.
1748 POWELL, GEORGE, George, Osborn.
1751 PRESCOTT, MOSES, (Willis, William, Moses), Thomas, Russell.
1752 PHILIPS, WM., Samuel, Elizabeth; Williams, Ann.
1752 POTTER, JOHN, William, John, Elizabeth.
1752 PLANNING, HUGH, Elizabeth; Hall, William, Elizabeth.
1752 PITTMAN, JOSEPH, Obedience, Joseph, John, Marsh, Southey.
1752 PETERS, WM. Elizabeth, Joseph.

R.

1785 RIGGS, GILES, Shadrack, David, Giles.
1786 RUSSELL, JOSIAH; Pearce, Mary.
1788 RICE, EPHRAIM, Rebecca, William.
1788 RIGGS, JOHN, Sarah, John, Miley,
1788 RUMLEY, EDWARD, Rhoda.
1788 ROYAL, JAMES, Robert W., Philip, Sarah.
1788 RICE, ZEBULON, Benjamin, John, James, Emanuel.
1790 ROOKE, BARTHOLOMEW, Haslin, Thomas.
1791 ROUNTREE, WILLIAM, Martha; Trisel, Jonathan.
1793 ROUNTREE, FRANCIS, Moses, William, Ann.
1792 REAL, PETER, Marie, Sarah, Holland; Snead, Elizabeth.
1794 RATTEBUM, JACOB, Nancy.
1796 RIGGS, DAVID, Jeremiah.

1799 REED, JAMES, Mary, Peter.
1799 REW, SOUTHEY, Edward, Thomas, Benly, William, Southey.
1800 RELL, MARY, Whitford, John.
1750 RIGNEY, BENJAMIN, Mary, Phoebe.
1751 RHODES, HENRY, Henry.
1751 REED, JOSEPH, William.
1753 RYAN, THOMAS, David, James, George, Mary, Martha, Thomas; Campbell, Elizabeth.
1753 RUSSELL, JOHN, James .
1744 RUSSELL, THOMAS, John, Jeremiah, Elizabeth.
1764 ROBERTS, JAMES, James, Mary, Cynthia.

S.

1786 SANFORD, DARCIS, Rhoda.
1786 SPARROW, FRANCIS, Deborah, William S.
1785 SAUNDERS, JAMES, Mary.
1789 STARLY, JOHN WRIGHT, Ann (wife) and children (not named).
1789 SLADE, SAMUEL, Mary, Lewis, Samuel.
1790 SHAPLEY, JOHN, John, Hannah, Mary.
1793 SMITH, JOHN, wife; Polly.
1793 SWAN, EVAN, Rachel, Ephraim, Shadrack.
1795 STEWART, JAMES, Andrew, Priscilla.
1796 SIMMONS, JAMES, James; Stewart, Isaac, John, Thomas.
1796 STEWART, NATHANIEL, David.
1797 SPARROW, HENRY, Elizabeth, William, Francis.
1797 SMITH, ARTHUR, Hannah, Stanton, John, Mary, Rebecca and Sarah.
1797 SPEIGHT, WILLIAM, John.
1798 STEWART, ALEX., Lydia.
1798 SPARROW, PAUL, Nancy, Robert, John, Paul.
1759 STREWS, WILLIAM, James, William, Penelope; Barrow, John.
1751 STREWS, THOMAS, Mary, John, Elizabeth, Ann, Frances, Thomas, Sarah.
1751 STANTON, HENRY, Lydia, Benjamin, John, Joseph, Hannah, Sarah; Albertson, Mary.
1751 STEEL, ALEX, Peter, James, Mary, Elizabeth. Margaret, Sarah, Annie, Rachel.
1752 SILVERTHORN, SEBASTIAN, John, Mary, Lydia, Sarah.
1751 SIMMONS, ANDREW, John, George, Mary.
1752 SHEETS, JACOB, Bud.
1752 SMALL, BYIMUS, Miriam, Benjamin, Jonas, Amos, Ephraim, Knight, John.
1751 STEVANS, EDWARD, Ephraim, Jacob, Edward.
1753 STRINGER, FRANCIS, Hannah, Elizabeth, Ralph,
1753 SMITH, THOMAS, James, Mary.
1745 STOEBACK, CHRISTINA, Mary M., Elizabeth.
1775 SLADE, DANIEL, Daniel, Eleazer, John, Dorcas Becton, John S.

T.

1787 TIGNOR, JAMES, Alley, William, Washington, Sarah.
1791 TAYLOR, ABSALOM, Absalom, Dave.
1793 TINGLE, JOSEPH, Mary, Shadrack, Thomas, Perry, Joseph, David.
1793 TRUITT, WM., Patience, James.
1795 TINGLE, SOLOMON, John, Mary.

1796 THOMAS, ABNER, Philip.
1796 TOOLEY, ADAM, Adam.
1795 TINKER, STEPHEN, Judith, James, Lucretia, Esther, Gracy, Sarah.
1798 TOLSON, BENJAMIN, Elizabeth, George, Frederick.
1750 TOMSON, JACOB, Thomas, Jacob, Mary.
1751 TUCKER, NATHANIEL, Henry.
1751 TAYLOR, ABRAHAM; Tucker, Prudence, Dinah, Abraham, Robert, Jacob, Joseph; Colton, Amy; Burgly, Rachel.

V.

1787 VEALE, JOHN, Elizabeth, Elijah, Bond, Mary, Nancy, Betsy.
1788 VENDRICK, JOHN, Rebecca, Harper, Peter, John, Francis, Abram, Daniel.
1789 VENDRICK, JOHN, Allis, John, William.

W.

1784 WHITAKER, BRYAN, Ann.
1788 WEBBER, THOMAS, Ann, Thomas, Francis.
1789 WHORTON, JAMES, David.
1789 WHORTON, JAMES, Christopher, James; Squires, Reddin; Tingle, Joseph, David; Burney, Joseph.
1789 WOOD, WM., Richard, Thomas, Sarah, Fanny, Elizabeth.
1790 WINGATE, THOMAS, Mary.
1791 WHITING, THOMAS, Eunice, Thomas; Shute, Sidney, Joseph.
1793 WRIGHT, STEPHEN, Nancy (wife); Nancy.
1791 WALLACE, STEPHEN, Solomon, John, Archibald, Beverly and Christopher.
1793 WOOD JEREMIAH, Gordon, Jesse; Market, Clair.
1795 WILKES, HUMPHREY, Sarah, Nancy.
1795 WARD, SARAH, Hannah.
1795 WISE, MATILDA, Kellum, Elizabeth; Brothers, Mary.
1796 WALLACE, ROBERT, Mary, Thomas, Stephen, Nancy.
1798 WILLIS, THOMAS, Rebecca.
1798 WILLIS, THOMAS, Jeremiah.
1798 WATSON, CATHERINE, Fanny, Betsy, Susette, Mary.
1798 WILLIS, JAMES, James, Joshua, Joseph, Isaac, Joel.
1750 WARD, JOHN, Michael, John, Elizabeth, Noble, David; Oversheet, Dorcas.
1750 WILSON, WILLIAM, Elizabeth, Mary; Jones, Frederick; Nixon, Richard.
1746 WILLIAMSON, CHARLES, Hannah.
1746 WARD, ENOCH, Mary (wife), Enoch, Ann Martha, Mary, Elizabeth, Sarah, Abigail, Susanna, Richard; Shackleford, James.
1751 WALLISS, JOHN, Richard.
1750 WOMBWELL, BENJAMIN, William, Nathan; Jordan, Benjamin.
1751 WINWRIGHT, ANN, Lovick, Thomas.
1752 WILLIAMS, ANTHONY, Stephen, Benjamin John, Mary; Carter, Edward.
1752 WALLISS, THOMAS S., Elizabeth, Richard M.

1752   WILSON, WILLIAM, Mary, Elizabeth; Jones, Frank.
1760   WINN, JAMES, William, Lassell, Edward, Vaile.
1750   WORSLEY, JOHN, Stephen, John, Abraham.

Y.

1793   YATES, DANIEL, Hester (wife), Sally, Hester, Susanna, Daniel, Peter R., David, Melchisidec, Abraham, Rebecca.
1750   YATES, JAMES, Mary.

CUMBERLAND COUNTY—WILLS

A.

1757 AINSWORTH, WILLIAM, Janet (wife); William, James P. and Leven.

1797 ARMSTRONG, ANN, John, George, Anne, Polly and Sarah.

1801 ADAM, ROBERT, Janet (wife); John, Eliza, Ann and Margaret Jr; Mary (sister); Mrs. Robert Adam (stepmother); John Hogg (friend).

1802 ARMSTRONG, THOMAS, Janet (wife); William, John, Farquhar, Thomas and Isabel.

1804 ATKINS, LEWIS, Molly (wife); Nancy, Joseph, Sarah, Samuel, Gray, Grace, Ica, John and Polly; Elizabeth Betha (sister).

1765 ARMSTRONG, THOMAS, Margaret (wife); William, John and Jean.

1759 AKINS, JAMES, Barbara (wife); James, Nancy, Elizabeth and Barbara.

1786 ARMSTRONG, GEORGE, Ann (wife); Jane, John, Margaret and Thomas.

1787 ALLEN, ROBERT, Mary (wife).

1796 ATKINS. ICA, Anne (wife); Lewis, Ica, John, Richard and James; Sarah Robinson and Grace Stephens (daughters); heirs of Nancy Parke (daughter); Ica Atkins (grandson).

1792 ARMOUR, ANDREW, Ann (wife); Helen and James and three daughters (not named).

1789 ARMSTRONG, ANDREW, Joanna and Charles Carrell (friends); Augustin Cicatry (friend).

1789 ALLEN, MARY, Mary Yarborough and Esther Exams (daughters); Matthew Mason (son by a former marriage).

1783 ADAMS, JOSEPH, Susanna (wife); Prudence; Mary Waid (Wade) (friend).

1765 APLEBURY, BRAZEY, Catherine (wife).

1808 AVERY, ALEXANDER, Wife; Esther, Winifred; other children (not named).

B.

1807 BELDEN, DANIEL, Ann (wife); Asa and Asal brothers);

1767 BETTIS, ELISHA, Wife (not named); Elijah, Irvin, Frances and Mary.

1809 BARGE, LEWIS, Christian (wife); George and Lewis; Polly Wilson (daughter).

1775 BLUE, DUNCAN, Duncan, Catherine, Elizabeth and Donald.

1794 BUTLER, MICHAEL, Eleanor (wife); Jacob, Mary, Barbara; James (brother).

1810 BLACK, DONALD, Catherine Ray (sister).

1794 BOLIN, WILLIAM, James (brother).

1790 BRAZIER, ELIJAH, Elijah and Laban; James Brazier· (grandson); Leah Brazier (grand-(brothers).

1810 BROADFOOT, ANDREW, Hetty (wife); Margaret; William and Andrew Broadfoot (nephews).

1812 BATTLE, JAMES, Lucy (wife(; James, Randolph, Lucy; James Burt (grandson).

1761 BUIE, NEIL, Catherine, John, Neil, and Hannibal; Margaret Horah (daughter).

1799 BUIE, GILBERT, Wife; Archibald, Neil, Gilbert Angus, Flora, Martha, Effie, Marion, Katie and Peggy.

1796 BUCKLY, JOHN, John Buckly (father).

1761 BROWN, DUNCAN, Ann (wife); Peter, Hugh, and Neil.

1799 BISHOP, WILLIAM, Father and mother (not named).

1792 BLACK, ARCHIBALD, Christian (wife); Malcolm, Donald, Angus and John.

1795 BULLOCK, JAMES, James, Thomas, Elisha, Seth, Lydia and Benjamin.

1795 BOWELL, LEWIS, Rebecca (wife); Abner and Lamis.

1761 BROWN, JOHN, Mary (wife); Mary, Elizabeth, Hamal, Margaret, Rosana and Jerusha.

1770 BARNES, JAMES, Sarah (wife); Elizabeth; Joshua and James Barnes, (cousins).

1772 BOYD, SAMUEL, Sarah (wife).

1794 BURNSIDE, JAMES, Margaret (wife).

1790 BLALOCK, CHARLES, Elizabeth (wife); William, Richard, Lorena, John, Elizabeth and Ann.

1801 BLACK, JAMES, Nancy (wife); Margaret, Marion, Duncan and Alexander.

1761 BLOCKER, MICHAEL, Nancy (wife); Michael.

1766 BLUE, MALCOLM, John, Duncan and four younger children (not named).

1798 BUMPAS, ROBERT, Elizabeth (wife); Samuel, John, Mary, James and Ann.

1800 BEARD, JOHN, Mary, Martha, Neil, Joseph, William and John.

1800 BUCHANAN, JOHN, JR. Fanny.

1801 BEARD, JAMES, Rachel (wife); Neil, Mary, John, Marion and James.

1801 BLACK, JAMES, Nancy (wife); Margaret, Marion, Duncan and Alexander.

1811 BUIE, ARCHIBALD, Catherine (wife); Catherine, Marion, Effie, Daniel, William and Archibald.

C.

1810 CULBREATH, PETER, Mary (wife); Effie, Peter, David and Nevin; Catherine and Mary Phares (daughters).

1811 CARTER, JESSE, Bramley (wife).

1808 CARRAWAY, MARGARET, Thomas; Elizabeth and Janet Carraway (grand daughters).

1806 CARVER, JESSE, Mary (wife); Susanna, Elizabeth, Sarah, Rebecca, Molly and William.

1815 CLARKE, CATHERINE, Mary and Jenny Clarke (sisters).

1814 CALVIN, JAMES, Margaret (wife); James, Henry, Robert, Mary.

1778 COLE, THOMAS, Lucy (wife); Patty, Celia, Jane, Rebecca, William, James and David; Mary Jackson and Sarah Harrod (daughters).

1796 CAMPBELL, DONALD, Wife; Donald, Nancy and Katherine.

1766 CAMPBELL, JEAN, David Smith and Neil Mc-
Neil, Nevin and Nancy Galbraith (children
by a former marriage).

1775 CAMPBELL, PATRICK, Mary (wife); Alexander, Neil, Duncan, Ann, Mary, Katherine;
Archibald Campbell (brother).

1775 CREECH, RICHARD, Mary (wife); Richard,
Lydia, Charles and Robert.

1797 CARVER, ROBERT, Elizabeth (wife); Elizabeth,
Mary, Sarah, Louisa, Nancy and Marshal.

1758 CLEVEN, TIMOTHY, John Stewart and Thomas
Armstrong (friends).

1794 CLARK, MALCOLM, Nancy (wife); Archibald,
Nancy, Sarah, Malcolm, Janet, Catherine,
Duncan, Robert and Henry.

1786 CHAMBERS, HENRY, Mary (wife); Robert and
Henry.

1799 CLARK, MARY, Luke and william; Elizabeth
Leger (daughter); Mary, Thomas and Elizabeth Council (grand daughters).

1757 CAMPBELL, JOHN, Alexander, Matthew and
Sarah.

1784 CAMPBELL, DONALD, Katherine (wife); Barbara, Christian, Margaret Isabel and Malcolm.

1791 CAMPBELL, ALEXANDER, Wife and children
(not named).

1784 CARTER, JOHN, Sarah (wife); James, Susanna and Catherine.

1798 CLARK, GILBERT, Ann (wife); Mary, Alexander, Archibald, Gilbert and David; Ann
Smith daughter); children of dead daughter
Flora.

1761 CLARK, ARCHIBALD, Margaret (wife); Hugh
Ray (brother).

1780 COLBRAITH, NEVEN, Effie (wife); Peter, Daniel and Archibald; Margaret Smith (daughter).

1770 CONELY, MICHAEL, Margaret (wife); Michael,
John, Ann, Henry and Bridget; Mary Morrison and Elizabeth Pickett (daughters).

1794 CARRAWAY, JOHN, Margaret (wife); Thomas,
William, John, James and Charles.

1793 CREAN, WILLIAM, Oliver, Bartholomer and
Mary Crean (brothers and sisters).

1765 CLARK, ARCHIBALD, Mother (not named);
Alexander and William Clark (nephews).

1807 CLARK, MARGARET, Mary Clark (sister).

1810 CLARK, MALCOLM, Mary, Sarah, Janet and
Catherine Clark (sisters); Duncan (brother).

1779 CAMPBELL, ALEXANDER, Polly, Kitty, Jean,
Colin and Donald.

1796 COLVIN, WILLIAM, John and William; Mary
Watson, Nancy Blue, Mary Galbraith and
Catherine McKay (daughters).

1760 CONNER, EDWARD, Lucretia (wife); Thomas.

1763 CAMPBELL, ARCHIBALD, Mary (wife); Edward,
Alexander and Katherine.

1767 CARVER, WILLIAM, Mary (wife); William,
Sampson, Samuel, Jesse, John and Mary.

1793 CLARK, ARCHIBALD, Catherine (wife); Daniel,
Archibald and Margaret.
Elizabeth, Mary and Margaret.

1767 CARVER, ROBERT, Isham, Ann, Milly, Susanna,
1800 CAMPBELL, DANIEL, Florence and Margaret
       Campbell (sisters); Margaret McKethan,
       Jean Anderson and Colin Campbell (nieces
       and nephew).
1802 CARMAN, JOSHUA, William R (son); Juliana
       Weeks and Joshua McLeod (friends).
1802 COLBRAITH, DUNCAN, Effie (wife); Barbara.
1804 CAMPBELL, COLIN, James Mumford (nephew);
       Fanny and Gilbert Eccles (friends).
1802 CAMPBELL, FARGUHARD, Rachel (wife);
       James, William and Robert; Janet Anthony,
       Ann Buchanan and Isabel Smith (daugh-
       ters).
1787 CAMPBELL, WILLIAM, James and Dugald
       Campbell (nephews); Jean Campbell (niece).
1776 CAMPBELL, WILLIAM, Isabella Campbell
       (niece); John, James and Dugald Campbell
       (nephews); Elizabeth Campbell (natural
       daughter).
1807 CLARK, JAMES, Alexander and John (bro-
       thers); Margaret, Catherine and Flora Clark
       (sisters; Euphemia Beck and Mary Clark
       (sisters).
1807 CLARK, LUKE, Saah (wife); Elizabeth Rich-
       ardson (daughter); Thomas Clark (nephew).

D.

1759 DICKERSON, ROBERT, Mary (wife); James,
       Michael, Willis and Robert.
1786 DUKEMINEER, JOHN, Hannah (wife); Han-
       nah; John and Rachel Dukemineer (grand-
       children).
1779 DAVIS, ARTHUR, Wife; Matthew and Ralph.
1781 DUKEMINEER, JOHN, Rachel (wife); John
       Dukemineer (grandson); Hannah Dukemi-
       neer (grand daughter).
1770 DELOP, WILLIAM, Robert (father).
1808 DONALDSON, ROBERT, Sarah (wife); Robert,
       Margaret Donaldson (sister); Margaret
       Buliff (niece); James Thorburn (nephew).

E.

1807 ELLIOTT, GEORGE, Mary (wife); Henry, Jean
       and Alexander.
1787 EMMETT, JAMES, Margaret (wife); mother
       (not named); Mary Mallett (friend).
1779 EDWARDS, JOSEPH, Susanna (wife); Joel,
       Bryan, Charles, Benjamin, Mary, Jean, Gilla,
       Lucy, Susanna and Nancy; Isham Edwards
       (grandson); Sarah Robinson (daughter).
1774 EVANS, GEORGE, Theophilus and David (bro-
       thers).
1784 EVANS, THOMAS, Mary (wife).
1803 EDWARDS, ROBERT, Joshua, Moses and Eliza-
       beth; Rhoda Kemp (daughter).
1806 EMMETT, MARGARET, Charlotte Nivoth
       (friend); Mary Jones (friend).
1796 ELKINS, FREDERICK, Young Elkins (grand-
       son); Bedie Warsack and Sally Elkins,
       (grandchildren).

F.

1757 FREDERICK, JOHN, Sarah (wife); Thomas, John and Alexander, Sarah Frederick (grand children).

1802 FINDLEY, DONALD, Wife; Nancy and Rebecca.

1803 FERGUSON, JOHN, Margaret (wife); John; Margaret McNeill (daughter).

1788 FOLSON, EBENEZER, Edith (wife); Israel, Ebenezer, Nathaniel, William and three daughters (not named).

1792 FALKNER, EPHRAIM, Elizabeth (wife); Ephraim and other children (not named).

1792 FRITT, JOHN, Dorcas (wife); Dorcas.

G.

1763 GIBSON, THOMAS, Mary (wife); Son (not named); Walter (brother).

1792 GARRACH, JOHN, Mary (wife); children (not named).

1795 GUESS, LUCY, Joseph McNeil (grandson); Mary McNeill (grand daughter).

1800 GIBSON, WILLIAM, Catherine (wife).

1800 GRAHA__, JOHN, Catherine; grand father and grand mother (not named).

1770 GRANTLAND, WILLIAM, Frances (mother).

1793 GREGORY, ALEXANDER, Catherine (wife); three McGregors (nephews) in Glasgow.

1794 GALESPIE, WILLIAM, Margaret (wife); David and John.

1783 GREEN, THOMAS, Susanna (wife); Joseph; Susanna Rowan (daughter).

1796 GREGORY, CATHERINE, John and Alexander and Neil McAllister (nephews); Alexander Phillips (nephew); William Gibson (nephew).

1785 GREEN, THOMAS, Wiife; Abrigail, Elizabeth, William and Stephen.

1793 GORDON, WILLIAM, Elizabeth (wife); Thomas, Lyddal, Langston, Richard, Martha, and Betsy; Jane Zachary and Lucy Martin (daughters).

1789 GILMORE, JOHN, Sophia (wife).

1771 GIVEN, JAMES, The Presbyterian minister (in charge of Andrew Shepperd.).

1797 GRAHAM, JOHN, Elizabeth (wife); Alexander, Archibald and Elizabeth.

1779 GRAHAM, DONALD, Wife; Betsy, Margaret, Effie and Mary, Joanna Campbell (granddaughter).

1800 GRAHAM, JOHN, Catherine; father and mother (not named); brothers (not named).

1801 GRAHAM, DONALD, Mary and Dugald; Archibald and Donald Graham (nephews).

1802 GIBSON, WILLIAM, Wife.

1809 GAMER, JOHN, Wife; Patience, Polly, Bedie, Allen, Jesse, William and Betsy.

1812 GRAHAM, ARCHIBALD, Mary (wife); children (not named).

H.

1810 HOLTON, NATHANIEL, Jane (wife); Leonard, Jane and Nancy; Sarah Buchanan (daughter).

1801 HOLT, FREDERICK, Rebecca (wife); John and David; Polly Burt and Betsy Utley (daughters); Nancy Bryan (grand daughter).

1757 HOWARD, ROBERT, Ruth (wife); Thomas.

1772 HANCOCK, JOHN, Susanna (wife); John and William.

1794 HOLTON, ABEL, Susanna (wife); Elizabeth, MaryAnn, William, John and James.

1777 HUGHES, THOMAS, Children (not named).

1761 HOWARD, SAMUEL, Wife; Thomas, John, Samuel, Robert and Jesse.

1793 HOWARD, EDWARD, Susanna (wife); Edward, Stephen, James, Jesse and Joseph.

1788 HORN, ENOCH, Wife; Levi and other children (not named).

1797 HOLMES, ARCHIBALD, Elizabeth (wife); Archibald, George, Jean, Peggy and Sarah.

1815 HOWIE, SAMUEL, Margaret (wife); Janet, Elizabeth, Mary, Jane, Martha, Samuel, John and David.

1807 HICKMAN, JESSE, Penelope (wife); William, Stephen and Tabitha; Nancy Colvin (daughter).

1809 HALLRIDGE, WILLIAM, Robert, Alexander and Mary (brothers and sister.)

I.

1763 INGLIS, JOHN, Elizabeth (wife); children (not named).

1797 INGRAM, JOHN, Sally Sinclair (niece); Esther Worthington and Robert Harris (friends).

J.

1804 JONES, THOMAS, Thomas, Joshua, Polly and Nelly; Rebecca McDaniel (daughter).

1804 JOHNSTON, ALEXANDER, Peter.

1799 JERRY, JOHN, Ann (wife).

K.

1798 KILLEN, THOMAS, Margaret and James.

1804 KENNEDY, WILLIAM, Daniel; William and Neil Kennedy (grandsons).

M.

1758 MUSE, JAMES, Sophia (wife); James, Lydia, Daniel, Anne, Barbara and Sophia; William Muse (grandson).

1800 McALL, ARCHIBALD, Hector, John and Mary.

1801 MURPHY, JOHN, Epha (wife); Esther, John and Cornelius; Mary Baker (daughter); Margaret Burnside (daughter); Nancy Dan (daughter; Jenny McNeill daughter.

1801 McDONALD, DANIEL, Margaret Anderson and Mary and Agnes Proctor (sisters).

1803 McMILLAN, EDWARD, Jean (wife); Malcolm and John.

1805 McINTYRE, GILBERT, Wife; Donald; Gilbert McCall (grandson).

1805 MALLETT, PETER, Sarah (wife); Elora H., Caroline, Henrietta, Sarah, Charles P., Peter J., Edward C., Giles W. and Lakerstedt.; Mary E. Jones (daughter).

1801 McNEIL, ARCHIBALD, John, Donald, Hector, Margaret and Neil; John, Donald and Lachlan McNeil (grandsons).

1758 McALLISTER, JOHN, Ann (wife); Angus and Catherine; Flora Phillips (daughters); Margaret Shears (daughter); Jane Cowan (daughter).

1776 McLEAN, JOHN, Margaret (wife); Hector.

1793 McKENNEY, MATTHEW, Sarah (wife); Howell, John, Matthew, Rintain, Sarah, Nancy and Amy.

1794 McKETHAN, JAMES, Dugald, Donald, John, James, Sarah and Ann.

1769 McKOY, ALEXANDER, Catherine (wife); John, Alexander and Neil.

1797 McKOY, ARCHIBALD, Katherine (wife); Julin, Malcolm, Archibald and Neil.

1763 McKOY, ARCHIBALD, Catherine Smith (daughter).

1764 McNEIL, NEIL, Margaret, Flora, Catherine, Roger, Harry, Mary and Amy.

1768 McNEIL, HECTOR, Marian (wife); Neil, John and Flora; Duncan and Archibald (brothers).

1773 McQUEEN, MURDOCH, Katrine (Katharine) McQueen (niece).

1801 McDANIEL, DANIEL, Margaret (wife); Mary Portor (sister); Agnes McDaniel (sister).

1783 McDUFFIE, JOHN, Effie (wife); George, Duncan, Malcolm and Dugald.

1795 McLERRAN, DUNCAN, Mary (wife); Daniel, Duncan, Archibald, Nevin, Elizabeth and Christian.

1767 McDOUL (McDOWELL), WILLIAM, Joanna (wife).

1766 McNEILL, NEILL, Katharine (wife); Robert and Isabel McNeil (nephew and niece).

1767 McFARLAND, JOHN, Wife; Duncan, Mary, Dugald, Margaret and John.

1797 McKAY, ARCHIBALD, Katherine (wife); Thomas, Margaret, Farquhar, Elizabeth, Isabella, Christian and Mary; Janet Shaw (daughter); Sarah McNeill (daughter); John McKay (nephew).

1797 MONROE, PATRICK, Flora (wife); Daniel (brother); John Monroe (nephew).

1798 McDANIEL, ABRAHAM, Daniel (brother).

1799 McKINNON, HECTOR, Neil (father).

1799 McKENZIE, KENNETH, Wife and three children (not named).

1799 McNEILL, JOHN ("Bluff John"), Nancy (wife); Polly, Hector, Henrietta and Dugald.

1808 McNEIL, DANIEL, Isabel (wife); Archibald, Margaret, Isobel, Nancy, Hector, Sarah and Barbara.

1776 McLEAN, HUGH, Margaret (wife); Hector; other children (not named).

N.

1774 NORTON, JOHN B. Anna (wife); Elijah, Jessaphey, Nancy, Zerubabel and John; Elizabeth Bathern (daughter).

R.

1800 ROBINSON, MARY, Susanna.

1797 ROBERTSON, ANDREW, Sally Donaldson (friend).

1798 ROBINSON, JOHN, SR., Susanna (wife); Joel, John and Mary; Sarah Gerley (daughter); Susanna Baker (daughter).

1799 REDDING TIMOTHY, Mary (wife); Robert and William; Elizabeth Brown (daughter); Nancy Tedder (grand daughter).

1799 ROWAN, ROBERT, Susanna (wife); Thomas; John Hay (son-in-law); William Barry Grove (stepson).

1752 RAEFORD, MATTHEW, Mourning (wife); Matthew, Mary, Anne, Mourning, Rebecca, Philip, William, Robert, Grace and Drusilla.

S.

1797 SPILLER, MARGARET, Husband; Betty (sister).

1798 SMYLIE, JAMES, James; Mary McIntosh (daughter).

1799 SPILLER, JAMES, Hardy Holmes, Daniel Dodd, Duncan McAuslan and Thomas Davis (friends).

1758 SMITH, DAVID, Robert; Hugh (brother).

T.

1800 TEDDER, THOMAS, Wife; children (not named).

U.

1808 UTLEY, WILLIAM, SR., Dorcas (wife).

W.

1800 WILDER, JOHN, William and Mary Ann; Lucretia Smith (daughter).

1798 WHITE, WILLIAM, Rachel (wife).

1802 WHITE, THOMAS, Isabella (wife).

Y.

1803 YARBOROUGH, ELIZABETH, Judith Taylor (daughter); Elizabeth Howard (daughter); Moses Gilmer (son); Frances Gay (daughter); Nimrod and Littleton (sons); Charlotte and Temperance Utley (friends); Catherine Gordon (friend).

CURRITUCK—WILLS

A.

1762 ARMSTRONG, SOLOMON, John, Jesse and James.
1774 ASHBY, SOLOMON, Elizabeth (wife), Abel and Solomon.
1777 ANGELL, URIAH, Millicent (wife).
1787 ASHBY, ELIZABETH, Abel, Solomon and Elizabeth.
1790 ALLAN, THOMAS, Thomas.
1796 ANSELL, JOHN, James and John.
1796 ADAMS, JOHN, Elizabeth (wife), Asa and Lamanor.
1799 ALLEN, JAMES, Mary (wife).
1798 ALLEN, MARY, Rachel and Ferrell.

B.

1761 BLOUNT, WILLIAM, Elizabeth and Rachel; Biggs, William.
1761 BOMP, WILLIAM, Mary (wife).
1762 BARBER, JOHN, Joshua, Letitia, Massenah and Sarah.
1762 BOWEN, JOSEPH, Edward, Tully and Benjamin.
1763 BURGESS, GEORGE, Rachel, Thomas and Job.
1766 BRIGHT, HENRY, John, Henry and Charles.
1768 BRAY, WILLIAM, Wallace, William and James.
1768 BRIGHT, SAMUEL, Burnham, Anna.
1768 BRICKHOUSE, BENJAMIN, Elizabeth and Betha.
1769 BRAY, WALLACE, Mary and William.
1770 BROWN, ADAM, Barbara, Frances, Peter and Bridget.
1771 BAUM, PETER, Smith, Peter; Litchfield, Abraham, Peter and Josiah.
1771 BENNETT, JOSEPH, Euphan and John.
1771 BALLENTINE, PETER, Sarah, Joseph, David and Peter.
1772 BOAN, JEAN, Barr, Elizabeth; White, Mary.
1772 BURNHAM, JAMES, Jacob and Samuel.
1774 BARNARD, SAMUEL, Samuel, John, Caleb, Jesse and Dinah.
1778 BOWREN, EDMUND, Mitchell, Joseph, Malachi, Mann and Edward.
1780 BRABBLE, WILLIAM, Nancy, Chloe and Franky.
1780 BRIGHT, JOHN, William and Willis.
1780 BAXTER, SARAH, Mary.
1782 BERNARD, WILLIAM, Margaret and Jesse.
1784 BAUM, MAURICE, Abraham.
1785 BARRETT, JOSIAH, Scarborough, Alice.
1786 BAXTER, JOSHUA, James and Samuel.
1786 BOWREN, JOSEPH, Darius, Daniel, Joseph and Mary.
1787 BENNETT, MOSES, Solomon, John, Moses and Matthew.
1788 BEASLEY, JACOB, Ann (wife).
1788 BURTON, HILARY, Benton.
1789 BRADLEY, JOHN, Charles.
1789 BRAY, WILLIAM, James.
1790 BALLANCE, CALEB, Anne, John and Caleb.
1791 BEASLEY, WILLIAM, William, Cornelius and Mordecai.

1792 BEACHAM, EDWARD, Mary (wife).
1792 BATES, JOHN, Dinah (wife).
1792 BURRUS, ROBERT, Mary, John and William.
1792 BONNEY, JONATHAN, Sarah, William and Gideon.
1793 BATCHELDOR, THOMAS, John.
1793 BARRETT, RICHARD, William and Elizabeth.
1793 BALL, REUBEN, Elizabeth.
1794 BRUNT, RICHARD, John, James and Richard.
1794 BALLENTINE, HENRY, Mary, Joseph, Henry and Davies.
1795 BENNETT, JESSE, Bridget and Hannah.
1795 BROOKS, WILLOUGHBY, John, Thomas, Isaac and Mary.
1796 BARNES, JONATHAN, Elizabeth (wife), Sarah and Benjamin.
1796 BRIGHT, SILAS, Frances (wife), Silas, Sarah, Elizabeth and Tully.
1796 BURNHAM, SAMUEL, Charlotte, James and Samuel.
1796 BALLANCE, WILLIAM, Barbara, William, John, Caleb, Wallace and Laban.
1799 BRAY, JAMES, Richard, William and Marian.
1795 BARRETT, JOHN, Bennett, Catron.
1794 BALLENTINE, HENRY, Bennett, Lydia.
1799 BENNETT, CARTER, Samuel and Elizabeth.
1799 BURRUS, JOHN, Gray, Griffith.

C

1762 CAPPS, DENNIS, Caleb, Mary, Dennis, Edward and Joanna.
1762 COOPER, OFLES, John and Sarah.
1765 CASON, LYDIA, Church, Joseph and Cobb; Stewart, Julian.
1772 COX, BENJAMIN, John, Anne and Frances.
1774 CAMPBELL, RICHARD, John, Thomas and Mary.
1776 CAMPBELL, JOSHUA, Elizabeth (wife); MacKay, Sarah.
1777 CARLING, JOB, Thomas.
1780 CALLIS, JOHN, Sarah (wife).
1780 CAMPBELL, SOLOMON, Moses and Lucy.
1784 CLARK, GEORGE, Henry and Berthier.
1785 CAMPBELL, THOMAS, John.
1789 CROCKTON, JOHN, Agnes (wife).
1792 CARD, ELIZABETH, Dough, Gideon.
1792 CREEF, WILLIAM, Lemuel.
1763 CASE, JOHN, Cornelius and Elizabeth; Hall, Jonathan.
1795 CAPPS, JOHN, Moses and Franky.
1796 CADON, JAMES, Sarah (wife).
1797 CREED, HENRY, Dinah (wife).
1799 COFFEE, GEORGE, Esther, William and Wheatley.
1795 CHAPLIN, JAMES, Polly, James, Henry, John, Spence and Caleb.
1795 CREEF, LYDIA,

D.

1766 DOWDY, DANIEL, Lulls, Jacob, Caleb and Benjamin.
1766 DAVIS, JOHN, George and Ephraim.
1778 DAVIS, EPHRAIM, Frances (wife).
1778 DOUGE, PETER, James, Bray, Jacquelin.

1782 DAVIS, JAMES, Baxter, Mary and Sarah.
1782 DOUGE, JAMES, Peter, James, Tully, Philip and Mitchell.
1788 DAVIS, JOSIAH, Cornelius.
1788 DOUGE, ANGELIA, Willoughby.
1788 DOUGLAS, ABEL, James.
1790 DOUGE, BENJAMIN, Wright.
1791 DOUGLAS, JAMES, James and Dempsey.
1792 DOUGH, GEORGE, Benjamin.
1799 DOUGH, TULLY, Elizabeth (wife), Samuel, James and Susanna.
1799 DOUGE, PETER, Philip and Samuel; Etheridge, Isaac.

E.

—— ETHERIDGE, PATIENCE, James, Jolly and Chloe; Crabb, Benjamin.
1777 EVANS, BENJAMIN, Jean (wife), Benjamin and John.
—— ETHERIDGE, ELMER, Caleb.
1780 ETHERIDGE, SAMUEL, Mary (wife).
1782 ETHERIDGE, JAMES, Jonah.
1784 ETHERIDGE, JOHN, John.
1785 ETHERIDGE, CALEB, Brickhouse, Benjamin, (friend).
1785 ETHERIDGE, AMOS, John and David.
1785 EVANS, HENRY, James.
1789 ETHERIDGE, JOHN, William, Samuel and Mary.
1792 ETHERIDGE, HENRY, Moses and Nealy.
1792 ETHERIDGE, AMOS, James and Hollowell.
1792 ETHERIDGE, SAMPSON, Sampson, Samuel, Annie and Simon.
1794 ETHERIDGE, RICHARD, Richard, Henry and William.
1796 EVANS, JOSEPH, Anne (wife), John and Joseph.
1798 ETHERIDGE, TIMOTHY, Samuel and Corsey.
1798 ETHERIDGE, MATTHIAS, Edney and Matthias.

F.

1761 FANSHAW, MOSES, Sarah (wife), Rebecca and Moses.
1762 FERREBEE, THOMAS, Elizabeth (wife), Eunice, Euphan and Franky.
1763 FANSHAW, RICHARD, Thomas, Dennis and Davis.
1773 FENTON, THOMAS, Richard, William and Larsus.
1780 FANSHAW, MOSES, Henry, Moses and Grace (wife).
1780 FENTON, RICHARD, Lydia (wife), Caleb.
1783 FERREBEE, WILLIAM, James, William, Samuel, Thomas and Elijah.
1785 FARROW, JACOB, Nancy (wife), Thomas.
1787 FERREBEE, JEAN, Nancy.
1789 FERREBEE, JAMES, Robert and Thomas.
1789 FARROW, JACOB, Elizabeth (wife), Thomas, Hezekiah, John and Barbara.
1792 FERREBEE, WILLIAM, Chloe (wife), Martha, Sarah, Mary and William.
1793 FERREBEE, ROBERT, William.
1796 FERREBEE, ELIZABETH, James, Thomas and Cooper.

1798 FARROW, HEZEKIAH, Christiana (wife), Edward, Hezekiah, James, Reuben and Sally.

G.

1761 GARRETT, JAMES, John and James.
1763 GAMEWELL, GEORGE, John, Katharine and Solomon.
1769 GREGORY, SAMUEL, Sarah (wife), Thomas, Samuel and Eliza.
1783 GIBBINS, WILLIAM, Urias, John and Elizabeth (wife).
1787 GRAY, LEMUEL, Stephen.
1790 GREGORY, GRIFFITH, Rachel (wife), Samuel and William.
1787 GAMEWELL, JAMES, Tamar (wife); James and John.
BANK 246 1-2
1794 GRAY, JOSHUA, William.
1795 GUTSON, ROBERT, Daniel and Michael.
1797 GREGORY, GRIFFITH, Willis, Griffith, Gideon and Enoch.
1798 GREGORY, JESSE, Mary (wife), Isaac, Caleb, Thomas and Lemuel.

H.

1762 HEATH, ROBERT, Aileen (wife), Robert, James, Margaret.
1763 HAMAR, JOSEPH, Thomas, Joseph and John.
1772 HUGHES, JOHN, Mary and Jenny.
1777 HALL, JOHN, Chaplin, Sophia.
—— HUTCHINS, THOMAS, John, Nathaniel, Thomas, Richard, James, William and Christopher.
1786 HALSTEAD, LEMUEL, Seth, Richard and Joshua.
1788 HOWELL, SYLVANUS, Lindsay, John.
1788 HAYMAN, THOMAS, Tamar (wife), Gideon and Sarah.
1792 HARRISON, JOSIAH, Winifred (wife).
1792 HALL, SPENCE, Nathan and Spence; Gregory, Sarah, Thomas and Director .
1792 HOWE, WILLIAM, Barbara (wife).
1793 HALSTEAD, JOHN, Matthias, John and Josiah.
1795 HEATH, ROBERT, Elizabeth (wife), Enoch and Ryland.
1796 HUMPHREYS, JOHN, Lydia (wife), John, Nancy and Mary.
1796 HALL, DIRECTOR, Nathaniel and Spence.
1797 HUMPHREYS, MARY, John and Nancy; Ferrebee, Lida.
1799 HALSTEAD, SETH, Mary (wife), Malachi, Thomas, Isaac and Anthony.

I.

1777 IVES, WILLIAM, Abigail (wife), Thomas.

J.

1762 JOHNSON, JONATHAN, Ashby, Solomon.
—— JASPER, THOMAS, Dorcas (wife), Samuel.
1768 JENKINS, JAMES, Dinah (wife), James and Love.
1771 JONES, SAMUEL, Mary (wife).
1772 JONES, JOHN, Sarah (wife), Bazilla, John and Zadok.

1774 JONES, FRANCES, Sarah; Morse, Caleb; Cox, Anne.
1774 JARVIS, WM., Elizabeth (wife), John and Fester.
1775 JONES, DAVID, Elizabeth (wife), William and Henry.
1776 JARVIS, JONATHAN, Thomas.
1780 JONES, TAYLOR, Sarah (wife), Malachi.
1783 JARVIS, SAMUEL, Mary (wife), Samuel and Patsy; Allen, Jarvis.
1784 JAMESON, GEORGE, George, Niel and John; Wilson, Molly.
1786 JONES, EVAN, Evan.
1788 JONES, ZADOK, John and Docksea [Eudoxia]; Willoughby, Parson and Elizabeth.
1788 JARVIS, JAMES, Mary (wife), William and James.
1791 JARVIS, MAXIMILIAN, Solomon.
1795 JENKINS, ELISHA, Simon and Ezekiel.
1795 JARVIS, THOMAS, Lydia (wife), Samuel, Richard, Jonathan and Thomas.
1796 JENNETT, JESSE, Fanny (wife).
1799 JONES, RANDAL, Mary (wife), Joseph.
1799 JONES, JOSEPH, Elizabeth (wife), Patsy and Cabron.
1799 JONES, RANDOLPH, Lovey (wife).

L.

1769 LITCHFIELD, EDWARD, Mary (wife), Abraham and Jacob.
1775 LINDSAY, DANIEL, Jonathan, Daniel and Berry.
1775 LINDSAY, JACOB, Peter; Gibson, Robert.
1776 LEE, DANIEL, Rasha (wife), Nathan, Linton, Daniel, John and Elias.
1781 LEE, WM., Mary (wife), William, Daniel, Thomas and Anne.
1783 LEE, THOMAS, Zebah (wife), Dempsey and Thomas.
1785 LEE, JOSIAH. Lydia (wife).
1789 LUFFMAN, DANIEL, Dinah (wife), William and Philip.
1790 LINDSAY, THOMAS, Charles and Susanna.
1792 LITCHFIELD, JACOB, John, Jacob and Ezekiel.
1795 LITCHFIELD, JOHN, Frank, John and Ezekiel.
1795 LITCHFIELD, ABSALOM, Mary (wife), Amy.
1795 LUFFMAN, JONATHAN, Thomas, Elizabeth (wife).
1798 LENTON, BENJAMIN, Augusta (wife), Elizabeth.
1799 LEMONT, ARTHUR, Mary (wife).
1799 LINDSAY, JOHN, Priscilla (wife), Joseph and Mary; Dough, Nancy.
1799 LEE, ASA, Mary (wife), Stephen and Fred; Wright, James and Thomas.

M.

1778 MIDGETT, JOSEPH, George and Christopher.
1782 MACLAMAHAN, MOSES, Sarah (wife).
1782 MOSES, RICHARD, Elizabeth (wife), Uriah and Richardson.
1782 MONMORIPTY, JEREMIAH, Parker, Peter and Elizabeth.

1782 MAY, THOMAS, George.
1782 MATESON, ELIJAH, Thomas and John.
1785 MAY, GEORGE, Joseph and Susanna (wife);
      Farquahar, George.
1785 MARCHANT, MALACHI, Lydia (wife), Edney
      and Jordan.
1785 MILLER, THOMAS, Thomas and William;
      Brooks, Mary; Taylor, Betty.
1788 MERCER, JOHN, Jeremiah, Perkins, Henry and
      Jeremiah.
1792 MIDGETT, JOHN, John and Christian.
1794 MONCRIEF, THOMAS, John and Lydia (wife).
1794 MORSE, ARCHIBALD, Lydia (wife); Solomon,
      Arthur and Willoughby.
1794 MORSE, CALEB, William and Hilary.
1795 MATTHIAS, MATHEW, Robert, Hilary, Joshua
      and Elizabeth.
1795 MILLER, WM., Francis and Upham.
1795 MIDGETT, BETHANY, Judy (wife), Daniel, Bar-
      ristor, Bethany and Jitnah.
1795 MAY, JOSEPH, Dorcas (wife), Frances and
      Fanny.
1797 MERCER, JEREMIAH, Winifred (wife), Thomas
      and Jeremiah.
1795 McCOY, WM., John.
1797 MERCHANT, CATHERINE, Thomas; Armstead,
      Martha; Whitehurst, Elizabeth.
1798 McPHERSON, DANIEL, Mary (wife), Robert,
      George and Asa.
1798 MACLAREN, JAMES, Mary (wife), Enoch.

N.

1771 NORTHERN, PHILIP, Philip, William and John.
1774 NICKENS, RICHARD, Rachel (wife), Edward
      and Leah.
1785 NICHOLS, NICHOLAS, Franky, James and
      Allie; Glasgow, Elizabeth.
1797 NICHOLAS, JAMES, Sally (wife), Elizabeth.
1797 NICHOLS, FRANKEY, Peggy; Cox, Nannie.

O.

1771 O'NEAL, CHRISTOPHER, John, William, Chris-
      topher and Thomas.
1777 O'DOWD, WM., Jacob and James.
1793 O'DOWDY, CALEB, Daniel, Thomas and Caleb.
1797 O'NEAL, MICHAEL, Nathan and Samuel.
1799 O'NEAL, WM., Bethany (wife), Mary, Wil-
      liam, Henry and Ivey.

P.

1765 PARKER, MARY, Harris and William.
1769 PARKER, JAMES, Thomas, James and Azilrikan.
1774 POYNER, JOSEPH, Ann (wife), James, Joseph
      and William.
1774 PORTWOOD, GILBERT, Mary (wife).
1775 POYNER, JAMES, Mary (wife), Robert and
      James.
1777 POPPLEWELL, WM., George.
1777 POYNER, ANNE, Lydia; Morse, Prudence.
1777 POYNER, NATHANIEL, Samuel, William and
      Alex.
1777 PARR, WM., Mary (wife), Daniel, Jesse, Wil-
      liam, Peter and Issachar.
1788 PADRICK, HENRY, Charity (wife), Henry and
      Berry.

1790 POYNER, WM., Joseph.
1791 POYNER, HUMPHREY, William and Thomas.
1792 PARKER, JEMIMA, Anne.
1795 POWERS, GEORGE, Mary (wife).
1795 POWERS, THOMAS, Whitehurst and Samuel.
1796 PERKINS, HENRY, Jeremiah.
1796 POWERS, WM., David, Caleb, William and Neal.
1796 POYNER, PETER, Robert and George; Powers, Abigail.
1796 POWERS, CURIFF, Elizabeth (wife).
1798 POYNER, ADAM, Diana (wife), Evan, Isaiah and Whitehurst.
1798 POWERS, THOMAS, Julian; Holt, Thomas; McLaren, Jesse.
1799 POYNER, JOSEPH, Joseph.

Q.

1799 QUIDLEY, THOMAS, Elizabeth (wife), Margaret, Sally, John and Dempsey.

R.

1778 RUSSELL, MILLIS, Lucy (wife), Thomas and Lemuel.
1783 ROBINSON, WM., William and Jean.
1784 ROBERTSON, ELIZABETH, Sarah (wife), Abner and Samuel.
1784 ROBB, THOMAS, Farrow, Hezekiah.
1784 RYAN, JAMES, Isabel (wife), Andrew and Duke.
——   ROBINSON, MARGARET, Thomas.
1799 RORINSON, WM. W., Mary (wife), Charles, Jonathan, Tully and Manliff.

S.

1766 SCOTT, WM., William.
1770 SIMPSON, SOLOMON, Mary (wife), Mebery.
1774 SHANNON, JAMES, Joyce (wife), William and Daniel.
1775 SANDERSON, LEMUEL, Mary (wife), Thomas and Lemuel.
1778 SANDERSON, THOMAS, Jesse, John and Lemuel; Poyner, Ann.
1784 SYKES, ABEL, Henry, Benjamin and John.
1784 SANDERSON, THOMAS, Anne (wife), John.
1785 SIMMONS, ROBERT, John.
1785 SHUGOLD, THOMAS, William and Grace (wife).
1785 SIMMONS, JOHN, Robert, John, Dennis and Amy.
1785 SIMMONS, SAMPSON, Mary (wife), Thomas, Sarah, John, Caleb and Jesse.
1786 STEWART, JOHN, Offiah (wife).
1787 SIMPSON, WM., Francis.
1787 SAWYER, TULLY, William, John and Millis; Winbury, Chloe.
1787 SANDERSON, JOSEPH, John, Lemuel, James and Lucy.
1787 SMITH, PERMINOS, Sarah (wife).
1790 STOW, MEISON, Acteon, Diana.
1791 SYKES, WALTER, Benjamin.
1792 SIMPSON, JAMES, James and Penina (wife).
1792 SANDERSON, JESSE, Thomas, Cobb and Lemuel.

1792 SMITH, ELI, Ann (wife), William.
1792 SMITH, SARAH, John.
1793 SAVAGE, LUTHER, George.
1793 STANLEY, RICHARD, Thomas and Evan; White, Mary Ann; Etheridge, Sarah.
1794 SLIGHT, HENRY, Mary (wife), Henry and William.
1795 STOW, JOSEPH, Comfort (wife), Mary.
1795 SIMMONS, JOHN, Jane (wife), Samuel, Jesse, William, James and Willis.
1796 SMITH, LABAN, Mary (wife), Hannah and Laban.
1797 SIMMONS, DORCAS, Taylor, Mary; O'Neal, Mary and Edney.
1797 SHUGOLD, TULLY, Grace (wife), and William.
1799 SCARBOROUGH, NANCY, Barsheba and Ada.

T.

1769 TATEM, THOMAS, Sarah (wife), William and Thomas.
—— TOWNSEND, JACOB, Esther (wife).
1783 THOMPSON, JOHN, John and William.
—— TOWNSEND, JOHN, Drusilla (wife).
1788 TURITON, ABNER, Dennis.
1790 THOMPSON, WILLIAM, Nathan and Mason.
1792 TURNER, SAMPSON, Sabonay (wife).
1793 THOMPSON, EVAN, Mary (wife), Evan.
1797 TILLETT, THOMAS, Isaac, Thomas and Samuel; Dowdy, Hannah.
1798 TAYLOR, EBENEZER, Susannah (wife); Joshua and George.
1798 TAYLOR, THOMAS, Jessie (wife); Samuel, James, William and Edward.

W.

1762 WILSON, FRANCES, Davis, Uptram.
1762 WILLIAMS, THOMAS, Anne (wife), William, Leda, Caleb and Zebulon.
—— WHITE, WM., Ann (wife), Abia and Lydia.
1767 WILLIAMS, STEPHEN, Sarah and Hollowell; Swann, Mary.
1767 WILLIAMS, CHARLES, John and Jacob.
1769 WARD, WM., Margaret (wife), Jonathan and Timothy.
—— WILLIAMS, WM., Thomas and James.
1769 WILKERSON, MARGARET, Elizabeth (wife), Thomas.
1771 WHEALEY, JOHN, Dinah (wife), Thomas, Robert, John, William and Willoughby.
1772 WOODHOUSE, JOHN, John and Lemuel; Sanderson, Mary.
1774 WICKER, RICHARD, John.
—— WEST, JOSHUA, William, Malachi, John and Willoughby.
1776 WILLIAMS, JOSEPH, Caleb, Joseph, James and Robert.
1777 WHITE, JOSHUA, Lydia (wife), Joshua, Patrick and Henry.
1780 WOODHOUSE, LEMUEL, William.
1780 WEST, NATHANIEL S., Rebecca (wife), Edward, Obadiah, Jonathan and Spencer.
1784 WABOL, WM., James and Thomas; Williams, Barbara; Smith, Mary, Sarah and Barbara.

1784 WRIGHT, HENRY, Elizabeth (wife), Thomas.
1785 WILLIAMSON, FRANCIS, Nancy and Long.
1787 WILLIAMS, NICHOLAS, Elias.
1788 WHITE, CALEB, Amy (wife); Dudley, Caleb.
1789 WILLIAMS, THOMAS, Elizabeth (wife), Susanna, Thomas, Christopher, John and Thomas.
1789 WEST, GEORGE D., Susanna (wife), Anna, Mary, Roland and Peggy.
1790 WHITEHURST, GIDEON, Samuel.
1792 WHEDBEE, JOHN, Major; Basnight, Elijah.
1792 WARD, JOHN, Mary and Charles.
1792 WICKER, JOHN, Sally (wife); Halstead, Mary.
1793 WALKER, CALEB, Lemuel and Caleb.
1793 WALKER, SPENCER, Sarah (wife).
1793 WILLIAMS, JAMES, Mary (wife).
1794 WILLIAMS, LUCRETIA, Dempsey and Robert.
1794 WHITE, HENRY, SR., Letitia (wife), Henry, Solomon, John and Caleb.
1795 WILLIAMS, HOLLOWELL, Mary (wife), John, Tully, Henry, Thomas and Hollowell.
1795 WHITE, MARY ANN, Thomas.
1795 WALKER, SAMUEL, Mary (wife).
1796 WILLIAMS, ELIZABETH, Sarah.
1796 WATERFIELD, MICHAEL, Mary (wife), Esther, Abraham, John, William and Ezekiel.
1798 WILLIAMS, JOHN, Charles; Barrett, Mary.
1798 WALKER, O'NEAL, Sarah (wife), Asa.
1798 WAHAB, THOMAS, Rachel (wife), Thomas; Cox, William; Farrow, Silas, Burrus and Allen.
1799 WRIGHT, GAMALIEL, Sally (wife), John and William.
1799 WICKER, WILLIAM, Jean (wife), Elizabeth, William and Lydia.
1799 WILLIAMS, CHARLES, Dinah (wife), John, Thomas, Daniel and Mary.

DUPLIN—WILLS

A.

1785 ALDERMAN, DANIEL, Abigail, David.
1785 ALLEN, HENRY, Henry, Leven, William, Ezekiel, Sabrough, Rhody, Ruth, Elizabeth, Sarah.
1771 ADKINSON, JOHN, Sarah, Timothy, Thomas, John, Mary, Rachel, Ann.

B.

1793 BRYAN, RIGDON, Kadar, wife; 2 children (not named); Dixon, Catherine; Whitfield, Charlotte, Curtis, Esther.
1799 BEST, JOHN, Hannah, Patty, Benjamin, Rebecca, Elizabeth, Absalom, Howell, Henry, Ethulorial, Redding.
1784 BROWN, EDWARD, Arthur, Sherrod, Prudence, Susannah, Mourning; Stephens, James.
1791 BOYETT, SAMUEL, Therby, John, Hardy.
1783 BELL, JOHN, Thomas, Archibald, John, wife Elizabeth.
1762 BLACKBORN, WILLIAM, Martha; Horrick, Jesse.
1775 BLAND, WILLIAM, William, James, Thomas, Charles, John, Joseph; Barker, Mary.
1781 BASS, RICHARD, William, Sarah, Richard, Mary, Andrew, Willis, Burrell, Elizabeth.
1783 BARBRIC, PETER, Pege, Allan, John, Sallie.
1791 BEST, WILLIAM, Catherine, John.
1768 BLACKMAN, JAMES, Elizabeth, Joab, Mary.
1716 BONEY, JACOB, wife, Jacob, John.
1780 BOYETTE, MOSES, Anne, Arthur; Stallings, Milas.
1762 BRIGHT, WILLIAM, Winders, John; Herring, Stephen.
1779 BRITTAIN, THOMAS, Edmond, wife, John, Catherine, Elizabeth, Thomas.
1769 BARNES, WILLIAM, Lewis, Mary.
1765 BURCH, JOSEPH, Ann, Charles.
1761 BIRD, JOHN, MICHAEL, Bethenia, Celia, John.
1766 BOYKIN, JOSEPH, Sarah, William, Fred, Eddy, John, Mary, David, wife.
1729 BELL, ARCHIBALD, Mary (wife); George, Oscar, Joseph, Mary; Jernigan, Namasa; Bond, Clara; Frazier, Sarah; Noble, Normana.

C.

1799 CAVENAUGH, SYLVESTER, William, James.
1796 CARR, JAMES, Susannah, Osborn, John, Nancy.
1788 CHASTEN, RICHARD, Agnes, Joseph, Benajah, William, Richard, Mary.
1788 CATTLE, ROBERT, Barbara.
1795 CARLETON, THOMAS, Rachel, Anna, Elizabeth, Lydia, Martha, Stephen, Thomas.
1781 CARR, JOSEPH, Barbara, William, James, John.
1798 CUMMINS, THOS., Thomas, Benjamin, Hugh, William, George, Aaron, James.
1770 CLARK, ARCHIBALD, Alice (wife).
1788 COOK, JOHN, Henry, Lewis, Catherine, Marie, Samuel.

1782 CRUMPLER, JOHN, Josiah, John, Rachel, Sarah, Noney, Elizabeth, Cajah.
1767 CLARK, JOHN, William, Archibald, John, Lewis, Elizabeth, Daniel, Nathan, Benjamin, David, James, Penelope.
1761 CARRILL, JOHN, Mary, John, Jasper, Dorcas, Rachel.
1799 COOK, JOHN, Reuben, Jesse, Thomas, Nathan, John; Blanton, Pheraba; Martin, Sarah, May; Pippin, Amy.
1783 CARTER, JOHN, Rachel, George.
1761 CANNADY, PATRICK, Patrick, Elizabeth, Sarah, Alex., Abigail, Abi, Zophia.
1781 CANNON, HENRY, David, Mary.

D.

1790 DICKSON, BENEDICT, Joseph, Susanna, Penny, William, Alfred, James.
1790 DICKSON, ROBERT, John, William, Robert; Bryan, Ann; Barbary, William; Hooks, Dickson.
1799 DOWD, EDMUND, Whittey, James, Sarah John.
1799 DUNCAN, EDMUND, Grace, William, Edmund, George; Reaves, Calvin, Anna.
1760 DAVIS, JOHN, Cook, John, Jr.
1793 DUNCAN, ISAAC, Leke (wife); William, Edmond, George.
1799 DOWNER, ALEX., McCanne, Sarah, Mary, Marcer, Nancy; Gilman, John.
1782 DUACKS, WILLIAM, Mary Jane, Presley, William, Robert, Celia, Rhoda, Henry, Elizabeth, Nannie; Cameron, Sarah.

E.

1784 ELLIOTT, WILLIAM, Zachariah, Elizabeth.

F.

1800 FOUNTAIN, JACOB, Mary (wife), Jacob, John, Mary, Sarah, Fanny.
1784 FUSSEL, BENJAMIN, Benjamin, John.
1788 FAISON, HENRY, Diana, Polly, Elias, Nancy, Patsy, Isham; Griffin, John.
1796 FALDS, JOSEPH, Elizabeth.

G.

1787 GRADY, JOHN, Mary, William, John, Alex, Louis, Fred, James; Goodman, Mary; Croom, Ann; Dawson, Isaac; Lovis, William.
1781 GRAY, JOHN, Elizabeth, Thomas, William, Ella, James.
1761 GAVIN, SAMUEL, Pateria, John, Samuel, Louis, Charles.
1784 GREEN, JAMES, Horden, Thomas; Hagin, Rachel.
1790 GRIMES, JOSEPH, Ellden, Charles, John, Joseph, James, Thomas.
1781 GRIMES, HUGH, Jesse, Joseph, John.
1794 GREY, SAMUEL, James, John, William; Byrd, Rachel, Nancy; Strikely, Pheraba; Beasley, Mary; Baker, Penn; Phillips, Sarah.
1789 GURGANUS, SAMUEL, Benjamin, Mary (wife), John, Cooper, Sarah, Betsy, Nancy.

1793 GARRISON, EPHRAIM, Polly, David, Thomas, Ephraim, James; Strickland, Elizabeth.

1774 GRISSON, BRYANT, Kornegay, William B.

H.

1774 HOLDEN, JEREMIAH, Alex, John; Campbell, Jane; Wells, Frederick.

1785 HICKS, THANKFUL, Tillie, Ann; Miller, Rebecca; Mills, Thankful, Mary, James, Shadrack, Frederick.

1775 HICKS, THOMAS, Wife, Rebecca, James, Leonard; Borden, Trankful, Ann, Laura, Betty, Sarah.

1764 HALL, THOMAS, Rachel, David, Elizabeth, Eloisa, Mary, Jemima, Noicy, Lucrecy.

1789 HALL, SARAH, Mary, Drury; Rhodes, James L.; William, Martha.

1761 HOLLY, JAMES, John, James, Lamos, Sarah.

1791 HARVALL, WM., Ruth, Gabriel, James.

1789 HEADRICK, JESSE, Mary, Nancy, Jesse, Richard, Elizabeth. Thiney, Sarah, Nancy.

1797 HERRING, STEPHEN, Stephen, Alex, Sarah, Samuel; Horne, Athalia; Henry, Elisha; Glisson, Daniel, Persis, Hella, Charity, Bryan, Sallie, Henry; New, Nancy.

1791 HUNTER, NICHOLAS, Hardy, Nicholas, Edmond, Mary, Ammey.

1797 HODGISON, AARON, Ann, Aaron, Louis, Joseph; Mills, Carlton; McCann, Pheraba; Powell, Esther.

1788 HOLLINGSWORTH, ELIZABETH, Sarah, Jacob, Henry, Ludia, Celia.

1790 HOLLINGSWORTH, JACOB, Henry, Willie; Harrell, Jacob, Henry; Pickett, Celia.

1791 HOLMES, GEORGE, Head, Harvey, Fred, William,George, John.

1791 HOLMES, EDWARD, John, Dorothy, Gabriel.

I.

1792 IVEY, JOHN, Leah, Elizabeth; Parr, Deucy; Brown, Jesse; Harrod, Sarah; Parker, Sarah; Smith, Charity.

1782 INGRAM, ABNER, Samuel, Elizabeth, John, Treechab.

J.

1796 JAMES, JAMES, Thomas E., Gabriel H., Thackey, Mary, Dwinny, Nancy T., Rebecca, Catherine; Shepperd, Thomas.

1796 JAMES, JOHN, Elizabeth, John, Lewis.

1715 JOHNSTON, JOHN, Use of the Poor.

1783 JOHNSTON, HANNAH, John Jr., Elizabeth, Hannah.

1762 JOHN, THOMAS, Wife; Thomas, Susanna, Margaret, Mary, David, John.

1788 JERNIGAN, THOMAS, June.

1782 JAMES, JOSEPH, Elizabeth, Elia, Margaret, Rachel; Sutton, Elizabeth; Sigleton, Mary; Moore, Rebekah.

K.

Arabella *Jane*

1765 KENAN, THOMAS, Elizabeth, Thomas, Michael, Annabella, Elizabeth, Penelope, Jane.

1783 KING, HENRY, Ann, Henry, Steve, Mary, Charles; Herring, Abraham.

1790 KENAN, ELIZABETH, James, Nellie, Michael; Morisy, Jesse; Torrence, Nancy, Elizabeth; Clinton, Penelope.

1784 KENNEDY, DUSSEY, Rhody, Rachel.

1792 KNOWLAS, ROBERT, Elizabeth, Emanuel, James, Francis, William.

L.

1799 LANIER, JOHN, Jesse, Lewis, James, Boyd, Benjamin, wife.

1798 LANIER, RENATEES, Mary, Robert, John; Merida, Alexander.

1787 LANIER, THOMAS, Wife, James, Elizabeth, Robert John, Fannie, Jessie, Stephen; Murray, Ann.

1782 LANE, ROBERT, wife; Shadrack; Renatees and wife, Henry, Lamb, John, Frances, Elinor.

M.

1761 MOLTON, JAMES, Scott, Mary; Carr, Mary, Frances, Jonathan; James, Margaret, Frances.

1790 MOLTON, JOHN, Abram, Mary, Sarah, Elizabeth, Catherine; Johnston, Thomas.

★— 1781 MERCER, JOHN, Rachel, Absalom, William, Joshua, Debry, Jonathan; Brockman, Nancy.

1795 MERRITT, JOSEPH, Elizabeth, William.

1790 MATCHET, SARAH, William.

1792 McGOWAN, WILLIAM, John, William, Robert, Edward, Mary, David.

1783 MATTHIS, EDWARD, Nancy, John, Rice, Margoun, Edward, James, Edah, Esther, Hanson, Thomas, Aliff, Tackus; Goff, Sarah, Elkins, Elizabeth; Fennell, Jenkins.

1766 MILLER, SARAH, George, Anthony.

1782 McLENDON, JESSE, Elizabeth, Henry, Jesse, William, Dennis, Sallie; Bell, Wilfion, Eshbie.

1774 MATCHET, JOHN, John, William, wife, Henry.

1787 MURPHEY, TIMOTHY, Barbara, William, Elizabeth, Timothy; Wells, Jacob.

1781 MURRAY, BETHANY, Springs, Sarah.

1798 MALLARD, GEORGE, Mary.

1797 MURRAY, JAMES, Wife, James, Arthur; Marshburn, Elizabeth; Jones, Sarah; Pickett, Esther; Williams, Charity.

1791 MOLTON, ABRAM, Sarah, John, Marshall, Abram, Dickson, Patience, Elizabeth; Hall, Abraham, William; Hill, James; Dickson, Joseph; Peacock, Jesse.

1771 MOORE, JOHN, Mary, Annie, Sarah, Backey. Maura, William.

1784 McINTYRE, ANDREW, James, Martha; Clinton, Andrew; Best, William.

1799 MORGAN, DORCAS, Newton, Isaac.

★ See Colonists of Carolina - Humphreys family p. 218 for copy of Will of John Mercer. m. J. W.

N.

1793 NEWTON, PATRICK, Mary, Ebey, Susanna, Major, James, Isaac, William; Parker, Brombly.

1780 NEW, JOHN, Betty, Tobias, John, William, Peggy, George, Winnie, Margaret.

1799 NORMENT, THOMAS, Catherine, Sally, Betsy Jane.

1799 NEWTON, ISAAC, Enoch, Isaac, Esther, Anne (wife), Anne, Mary, James, Jeremiah; Alderman, Sarah; Herring, Phoebe; Williams, Mary; Roey, Elizabeth; Morgan, Dorcas.

O.

1759 OUTLAW, EDWARD, Wife; Alice, James, Elizabeth, Edward, William, Mary, Anna.

1780 OATES, JETHRO, Lydia, Amy, Rebecca, Jesse, Jethro, Elizabeth, Michael, Susanna, John.

P.

1780 PARKER, WILLIAM, Jerusha, Susanna; Jenkins, Mary; Cherry, Esther.

1762 POPE, THOMAS, Thomas, James, Obadiah, Celia, Constance, Jesse, William, Robert; Clark, Ann; Bueston, Patience; Bailey, Mary.

1788 PARKER, JOHN, Peter, Elizabeth, Sarah, Rachel, Mary.

1759 PARISH, WM., Thomas, Amy, Jeremiah, Henry, Edward, Charles, Judith, Sarah, Nancy, William, John.

1769 POWELL, PATRICK, Mary M., John.

1795 PHILLIPS, JOHN, Dorothy, Thomas, Frances, Mary, John, Benjamin; Best, Ruth.

1784 PETERS, SAMUEL, James, Ann, Samuel, Christian, John, Rebecca, Jesse, Elias, Damaris; New, Elizabeth.

1791 PEARSE, SARAH, Isbam, Sarah, Mary.

1791 PROWSE, JOHN, Elizabeth, Thomas.

1778 PUMPHREY, SILVANUS, Ann, Nancy, Sally, John, Jesse.

R.

1765 ROUTLEDGE, NICHOLAS, Ann.

1765 ROUTLEDGE, WILLIAM, Thomas, Mary, Elinor, Catherine, Elizabeth; Evans, William.

1791 RUECHEY, ADAM, Cox, Samuel, John, Margaret, Joseph, James.

1783 RUNNELS, SHADRACK, Mary, Robert, Willis.

S.

1791 SLOAN, DAVID, Nancy, David.

1791 SHUFFIELD, JOHN, Ephriam, William, Elizabeth, Wright, Isham, Bryan, West, Arthur, Nancy, Louise, Polly, Catherine, Tabitha; Grady, William.

1798 STROUD, LISTON, JR., Hannah, Louis, Celia, William, Isaac.

1799 SMITH, GEORGE, JR., Nancy, Jesse; Jones, Bryan, George, David.

1795   SMITH, ROGER, John, Sarah.
1781   SCOTT, JOSEPH, Jonathan, Jerusha, Nehemiah, Peggy, Ada, Ashea, Mary, Wife, Joshua, Joseph.
1762   SNELL, JAMES, Elizabeth, Roger.
1784   SLOAN, DAVID, Margaret, John, David, Gibson, Susanna; Brown, Polly.
1767   SLOCUMB, SAMUEL, Mildred.
1770   SULLIVAN, DANIEL, Amy, Elizabeth, John. Owen, Grant.

T.

1788   TAYLOR, JACOR, Elizabeth, John, Jacob, Jonathan.
1782   TREADWELL, ADMIRAN, Adrois, Phoebe, Enos.
1782   THOMAS, WILLIAM, Isaac, Riley, Billis, Richard, Phyllis, William.

W.

1796   WORSLEY, JOHN, Elizabeth, William, Charlotte, Pedenn.
1774   WILLIAMS, RICHARD, Lydia; Daughtry, Joshua.
1792   WILKINS, JOHN, Mary, Benjamin, Michael, James, Siddy, Jane, William.
1761   WILKINS, JOHN, Prudence, James, John.
1795   WORLEY, ANN, Loftin; Sowill, Ann; Miller, Elizabeth; Smith, William.
1790   WILLIAMS, JOHN, Priscilla, Zilphia, Prudence, Seavey, Patience, Jacob, Lewis, Jesse, Fountain, John.
1775   WESTON, ABSALOM, Reuben, John, Isham.
1769   WESTON, EDWARD, Reuben, Benjamin, Absalom.
1796   WARD, LUKE, Bridget, Luke, Penny.
1774   WRIGHT, ROBERT, Sarah, Frances, Jane, Robert.
1795   WEAL, JOSEPH, Mary, Dicy, Dolly, Elizabeth, James, Joseph, Samuel.
1761   WILKERSON, MARGARET, Sillivan, David; Bennett, Richard.
1775   WILIAM, THOMAS, Butler, Charles.
1777   WARD, JOHN, Sampson, Jesse, John, Sarah, Paul.
1799   WILLIAMS, JAMES, Enoch, James, Elizabeth, Burwell, Bertha, Zilla.

EDGECOMBE—WILLS

A.

1763 ALLEN, SAMUEL, Dempsey (son); Wallis, Caleb.
1762 ALLEN, ROGER, Elizabeth (wife); Mary and Elizabeth.
1763 ALLEN, JOHN, Alce (wife); children (not named).
1768 ANDREWS, ELIZABETH, Nicholson, Benjamin.
1772 ANDREWS, JESSE, Amelia, Cullen and Allen.
1790 ANDERSON, WILLIAM, Mourning and Henry.
1792 AMASON, THOMAS, William and Christiana.
1797 AMASON, WM., Sarah and John.
1798 ARMSTRONG, ROBERT, Mary and Matthew.
1799 ADAMS, HOPEWELL, James and William.

B.

1760 BUNN, JOHN, David and John.
1760 BOND, HENRY, Sons of Susan, Lewis, William and Maria Bond.
1761 BARNES, THOMAS, John, Britton, Arthur.
1763 BRYANT, WILLIAM, Samuel; Benjamin and Smith, William and Sarah.
1762 BARNES, EDWARD, Patience, Elizabeth, Jacob, Michael and Sarah. William.
1763 BELL, THOMAS, Brittain and Martha.
1764 BARNES, JACOB, Jesse, James, Joseph, Jacob. Juland, Archelaus and Abraham.
1765 BRASWELL, JAMES, Simon.
1767 BLACKWELL, BEORGE, Hardia (wife); Ann, Edmond, William and George.
1772 BRASWELL, RICHARD, Sampson and Solomon.
1772 BRADLEY, JOHN, Elizabeth, Burwell, John and Joseph.
1774 BATTLE, JOHN, William and John.
1777 BARRON, THOMAS, James, Thomas and Barnaby.
1780 BUNN, MICHAEL, Ann, Aaron and Michael; Swinson, Fred.
1780 BILLEAMY, WM., Mary, John, William and Alex.
1780 BALDIN, JONATHAN, Sarah.
1782 BRADDY, PATRICK, Job.
1782 BULLUCK, DAVID, Robert H.
1783 BRASWELL, JAMES, Nathan, James, Abner and Burrell.
1784 BROWNRIGG, GEORGE, George, Jr.
1785 BRYAN, THOMAS, Evan, Henderson and Faithful.
1786 BAKER, MOSES, Jesse.
1786 BOOTH, THOMAS, SR., James, Benjamin and Robert.
1787 BILBRE, MARGARET, Alex and Sarah.
1788 BLACKLEDGE, LOUISA, Blount and Richard.
1787 BIGNALL, ROBERT, Robert and Edward.
1788 BAKER, JESSE, Jonathan, Moses, Aaron and David.
1789 BOLTON, RICHARD, John, Mary, Richard, Isaac and Luke.
1789 BIGGS, JOHN, James and William.
1790 BARLOW, DAVID, Lewis, David and Benjamin.

1790 BALL, RICHARD, Mildred, Benjamin and John.
1791 BASHFORD, ALEX, Ann, Mary, Alex, James and George.
1792 BARNES, ABSALOM, Noah and Jacob.
1792 BRASWELL, BENJAMIN, Mary, James, John, Simon, Sader and Permenter.
1793 BIGNALL, ROBERT, Elizabeth and John.
1793 BRYANT, GALE, Elizabeth; Brand, Sarah; Jordan, Eulah.
1793 BELL, JOSHUA, Fred, Joshua, Thomas, Whitmel, Benjamin and Joseph; Wright, Reason.
1794 BELL, JOHN, Elizabeth, Jonas and Richard.
1794 BLOODWORTH, WM., wife; William, Hardy. Jesse and Timothy.
1794 BROADRIBBS, THOMAS, Michael B.
1795 BIGNALL, ELIZA, Robert E. B.; Baker, Blake.
1795 BRIDGERS, BRITON, wife; William and John.
1796 BOAZMAN, JAMES, Martin and Josiah.
1796 BATTLE, JOHN, Frances, Joseph, David, Elisha and John.
1797 BROWN, JAMES, Celia, Sarah, Samuel and James.
1797 BELLAMY, JOHN, Sally, William and John.
1797 BRYAN, WM., Lezanar, Turner and Bart.
1799 BATTLE, ELISHA, Dempsey.
1799 BENTLEY, JOSHUA, Martha; Turnal, Martha and Joshua.
1800 BAREFOOT, JEPTHAH, Senath, Jepthah, John, Jonathan and Dillon.

C.

1760 COLEMAN, MOSES, John, Moses, Mary and Amos.
1761 COLEMAN, ROBERT, Susanna and Robert.
1761 COLEMAN, CHARLES, Abigail, Jonathan, Charles and Aaron.
1761 CANE, WM., Archibald and William.
1761 COLEMAN, CHARLES, Jonathan, Aaron, Sarah and Patience.
1761 CAIN, JAMES, James, Hardy and Jacob.
1762 COLWELL, JOHN, William and John.
1770 COFFIELD, BENJAMIN, Gresham and Benjamin.
1772 CULPEPPER, BENJAMIN, Elizabeth and Erasmus; Whitehead, Rahab; Manning, Martha.
1774 COUNCIL, JOSHUA, Christian.
1774 CAIN, HARDY, James.
1776 CARLILE, SARAH, William, Richard and Joseph.
1777 CARTER, KINDRED, Mary, Uron and Carter.
1779 CARTER, JESSE, Morgan, Sarah.
1779 CROCKER, DREWRY, Anne and Sally; Pender, Mary; Pury, Molly.
1780 CARTWRIGHT, JOHN, Sarah (wife); Susanna, Sarah, Thomas and Hezekiah.
1781 COTTEN, AMOS, Zilpah, George, Wimberly, Joseph and James.
1781 CUTCHINS, THOMAS, Mary and Thomas.
1785 CLARK, HENRY, Frances and Nathan.
1785 COKER, CALEB, Jacob and Ezekiel.
1786 CARLILE, ROBERT, Sarah, Simon and Edwin.
1788 CROMWELL, ALEX, Smith, Vinson.
1788 CLARK, HENRY, Mary and Richard.
1789 COHOON, JOHN, Joel, Simon and Priscilla.

1790 COHOON, WM., wife; Treasy and Solomon.
1793 COPPEDGE, AUGUSTIN, Charlotte, Willmuth, Mary and Augustin.
1794 CAVENAH, MARY, Charles.
1795 COLEMAN, ROBERT, John and Grace.
1795 CROMWELL, THOMAS, Celia, Elisha, Oliver and Charles.
1796 COKER, JAMES, Mary and Nathaniel.
1799 COCKBURN, GEORGE, Frances, George and ~~Thomas.~~ *Theophilus*

D.

1760 DEW, JOHN, Abraham, John, Arthur, Sarah, Priscilla and Mary.
1760 DELOACH, SAMUEL, Mary, William, Averilla, Jesse, Samuel, Molly, John and Solomon.
1774 DELOACH, MARY, Jesse, John and Samuel; Barnes, Celia; Bloodworth, Milly.
1779 DICKENS, CHRISTOPHER, Key, Mary.
1780 DICKINSON, JOHN, Jane and Thomas.
1785 DRAKE, LAZARUS, Sarah, Drury, Hines and David.
1787 DAUGHERTY, SAMUEL, SR., Joseph and Elizabeth.
1788 DAUGHTIE, DEMPSEY, Daniel.
1789 DIGGS, ROBERT, Elizabeth and Sterling.
1790 DIXON, THOMAS, William.
1791 DICKEN, EPHRAIM, Father.
1793 DUNN, JOHN, Ann, Stephen, Lamon, Jonah and James.
1794 DICKEN, BENJAMIN, Catharine, James and Turner.
1796 DAVIS, EMORY, David.
1799 DAVIS, JOHN, Ann and Aaron.
1799 DAVIS, JOSEPH, Noah.

E.

1762 EVANS, ABRAHAM, John, Abraham, Elizabeth, Sarah, Ledy and Anne.
1766 EVANS, ELIZABETH, John, Abraham and Sarah.
1769 ELINOR, FRANCIS, Honour, William, Francis and Thomas.
1775 EXUM, JOHN, Benjamin and Etheldred.
1778 EWING, GUSTAVUS, Judith, John and Elizabeth.
1779 EXUM, ETHELDRED, Etheldred.
1785 EXUM, MICAJAH, John.
1795 EXUM, WM., Mary; Bellamy, Sarah.
1796 EDWARDS, MICAJAH, Elizabeth and Littleberry.
1796 EXUM, BARNABY, Williamson and William.
1798 ELINOR, WM., Sarah, James, Etheldred and Benjamin.

F.

1761 FORT, JOHN, Jacob and Joseph.
1761 FORT, ELIAS, Catherine, Joseph, William and Elias.
1761 FLOYD, FRANCIS, Elizabeth, Parham and Cyrus.
1761 FORT, GEORGE, Mary, Jacob, Joseph and Priscilla.

1766   FLOWERS, JACOB, Hardy and Mary.
1769   FERGUSON, JAMES, Margaret and Joseph.
1775   FLOWERS, EDWARD, John.
1780   FORT, JOHN, William, John and Fred.
1785   FARMER, THOMAS, Joseph, Jesse and Thomas.
1791   FORT, JOSEPH, Elizabeth, George and John.
1792   FOXHALL, THOMAS, John and Thomas.
1793   FLENAGIN, JOHN, Margaret; Mitchell, Charity and children.
1798   FOXHALL, THOMAS, Lucy and William.
1799   FLORY, LAZARUS, Jesse and William.

G.

1760   GARNER, JOHN, John, Jonathan and Absalom.
1761   GAY, JOHN, Pittman, Thomas.
1761   GRIFFIN, JOHN, Lewis, Hardy, Joseph, Demsey, Mildred, Anna, May and Delilah.
1761   GAY, JOHN, William.
1762   GOODSON, THOMAS, Winnie and Elizabeth; Merritt, Mary and Elizabeth; Gunter, Sarah.
1768   GLOVER, GEORGE, Faithful, John and Porsons.
1770   GOSNEY, JOHN, Martha.
1771   GEORGE, ELIAS, Martha and William .
1777   GRAY, JOHN, Joseph and James.
1777   GRAY, ROBERT, Etheldred.
1781   GOODWIN, WILLIAM, Tabitha (wife) and children (not named).
1788   GADDY, THOMAS, Thomas.
1789   GARDNER, GEORGE, Mary, William and George.
1789   GRICHRIST, THOMAS, Martha and Allen; Jones, Willie and Allen.
1790   GRAY, ETHELDRED, William R., Charles and Thomas.
1792   GAY, HENRY, Barnes, Stephen.
1793   GILL, TAYLOR, Molly, William T., Thomas and Nancy.
1796   GWIN, DANIEL, Elizabeth, William and Polly.
1796   GERRARD, CHARLES, Elizabeth and George; University of N. C.; Simon, Dinah and Benjamin.
1798   GAY, WILLIAM, Ann.
1798   GARNER, ABSOLOM, Jenny and Lasens.
1799   GRIFFIS, JOHN, William.

H.

1761   HORN, HENRY, Elizabeth.
1763   HUDNALL, ROBERT, Willis.
1763   HARRELL, THOMAS, Simon, Edward and Sabra.
1764   HILLIARD, JACOB, Sarah, Elizabeth and Jeremiah.
1767   HENDRICK, WILLIAM, Joshua, William and Sarah.
1766   HATCHER, JOHN, Jeremiah, Dorothy and Sarah.
1770   HARWOOD, JOSEPH, Joseph, Absolom and Sarah.
1772   HALL, JAMES, wife and children (not named).
1774   HARE, JESSE, Bettie, Elizabeth, Mary Ann, King, Annas and Anna.
1780   HAYWOOD, WILLIAM, Charity, John, Sherwood, William H. and Stephen.

1780 HAYWOOD, SHERWOOD, Hannah, Adam and Sherwood.
1781 HINES, RICHARD, Jesse and Mary.
1783 HINES, PETER, Henry and Peter.
1783 HERN, JAMES, Elizabeth (wife); and children (not named).
1784 HARRIS, ARTHUR, Lydia and Thomas.
1785 HART, HENRY, Joseph and Richard.
1785 HORN, JOEL, Ann and Elijah.
1786 HARRIS, THOMAS, Sarah and William.
1788 HEARN, MICHAEL, wife; Michael.
1789 HOGG, THOMAS, Samuel, Eliza, Samuel and John Baptist.
1791 HANSE, JOHN, John, Israel, Isaac and Joseph.
1791 HALL, CHARLES, Thomas and Ralph.
1795 HORN, WM., Ruth, Jemima, Charity and Rachel.
1795 HICKMAN, NATHANIEL, Sarah, Nathaniel, William and Snowden.
1795 HYMAN, THOMAS, Mary, Duggan, Elizabeth.
1799 HOLLAND, JACOB, Peggy, James, Richard, Jacob, Lamon, David, Hardy and Delolacan.
1783 HYETT, THOMAS, Willis, John and Thomas.

I.

1762 IVEY, ADAM, Lewis and Benjamin.
1772 IRWIN, ANDREW, John, Jeremiah, James, Mary and Andrew.
1774 INGE, JOSEPH, Anne, Joseph, Christopher and Matthew.
1778 IRWIN, HENRY, Henry, Lewis, John A. and Elizabeth.

J.

1763 JOHNSON, BENJAMIN, James and Cornelius.
1779 JOHNSTON, JONAS, William and Esther.
1782 JELKS, WM., Ann and Lemuel.
1782 JOHNSTON, JACOB, Jacob, Amos and Jordan.
1789 JOHNSTON, SIMON, Martha and Jesse.
1791 JORDAN, JOSHUA, Edey, Jesse and Stephen.
1794 JORDAN, CORNELIUS, Joshua, Henry and Levi.
1796 JONES, HARDY, Hannah and Abraham.
1799 JACKSON, JOHN J., Charlotte and Nancy.

K.

1761 KNIGHT, ROBERT, Spier, Terence, Penelope and Francis.
1765 KELLY, ALEX, Margaret.
1769 KING, WM., Elizabeth (wife) and children (not named).
1770 KNIGHT, JOHN, Isabella and James.
1772 KITCHIN, BOAZ, William and Boaz.
1779 KINCHEN, WM., Sarah and Matthew.
1781 KNIGHT, MOSES, Allen and John C.
1783 KELLY, JOHN, Eliza and Joseph.
1785 KITCHIN, MARY, Jethro.
1793 KILLIBREW, JOSHUA, Susanna (wife) and children (not named).
1794 KNIGHT, JAMES, James and William; and Jacob Knight's children.

L.

1762 LEE, SOLOMON, Richard and Brian.
1765 LENOIR, THOMAS, Isaac, Thomas, Mourning, William, Lewis and John.
1773 LOWRY, ROBERT, Amos and John.
1774 LEE, JOSHUA, Eleanor and Mary Pope.
1777 LAKEY, RICHARD, Mary and Christopher.
1777 LEE, JAMES, William, Root, Travis, Winnie and James.
1777 LAWRENCE, EPHRAIM, Betty and Jesse.
1780 LANGSTON, LEONARD, Bandy, James; Bolton, Luke.
1781 LLOYD, NICHOLAS, Sarah, Roderick and Francis.
1788 LYNCH, WM., Jordan, McDominick.
1789 LITTLE, ABRAHAM, William, Jesse and John.
1789 LANGLEY, WM., William.
1789 LAIN, JAMES, SR., Sarah and James.
1791 LITTLE, WM., Mary and Asa.
1791 LOHON, ELIZABETH, Coker, James Jr.
1793 LANCASTER, BENJAMIN, Benjamin and Elijah.
1794 LODGE, LEWIS, Mary, John, Robert and Riddick.
1794 LLEWELLYN, JOHN, John.
1794 LAWRENCE, THOMAS, Comfort, Lydia, Lucy, Sarah and Thomas.
1794 LITTLE, WM., Exum, Noe and Elizabeth.
1795 LAWRENCE, JOHN, Absel, John, Joshua, David, Riddick, Mary and Pheraba.
1796 LEWIS, EXUM, Thomas, Green and Bartholomew.

M.

1761 MAUND, WM., Hardie.
1768 MERRITT, THOMAS, William, Benjamin, Mary I., Martha, Margaret, Barbara , Fanny, Shalaty and James.
1769 McDANIEL, DANIEL, David, Camel, Duncan and John.
1776 MOORE, JOSEPH, Ann and Ezekiel.
1778 MIAL, JOHN, Norsworthy.
1778 MERRITT, MARY, Emanuel.
1778 MORRIS, JESSE, Cheston, Henry, Samuel, James, Jabez and Susanna.
1782 MEWBORNE, THOMAS, George and Thomas.
1784 McMILLAN, WM., Nelly and Robert.
1789 MOORE, AMOS, Elizabeth and Newton.
1792 McDANIEL, DANIEL, John, Mary Ann, Charles; Mary Ann (wife).
1792 MORGAN, JOSEPH, Mary, John and David.
1794 MOORE, SAMUEL, Ellender and Jemima.
1795 MORGAN, WM., SR., William.

N.

1767 NELSON, JAMES, Charity, Violet and Wilson.
1779 NEWSOM, THOMAS, Hannah and Joseph.
1781 NORSWORTHY, WM., John.
1793 NORTHOM, WM., Peter, Katie, Nellie and Lucy.
1799 NICHOLSON, JOHN, Penelope, Timothy, Sarah, Martha, Mary, Pheraba, Eliza and Ann.

O.

1784   O'NEAL, JOHN, Sarah.

P.

1760   PITTMAN, MOSES, Elizabeth, James, Moses and Mary.
1761   PARKER, JOHN, Gabriel.
1762   PRIDGEN, WM., Thomas, Jesse and William.
1763   PITTMAN, JOSEPH, Jethro, Ann and Chloe.
1772   POPE, JACOB, Jane, Elijah and Pilgrim.
1772   PROCTOR, JOHN, John, Shadrack, Aaron, Sampson and Moses.
1774   PARKER, FRANCIS, wife; Francis.
1777   POWELL, NATHANIEL, Nathan and Nathaniel.
1780   PROCTOR, WILLIAM, Jane, Stephen, Josey and Morris.
1781   PENNY, THOMAS, Malachi and John.
1781   PRICE, THOMAS, Elizabeth and Eliza.
1781   PARKER, SIMON, Jethro.
1784   PHILIPS, JOSEPH, Etheldred, Benjamin, Exum, Matthew, Sarah and Joseph.
1784   PHILIPS, JOHN, Sarah (wife), and children (not named).
1785   PROCTOR, JOSHUA, Jacob.
1786   PERRIT, LEWIS, Solomon.
1786   PETTEWAY, WM., Elizabeth; Barlow, David.
1789   PERMENTER, JAMES, Nathaniel and Margaret; Quinn, John.
1790   PHILIPS, ARTHUR, Elizabeth and Sarah; Adkins, John.
1791   PIPPIN, JOSEPH, Barbara (wife) and children (not named).
1792   PRICE, ELIJAH, wife and children (not named).
1793   PRICE, WM , Sarah, Mackingain, Barbara, James, William and John.
1793   PITTMAN, JESSE, Huhman.
1794   POWELL, WM., Nancy. Zachariah, John, Wm., George, Jesse and Condall; Coleman, Sarah; Noane, Christian.
1794   PROCTOR, JOHN, Ede and John.
1795   PHILIPS, ETHELDRED, Exum and Eaton.
1797   PITT, JAMES, Ann, Richard and Etheldred.
1798   PEELLE, ABNER, John.
1799   PITT, ETHELDRED, Richard.
1799   PITTMAN, ELIJAH, Harrison, Graham and Benjamin.

R.

1760   ROSS, WILLIAM, Daniel.
1760   RICKS, ISAAC, James and John.
1761   ROSS, DANIEL, Andrew.
1761   ROW, WM., Christian.
1761   ROSS, ANDREW, Sarah, Judith, Ann, Mary, Esther and Elizabeth.
1771   RICHMOND, SKIPWITH, Sarah; Mearns, William, Skipwith.
1775   RICKS, BENJAMIN, Patience and Abraham.
1776   ROBINS, THOMAS, William, Rowland and Simon.
1781   ROSS, DANIEL, Sarah and Daniel.

1781 ROBBINS, WM , John.
1784 ROBINSON, JONATHAN, Patience, Willis, Wiley, John and Reddin.
1792 RENN, WM., David and Archibald.
1792 RICKS, JAMES, Phoebe, Robert, Eli, Henry
and Josiah.
1795 RENN, JAMES, David.
1795 RUFFIN, BENJAMIN, Sarah, John and Lamon.
1799 RODGERS, TRISTRAM, Daniel, Willis and Levi.

S.

1761 SORNES, WM., John, Benjamin and Henry.
1761 SELLERS, BENJAMIN, Sarah, Simon and Je-
honias.
1761 SPEER, JAMES, William W., David, Elizabeth
and Kindred.
1762 SUMMERALL, JACOB, Rosanna, Mary, and
Sarah.
1764 SINGLETON, JAMES, Mary and John.
1764 SMITH, JOSEPH, Elizabeth, Archibald, Nea-
mesha and Abram.
1764 SESSUMS, NICHOLAS, Elizabeth, William and
Thomas.
1769 SESSUMS, RICHARD, Jacob, Isaac and Solomon.
1772 SAUL, ABRAHAM, Absalom and Abraham.
1774 STOCKDALE, JOHN, Ann (wife).
1774 SCARBOROUGH, DAVID, Sarah, Joseph, Labe,
Nancy and Hardy.
1778 SHERROD, WM., Unity (wife); children (not
named).
1778 SURGENER, ROBERT, Catherine and John.
1778 SHIP, RICHARD, Elizabeth, Ephraim and
Teller.
1780 STALLINGS, JOHN, Juda and Simon.
1780 SUGG, LEMUEL, Noah, Lemuel, Davis, Reading,
and Mary.
1782 SPELL, DREWRY, Joel and Lewis.
1784 STOKES, JOHN, William, Marcus and Demsey.
1784 STOKES, MARCUS, Martin and Marcus.
1784 SPELL, JOHN, Elizabeth, Lewis and John.
1785 SESSUMS, ISAAC, Richard.
1785 SUMMER, JOSEPH, Anna, John, Joseph and
Charlotte.
1788 SUGG, WILLIAM, Josiah and Mary.
1790 STEPHENS, SHADRACK, Lucy, George and
James.
1790 SPIER, JOHN, John.
1792 STALLINGS, ELISHA, Mary, Hardy, Orpha,
Reddick, Lot, Joseph, Elijah and Nathan.
1792 SESSUMS, JACOB, Frances, Alex., Robert and
Jacob.
1794 SAVIDGE, STERLING, Susanna, Sterling K.,
Jesse and Lovelace.
1795 SUMNER, JOSEPH, Martha, Duke, Tobias, Exum, Joseph and Jacob.
1795 SIMMS, JOSEPH, Simon, Benjamin, William
and Garry.
1795 SARSNETT, RICHARD, John, Joshua, Zachariah
and Henrietta.
1796 SAVIDGE, ROBERT, Rhoda, William and Mary.
1797 SUMNER, JOHN, Mary, Joseph, Exum and
Daniel. *son John Jr.; +*
1798 SOUTHERLAND, JOHN, James; *Martha*
dau., Abby; dau., Sally.

1799 SPIER, WRIGHT, Elizabeth and Wiley.
1799 SHARP, JOHN, Joshua and Ann.

T.

1761 TOOLE, LAWRENCE, Sabra, Lawrence, Henry I., and Geraldus.
1765 TAYLOR, ARTHUR, John, Wilson, Drury and Christopher.
1770 THOMAS, MICAJAH, Mourning, Bathsheba and Micajah.
1774 TAYLOR, THOMAS, William.
1775 THOMAS, JONATHAN, Mary and Jonathan.
1776 THOMAS, WILLIAM, Elizabeth, James and Nancy Hilliard.
1783 TAYLOR, JAMES, Samuel and James.
1786 TAYLOR, WILLIAM, Mary and David; Thorn, Mary; Whitley, Rachel.
1788 THOMAS, PHILIP, Jacob, Ann and Mary.
1789 THOMAS, JOHN, Theophilus.
1789 TART, JONATHAN, Martha, Elnathan, Enos, James and Catherine.
1789 THORN, NICHOLAS, Rachel.
1791 TREVATHAN, ROBERT, Robert.
1791 THOMPSON, JOHN, Ann.
1792 THOMPSON, ELIZABETH, John.
1793 THORP, SOLOMON, Brady, Job.
1796 TART, ELNATHAN, Obedience, James and Thomas.

U.

1761 UMPHREY, ROBERT, Thomas and Matthew.

V.

1762 VICKERS, RALPH, Sarah, Abraham, John and Ralph.
1783 VICKERS, SARAH, Abraham.
1784 VICKERS, JOHN, John, David, George and Benjamin.

W.

1761 WALL, GURARD, Dorset, Elijah, Elisha, Moses, Rachel and James.
1761 WILLIAMSON, HARDY, Bellajah and Laureny.
1761 WALL, ELIJAH, Elisha.
1761 WHITTINTON, RICHARD, Richard.
1761 WALL, DORSET, Massey and Fanny.
1763 WRIGHT, WM., Clamandtanor (wife); Clamandtanor R,, after her mother's death.
1764 WILLIAMS, PILGRIM, Rowland and Jonas.
1765 WOODARD, JOHN, Margaret and John.
1766 WHEATLEY, GEORGE, Nathan, George, Elizabeth.
1766 WILLS, THOMAS, Willis, Willoughby, Thomas B. and William.
1772 WHELESS, BENJAMIN, Mildred, Amos, William, Jesse and Sarah.
1774 WIGGINS, RICHARD, Sarah.
1775 WELDS, STEPHEN, Priscilla, Stephen, Redman, Fred, Solomon and Joshua.
1776 WILLIS, WM., Thomas.
1779 WALL, JOHN, Jesse.
1779 WILSON, ISAAC, William, James, Willie and John.

1779 WILLIAMS, ARTHUR, Absalom, Noah, Unity, Joseph, Henry, Sarah and Nancy.
1782 WHITE, GEORGE, William and Benjamin.
1783 WHITE, ARCHIBALD, Murfree, William A., Henry and Archibald.
1785 WEBB, JOHN, John, Thomas and William.
1785 WOOD, JOSEPH, John H. and Ann.
1789 WILLIAMS, JAMES, John, Matthew, James and Etheldred.
1790 WIMBERLY, GEORGE, Joseph, George, Jonathan and Mourning.
1792 WOOTEN, WILLIAM, Ann and James.
1792 WINSTEAD, RICHARD, Susanna (wife); children (not named).
1793 WILLIAMS, BENJAMIN, Simon, Elisha, Mary and Benjamin.
1793 WILLIAMS, JOHN, Benjamin, Jesse, Mibre, Nancy, John, Drury and Betsy.
1794 WIGGINS, JAMES, Winifred (wife) and children.
1798 WILLIAMS, JOSHUA, Esther and Colding.
1798 WOODARD, ELISHA, John, Elisha and David.

FRANKLIN

A.

1799 ARNOLD, JAMES, Peterson, Sally, Lewis, Wyatt.
1798 ARENDELL, BRIDGES, Thomas, Elizabeth (wife); Franky, Sally, Rowena, Elizabeth, Nancy, Polly.
1797 ARENDELL, THOMAS, Bridges, Ede, Thomas, Ada.
1792 ALFORD, LODOWICK, Samuel, Bailey, Kinchin, Goodrich.

B.

1789 BELL, BENJAMIN, Lucy (wife), Benjamin, Nancy, Patsy, Polly, Tempe.
1791 BROWN, COLLINS, Barrow, Mary; Green, Mary.
1792 BRADLEY, FRANCIS, Nancy, John, James, Francis, Catson, Rebecca, Mary.
1799 BOON, WILLIAM, Rebecca (wife); Benjamin, Sion, Kinchin, Willis.
1799 BEVERS, GILES, James, Franky, Betsy, Benjamin, Polly, Sarah, Jesse, William, Patsy.
1794 BUTLER, JOHN, Micajah, Barnaba, Macha, Agatha, Chloe, Elizabeth.
1795 BUTLER, ROBERT, Asa.
1795 BUNN, THOMAS, Suckey (wife).
1796 BOON, SARAH, Rayford.

C.

1790 CROCKER, JACOB, wife (not named); children (not named).
1788 CROWDER, BARTHOLOMEW, Ruth (wife); Elizabeth, Nancy and Bartholomew.
1792 CONYERS, RICHARD, Joel, Ephraim, Amy, William.
1794 COOPER, KANNAN, Sarah (wife); Kannan, James, Hollandberry, Clorimond, Elvira.
1794 CARLISLE, EDWARD, Sally, Nancy, Tabitha, Jemima, James.

D.

1789 DUNN, WILLIAM, Lucy (wife); William.
1794 DAVIS, RANSOM, wife (not named) children (not named).
1793 DENTON, WILLIAM, William, Chloe, Peter, Anna (wife).
1797 DAVIS, LOUIS, Sarah (wife).
1795 DENLY, JAMES, Patience, Priscilla, Keziah, Nancy, Elijah.
1800 DUKE, BRITTON, Anna (wife); Nelson, Robert, Bennett, Dalen.

F.

1793 FINCH, JOHN, Susanna (wife).
1793 FERRELL, BRYANT, William, Nancy, James, Orril, Polly, Cuthbert, Rebecca, Theodoric.
1786 FERRELL, JOHN, Ann (wife); Bryant, William, Sarah, Ann.
1795 FLOYD, ANN, Jackson, Ann, Mahalah.

G.

1791 GREEN, JOHN, Tabitha (wife).
1794 GORDAN, JOHN, Jessie (wife).
1797 GANT, JAMES, Elizabeth (wife).
1794 GAY, JOHN, Lucretia (wife); Thomas, James.
1784 GAY, THOMAS, Patience (wife), Joshua, John, Allen, Gilbert.
1779 GHOLSON, JOHN, Francis.

H.

1795 HOGG, JOHN, Matthew, Daniel, Mary (wife), Elizabeth, Jenny, Peggy, Charles, John, James.
1786 HARRIS, MOSES, James, John, Elizabeth (wife).
1787 HOUZE, WILLIAM, Isaac (brother); Isham (brother).
1784 HILL, WILLIAM, Polly (wife), William, Samuel, James, Charles.
1790 HILL, BENJAMIN, Mary (wife); Sally, Elizabeth, Collier, Benjamin, Robert.
1790 HUNT, THOMAS, John, Sarah, Henry.
1792 HUCKABY, SAMUEL, Lydia (wife); Fuller, William, Polly, Pheraba, Elizabeth.
1792 HOUSE, ISAAC, James, Amy, Elizabeth, Mary, Tabitha, Wilson, John, James, Isaac, Isham.
1791 HOWELL, ARTHUR, Jesse, Margaret (wife).
1794 HAM, RICHARD, Dinah (wife).
1795 HIGHT, JOHN, William, Robert, Elizabeth, Lively.
1791 HILL, BENNETT, Martha (wife); children (not named).
1784 HILSMAN, BENNETT, Hind, Mary, Hannah.

I.

1795 INGRAM, THOMAS, Mary (wife).
1796 IVEY, CHARLES, Gathwhitt, Anthony, Ruth, Polly, Milly.

J.

1794 JEFFREYS, DAVID, Barbara (wife); Ann, Sarah, Hicksey, Martha.
1793 JEFFREYS, OSBORN, William, Simon, Peggy, Osborn, David, Mary, Paul.
1793 JONAKIN, ELIZABETH, Lula, Thomas.
1799 JARROTT, NATHANIEL, Nelly (wife).
1794 JONES, LEWELLEN, William.
1796 JONES, FREDERICK, wife (not named).

K.

1793 KINCHIN, JOHN, Henry M., Peggy, wife (not named).

L.

1793 LUNSFORD, LINUM, William.

M.

1785 MAYO, JAMES, Osborne, Betsy.
1788 MILNER, PATEWELLS, John, Allen, James, Mary, Janet, Benjamin, William.

1791 MABRY, JESSE, Sally (wife); children (not named).
1791 MASSEY, HEZEKIAH, Burgess, Martha (wife); Charity, Hezekiah, John, Joseph, Lydia.
1793 MITCHELL, JOHN, Elizabeth (wife); Thomas, Patty, Judah, Norsworthy.
1793 MARTIN, JOHN, John Jr., Elizabeth (wife).
1797 MOODY, EPPES, Tabb, Sarah.
1794 MASSEY, PITTEPOOL, Eli, Asa, Warren, Celia (wife).

N.

1796 NEAL, JEREMIAH, Aaron, Moses, Mary (wife).
1797 NELMS, PRESLEY, Presley, Eben, Elizabeth.

O.

1796 OWNBY, THOMAS, Anna (wife); Walter, Willoughby.

P.

1785 PEYTON, ROBERT, Anne (wife), children (not named), James (brother).
1789 PARE, WILLIAM, Jemima (wife); George, Martha, Bedie, Edie, Mary, Winifred,, Taylor, Sarah, Abraham.
1790 PERRY, NATHANIEL, Ephraim.
1793 PIERCE, JAMES, Mary (wife); Bedie, Penny, Patsy, Willie.
1795 PASCHAL, ISAIAH, Ann (wife); George, William.
1797 PARKS, MOSES, Hunt, Hannah.
1785 POPE, JOHN, wife (not named); Alford, John.
1796 PURY, JOHN, Jeremiah.

R.

1796 RAILEY, MORRIS, Mary (wife); Nelly, Robert.
1790 RUSH, SARAH, Benjamin (husband); Bledsoe, Moses (brother).
1793 RANSOM, JOHN, John, Jr., Reuben.
1795 RICHARDS, WILLIAM, Mary (wife), Major, William, Benjamin.
1796 RICHARDS, JOHN, Frances (wife); Willis, Burrell, John, William.

S.

1787 SMITH, JOHN, Benjamin, John, Joseph, Elizabeth (wife), William.
1789 STOKES, DAVID, Archibald, Sarah (wife), Lucy, Mary.
1790 STILES, WILLIAM, Esther (wife); children (not named).
1793 SLEDGE, ISHAM, Willey, Levi, Sabrina, Littleton, Tabitha (wife).
1793 SMITH, ELIZABETH H., Joseph, Lucy, Sally.
1794 SMITH, JOHN, William.
1797 SIMMONS, HENRY, Benjamin.
1795 SIMMONS, WILLIAM, Elizabeth (wife), Mary, Ann, Agnes, Henry, John.
1795 STALLINGS, ELIAS, Ann (wife); Shadrack, Meshach, Daniel, Elijah, Penelope, Elisha, Delilah, Winnie, Kerenhappuch, Matilda.

1798 SMITH, JOHN, Elizabeth (wife), Benjamin, Joseph, William, Margaret, May.

T.

1787 THORNTON, JOHN, Elizabeth (wife), Agga, Joshua, Yancey.

1785 TAYLOR, JOHN, Mourning, Mary (wife).

1790 TANT, WILLIAM, Anna (wife); Jerry, Drew-

1799 THARRINGTON, THOMAS, John, Sarah. ry, Patty, Susanna.

1792 TAYLOR, ETHELRED, Samuel (brother); and other brothers and sisters.

1793 THOMAS, BENJAMIN, Katherine (wife): William, Thomas, John, Benjamin, Hannah, Anne, Elizabeth.

W.

1787 ✳WINSTON, ANTHONY, Mary (wife).

1788 WOOTEN, SARAH, Weldon, Pines.

1794 WYNNE, KNIBB, Polly (wife).

1794 WILLIAMS, BENJAMIN, Mary (wife); John, Peggy, William, Patsy.

Y.

1794 YARBOROUGH, HENRY, Elizabeth (wife); Frances, Archibald, Charles, David, Henry, Nancy M.

*Had sons John, Isaac, Moses, dau. Sarah High, son-in-law Robert High. All given in certified copy of Anthony Winston's will, as.

GATES—WILLS

A.

1794 ALLEN, SARAH, William, Alice (sister); Williams, Elizabeth (niece).

B.

1781 BENTON, JOHN, Jesse, Elizabeth (wife).

1782 BLANCHARD, SARAH, Alsila, Millicent and Absalom.

1782 BARNES, THOMAS, Milly, Sarah, Bethany, Benjamin, Thomas, Elizabeth, Richard, Lottie, Katie and Betty.

1786 BRINKLEY, JOHN, Wife (not named), David, Jacob, Simeon, Elisha and Hetty.

1785 BLANCHARD, ABSALOM, Mary (wife), William, Fred, Sarah and Mary.

1785 BENTON, JOHN, Mary (wife), Jesse, Mary, Jeremiah, Samuel and Martha.

1786 BRINKLEY, JOHN, Wife (not named), David, Jacob, Simeon, Elisha.

1789 BAGLEY, JACOB, Celia (wife), Doctor, Henry and Trotman.

1791 BRADY, JAMES, Mary (wife), Lewis, Ruth, James, Joseph, Mary.

1781 BRINKLEY, IMARAH, Peter, John, Isabel.

1800 BENTON, JOHN, Norfleet, Polly (sister).

1790 BRINKLEY, JOSEPH, Brinkley, James and Susanna (grandchildren).

1796 BROWN, MARY, Harris, John (son); Wills, Margaret (daughter).

1805 BENTON, MILES, Nancy (wife), John, Suckey, Elizabeth, Patsy, Jethro, Henry and Mary; (and for a public school house and the pay of a teacher).

1791 BERRIMAN, BENJAMIN, Bennett, Christian (daughter).

1791 BENTON, ISAAC, Nanny (wife), David and Jacob.

1793 BENTON, MOSES, Absilla (wife), Absalom, Seth, James, William, Charity, Mills, Christian, Theresa and Joseph.

1796 BETHEY, JAMES, John (brother); Parker, Ann (sister); Cross, Mary and Priscilla (sisters).

1796 BARCLIFT, WILLIAM B., Barnes, James (uncle).

1799 BROWN, CHRISTIAN, James, Willis, Polly, Nancy, Louisa, Elizabeth and Robert.

1797 BENTON, ROBERT F., Jesse and Jeremiah (brothers); Mary (mother); Mary (sister); Jesse and John (grandsons).

1799 BETHEY, JOHN, Mary (wife), Elizabeth and Mary.

1795 BOND, RICHARD, Richard, Judah, Jerusha, Christian, William.

1796 BALLARD, JETHRO, Elizabeth (wife), Thomas W., Richard H., Martha, Elizabeth, Judah and Lucinda.

—— BLANCHARD, AARON, Dempsey, Aaron, Huldah, Leah, Ben, Barnes, Henry, Pelatiah, Mahala.

1776 BRINKLEY, MARY, (Perquimans), Peter, John, Isabel (children); Brinkley, Thomas, James, John, Peter and Penelope (grandchildren).

C.

1792 CROSS, MARY, Abel (husband); children (not named).

1782 COSTEN, DEMPSEY, Christian (wife), Isaac, Thomas, Nathaniel, Sibbea, Sarah, Leah and Benjamin.

1800 COSTEN, CHRISTIAN, Dempsey, Benjamin, Isaac, James, Leah, Elizabeth, Thomas and Polly.

1799 CULLENS, JONATHAN, Thomas, Nathan, Sally, Betsy, Patsy, Molly and Ruth.

1791 COSTEN, JAMES, Elizabeth (wife), Leah, Susanna, Thomas, Mary (children); Costen, Nathaniel and Benjamin (grandchildren).

D.

1797 DAVIS, JAMES, Keziah (wife); Overman, Henry and James (nephews).

1788 DOUGHTIE, DANIEL, John, Leah (children); Doughtie, Edward and William (nephews).

1782 DAVIS, GARRETT, Hester (wife); Mansfield, Thomas (son-in-law).

1786 DUNN, SARAH, George (husband); Catherine (daughter).

1791 DOUGHTIE, EDWARD, William (brother); Sarah (sister); Leah and John (children).

1786 DUNN, SARAH, George (husband); Catherine (daughter).

1792 DAVIS, JOHN, Sarah (wife), Ruth, Asenath, Celia, David, John, Judith, Moses, Rachel, Miriam.

E.

1798 ELLIS, WILLIAM, Julia, Jesse, Shadrack, Jacob, Eli, Samuel, Jcseoh and Sarah.

1798 ELLIS, MARY, Reuben, John, William and Esther.

1781 EASON, WILLIAM, ——————.

1788 EASON, JESSE, Christian, Alexander, Elizabeth, Jane and Jesse.

1781 EASON, WILLIAM, (wife), William, Mary, Sarah, Fred, Hardy and Solomon.

F.

1784 FELTON, MARY, Smith, Sally (niece); Thomas, John (nephew).

1785 FULLINGTON, THOMAS, Judith (wife), Matthias, Mary, Rachel, Sarah, Elizabeth and Millicent.

1785 FELTON, MARY, Emith, Celia (neice); Thomas, John (nephew).

1794 FIGG, JOSEPH, James, Willis and Ann.

1781 FREEMAN, WILLIAM, Christian (wife), John, Moses, King, Sarah, Susanna, Mary, William and James.

G.

1783 GOODMAN, HENRY, William, Joel, Ann, Rose, John, David, .Sarah, Mary, Joel, Cyprian and William.

1791 GALLING, WILLIAM, Wife (not named), John, William, Edward and Mary.
1795 GOODMAN, JOEL, Cyprian, William and Mary (brothers and sisters).
1781 GWINN, WILLIAM, Daniel and other children (not named).
1787 GORDON, JOHN, Jacob, Benjamin and Sarah.
1782 GOODMAN, WILLIAM, Henry, William, Mary, Elizabeth and Charity.
1781 GARRETT, JAMES, Ruth (wife), Nancy.
1782 GREEN, SAMUEL, Jehoda (wife), Sarah, Keziah, Samuel, Abraham.
1783 GOODMAN, HENRY, William, Joel, Ann, Rose, Henry, Timothy, Sarah and Charity.
1784 GREGORY, JOHN, Thomas, John, Nancy (brothers and sister).

H.

1786 HOBBS, GREY, Patience (wife), William, Jesse, Moses and Tamar.
1788 HARE, MARY, John, Ann and Thomas.
1794 HARE, MOSES, Moses, Winston, Simon and Jenny.
1793 HARE, MOSES, Honour (wife), Moses, Joseph, Elisha and Bridget.
1796 HINTON, WILLIAM, Mary (wife), Elizabeth, Noah and William.
1794 HAYES, WILLIAM, Mary (wife), James, Daniel, Wright, Jacob, Dorcas, Milly and Sarah.
1794 HURDLE, ELIZABETH, Elizabeth, Senath, Ruth, Thomas, Abraham, William and Rachel.
1797 HUNTER, THOMAS, Elisha, Isaac, Ann and Christian.
1796 HARRELL, CHRISTIAN, Mary (mother).
1781 HUNTER, ALCE (Alsey), Theophilus, William, John and Mary.
1784 HARRELL, JETHRO, Ann (wife), Nancy, Milly, Betsy, Mary, Reuben.
1784 HAYS, WILLIAM, Mary (wife), James, Daniel, Sarah, Dorcas, Milly, Jacob and Wright.
1784 HUNTER, JACOB, Sarah (wife), Isaac, Leah, and Elizabeth.
1786 HYATT, SOLO__ON, Rebecca (wife), Thomas, Elisha, Jesse, Merica, Ann and Celia.
1786 HUNTER, ELISHA, Ann (wife), Thomas and Celia.
1781 HILL, HENRY, Henry, Clement, Charity, David and Hambrick.

J.

1785 JONES, JOSEPH, Edah (wife), James, John, William and Keziah.
1795 JONES, DAVID, Hezekiah, James, David, Pheraba, Judith and Esther.

K.

1782 KING, HENRY, Mary (wife), William, John, Elizabeth, Mary and Sarah.
1781 KNOX, AMAN, Mary (wife), John, Elizabeth. _dau. of later._
~~1795~~ KING, SOLOMON, Abigail (wife), Mary, Elizabeth, Abigail.
1794

L.

1793 LEWIS, PHILIP, Elizabeth (wife), Luke, Mills, John and Luten (brothers).

1781 LASSITER, ANN, Christian (wife), Aaron, Josiah, Rose, Mary, Ezekiel, Christian.

1796 LASSITER, GEORGE, Anne, Treasy, Mary, Rachel, Aaron, Moses and George.

1778 LASSITER, ROBERT, Prudence (wife).

1781 LASSITER, AARON, Christian (wife), Aaron, Michael, Josiah, Rose, Antamerica, Ann, Mary, Ezekiel and Christian.

1791 LAWRENCE, RACHEL, Michael (husband).

1795 LASSITER, SARAH, James, Henry, Peggy.

1793 LASSITER, MICHAEL, Jethro, William and Bethany.

1796 LEWIS, WILLIAM, Leah (wife), John.

M.

1798 MATHIAS, WILLIAM, Penelope (wife), John, William and Elisha.

1778 MARTIN, ABEL, Elizabeth (wife), David.

1786 MILDER, JOHN, Rachel (wife), Robert, Reuben, William.

1783 MURFREE, EVAN, (no will).

1789 MINCHEW, MAXEY, Elizabeth (wife), Zachary, Zanra and Theresa, Clowey, Judah and Bond.

N.

1784 NESBIT, JOSEPH, Sarah (wife).

1798 NORFLEET, JAMES, Sarah (wife), Sarah, Mary, Elizabeth and Felicia.

1780 NORFLEET, JACOB, (Chowan), Elizabeth (wife), Kinchen, Esther, Elizabeth, Pleasant.

O.

1762 ODOM, JACOB, Sarah (wife), Jacob, Asa, Cader, Elisha and Absilla.

1794 ODOM, WILLIAM, Jemima (wife), Uriah, John, William, Mary.

1796 OUTLAW, JAMES, David and George.

P.

1799 PARKER, ELIZABETH, Parker, Isaac (brother).

1794 PHELPS, JAMES, SR., Renthy (wife), Kinchen, James, Luten, Henry, Micajah, William and Jesse.

1798 PEARCE, CHRISTOPHER, Dorcas (wife), Isaac, William, Sarah, Rachel.

1793 PARKER, ROSANNA, James and Sarah.

1781 PARKER, DANIEL, Sarah, Dempsey, Isaac and Robert.

1789 PARKER, WILLIAM, Elizabeth (wife), John, William, Willis, Kedar, Treacy, James and Hugh.

1789 PARKER, JOSEPH, Katharine (wife), Joseph, David, John, Cader, James and Priscilla.

1791 PARKER, FRANCIS, Febury (Phoebe) (wife), Miles, Weeday.

1788 POWELL, JACOB, Ann (wife), Kedar, James, Daniel, John, Robert, William, David, Rachel, Barsheba, Mary, Christian and Elizabeth.

1782 POWELL, WILLIAM, Kader and Isaac (brothers); other brothers and sisters (not named).

1793 PARKER, ELISHA, Esther (wife), Peter, Elizabeth, Mary, John, Jesse, Peggy, Elisha, Christian and Nancy.

1789 PILAND, THOMAS, Stephen, Thomas, Willis and Peggy.

1787 PILAND, JAMES, Thomas, James, John.

1796 PILAND, GEORGE, Wife (not named), Catherine, Eleanor, Edward, Mary and Mildred.

R.

1797 RIDDICK, NATHANAEL, Mary (mother); David and Mills (brothers); Elza (sister).

1792 RIDDICK, CHRISTOPHER, Sarah (wife), William, Mary, Ann, Penelope and Zilla.

1797 RICE, ELIZABETH, Laodicia (daughter).

1784 RIDDICK, KEDAR, Eliza (wife), Thomas, Edward, James and Sarah.

1785 ROSS, JOHN, Bethany (wife), Susanna, Solomon, Sarah and Mary.

1785 ROGERS, DANIEL, Millie (wife), Timothy, Benjamin and Daniel.

1786 RIDDICK, JAMES, Sarah (wife); Children of brother Kader and sisters, Mary and Sarah Riddick.

1791 RICE, JOHN, Peggy (wife), Thomas and Ann.

1792 RODGERS, ZILPAH, Philip, Lot, Annn, Enos, Jonathan and Absola.

1781 ROUNTREE, THOMAS, Seth, Christian, Leah, Lavinia, Rachel, Priscilla and Peniah.

1785 ROSS, JOHN, Bethany (wife), Susanna, Solomon, Sarah and Mary.

S.

1785 SAUNDERS, FRANCIS, Charity (wife), Zilpah, Anne, Abraham and Francis.

1790 SMALL, JOSHUA, Charity (wife), David, James, John and Mary.

1787 SMITH, HENRY, Mary (wife), Mary, Jonah, Dorothea, Marcy, Jonathan and Henry.

1779 SUMNER, DEMPSEY, Martha wife), Dempsey, Edwin, James, Mary, Jethro, Theresa and Letitia.

1793 SUMNER, JETHRO, Barsheba (wife), David.

1781 SPIVEY, ELIJAH, Sarah (wife), Elizabeth, Sarah, Rachel, Judith and Elijah.

1789 SPIVEY, JACOB, Zilpah (wife), Francis and William, Cynthia and Absilla.

1792 SPEIGHT, JOSEPH, Anna (wife), Francis and Henry.

1786 SPIVEY, JESSE, Mary (wife), Zachariah.

1792 SPEIGHT, MOSES, Moses and Aaron.

1792 SPIVEY, MOSES, Sarah and Priscilla.

T.

1787 THOMAS, STEVEN, Rachel (sister); Jacob (brother).

1779 TUGWELL, JOSEPH, Elizabeth wife), James, Mary.
1790 TAYLOR, ROBERT, Christian (wife), Penina, Christian, William, Sarah and Mary.
1791 TROTMAN, THOMAS, Rachel (wife), Polly, Absilla, Thomas, Joseph, Love and Willis.
1791 TROTMAN, RACHEL, William, Benjamin and Sarah.
1790 TROTMAN, AMOS, Wife (not named), Amos, Celia, Sarah, Elisha and Edward.
1779 TUGWELL, JOSEPH, Elizabeth (wife), James and Mary.

U.

1784 URMPHLET, WILLIAM, Sarah, Susanna, Martha, Mary, David and Job.

V.

1793 VANN, DORCAS, Langston, Isaac, Dempsey and Judah.
1788 VANN, WILLIAM, Rachel (wife), children (not named).

W.

1795 WILLIAMS, MOSES, Dorothy (wife).
1791 WALTERS, SARAH, Mary (wife), Brian, Hezekiah, Sarah, Edith and Jacob.
1797 WIGGINS, BRIDGET, Judith and Edith.
1796 WARREN, WILLIAM, Mary (mother); brothers and sisters (not named).
1784 WALTERS, JAMES B., William (father); Susanna (mother).
1789 WARREN, EDWARD, Mary (wife), William, Ruth, John, Robert, Elizabeth and Mary.
1792 WHITE, JOHN, Elizabeth (wife), nephews,
1792 WHITE, JOHN, Elizabeth (wife); George, Thomas and Joshua White (nephews).
1788 WALTERS, THOMAS, Miles (son).

GRANVILLE—WILLS

See also p. 327 et seq.

A.

1780 ADCOCK, LEONARD, John, Bolton, Josebud, Sarah, Elizabeth, Robert; Connaway, Edward.

1785 ANDERSON, LEWIS, Shadrach, Lewis, Lydia; Tobourn, Elisha; Tyler, Sarah; Boss, Tamar, Mary.

*1786 ALLEN, WM., Frances (wife); Mary, Frances, Mildred, Thomas, Grant, William.

1797 ALLISON, ROBERT, Janet, Robert, John, Mary, Robin.

1797 ADCOCK, ROBERT, Solomon, Elizabeth; Hester, Mary.

1798 ADCOCK, LEONARD, Mary, Linson, Leonard, Mary, Chloe, Elizabeth, Susanna, Edamiah.

1799 ADCOCK, EDWARD, Tabitha (wife) and children (not named).

*See Will-Complete-in F.C.

B.

1782 BOYD, ROBERT, Robert, John, Rachel, Thomas, Sarah.

1783 BULLOCK, JAMES, Sarah, Jeremiah, Joshua, Charles, Samuel, James, George; Cook, Priscilla, Nancy.

1783 BRISTOW, GEORGE, Elizabeth, Averilla, James, John, George, Philemon.

1785 BYARS, GEORGE, Nicholas, Barbara, Mary; Horeman, Mary; Glimp, George.

1786 BENNETT, RICHARD, Anne, Micajah, William, Peter, Barlette, Lewis.

1786 BRADFORD, THOMAS, Philemon, David, Mary, Thomas, Ephraim, Richard, Benjamin, Sarah, Seaby.

1787 BREECE, GEORGE, Anne, Pulliam, John, Barnett; Boyd, William; Willis, Mary.

1789 BUCHAMAN, WM., wife and children (no names).

1789 BURDEN, THOMAS, Elizabeth, Thomas; children of Abraham Burden.

1790 BRASFIELD, GEORGE, Elizabeth, Caleb, Nancy, George, Willie, Patty.

1792 BURDEN, ELIZABETH, Lyne, James, Mary, Patillo, Henry, Mary; Dorcas (a negro girl) Molly (ditto).

1793 BOTTOMS, THOMAS L., Lydia, William, Samuel; Wallace, Rene.

1794 BALL, DANIEL, William, Daniel, Osborn, James, Elijah, Pheraba.

1795 BRUCE, AMY, Rose, Frederick, William, Howell.

1796 BULLOCK, WILLIAM, wife Elizabeth, son William, gr. son James; Boyd, Frances; Lewis, James. daus Frances Boyd Elizabeth Maclin, & stepson James Lewis gr. son James son of dec. son

1798 BISHOP, JAMES, Mary, Philip, Jenny.

1799 BYERS, JAMES, Sally, Betsey, Katie, Nancy, Lucy.

1800 BOYD, JOSEPH, Branchwood; Talley, Mary; Freeman, Patty.

C.

1775 CLEMENTS, PEYTON, Elizabeth, Thomas, William, Tyree, Jessie, Philip, Grisell.
1777 CHAVIS, GIBEA, William, Nancy.
1778 CRITCHER, THOMAS, Esther, Thomas, Sally, James, Jenny, John G.
1799 COLDDOUGH, WILLIAM, Dolly, Elizabeth, John, Alexander; wife, (not named).
1780 CURRIN, HUGH, William.
1780 CASH, JOSEPH, Howard, Peter, James, Elisha, Comfort, Phebe, Elizabeth, Joseph.
1781 CUZART, ANTHONY, Jesse, Jeremiah, Joshua; (wife).
1782 CURRIN, JAMES, Elizabeth W.; Hugh, James, Mary, Betsy, Catherine, Nancy, Keziah, Agnes, Jean.
1782 CARROLL, WM., Elizabeth, Jesse, Mary, Thomas, John, William.
1785 COLLINS, LEWIS, Elizabeth, Edward, Lewis, Willey, Diana.
1787 CHAMPION, JOHN, Charles, Susanna, Richard, Joseph, John, William.
1789 CROWDER, HILLKIN, Lydia.
1789 CRAFT, THOMAS, Elizabeth, John; Hanks, Ann, Elizabeth; Dreskell, Barbara.
1789 CULVERHOUSE, THOMAS W., Elizabeth, Thomas; Hull, Ann; Gilmore, Jeremiah.
1791 CHAMPION, CHARLES, John, Richard, Elizabeth, Charles, Mary, Allen.
1791 CHANDLER, HENRY R., Scholars (not named).
1795 CRAWBY, ANNE A., Hannah, Burwell, Armistead and Anne S.; Green, Lewis.
1795 CHAMPION, JOSEPH, Mary, Richard, Joseph, Merritt, Nancy.
1796 CAVENDISH, GEORGE, Bryant, John, Elizabeth, Margaret, Tommy, Nancy, Gerrel, Needham, Neddy, Sarah.
1796 COOK, ISHAM, Ann, John, Shem, Claiborne, Rowland, Ann.
1796 COOKE, WM., Rebecca, James, Elizabeth, Benjamin, William.
1800 CARDWELL, THOMAS, Thomas, Leonard, William, John.

D.

1779 DREWRY, ELLIS, Annie, William; Vowel, Obey.
1779 DANIEL, JOHN, Martin, Celia.
1785 DANIEL, JAMES, John, William, Reuben, Richard, Joseph, Ann, Sarah; Royster, Mary.
1791 DODSON, WM., Frances (wife), William, Charles, Frances, Polly, Holly.
1795 DUTY, RICHARD, Elizabeth (wife); George, Richard, Ann, Benjamin, Thomas, Isabel, Rachel, Elizabeth, Samuel, Sarah.
1796 DODSON, THOMAS, William, Charles, Holley; Fleming, Polly.
1799 DODSON, CHARLES, Elizabeth, Stephen, Polly, Lucy, Betsy; Smith, John, Nancy.

E.

1784 ESTRIDGE, EPHRAIM, Sarah (wife); children (not named).

1792 EDWARDS, JOHN, Pumphret W., Daniel, Nancy.
1792 EDWARDS, THOMAS, Sarah, William, Elizabeth, Charles, John, Nancy, Thomas, Judith.
1794 EASTWARD, SARAH, Mary, Lewis, Keziah, Mary (wife); Israel, Lydia, Rebecca, John, Abraham, Charles.
1797 EARL, JOHN, Agnes, John, Rebecca, Elizabeth.
1799 EMERY, EPHRAIM, Edmund, Martha.

F.

1784 FRAZIER, MARTHA, Sarah, Isabel, Rachel, Ruth, Shadrack, Ransom, Lewis, Greyhill, Judith, Sarah, Michael.
1788 FARRAR, WM., Lucy, George, Susanna, Sarah, Judith.
1792 FARRAR, WILLIAM, Esther (wife); Penny, Susanna, Joshua, Thomas.
1793 FULLER, SAMUEL, Pheraby, William, Sarah, Spivey, Washington.
1793 FRAZER, WILLIAM, Mary (wife), Ann, Malachi, Daniel, William, Charity, John, Elizabeth, Arthur, Sowell, Willie, Sarah.
1796 FOWLER, HENRY, Rebecca, Elizabeth, Hanson, Charles, Allen, Henry, Lewis.
1800 FULLER, HENRY, Judith, Littleton, Britain, Christian, Jones, Samuel, John, Jonathan.

G.

1786 GLOVER, JOSEPH, William, John, Jacob, Ransom, Phebe, Daniel, Robert, David.
1786 GROVES, WM., Nancy, Henry, William, Lydia, Nathaniel, Anna, Martha, Mary.
1789 GATES, LOVIT, Diana (wife); Read, Lovit.
1789 GRAVES, JOHN W., Mary, John, Rachel, William.
1790 GRIMSBY, WM., Margaret, James, Elisha.
1791 GOODLOE, ROBERT, William.
1793 GOOCH, JOHN, Gideon, Joseph, John, Rowland, William.
1797 GOODLOE, ROBERT, Sarah, William, John H., Henry, David S.; Samuel.
1797 GROVES, HENRY, Rachel, Betsy, Ralph, David; Yancey, Mary.
1799 GUY, BENJAMIN, Elizabeth, Nancy, Mary, Eunice, James, Isaiah.
1800 GOOCH, GIDEON, Mary, John, Elizabeth, Gideon, Judith; Terry, Mary, Nancy.

H.

1772 HICKS, SAMUEL, Diana, Solomon, Bishop, Samuel, Henry.
1774 HARRISON, BENJAMIN, Alsey, Samuel, Benjamin, Ellen, Venion.
1774 HOLSTON, NICHOLAS, Jacob, John, Catherine, Mary, Susanna, Barbara, Elizabeth.
1774 HESTER, WM., Mary (wife), Robert, Bensamen Francis, Mary, Zachariah, Temperance, John, Nancy, Lucy.
1778 HASEBRIG, JAMES, Rice, Babil, and wife.
1775 HUCKABY, SAMUEL, William, Mary, Sukey, Samuel, Elizabeth.

1779 HOWARD, JOHN, David, Benjamin, Sarah, Mary; Davis, Sarah

1780 HARRIS, THOMAS, Robert, Gilley, Mary, Penny, Samuel, Ellyfare

1781 HUDSPETH, GILES, John, Giles.

1783 HENDERSON, SAMUEL, Elizabeth, Pleasant.

1786 HENDERSON, RICHARD, Elizabeth, John, Richard, Archibald, Fanny, Elizabeth.

1795 HARRIS, ROBERT, Mary, Christopher, Sherwood, Robert, David, Samuel, Timender.

1786 HUNT, WILLIAM, Rose, James, Samuel, William.

1787 HARPER, JESSE, Diana (wife), Frances, Robert G., Lettice, Diana, Katie, Mary.

1787 HARRIS, RICHARD, Richard, Charles, Samuel, Tyre, Priscilla.

1787 HATCHER, JOHN, Mary, Thomas, John, Joshua.

1787 HANKS, WM., Elijah, William, Susanna, Argil; Moore, Hannah.

1789 HUNT, JOHN, wife and children (not named).

1791 HOWELL, THOMAS, Rebecca, Thomas, John, Robert. Keziah, Forchin, Mary, Elizabeth.

1791 HOOKER, JOHN, Temperance, Thomas, William.

1791 HUNT, JAMES, Ann, Michael, Frances.

1792 HENDERSON, ELIZABETH, Elizabeth; McCoy, Fanny.

1792 HICKS, ROBERT SR., Sarah, Betsey, Lucretia; Cooper, Abigail.

1792 HARGROVE, JOHN, Annie (wife), John, William, Molly, Annie.

1792 HAYS, JOSEPH, Samuel, Jesse, Stephen, Simon, Sarah, Temperance, Mary, Lucy, Lewis.

1794 HOLSTON, JACOB, Catherine, John.

1795 HANKS, WM., Sally, William.

1796 HUDSPETH, CARTER, Margaret, Solomon, Sarah, Richard.

1798 HUNT, JAMES, Sarah (wife); James, David.

1798 HANKS, ELIJAH, Samuel, David, Thomas, John, William, Betsy.

1799 HUNT, SAMUEL, Sarah, John, Grover, Samuel.

1797 HAYS, JOSHUA, Sarah, Henry, Joshua, Sylvia, John.

1797 HICKS, WM., Mourning, Abner.

I.

1797 IRBY, WM., John, Elizabeth, Peter.

J.

1781 JORDAN, MARCELLUS B., Nancy, Arthur and other children (not named).

1782 JONES, EDMUND, Sarah (wife), and children (not named).

1790 JENKINS, JAMES, Patty, Elias, Joshua, Joseph, John, Elizabeth, James, Wilson, Samuel, Mansfield.

1792 JONES, AMBROSE, Catherine, Gabriel, James, Ambrose, Stephen, Reuben.

1793 JORDAN, ARTHUR, Elizabeth, Thomas, Marcellus, Penelope, Jane, Charlotte, Nimrod, Martha.

1795 JOHNSON, JAMES, Elizabeth, John, Talton, Absalom, Isaac, Betsy, Sally.

1780 JOHNSTON, MATHEW, Elizabeth, Isham, Susanna, Archer, James, Judith.

1796 JONES, MICHAEL, Harrison, William, Kersey, Mary.

1797 JOHNSTON, GIDEON, Zilpha, Rebecca, Jonathan, Gideon, Sugar.

1797 JOHNSON, JONATHAN, Mary, James, Gideon, William; Hobgood, Sally.

K.

1783 KNOTT, JAMES, John, David, Mary.

1796 KNOWLAND, EDWARD, Hampton, John.

1799 KNOTT, JOHN, James, John, William, Len, David, Thomas, Lucy, Francis.

L.

1779 LEITH, SARAH, Parish of Pitsworth; Starke, Thomas, Turner and William; Smith, Lawrence, Ann and Guy.

1781 LEWIS, ROBERT, James, Frances (wife).

1785 LINSEY, LEONARD, Sarah (wife); Elisha.

1787 LEAVESTOR, GEORGE, Rebecca, Davis, James, John, Susanna, Temperance, Jemima.

1799 LEWIS, HOWELL, Charles, Willis, Betsy.

1791 LOYD, EDWARD,. Mary (wife), Charlotte, Nancy, Nicholas, William, Parrott, Joshua.

1792 LINDSEY, ELISHA, Elizabeth, Weatt, John.

1793 LOYD, MARY, Joshua, Mary, Charlotte, Nancy, Nicholas, William, Garratt.

1798 LEWIS, CHARLES, Mary (wife); children (not named).

1799 LYNE, HENRY, Henry, Edmond, James.

M.

1774 MOORE, EDWARD, William, James, Dinah, Edward, Richard, Elizabeth, Samuel, Dempsey, Noah, Elijah, John.

1775 MALONE, ISHAM, George, Hal, Nathaniel, Molly, Deloney, Daniel, Judith.

1778 MAYFIELD, ABRAHAM, Elizabeth, Valentine, Abraham.

1777 MERRITT, BENJAMIN, Ephraim; Boyd, Ephraim, Rose; Langston, Alice.

1777 MITCHELL, JAMES, Joseph, David, John, Abraham, Junius, Randal, Elizabeth.

1781 MITCHELL, DAVID, Drewry, Jean, Jesse, Martha, Anne, Mary, Susanna.

1786 MORGAN, JOHN, Ridley, John, Elizabeth, Betsy, Rebecca, Sally, Mollie.

1787 MITCHELL, JOHN, Phillis.

1788 MORSE, SAMUEL, Allen, Willis, Martha, Phillis (wife).

1789 MERRYMAN, CHARLES, William, Millicent (wife); Benjamin. *wife*

Court 1790 MITCHELL, DAVID, Hannah, Elijah, Charles, Milly, David, Thomas, John. *and also given in will* *

1791 MAYFIELD, VALENTINE, Winifred (wife); children (not named).

1792 MORSE, SAMUEL, Elizabeth, John, Samuel.

1792 MITCHELL, PHILLIS, William, Samuel F.; Sneed, Mary and Archibald.

* daue. Martha Walker, Susan Moore, Elizabeth Saunders and Hannah Saunders, wife of James Saunders

1794   MILTON, HENRY, Haggai (wife) and children (not named).
1795   MARTIN, JOSEPH, James.
1796   MOORE, JOHN, Alexander, Seth, Molly.
1799   MUTTER, THOMAS, John, Margaret, Elizabeth, Thomas, Elizabeth.

N.

1783   NEWPORT, PETER, Jenny, Lavinia, Sarah, rances.
1783   NORWOOD, NATHANIEL, John, Gilliam, Jordan, Mary, Benjamin; Glover, Penelope.
1785   NEVILLE, JOHN, Elizabeth (wife) and children (not named).
1798   NEWBY, THOMAS, Mary, Keziah, Drusilla, Priscilla, Thomas, John, Henry, Zaccheus, James, Betsy, Alis, Bathsheba.

O.

1794   OWEN, WILLIAM, Catherine, Judy, Jacob, Daniel, John W., Shadrach.
1795   OWENS, JAMES, Sarah, Susanna, Frederick, William, Denny.

P.

1778   POTTER, WILLIAM, Elizabeth, Margaret.
1780   PARKER, CADER, Samuel, Elijah, George, Jemima, Elizabeth, Pheraba.
1784   PEAKE, LEONARD, Lucy, Samuel, Charles; Abercomby, Abner; Burford, Leonard.
1787   PIERCE, SOLOMON, Nancy, Sally, Elizabeth, William, Elijah.
1787   PHILPOT, THOMAS, William; Colbert, Martha; Bradley, Mary.
1788   PARKER, JONATHAN, Jesse, Elizabeth, Ann, Samuel, Elijah, George.
1788   PENN, JOHN, William; Taylor, Lucy.
1789   PETTYPOOL, SETH, Elizabeth, Mary, Sarah, Jane, Nancy, William, John, Seth, Young, Jesse, Claiborne, Philip.
1791   PARRISH, BRISSY, Noel, David, Agga, Justice, George, Humphrey, John.
1794   PARRISH, ELIJAH, Polly, Shadrach, Lankford, Ralph, Willis, Absalom, Lucy, Labon, Agnes.
1799   POOL, THOMAS, Elizabeth, Sarah, William, Burgess, Thomas, Obedience.

R.

1774   ROBINSON, JOHN, John, Nicholas, Mark, Ruth, Robert, Nathaniel, Susanna, Marv. Francis.
1777   ROBERTS, JESSE, Celia, Willis.
1778   RAGLAND, EVAN, Amy, Reuben, Benjamin, William, Evan, Stephen, George.
1781   RAY, DAVID, Isabella.
1790   RAGLAND, AMY, William, Reuben; Glass, Amy.
1799   ROBERTS, WILLIAM, Elizabeth, Isaac, Philip, Nancy ;Parish, Mary.

S.

1775   SCURRY, GIDEON, Catron, Thomas, Eli, Jesse.
1778   STAINBACK, JAMES, William, Frances.
1778   SNELLING, ALEX, Bennett, Frances, Anna Catron, Elizabeth, Ann.

1781 STOVALL, JOHN, Bartholomew, Josiah, William, Drury, Rebecca, Susanna, Mary, Benjamin, John, George.

1784 SHEARMON, JOHN SR., Catherine, Michael, John.

1784 SEAREY, BARTLETT, Lucy, Samuel.

1787 SEAREY, JOHN, John, William, Bartlett, Elizabeth, Richard.

1787 SMITH, GUY, John, Guy, William.

1788 SMITH, DAVID, Joseph, Charles, David.

1788 SPEARS, PHILIP H., Penny, Martha, James H.

1790 SMITH, THOMAS, Isaiah, Goodman, Elizabeth, Thomas, Herbert, John.

1790 SPEARS, WILLIAM, Jesse, William, James H., Martha, John.

1797 SHEMWELL, JAMES, Samuel, James, Anna, Rebecca, Ellender, Joseph, Mary.

1798 STARK, JAMES, Jean, Rowland, John, William, Sally.

T.

1777 TRAYLOR, WILLIAM, Hollandbury (son) and children.

1780 TAYLOR, JOHN SR., Joseph, John, Elizabeth, James, Edmund, William; Penn, John, Philip, Moses, Thomas, Catherine, Mary.

1780 TILLMAN, GEORGE, William, Elizabeth, John, Polly; wife.

1782 TUDOR, JOHN, Elizabeth, Valentine, Bloomer, Daniel, Henry, John.

1787 TAYLOR, JOHN, Elizabeth, Edmund, William, Joseph, Philip, James, John; Penn, Moses, Mary, John.

1798 TAYLOR, ELIZABETH, Tyne, James, Lucy; Penn, Susanna, William.

1799 TERRY, JAMES, William, Stephen, James, John.

V.

1799 VASS, FANNY, Thomas.

W.

1774 WHITLOCK, GEORGE, Mary, Anne M., John N., Jeremiah M.

1774 WARD, BENJAMIN, William, Susanna, Elizabeth, Mary, Rebecca.

1774 WILLIAMS, JOSEPH, Sarah, Mary.

1777 WILLIAMS, WILLIAM, John, Samuel, Phillis, Mary, Betsy, Sally.

1783 WRIGHT, WINFIELD, Hannah, Susanna, Mary P., Winfield, Thomas, John, William, Benjamin.

1785 WADE, BENJAMIN, Anne (wife) and children (not named).

1788 WINNINGHAM, SHERWOOD, Thomas; Austin, Valentine.

1791 WALKER, SOLOMON, Martha (wife), John and other children (not named). Lucy m — Hillard and

1792 WRIGHT, HANNAH, Judge, James, Israel, Hanna, Rebecca.

Susannah m — Potter, Elisabeth m — Lewis, Hannah mildred and martha ch. of Solomon and named in settlement of estate. Feb. Churt 1802, April 20, 1802 signed. Certified copy examined a.g. Copydated aug 1927

1792 WHITE, GEORGE, Susanna, William, John, Coleman R., Philip, Ann R., Garrott, Joshua, Joseph.
1793 WHITE, MARK, wife; James.
1795 WEBB, MARY, William, John, James.
1795 WEAVER, JOHN, Fred, William, Arimanus, Robert, Anne.
1797 WALLER, ZEPHANIAH, Job, Sarah, John, Zephaniah.
1799 WIGGINS, THOMAS, Frances, Thomas, Fred.
1799 WILLIAMS, JOHN, Agnes; Burton, John W., Frank, Agatha, Robert; Henderson. Leonard.

Y.

1779 YANCEY, JAMES, Bartlett, Philip, Thomas, Thornton; Sanders, Jesse, Jenny; Baynes, Nancy.
1797 YOUNG, JOHN, Rachel, Francis, Henry, Millicent, Elizabeth, James, John Smith Young (all minors) dau Jane Taylor. Dated 8-19-1797. pro Nov. Ct. 1797.

HALIFAX—WILLS

A.

1765 ANDREWS, WM. H., Mary (wife).

1761 ANDREWS, WM., Henry, William H., Abner, Isham, Micajah, Sarah, Catherine and Jesse.

1766 ALSOBROOK, SAMUEL, Mary, Hewett and David.

1778 AARON, MICHAEL, Anne (wife).

1781 ALLEN, JAMES, James, William, Taylor, John and Mary.

1791 ALLEN, JAMES, Mary (wife); William and Taylor.

1781 LISTON, JOSEPH, John, Philip, Warren, Willis, John J., Joseph J., Henry and Mary.

1784 ALSTON, JOHN, Ann H. (wife), Gideon, Willis, Priscilla, Ann H. and Robert.

1795 ALSOBROOK, DREWRY, Haynes, Turner, Henry, Drewry and Nancy (nephews); Celia (wife).

1781 ALSOBROOK, JOHN, James, Drury, David, William, Mabel, Celia and Elizabeth.

1786 ATKINSON, JAMES, James, Patience, Elizabeth, Polly, Lucy, Olive, and Sallie.

1788 APPLEWHITE, MARTHA, Wilkins, Pheraba; Whitehead, Martha, John, Tobias, Betsy and Jonah.

1793 ADAMS, JAMES, Tabitha (wife), Frederic.

1798 ADAMS, JOHN, Sallie, James, John, Hardiman, Polly and Rebecca.

1794 AXUM, MARY, William J. and Joseph H.

1798 AMIS, THOMAS, Bennehan, _Rebecca_ and Thomas D. Marshall, Sterling; Rhymer, Jesse.

niece and nephew

B.

1760 BECK, MOSES, John; Winston, Mary (daughter).

1761 BECK, JOHN, John, Marly and Mourning (wife).

1762 BOYKIN, JOHN, Benjamin, Joseph and Chaney.

1762 BELL, GEORGE, Ann (wife); Elias and Ann.

1762 BAILEY, RICHARD, Rebecca (wife), Lewis, Thomas and Philip.

1762 BRUCE, PETER, Mary (wife), Peter and Jean; Fountain, Ann.

1762 BRYANT, WM., Jesse, William, Jean, Penelope, Sally and Catherine.

1763 BYNUM, JAMES, William, John and Nicholas

1763 BUTLER, JOSEPH, Joseph, Samuel, Stephen, Sarah, Anna, Mary Ann, Ellis, Susanna and Dorothy.

1763 BULL, THOMAS, Susanna, Thomas, Henry, Susanna (wife), Anne, Jesse and Rachel.

1764 BROWN, SAMUEL, Ann (wife); Williams, Willis and William.

1764 BRADLEY, HENRY, Ales (wife), Samuel, William and Mary.

1768 BRANTLEY, EDWARD, Edward, Lewis, William, Robert, Benjamin, Martha, Mary, Patty and Anna.

1768 BAYLISS, JOHN, Benjamin, Burwell, William, Thomas, John, Isham, Britain, Elizabeth,

Mary, Ann, Rebecca and Amy.

1769 BAKER, BLAKE, Mary, Zadok, Mary B. and Elizabeth.

1772 BELL, ANN, Blount, Sarah.

1774 BRADLEY, JOSEPH, Elizabeth, Benjamin, Sarah and Joseph.

1775 BALLARD, WM., Walter O., Devereux, Salusmith, William S. and Elizabeth.

1775 BRANTLEY, PHILIP, Mary (wife), Lewis and William.

1775 BELL, BENJAMIN, Marmaduke, Arthur and Sarah.

1775 BARNES, JAMES, Catherine (wife), James.

1775 BELL, ARTHUR, Arthur, Joshua, Shadrack, Elisha, Lucy, Absilla, Mary and Sarah.

1778 BLACKBURN, JOHN, William, Absalom, Benjamin, Sally and Patience.

1778 BARNES, WM., Martha (wife), Mildred and Thomas.

1785 BURGESS, WM., Penelope (wife), Bryant, Cullen, Milisha, Betsy, Mourning, Winnie, Dempsey, John, William, Sallie and Catherine.

1794 BURGESS, THOMAS, Mary (wife); Lovatt, Henry J., and Anna M.

1782 BRADLEY, BENJAMIN, Sarah (wife).

1788 BRADLEY, JOHN, Eleanor (wife).

1790 BRADLEY, ELEANOR, Keziah, Samuel, Mary P., Temperance and Lydia.

1783 BISHOP, WM., William, John, Moses, Keziah, Sarah, Jonathan, Polly, Drusilla, Sallie, Betsy, Patsy and Hardiman.

1784 BELL, JOSHUA, Elisha, Shadrack and Lucy; Atherton, Penelope.

1797 BELL, MARMADUKE, Martha (wife); Benjamin and Milly.

1791 BELL, ELISHA, Sarah (wife), Shadrack.

1784 BENNETT, WM., Thomas and Susanna.

1784 BIRD, PETER, Charity (wife), Peter, Allen, Mary and Nancy.

1783 BARKER, STEPHEN, Mary, Stephen, William and Sarah.

1782 BARKER, JOSHUA, Martha (wife), Edmund, Nancy, William, Stephen and Sarah.

1785 BRYAN, JAMES, Lucy (wife), Sarah, Mary and James.

1786 BASS, JOHN, Ann (wife), Isaac and Jacob.

1790 BARROW, JACOB, Thomas, Milly, Betsy, Pheraba and Sallie.

1787 BARROW, WM., Olive (wife), William, Robert, Bartholomew, Mary, Sarah, Ruffin and Bennett.

1787 BRADFORD, JOHN, Elizabeth (wife), Henry, Joseph, John, Richard H., William, Elizabeth, Tabitha, Ann, Sarah, Mary and Martha.

1785 BRYANT, NEEDHAM, Mina (wife), Nancy and Nicholas.

1788 BARKSDALE, CARY, William and Hiram.

1788 BURT, JOSEPH, John, Joseph, Stephen, William, James, Richard, Elizabeth and Mary.

1793 BURT, STEPHEN, John, William and Jesse.

1789 BRICKLE, JOHN, Nancy (wife), William, Jeremiah, John, Patsy, Abigail and Sally.

1790 BERRYMAN, JOSIAH, John and Balaam.

1794 BERRYMAN, JOHN, Priscilla (wife), John.
1791 BARBER, JOSHUA, Jesse.
1794 BROUCH, WM. SR., Elizabeth (wife), Nicholas. John.
1794 BROUCH, JOHN SR., Elizabeth (wife) Patience, Joseph, James, John, Washington and William.
1794 BULL, THOMAS, Sarah (wife).
1795 BRANTLEY, ROBERT, Martha (wife), Robert and Thomas.
1799 BBANTLEY, LEWIS, Robert, Patty, H. L., B. J., Betsy and Dolly.
1795 BRUCE, WM., Christian (wife), Matthew and Alcey.
1796 BRINKLEY, WM., Hunt, Charity, Wm. B., Robert, Sarah and Polly.
1797 BRINKLEY, WM., William, Abraham, Tabitha.
1799 BRINKLEY, JUDITH, Robert, William H., Leah, William and Sally.
1797 BROWN, WM., Elizabeth (wife), Zilphia, Anne, Mary and William.
1797 BAKER, DAVID, Sylvester and John.
1799 BAKER, JAMES, Winifred, Sallie and James.

C.

1760 CURETON, RICHARD, John and Thomas.
1760 CONNELL, MICHAEL, Mary (wife), Thomas, Sarah, Winnie, Katie and Davis.
1761 CRUDUP, MARY, Mary C. (wife), Isaiah and George.
1761 CROWELL, JOHN, Elizabeth (wife), Edward, John, Joseph and Mary.
1762 CORLEW, JOHN, Keziah (wife), John, Philip and William.
1762 CAIN, WM., Rebecca (wife).
1768 CHAPMAN, JOHN, Ann (wife).
1764 CRUDUP, GEORGE, Isaiah and Mary.
1769 COOLEY, JOHN, John and Martha.
1769 CHAMPION, BENJAMIN, William and John.
1772 COX, WM., Mary (wife), John, Sinah and Prufley.
1772 CROKER, ARTHUR, Drury, Milly and Dowsabell.
1772 COTTON, JOSEPH, Joseph, Amos, Willis, William, Sabra and Mary.
1774 CHAMPION, JOHN, Celia, Thomas and Wm.
1776 CARTER, JAMES, David, William, Charity and Thomas.
1776 CARTER, CORNELIUS, William W., Jane and Cruise.
1777 CROWLEY, DAVID, Daniel, David and Sallie.
1777 CARTER, ELIZABETH, David, Thomas, William, Charity and Jane.
1778 CROSSLAND, EDWARD, Edward, Sarah, Joshua, Sarah (wife), Rebecca.
1782 COUPLAND, WM., Mary and Charlotte.
1786 COUPLAND, SAMUEL, Jane (wife), Samuel, Ann, Mary, Martha and Bouldin.
1784 CONE, JOHN, Winnie (wife), John, Richard, Elizabeth and Frances.
1784 COX, JOHN, Elizabeth (wife), Charles, Joseph, Mary, Ann and Phoebe.
1785 CHAMPION, BENJAMIN, Sarah, John, Thomas and Gordon.

1785 COLEY, ROBERT, Frances (wife), Francis and
William.
1787 COUNSEL, NATHAN, Mary (wife), Lydia,
John, David, Polly, Dudley and Chase.
1787 CHATHAM, BENJAMIN, Edward, Franky, Berry and Rookins.
1785 COTTEN, HENRY, Elizabeth, Sarah and James.
1796 COTTEN, JOAB, James, Josiah, Whitmel, Robert, John, Mary, Dorothy and Anna.
1797 COTTEN, WM., Mary (wife).
1785 CORLEW, JOHN, Mary, Frances, Catherine
and William.
1792 CROWELL, EDWARD, Martha (wife), Samuel,
Benjamin, Edward, Thomas, Mary and Martha.
1793 CROWELL, THOMAS, Mary (wife), Benjamin,
Edward, Hannah, Sarah, Mary and Martha.
1793 CARNEY, RICHARD, Mary (wife), Richard
and S. W.
1794 COOPER, THOMAS, Rachel, Mary, Nanny.
1794 COOPER, JOHN, Samuel, Thomas, Sophia,
John, Zaccheus, James and Franky.
1795 CARTER, JOSEPH, John, Richard.
1796 CARTER, BENJAMIN, Mary (wife).
1798 CARTER, ROBERT, Sarah, Jacob and Robert.
1798 CARTER, JACOB, Nancy, Rebecca and Holly.
1799 CARTER, SARAH, Philip and Jesse.

D.

1760 DRURY, CHARLES, Martha (wife), Henry,
Charles, Willis and Peggy.
1760 DAVIS, LEWIS, John, Martha and Lewis.
1760 DAVIS, MARTHA, Whitehead, Nathan and
Sarah; Lewis, Lewis.
1761 DAVIS, JOHN, Samuel, Mary, Sarah and Lucy.
1761 DOUGLAS, WM., Robert, John and William.
1765 DAVIS, THOMAS, Fred, Goodman, Hartwell,
Dolphin, Thomas, Archibald and Dion.
1764 DICKENS, DAVID, Jane (wife).
1766 DOUGLAS, WM., Edward.
1764 DAVIS, WM., Francis.
1766 DUNCAN, WM., William, Ann, George, John
and James.
1770 DAVIS, THOMAS, Sarah and Thomas.
1771 DYAR, JAMES, Helena (wife), Joseph, George,
John and James.
1772 DEW, JOHN, Mary (wife).
1778 DAMERON, JOHN, Sarah (wife), Christopher,
John, Joseph, Sarah, Judith and Tigner.
1778 DEEN, THOMAS, Isaac, Fred, Jane, Winifred
and Sally.
1781 DUDLEY, CHRISTOPHER, Christopher, Sarah,
Ransom, Linton, Guilford, Agatha and Elizabeth.
1781 DAVIS, FRANCIS, Ann (wife), Frances, Sarah, Mary and Rebecca.
1781 DAVIS, OROONDATES, Mary (wife), Mary and
Elizabeth.
1790 DAVIS, ARTHUR, John, Benjamin and Patience.
1782 DANIEL, JOHN, Silvia (wife), Mary and
Bethany.
1789 DANIEL, JAMES, Patsy, Elizabeth and West.

1795 DANIEL, AMBROSE, Sarah (wife), Chloe, Jesse, Sarah, John, Joseph, Sion, Ambrose, Mary, Brittain and Willis.
1789 DUBERRY, JOILES, Daniel.
1791 DOLES, SARAH, William, Patience and John.
1793 DOWNS, WM., William, Sarah, Mary, Frances, Lucy, David and John.
1794 DICKENS, BENJAMIN, Martha (wife), Delpha, Benjamin, Lewis, William, Ephraim, Richard and Ann.
1794 DAVIDSON, JAMES, Sallie and Nancy.
1794 DOE, ELIZABETH, Nancy.
1797 DAFFIN, GEORGE, Peggy and Dolly.
1798 DIXON, ELISHA, Williams, William; Hogues, Elisha and James.

E.

1764 EMRY, GREEN, Ephraim, John, Mary, Lucy, Phoebe, Martha, Edmond and Sarah.
1762 EVERITT, WM., James, John and Samuel.
1768 EASLEY, RODERICK, Elizabeth (wife), Roderick and Benjamin.
1774 ELLIS, JOHN, Mary (wife), James, Jane and John.
1774 EASTHAM, GEORGE, William, Edward, James, Miriam and Elizabeth.
1765 ELBANK, JOHN, Eliza (wife).
1784 EDWARDS, CULLEN, John and Cullen.
1793 EDWARDS, MARTHA, Ann, Dorothy and John.
1794 EDWARDS, JOSEPH, Jarratt, Mary Ann, Joseph, John, Peter, Jonathan, Ann, Jesse and Sturton.
1797 EDWARDS, JESSE, Mary (wife), Henry, Martha, Sally and Penny.
1783 ELBECK, HENRY, Jane and Montfort.
1790 ELBECK, MONTFORT, SR., Mary (wife), Anna Maria, Montfort, John, Penelope, Susanna and Mary; Frohock, Elizabeth.
1786 EDMONDS, WM., Elizabeth (wife), Charles and Benjamin.
1796 ETHERIDGE, AARON, Emily (wife), William, Mary and Martha.
1795 ETHERIDGE, WM., Elizabeth and Catron.
1795 ETHERIDGE, UNITY, Celia.
1792 EDMONDSON, THOMAS, Elizabeth (wife), William, Judah, Ambrose, Humphrey, Sallie, Thomas, Daniel and Willie.
1795 EDMONDSON, BRYAN, Sallie (wife).
1792 EMORY, EDWARD, John, Aaron and Rebecca.
1797 EVERETT, JESSE, Joanna (wife), John, David, Mary, Nancy.
1799 EASLEY, JAMES, Frances (wife).

F.

1764 FERGUSON, WM., Jane (wife), Sarah.
1763 FUQUA, WM., Prudence (wife).
1766 FOREMAN, WM., Benjamin, Judah, Hester and Pheraba.
1766 FORT, ELIAS, Elias, John, Mary, Jesse, Lucy, Priscilla and Micajah.
1774 FREEAR, RICHARD, Winifred (wife), Robert, Richard and Margaret.
1785 FORT, ANN, Absilla.

1798 FLUELLEN, RICHARD, Obadiah, Thomas, Rich-
and and Mary.
1787 FAUCETT, JAMES, Mary (wife), William,
James and John.
1793 FORT, IBELL, William, Daniel.
1795 FORT, WILLIS, Penny (wife), Betsy, Charlotte and Nancy.
1794 FREEAR, ROBERT, Richard.

G.

1761 GREEN, WM., William, Thomas, John, Amy
and Robert.
1763 GAINES, SAMUEL, Samuel, William and Mary.
1764 GRICE, JOHN, Moses, William, Ann, Mary,
Robert, Jonathan and Elizabeth.
1764 GOODWIN, GEORGE, Martha (wife), Josiah.
1771 GARNER, WM., Ann (wife).
1772 GREEN, THOMAS, Hannah (wife), Benjamin,
Sarah, Elizabeth and Hervey.
1777 GRAY, SAMUEL, Ann (wife), Henry, John,
Ann, Lucy and Sallie.
1777 GARDNER, THOMAS, George, John, Sterling,
William, Thomas, Pryor and Camp.
1783 GEE, JAMES, Rebecca and Henry.
1783 GARLAND, PATRICK, Henry, Thomas, Miriam
and Mary.
1787 GRIFFIN, EZBEEL, James, Mary, Winifred,
Michael, Eli and Brinkley.
1787 GREEN, JAMES W., Martha C. (wife), Allen J.
and Furnifold.
1797 GREEN, ANN H., Alston, Gideon, Willis,
Priscilla and R. W. (relatives).
1788 GILL, THOMAS, Elizabeth (wife), Priscilla
and James.
1789 GOOD, THOMAS, Elizabeth (wife).
1792 GRANT, JAMES, Martha and James.
1793 GILMOUR, JOHN, Mary (wife), William and
H. C.
1797 GRAY, JOSEPH, John A.
1797 GRAY, JAMES, Joseph and John.
1798 GRIFFIS, ANN, Harrison, Winnie.
1752 GOOD, JOHN, Mary (wife).

H.

1761 HAYES, PETER, Charles, Siler, Millie, Willie,
Reuben and Martha.
1761 HAWS, HENRY, Henry.
1762 HOBGOOD, WM., Sarah (wife).
1763 HARDY, HUGH, Bethiah (wife).
1763 HOUSE, WM., Isaac, Mary, Annie and Wm.
1763 HOBGOOD, MICAJAH, John.
1765 HACKNEY, JENNINGS, William.
1765 HILL, ROBERT, Tabitha (wife), Green, Sion,
Abner and Milory.
1765 HANCOCK, JAMES, Mary (wife), William and
James.
1765 HEATH, JOHN, William, Abraham, Adam,
Moses, James, Mary, Elizabeth, Jesse and
Sarah.
1766 HARPER, HENRY, Rachel (wife), Isaac, Joseph, Samuel, Ambrose, James, Tabitha, Mary
and Henry.
1769 HURST, PHILIP, Baker, Blake; Green, Wm.;

1796 PRITCHETT, THOMAS, Sallie (wife), Nancy, Elisha and Sterling. Shelton, Burwell; Stone, Mary.

1769 HILL, THOMAS, George, James, Nancy, Comfort, Anas, Moses and Slaughter.

1772 HIGHSMITH, DANIEL, Ann (wife), Daniel, James, William and Dorcas.

1772 HARRIS, WM., Simon, Matthew, Henry, Patience, Charity and Martha.

1773 HEATH, THOMAS, Absalom, Richard, Ann, Mary, Adam, and Sarah.

1774 HARDY, JOHN, Benjamin, Elizabeth, Mary, Penelope, Tabitha, Martha and Deborah.

1777 HARGROVE, WM., Sarah (wife), John and Thomas.

1777 HEWITT, BENJAMIN, Jane (wife), Sarah.

1777 HOWELL, THOMAS, Ann, William and Thomas.

1778 HARRISON, SIMON, Daniel, William and Joseph.

1778 HARDEE, CURTIS, Thomas, John, Curtis, Elizabeth, Anna, Louisa and David.

1781 HOGUN, JAMES, Ruth (wife), Lemuel.

1781 HINTON, JAMES, Robert, Sally J., James, Christopher and Winnie.

1783 HOBGOOD, JOHN, Lemuel, Elijah, Micajah, Samuel, Frances, John, Elizabeth, Ruthemah and William.

1783 HORN, RICHARD, Sarah (wife), James, Henry, Rhoda, Patience, Hannah and Howell.

1783 HARRISS, TEMPERANCE, Norfleet Pheraba. Mary, Samuel, Elizabeth and James.

1788 HARRISS, GIDEON, Benjamin, Henrietta and Warren.

1788 HARRISS, ELIAS, Asa, Abner, Frances, Catherine, Phoebe, Mary, Hugh, Arthur and Sion.

1709 HARRIS, ROE, Elizabeth (wife).

1795 HARRIS, THOMAS, Elizabeth (wife), Nancy, Mary and Phoebe.

1788 HARRIS, GIDEON, Mason, Nathaniel.

1799 HARRIS, DRURY, Priscilla, Nancy, Jacob, Kinchin, Thomas and Carter.

1783 HALL, IGNATIUS, Mary (wife), Ignatius, Thomas L., Robert and Anna.

1799 HALL, MARY, Ignatius.

1799 HALL, THEODORICK, Moody, Elizabeth, Fred and Robert; Moss, Rebecca and Mial; Allen, William.

1787 HILLIARD, MARGARET, John and Wm.

1787 HAYNES, CHRISTOPHER, Lucy (wife).

1796 HAYNES, THOMAS, Christopher, Thomas, Eaton and Mary.

1789 HULIN, JOHN, Ann (wife), Thomas, John, Robert and Elizabeth.

1789 HULIN, MARY, Ann and John.

1791 HULIN, ROBERT, Mary (wife), Ann.

1789 HILL, THOMAS, Sarah (wife), Thomas, Benjamin, Robert and Richard.

1793 HILL, SARAH, McNeill, Fannie; Long, Nanny; Lassiter, Christian.

1798 HILL, WM., Wm. W., Vely, Charlotte, Mary, Elizabeth, Margaret and Dorothy.

1799 HILL, COLLIER, Robert, Thomas and Benjamin.

1789 HAMLIN, CHARLES, Martha (wife), Nancy and Wood J.

1791 HARDEN, JAMES, Elizabeth (wife), John and Eleanor.

1791 HARDEN, WM., Mary (wife), John, Elizabeth and Nelly.

1793 HADLEY, JOSEPH, Lydia (wife), Sarah, Mildred, Henry, Wm. D., Martha, Valentine and J. J.

1794 HOLT, THOMAS, Ann (wife), Joseph, James, Thomas and Arrington.

1797 HAIL, ARIS, Sarah (wife), Nancy.

1797 HAIL, ROBERT, William, Judith, Samuel and Thomas.

1795 HORTON, SAMUEL, Winifred (wife), Junius, Jane, Esther and Willie.

1795 HUBANK (Eubanks), JOSEPH, George and Joseph.

1795 HATHAWAY, WM., Elizabeth (wife), Sallie, Thomas and Jesse.

1795 HEATH, JOHN, Mary (wife), James, Moses, Adam and Jesse.

1796 HOWELL, THOMAS, Nathan.

1796 HUMPHREYS, ELIJAH, Judith (wife), George. and Judith.

1798 HANCOCK, HENRY, Bell, Celia and Lemuel.

I.

1774 IVEY, JOHN, Sarah (wife), Robert.

1787 IVES, TIMOTHY, John, Timothy and Dinah.

1795 IRBY, ELIZABETH, Powell, Daniel and Rasous.

J.

1760 JONES, PETER, wife and children (not named).

1761 JUDGE, JAMES, wife (not named).

1761 JACKSON, JAMES, Thomas, James, John, Ann, Lucy, Ann (wife), Jacob, Elizabeth and Richard.

1762 JONES, WM., Frances (wife).

1762 JACKSON, EDWARD, Jacob, Joanna, Green, Hays, Mary, Patty, Mary (wife), Isaac, William and John.

1765 JOHNSON, PETER, Egbert.

1770 JOYNER, JOSHUA, Patience (wife), John, Joshua and Mary.

1770 JOYNER, NATHAN, Joseph, Joshua, Theophilus, Ann and Bridgerman.

1770 JOYNER, JOHN, Martha (wife), Henry and Martha.

1772 JONES, WM. T., Haywood, Betsy, John, Polly and Egbert; Burgess. William.

1774 JOHNSON, STERLING, Rebecca (wife), Robert.

1774 JOYNER, JOSEPH, Nathan, Mary and Olive.

1778 JONES, JAMES, Sarah (wife), John, Fred, James and Archritain.

1787 JACKSON, ISAAC, Elizabeth (wife), William, Lucy, David and Nancy.

1784 JACKSON, THOMAS, Mary (wife), Edward, Sarah and Judah.

1785 JOYNER, PATIENCE, John.

1794 JOYNER, JOEL, Molly (wife), Eli, Joel, Elizabeth, Nancy, Pheraba, Sallie and Olive.

1796 JOYNER, BRIDGERMAN, Theophilus, Henry, Andrew, Robert, Martha, Mary, Alcy, and Harriet.
1785 JARVIS, WM., Catherine (wife), Patience and Sarah.
1787 JOSEY, JAMES, Peggy (wife), Robert, James, John, Olive, Mary and Sarah.
1795 JOSEY, JAMES, Lydia (wife).
1782 JONES, DAVID, Joshua, John, Elizabeth, Anne and Sarah.
1792 JONES, SARAH, Albritton.
1793 JONES, WM., William, Henry, Brittain, Simon, Sarah, Winifred, Anne, Silvia and Elizabeth.
1794 JONES, JOHN, John, Willie, Robert, Judith and Nancy.
1794 JONES, WM., Mary (wife).
1794 JONES, ROBERT, Rachel (wife), John.
1785 JOHNSTON, ELIZABETH, Taylor, Elizabeth; Doc, Elizabeth; Rawlings, Hannah.
1791 JOHNSTON, ABRAM, Lavinia and Roper.
1791 JOHNSTON, ABRAHAM, William, John, Abraham and Susanna.

K.

1759 KEELING, GEORGE, George, Elizabeth, Ann, Agatha and Francis.
1764 KEARNEY, THOMAS, Sarah (wife), Edmond and Philip.
1775 KNIGHT, FRED, Martha (wife); John.
1777 KING, WM., Martha (wife), Thomas M., Martha and William.
1794 KAY, RICHARD, Lucy (wife), Frances, Richard, Mary and Betsy.
1798 KING, EDWARD, Ann (wife).

L.

1760 LEWIS, RICHARD, Nicholas, Thomas, William and Ann.
1760 LONG, JOHN, John, Prudence (wife); Henry.
1764 LATTIMORE, MARY, Ann.
1762 LOVELL, JAMES, James, Elizabeth, Jane, Malachi and Ann.
1762 LANE, BARNABAS, Wife (not named), Martin.
1764 LANGLEY, THOMAS, Lucy (wife).
1764 LINTON, JOHN, Montfort, Joseph.
1766 LANE, JOHN, John.
1768 LANGSDILL, RICHARD, Elizabeth (wife); Richard, William, Winifred, John and Benjamin.
1775 LONG, JOSEPH, Mary (wife).
1776 LANE, JOHN, David, Mourning (wife), Julian, David.
1777 LANE, JOSEPH, Joseph, James, Jesse, Henry and Joel.
1781 LESLIE, JAMES, Mary (wife), Robert and Sarah.
1786 LANE, WM., William, Joseph, Elizabeth and Tabitha.
1790 LANE, DAVID, David.
1798 LANE, LEVI, Martha (wife), Elizabeth and Isaac.

1788 LEEK, JOSEPH, Sallie (wife), Tempe, Josiah, John, Isaac, Dize and Ellenback.
1788 LONG, GILES, Elizabeth (wife).
1798 LONG, NICHOLAS, SR., Nicholas, Lunsford, Richard H., J. J., Lemuel, McKenzie, George W., Martha E., and Mary.
1789 LEWIS, MORGAN, Lucy (wife), John, Morgan, Charles, Warner, Elizabeth and Lucy.
1789 LOCK, JOHN, John, Jonathan, Dorothy.
1789 LOWRY, THOMAS, Ann (wife), Benjamin and William.
1793 LOWE, WM., JR., Sallie (wife).

M.

1760 MARTIN, THOMAS, William.
1761 MERRITT, BENJAMIN, Mary (wife), Nathan, Ephraim, Sarah and Mary.
1762 MATHIS, JAMES, Charles.
1764 MARTIN, JAMES, William, Susanna, Mary, Henry, Patrick and Lucy.
1765 MATHIS, THOMAS, Charles, James, Milly and Benjamin.
1765 MERRITT, MARY, Ephraim, Matthew and Benjamin.
1766 MORELAND, JOHN, Edward, William, Frances, Jane and Mary.
1768 MATHIS, ISAAC, Mary (wife), Thomas, Jean, Isaac, Mary, Sarah, Robert, Peter.
1775 MARTIN, JOHN, Susanna (wife).
1774 MERRYMAN, BENJAMIN, Frances (wife); Thomas, Benjamin and Margaret.
1775 MATTHEWS, JAMES, Ann (wife), Richard, Susanna and Delilah.
1777 MORRISS, THOMAS, Mary (wife), Lovey, Daniel, Mitchell, Samuel and Mary.
1777 MARTIN, AMBROSE, Sarah (wife), Henry, John, Thomas, Patty, Reading, and Mary.
1777 MONTFORT, JOSEPH, Henry, Priscilla, Mary and Elizabeth.
1778 MERRITT, MARY, Molly, Amy and Sale.
1781 MERRITT, RICHARD, Sarah, James, Richard, Ephraim, Annie, Mary, Amy and Waddill.
1784 MERRITT, WM., Richard, Thomas and Absalom.
1789 MERRITT, EPHRAIM, Nathaniel, Jeremiah and Holly.
1794 MERRITT, THOMAS, Mary (wife), Fred, Shadrack and Madrock.
1782 MATHIAS, ROPES, Oroondates, Mark, Sallie, Nancy, Betsy and Hartwell.
1782 MARSHALL, THOMAS, Nancy, Charity and Ransom.
1785 MARSHALL, DAVID, William, Stephen, Catherine, Ann, Lucy, Mary, Janie, Betsy, Susanna, Sarah and Patty.
1799 MARSHALL, JOHN, Elizabeth (wife), John, Allen and Starling.
1783 MORRISS, GRIFFIN, Sarah and Griffin.
1799 MORRISS, HEZEKIAH, Aquilla, Priscilla and Winnie.
1784 MORGAN, PETER, Peter.
1784 MASON, ELIZABETH, Thomas and Turner.
1785 MALLARD, JOHN, John, Joseph, Elizabeth, Margery, Thornton and Dinah.

1786 MOY, THOMAS, Elizabeth (wife).
1788 MARTIN, JAMES, Patrick, Mary, Amy, Elizabeth, Temperance and Susanna.
1788 MARTIN, WM., Lucy (wife), Susanna, Ann Maria and William J.
1789 MOORE, JAMES, Ann (wife), Richard and Elijah.
1794 MOORE, CHARLES, Mary (wife), Wm. B., Martha and Elizabeth.
1791 MITCHELL, ABRAM, Thomas, Mary and Dorothy.
1794 MANGUM, JOHN, Jane (wife), Henry, Elizabeth and Lucy.
1795 MONCRIEF, WM., Martha (wife).
1795 MUIR, WM., Elizabeth (wife), Robert.
1795 MOTLEY, ROBERT, Henry, John and Thomas.
1795 MAHONEY, WM., John, Jesse, George, James, Dennis and Leon.
1796 MONTFORT, RICHARD, Ann (wife), Sallie, John, William, Thomas, Samuel, Geoffrey, Polly and Joseph.
1796 MILES, THOMAS, Thomas and Benjamin.
1797 MASON, WM., Eleanor (wife), Samuel, Elisha, Joseph, Elizabeth, Sarah, Eleanor, Susanna, William, Gabriel, Mary and John.
1798 MALLORY, FRANCIS, John, Francis, James, William and Elizabeth.
1761 McKENNIE, BARNABY, Ann (wife), Patience and Martha.
1786 McCLANACHAN, WM., Jane (wife), John, Margaret and William.
1797 McDOUGALL, JOHN, Sloan, John.
1797 McCLELLAN, JOHN, William and David.
1798 McCULLOCH, ALEX., Sarah (wife), Mary, Elizabeth, Samuel, Benjamin and Alexander.
1782 McKINNEY, SARAH, Elliott, John, Upshur, Lovey and Fannie; Hodges, Martha.

N.

1763 NORSFORD, SUSANNA, Harrell, Abraham and Siserah; Campbell, Jack.
1768 NELMS, JOSHUA, Sarah (wife).
1769 NELMS, JOSHUA, Sarah (wife), Jeremiah, William, Nancy and Parismus.
1774 NELMS, PARISMUS, Nancy (wife), Milly, Betsy and Nancy.
1775 NICHOLSON, LEMUEL, Thomas, John, Joseph W., Absalom, Pheraba, Abigail and Bathsheba.
1775 NICHOLSON, ANN, Lemuel, Bathsheba, John, Elizabeth and Thomas.
1790 NICHOLS, LUKE, Susanna (wife), James.
1795 NORWOOD, RICHARD, Lydia (wife).
1795 NORWOOD, SAMUEL, Richard and Lydia.
1796 NOBBIN, WM,. Ann (wife); Christopher, Lucy, William and Mary.
1799 NELLOMS (Nelms), MEREDITH, John L., Polly, F. T., Sallie and Lucy.

O.

1795 OVERSTREET, HENRY, Jane (wife), James, Richard and J. D.

P.

1758 PERRY, JOHN, William.

1761 POWELL, NATHAN, Nathan, Elizabeth, Willis, Jordan, Dempsey and Patty.

1762 POPE, THOMAS, Amos and Edeh.

1762 POPE, THOMAS, Thomas, James, Sally, Constance, Robert, Mary and Obadiah.

1762 POPE, WINIFRED, Jesse, Louise, Tabitha and Ann.

1763 POWELLS, NATHAN, Gordon.

1763 POPE, RICHARD, Jordan and William.

1763 PIERCE, JOSEPH, William, Joseph and Priscilla.

1764 PRESSGRAVES, GEORGE, Robert.

1764 PARIS, JOHN, Mary (wife), Mary.

1764 POPE, HENRY, Tabitha (wife), Willis, John, Henry and B.

1766 PARK, JOHN, John, Joseph and Moses.

1767 POWELL, RICHARD, Harry, Pheraba, Mary and Richard.

1770 PRYOR, JOHN, Luke and Lucretia.

1770 PITTS, WALTER, Thaddeus, Mark, Lewis, Henry and John.

1770 POWELL, SALMON, Rebecca (wife), John, Benjamin, William, Mary, Rebecca and Whitley.

1771 PERKINS, WM., Sarah (wife).

1771 PERRY, JAMES, Jacob, Jesse, John, James, William, Rawls, Alice, Patience, Mary, Ann, Christian, Grace, Charity, Philip and Patience (wife).

1771 PERRY, PATIENCE, John.

1772 POPE, WM., Martha (wife), John, William, Benjamin and Ann.

1778 PARSONS, JAMES, William, Joseph, Mary and Susanna.

1779 PAU, GEORGE, Job and William.

1782 PITTMAN, MARTHA, Sarah.

1787 PITTMAN, AMBROSE, Lila (wife), Elisha, Elijah, Arthur, Miller, Willie and John.

1789 PEMBERTON, RICHARD, Elizabeth (wife), William, Jesse and Joshua.

1785 PASSMORE, ROBERT, John, Amy, Houseman, Susanna, Betty, Polly and Alexander.

1787 POWERS, JOHN, Edith (wife), James, Moses and William.

1785 PASS, WM., Samuel, William, Willis, Nelson and Nancy.

1790 PARKER, JAMES, Sarah (wife), Eliazbeth, Susanna and James.

1791 PASTEUR, JAMES, Susanna (wife), Elizabeth, Rachel and Charles.

1794 PASTEUR, CHARLES, Martha (wife), Francis, J. J., Ann and Sarah.

1791 PUGH, DAVID, Elizabeth (wife), John, William, Thomas, Peggy and Eaton.

1795 PULLIN, WM., Charlotte (wife), William, Chloe, Leroy, Chancy, Clara, Eaton and Ludwell.

1799 PITTMAN, MILLY, Elisha, Arthur, John, Zilphia, Thomas and Sarah.

1793 POWELL, JORDAN, Elizabeth (wife), Willis.

1785 POWELL, JOHN, John, Ptolemy, William and Mary.
1798 POWELL, JOHN, wife (not named).
1783 PERRY, JOHN, Joseph and James.
1793 PERRY, HUBBARD, Mary and Hartwell.
1783 PRITCHETT, JOHN, Sarah (wife), Sterling and George C.
1795 PACE, THOMAS, Martha (wife), William, Nancy, James and Hardy.
1795 PARTIN, JOHN, Robert, Barnaby, Charles, Lucy, Sarah, Elizabeth, Mary and Priscilla.
1796 PURNALL, JOHN, Penny (wife), William, John, Henry, David and Patrick.
1797 PEARCE, WM., Mary (wife), Elizabeth.
1798 PEARCE, MARY, Whitaker, Robert, Lunsford, Dudley and Thomas.
1797 PONS, JOHN, Mary.
1797 PERKINS, HENRY, Joshua, James, Charles B., Ann, Moses, Thomas, William, Abigail and H. S. J.
1798 POPE, ELIJAH, Henry, Jacob, Upham, William, Elijah, Patience, Penelope, Sallie, Hardy and Charlotte.
1799 POPE, HARDIE, Benjamin and William H.

Q

1794 QUALLS, PETER, Mary (wife), James, Henry, Peter and Margaret.
1795 QUALLS, JAMES, Milla, Alfred and Peter.

R.

1760 ROZAR, DAVID, Ann (wife), John, David, Shadrack, Sarah and Mashack.
1760 RAWLS, WILLIAM, Priscilla (wife), Philip, John, Elisha, Willis, Ann, Mary and Diana.
1761 RONARD, ROBERT, Barbara (wife), James and William.
1764 ROBERTSON, HENRY, Ann (wife), Henry, Peter and Suckey.
1764 ROGERS, DAVID, Montfort, Joheph.
1763 RUSSELL, JEFFREY, Jackson, William.
1767 READE, HARMAN, Mary (wife), Jesse.
1771 REED, SUSANNA, Katherine.
1771 ROBINSON, WM., Sarah and Elizabeth.
1774 ROBERTSON, ANNE, Peter, Suckey and Henry.
1777 RICKMAN, RORERT, Mark and Nathan.
1777 RONE, WM., John, Lewis, Jesse and Sarah.
1778 RAWLS, MICAJAH, Reves, John and Jesse.
1778 RICKS, SARAH, John, Isaac, Mary, Richard and Betsy.
1787 RICKS, JOHN, Elizabeth (wife), Abraham, Robert, Sarah and Mary.
1781 READ, MARY, James.
1782 RORIE, JOHN, William and Zachariah.
1790 ROGERS, THOMAS, Charity (wife), Biddy, Stephen, Shadrack, William, John, Thomas, Pleasant, Randolph, Sally, Betty, Polly, Keziah and Elizabeth.
1794 ROBERTSON, RANDALL, Mary (wife), Martha D. and John.
1794 ROAN, JESSE, Judith (wife), Elizabeth and John.

1787 RUTLAND, SHADRACK, Elizabeth (wife), Martha, Dolly and Shadrack.
1797 ROOPER, JOHN, Zilpha (wife), Bethea.
1798 RICHARDSON, WM., Elijah, Mathew, Henry and William.

S.

1760 SHERROD, BENJAMIN, Benjamin, Richard and Patience.
1761 SAXON, ARTHULUS, Benjamin, Charles, Benajah, Temple and Samuel.
1761 SILLS, WM., John, Isham, Peter, Morris, Lambert, Drury, David and Sarah.
1762 SMITH, JAMES, Frances (wife), James and Jeremiah.
1765 STRICKLAND, MOSES, wife (not named).
1762 SMITH, DREW, Elizabeth (wife), Priscilla, Millia, Temperance and Ann.
1766 SMITH, GEORGE, Ann (wife), Rachel and George.
1766 SAXON, SAMUEL, Benjamin, Charles, John, Mary and Benajah.
1763 STRAUGHAN, DAVID, Elizabeth (wife), John, David and Margaret.
1769 STEVENSON, JOSEPH, Martha (wife).
1770 SMALLY, MICHAEL, Ann, Michael, Nancy, William, Patty, James and John.
1770 STATON, THOMAS, Nehemiah, Ann, Jesse, Sarah, Ezekiel, Arthur and Sadok.
1771 STEELE, THOMAS, Elizabeth (wife).
1771 STURDIVANT, BIGGONES, wife (not named).
1772 SPEARS, HEZEKIAH, Joseph and Margery.
1772 SMITH, JOHN, John M., Betsy, Jesse, William and Sallie.
1774 SCOTT, FRANCIS, Sarah and Resom.
1777 SMITH, WM., William, Elizabeth, Agnes and Mary.
1777 STORY, JAMES, Sarah (wife); William and Martha.
1777 SUMMER, DAVID, James and William.
1777 SHEPPARD, SAMPSON, Martha (wife), Robert.
1777 SIKES, JAMES, Daniel, Nathan, Jacob and Sarah.
1783 STURDIVANT, SARAH, Amanda and John.
1783 STEEL, TABITHA, Goodwin, Jesse, Sarah, George and Gideon.
1789 SMITH, AMY, Mary.
1789 SMITH, JOHN, John, Major, Elizabeth, Samuel and Mary.
1784 SMITH, THOMAS, Phoebe and Tempe.
1789 SMITH, ARTHUR, Arthur, Ann, William and Drew.
1791 SMITH, WM., EDMUNDS, Elizabeth; Howes, Judith; Powell, Mary.
1794 SMITH, PETER, Mary (wife), Zachariah, Uriah, Peter and John.
1797 SMITH, SAMUEL, Thomas, Samuel, Nancy, Peggy and Martha.
1798 SMITH, THOMAS, Rebecca (wife), Thomas, Isham, Josiah, Nancy, Miles.
1792 SMITH, WM., Pattie (wife).
1785 SCOTT, JAMES, Rachel (wife),

1786 SHELTON, LODOMAN, Patty, Hannah, Ruth, Willis and Burrell.
1786 STAMPER, ELIZABETH, Robert, John and Sarah.
1785 SUMNER, WM., Jethro, Seth, Mary T., Penolope, James and David.
1789 SIMMONS, LACY, Zadok, Ann, Mary and Sarah.
1790 SHAW, JAMES, Sarah (wife), Thomas, Henry, Peyton and Sallie.
1790 SHAW, JOHN, Robert and Elliott.
1791 SPEAR, NATHAN, Mary (wife), John.
1792 SCARLOCK, THOMAS, James and George.
1794 SOUTHERLAND, JOHN, Pattie (wife), Nancy, Bettie, John and James.
1794 SANDERS, SAMUEL, Leah (wife).
1796 STORY, SARAH, George, James, William, Martha and Sarah.
1797 STRICKLAND, HERMAN, John, Elizabeth, James, Herman, Lucy and Ruth.
1797 SLATTER, ELIZABETH, Harden, Lucy.
1798 SANDS, BARHAM, Samuel, Elizabeth and Peggy.
1799 SLAUGHTER, JAMES, Thomas and D. R.

T.

1760 TOMSON, JOHN, Mary (wife), Sarah, Elizabeth, Anness, Richard, William and Pigeten.
1764 TROUBLEVIL (DURBEVILLE), WALTER, Joseph, Isaac, Mary Jane, Martha, Jonathan and Ellett.
1763 TAYLOR, ROGER, Cary, Suffea (Sophia).
1763 THOMAS, JORDAN, Ann (wife), William and John.
1762 TAYLOR, WM., Thomas T., Mary, Joshua, John, Esther, Catherine and Elizabeth.
1765 TATUM, JOSHUA, Christopher, Howell, Joshua, Elizabeth and Amy.
1766 TROUGHTON, ANDREW, Mary, James, Elsie, Charles, Stagg, Swan and Mannie.
1770 TAYLOR, JOHN, Ann (wife), Frankey.
1771 TUCKER, WM. W., Priscilla (wife), Martha, Mary, Sterling and Fanny.
1771 THOMPSON, WM. R., Martha (wife), William, Charles, Agnes, John, Elizabeth, Sarah, Lucy and Nancy.
1771 TOMBLEYS, HENNING, Riddick, Peggy; Meadows, Mary; Davis, Elizabeth.
1772 TAYLOR, JAMES, Thomas, Dorcas, Fullard, Sukey, Goodwin, Katie, Judah and John.
1772 TIPPETT, PHILIP, Erasmus, Clara and Jane.
1777 TURNER, GEORGE, James, Nathan, Elizabeth and Lucy.
1783 TURNER, NATHAN, James, George, Lucy, Joseph and Susanna.
1786 TURNER, WM., Winnie, Edwin, Fielding, William, Henry and Mary.
1788 TURNER, FIELDING, Elizabeth (wife), James, Fielding, Edwin, Peter, John, Henry, William and Mary.
1790 TURNER, THOMAS, Sarah (wife).
1795 TURNER, EDWIN, Temperance (wife), Martha, Mary, Edwin and Dorcas.
1796 TURNER, JESSE, Pheraba.

1783 TROUGHTON, MARY, Martin, Lucy; Bullock, Susanna.
1784 TAYLOR, JOSEPH, Mary (wife), Cyrus, John, Sarah and Jeremiah.
1785 TAYLOR, WM., Charity (wife), John.
1792 TAYLOR, MARY, Jeremiah, John and Mary.
1785 TULLOCK, THOMAS, Susanna (wife), John.
1787 THOMAS, THOMAS, William, John, Levi, Major, Desdemona, Benjamin, Jesse, Henry, Bosten, Mason, Elkanah and Sion.
1791 TABB, THOMAS, Martha (wife); Jones, Thomas.
1795 TILLERY, JOHN, George and Eppy.
1798 TILLERY, EPPY, Velie (wife), Betsy, Nancy, David, Thomas, John, Judith, Alex., Samuel and Polly.

V.

1761 VAULX, JAMES, Mary (wife), Daniel and Elizabeth.
1782 VALENTINE, DANIEL, Mary (wife), Joshua.
1783 VICK, BENJAMIN, Mary (wife), Benjamin and Josiah.
1798 VINSON, JOHN, Letitia (wife), Mary, Rebecca, Nancy and Warren.

W.

1761 WILLIAMS, JOSHUA, Thomas, Temperance, Sarah (wife), Elisha, Sarah.
1761 WHEELER, JOSEPH, John, James, Elizabeth and Joseph.
1761 WYATT, JACOB, Rhoda (wife), Jesse, Christiana and Mary.
1764 WOOTEN, BENJAMIN, Elizabeth (wife), Thomas, John, Mary and Priscilla.
1764 WILLIAMS, JANE, Sampson, Samuel, William, Chloe and George.
1764 WILLIAMSON, ROBERT, George, Frances and John.
1762 WEATHERSBEE, WYATT, Wade, Thomas, William and Mary.
1762 WILKINS, THOMAS, Thomas, William, Robert, John, James, Lucy, and Sarah.
1762 WALLER, JOHN, Ann (wife), Robert, William, Nancy, Matthew, Susie and Patsy.
1765 WHITEHEAD, WM., Arthur, Cullen, Lewis, Abby, Martha, Rachel, Rebecca, Temperance and Priscilla.
1765 WHITAKER, ROBERT, John, Robert, Lawrence, Benton, Thomas, William, Sarah and Lucy.
1788 WINTER, THOMAS, Mary (wife), Henry.
1766 WILLIAMS, FRANCIS, Sarah (wife), Charles, Frances, Betty Ann, Mary Ann, Jemima Ann and Sarah Ann.
1766 WHITEHEAD, ABRAHAM, William, Tobias, Jacob, Arthur and Lazarus.
1770 WILLIAMS, SOLOMON, Charles, Elisha, Lydia, Mennia, Lucy, Sarah and Elizabeth.
1771 WALLACE, MICHAEL, John, William, Charles, Bartholomew, Patrick, Sarah, Elizabeth, Michael and Rachel.
1771 WILLIAMS, JOHN, Mary (wife).
1772 WALKER, WM., Jane (wife), William, Sukey and Winifred.

1773 WILLIAMS, LYDIA, Elizabeth, Lucy and Jemima.

1774 WHITEHEAD, TOBIAS, Ann (wife), Catherine, Penelope, Mary, Elizabeth and Sarah.

1774 WILLIAMS, JACOB, Mary (wife), Sarah and John.

1774 WILLIAMS, WILSON, Ann (wife), Jesse, Eli, Isaac and Martha.

1774 WIGGINS, THOMAS, Mary Ann (wife).

1775 WRIGHT, WINIFRED, Patience, James, Roderick, Nancy and Alice.

1776 WINGFIELD, LAWRENCE, William.

1776 WOMACK, WM., Thomas, Fred, James and Brittain.

1781 WHITEHEAD, JOSEPH, Pheraba (wife), Tobias, John, Martha and Elizabeth.

1781 WATSON, WM., Mary (wife), Charles, Alexander and Mary.

1791 WATSON, JOHN, Mary (wife).

1782 WELDON, SAMUEL, Penelope (wife). Benjamin, William and Martha.

1783 WILLIAMS, LUCY, Lawrence, Elisha, Elizabeth and Charles.

1785 WELDON, WELDON, David, Betty and Nancy.

1785 WILLIAMS, ANNE, Hill, Charity; Lewis, Thomas, William and Hannah.

1792 WILLIAMS, JOHN, Elizabeth (wife), Robert.

1795 WILLIAMS, JOHN, Nicholas, Sallie, Rebecca and Lucy.

1796 WILLIAMS, JESSE, Silvia (wife).

1798 WILLIAMS, CHARLES, John, Elizabeth and J. J.

1785 WYATT, JAMES, John, Jonah and James.

1787 WYATT, JAMES, Sarah (wife), James, Christian and Elizabeth.

1794 WYATT J. J., Sallie (wife), Thomas and Betty.

1787 WHEELESS, JOSEPH, Hardy, Sion and Mollie.

1787 WARREN, GEORGE, Celia (wife), Cornelia, Mary, Elizabeth, Ann, Enoch and Elijah.

1787 WRIGHT, MARTHA, Augustus, Sarah, Priscilla, Minnie, Mary.

1795 WINTER, JOSEPH, William, Betty, Polly, Penny and Ruth.

1739 WEST, ISRAEL, Priscilla (wife).

1791 WIGGINS, WM., Priscilla (wife), William, Arthur, Lemuel and Edmund.

1793 WOOTTEN, WM., Frances (wife) Ann, James, John, William and Elizabeth.

1795 WARLEY, JOHN, Elizabeth, Lovick, Anne, John, Sarah, Joseph and Robert.

1795 WALKER, JOEL, Henry, Daniel and Polly.

1798 WHITMELL, THOMAS B., Anne (wife), Anne S., Thomas W., Drew S.

1799 WILLIS, AUGUSTIN, Lewis, Ann, John and Anne.

1799 WALL, ROBERT, David and Burgess.

Y.

1760 YANCY, JECONIAS, Hannah (wife).

1764 YEWEL, SAMUEL, Hogg, James.

1781 YOUNG, JOHN, Thomas, Marmaduke, Jarrod, Francis, Sarah, William, Louisa, Pheraba and Ruth.

1794 YOUNG, GEORGE, Elizabeth (wife), Martha and Willis.

1795 YOUNG, DOLPHIN D., Mary (wife), Absilla, Drew, James, and General.

1795 YOUNG, MARMADUKE, Thomas, George, John and Turner.

1798 YARBOROUGH, GEORGE, Elizabeth (wife), Samuel, George, James, William, Tabitha and Moses.

HYDE—WILLS

A.

1774 ARTHUR, JAMES, Mary (wife), John, Abigail, Asenath, Abraham and Jeremiah.

1782 ALLEN, JOHN, Zachariah, Lucretia, Sarah and May.

1785 ADAMS, WM , Ann, John and William.

1786 ALDERSON, LEVI. John and Simon.

1786 ALLEN, JOHN, Hannah, Sally, Zedekiah, Isaac, Raphael, James, Jesse, Jeremiah, Josiah and Jacob.

1794 ABRANER, JOHN, Robert, Edah, Sarah, William and John.

B.

1772 BAILEY, HENRY, Abraham, Thomas, Archelaus, Dinah and David.

1775 BELOST, ABBOT, James, Robert, Thomas.

1775 BOYD, ROBERT, Thomas, Robert, William and Joseph.

1775 BELL, WM., Chesanah, William and Richard D.

1780 BATCHELDER, JAMES, Rebecca, Thomas, Sarah, Benjamin and Rosanna.

1785 BATSON, MARY, Elizabeth.

1786 BELOAT, THOMAS, Sabra, Tamar (wife), Margaret and Tamar.

1786 BELL, ABRAM, Asenath, Mary, Hannah and John.

1786 BORROW, GEORGE, Thomas and Mary.

1789 BAILEY, THOMAS, Simon, Jerusha and Borah.

1790 BAILEY, BETHUEL, Mary (wife), Barbara, Mary, Margaret, Sarah, Mourning, Truelove, Samuel and Buthael.

1790 BELL, GEORGE, Nancy (wife), Sidney, Jonathan, Ollie, Mary, Uriah, Littleton, Edward, Dorcas, James, Cornelius, Elizabeth, Walter and Eleanor.

1793 BURGESS, MALACHI, Lydia, Timothy, Mary, Letitia and Sukey.

1794 BOOMER, WM., Nancy (wife), Benjamin, Tabitha, Elizabeth and Nelly.

1796 BORROW, ZACHARIAH, Bozer, Ann, Prusha, Eunice and Louis.

1797 BAILEY, DAVID, Reading, Sidney, Mary and Susanna.

1797 BROOK, STEPHEN, Isaac, William, Stephen, Jacob, Esther, Charity and Sarah.

1798 BAILEY, JAMES, Dorcas (wife), Nancy, James and Richard.

1798 BEACHAM, WM , Morris, William, John, Lurany, Polly, Sally, Ephraim and Jesse.

C.

1771 CARAWAN, JOSHUA, Joseph, John, Patrick, William, Rachel, Joseph and Ephraim.

1772 COX, JOSEPH, Aaron, David, Rosanna, Truelove, Charity, Mary, Ann and Elizabeth.

1774 CLEVES, JOHN, Hannah, Mary, Nancy and Sarah.

1774 CONNER, JACOB, Jacob, Elizabeth, Mourning and Mary.

1783 CAMPBELL, WM., Vened, William, Odur and
      Noah.
1785 COX, WM., Jesse, Shadrack, Abram, Eliza-
      beth, Winifred and John.
1784 CUTRELL, PETER, Daniel, Jacob, Peter, Ben-
      jamin, Keziah, Lydia, Mary, Keziah (wife).
1785 CORDING, WM., Moses, Asa, Dinah, John W.
      and William.
1786 CLARK, MAJOR, William, Henry, Samuel and
      Mary.
1786 CHAMBERS, EZEKIEL, Elizabeth (wife), John,
      Elizabeth and Mary.
1786 CLAYTON, JOHN, Thomas, Elliott and Jemima.
1786 COLLINS, HENRY, Sarah and Margaret S.
1791 CARAWAN, JOHN, Joseph, Ephraim, Mary and
      Frances.
1791 CUTRELL, CHARLES, Joseph, Silence, Andrew,
      Charles, Chloe and Francis.
1791 CHAVIS, THOMAS, Hannah, Mary and John.
1795 CLEAVES, JAMES, Lydia and Elizabeth.
1795 COLLINS, SARAH, Margaret S.
1796 CAPPS, JAMES, Ruth, Thomas, Sarah, Lydia,
      Renbrook, Christopher and Henry.

D.

1794 DAVIS, WM., Dorcas (wife), Edward and
      John.
1785 DANIELS, SOPHIA, John.
1786 DIXON, JOHN, George, John, Elizabeth, Dor-
      cas.
1790 DUKE, GEORGE, John, Duke, Fanny, Martin,
      Ann and Sarah.
1789 DAILY, SAMUEL, George and William.
1789 DURDEN, JACOB, Rachel, Daniel, Rhoda,
      Elisha, Jacob and Eliza.
1791 DAILY, THOMAS, Elizabeth, Samuel, John,
      Thomas and William.
1795 DAVIS, SAMUEL, Jane (wife), John, James,
      Winfield, Jesse and Anna.
1796 DURDEN, DANIEL, Tony.
1797 DAVIS, JOHN, Daniel, William, Abi, Charity,
      Molly, Priscilla and Jerusha.
1797 DAVIS, DORCAS, William, Hasir and Dorcas.

E.

1770 ESTER, WM, Catherine (wife), John, Sarah,
      Ally and Hufany.
1770 EBERN, ANN, William.
1770 ELSBREN, JOHN, Edna, David, Ephraim and
      Emanuel.
1781 ENLOE, MARY, Gladding, Elizabeth; Wade,
      Zilpha.
1775 ENLOE, ABRAHAM, William, Sebastian, Zil-
      pha and Mary.
1775 EMORY, STEPHEN, Lena (wife).
1775 ELLISON, THOMAS, Ann (wife), Robert W.,
      Thomas and Alderson.
1775 ETHERIDGE, SAMUEL, Lydia, Thomas, Samuel,
      Susanna, John and Dinah.
1784 EBERN, WM,. Nathaniel, William, Israel,
      Mary, Cullen and Rebecca.

1785 EBERN, AARON, Zenith, Aaron, Littleton, Edmond, Elizabeth (wife), Elizabeth, Anna, Mourning, and Rebecca.

1789 EBERN, EPHRAIM, Mary, Henry, John, Ephraim, Wilhelma, Charity and Lydia.

1789 EBERN, HENRY, Ephraim, Henry, Jehoiakim, Joachim, John, Samuel.

1794 EBERN, REBECCA, William, Mourning, Mary, Patty and Ephraim.

1796 EBERN, JOHN, Archadah, Zachariah, Elizabeth and Benjamin.

1797 EBERN, JAMES, Margaret (wife), Ann, John, James, Penelope, Enoch and Hosea.

1799 EBERN, ENOCH, Hosea, Ann, James, Margaret, Penelope and Moses.

F.

1770 FORTESCUE, SIMON, John, Simon, Patty and Grace.

1771 FOREMAN, LAZARUS, Margaret (wife), Mary, Noah, Charity, Isaiah, and Abednego.

1774 FOREMAN, CALEB, Abigail (wife), Fred, Thomas, Elizabeth, Mary, Edna and Rebecca.

1775 FORTESCUE, BELL, Agnes (wife), Simon, Bell, Dickson, Mary and Barbara.

1776 FOREMAN, JOSHUA, Rebecca, Caleb, John, Martha, Benjamin, Caleb and Archadah. Martha.

1776 FOREMAN, MARTIN, Rebecca, Uel, Ormond, Martha, Benjamin, Caleb and Archady.

1785 FOREMAN, JOSEPH, Uriah, Sarah, Joshua and Rebecca.

1786 FISHER, ROBINSON, Timothy, Hezekiah, Zachariah, Martin, George, Mary and Elizabeth.

1786 FOREMAN, CALEB, Elizabeth (wife), James and Rebecca.

1796 FOREMAN, LAZARUS, Elizabeth (wife), Archadah, Hardy, Olive and Essber.

1797 FARROW, JOHN, Naomi (wife), William, Jeremiah, Charity, Sarah and David.

G.

1772 GURGANUS, DAVID, Mary, Jonathan, Samuel, Lydia and Abigail.

1777 GIBBS, HENRY, SR., Henry, Jemima, Robert, Elizabeth, Joseph and Jane.

1777 GIBBS, WM., SR., William, Selby, Jeremiah, Benjamin, Thomas, Elizabeth, Ann, Rebecca and Cassandra.

1784 GREEN, DAVID, Ezekiel and Bridget.

1794 GURGANUS, WM., Abner, and Zilpha.

1794 GAYLORD, THOMAS, Rosanna, Edward S., Thomas, Stephen, Benjamin, Winfield and James.

1791 GAYLORD, WINFIELD, Keziah, Mearna, Bersheba, Henry and John.

1794 GIBBS, ROBERT, John, Robert, Thomas, Samuel, William, and Rachel.

1794 GAYLORD, ROSANNA, Batchelor, Sarah; Truelove, William.

1798 GURGANUS, JONATHAN, Wife and children (not named).

1798 GALLOWAY, ABRAHAM, Henry and Margaret.

H.

1770 HARVEY, PETER, Samuel, Mary, Peter and Jorman.

1771 HOLLOWELL, JOSEPH, Arthur and Mary.

1772 HARRIS, WM., William, Peter, John, Amy, Lucretia, Rebecca, Mary and Sarah.

1774 HUSSEY, HENRY, Thomas, Winifred and Mary.

1774 HOPKINS, ANDREW, George, John, William, Elizabeth, Peggy, Mary and Margaret.

1774 HAMILTON, JAMES, Sexton, William and Rebecca.

1775 HARRIS, THOMAS, Elizabeth, Rachel, William, John, Ezekiel and Jesse.

1775 HENRY, ROBERT, Hugh, Margaret (wife), Jane, Frank, Margaret, Samuel, Mary and Robert.

1775 HALL, JOHN, James, John, Thomas, William, Benjamin, Jemima and Mary.

1785 HOLLOWELL, BENJAMIN, Margaret, Benjamin and Denson.

1786 HUSSEY, MARY, Thomas.

1786 HARRIS, PETER, Elizabeth (wife), David, Ebenezer, Gibson, Amy, Lydia and Elizabeth.

1791 HENRY, JOHN, John, Robert, Margaret, Samuel and Phoebe.

1795 HAMMOND, BOAZ, Tamar (wife), Sabra, Margaret and Winifred.

1798 HERBERT, IGNATIUS, Sarah (wife), James and Thomas.

1799 HAYWOOD, WM., James, Martha, Ann and Tabitha.

J.

1770 JONES, ELIZABETH, Richard.

1770 JASPER, JONATHAN, Elizabeth (wife), James, Sheldon, Valentine and Samuel.

1774 JENNETT, JOHN, Sarah, Robert, John, Lurana and Mary.

1775 JORDAN, JOHN, Thomas and John.

1782 JONES, HENRY, Tooley, Mary.

1774 JOLLY, PHILIP, Adam, Philip and Thomas.

1785 JEWELL, BENJAMIN, Mary, Ebenezer, Zedekiah, Jemima and Stephen.

1786 JORDAN, THOMAS, Richard, Abraham, John, James, Rotheus, Zachariah, Dinah, Thomas, John, Mary, Sarah, Margaret, Elizabeth and Ann.

1788 JONES, ABRAHAM, Abraham, Henry G., Daniel, Mary and Rebecca.

1792 JONES, SOLOMON, Bartholomew, Cornelius, Delancy, Jincy and Dinah.

1792 JONES, MORRIS, Morris, Mary, Prudence and Susanna.

1792 JEWELL, MARY, Jemima, Stephen, and Ebenezer.

1794 JASPER, WM. R., Jehail, John, Richard, Hannah, Elizabeth and William.

1795 JENNETT, JOSEPH, Angelica (wife).

1796 JASPER, ELIZABETH, Samuel, James and Winifred.

1796 JASPER, JAMES, Anne (wife), John, James, Jack and Bryan.
1797 JONES, SUSANNA, Morris.

K.

1797 KIFFS, SETH, Sarah, Robert, Zachariah, Margaret and David.

L.

1783 LOCKHART, JOHN, Ann (wife), Jordan, Julia and Jesse.
1784 LATHAM, ROTHEUS, Sarah, Phineas, Daniel, Jesse, Harding, Rotheus, Elizabeth and Fenetras.
1790 LACY, PARKER, Isaac, Adam, Agnes and Ann. Elizabeth and Fenetras.
1794 LINTON, JOHN, Elizabeth, Zachariah, Burrage, Nancy, Betsy, John and Barbara.
1794 LATHAM, SARAH, Martin, Hosea and Rotheus; Smith, Margaret.

M.

1771 MALLISON, JOHN, William and Eleanor.
1771 MORDICK, LEVI, Benjamin, Bridget, Mitchell, Louisa and John.
1772 MASON, BENJAMIN, Daniel, Christopher, Morris, Benjamin, Sarah and Elizabeth.
1772 McTWAIN, EDWARD, Edward, John, Jeconias. Elizabeth (wife), Martha, Elizabeth, Ann and Margaret.
1781 MOORE, WM., Mary (wife), John and William.
1783 MARTIN, BENJAMIN, Foreman, Rebecca; Hancock, Edna.
1787 MASON, JOHN, John, James, Susanna, Thomas, Sarah, Benjamin and Martha.
1795 MASON, SAMUEL, Charlotte (wife), David, Samuel, Drusilla and Agnes.

N.

1793 NEAL, BENJAMIN, Nancy (wife), Sarah, Hannah, Mary and Margaret.

O

1795 O'NEAL, JOHN, SR., Christopher, William, Ephraim, John, Robert and Mary.

P.

1772 POOL, THOMAS, John, Thomas and Sarah.
1795 PORTER, WM., Jane (wife), William.

R.

1771 READ, CHARLES, George, Ann, Samuel, Lucy and Mary.
1786 RUE, MARK, Frederick.
1788 RUE, RACHEL, Solomon, Mary Ann, Jabtha and Phanuel.
1790 RICHARDS, THOMAS, Shadrack, Lydia, Thomas, Brittain and Olivet.
1792 RUE, THOMAS, Sally (wife), Mary and Southey.
1795 RICHARDS, HENRY, Betsy and Willsty.

S.

1772 SLADE, BENJAMIN, David, Nathan, Stephen, Furnifold, Samuel and Enoch.

1774 SMITH, JOHN, Sarah (wife), John, Benjamin, Sidney, Sarah, Mary, Elizabeth and Thomas.

1775 SILVERTHORN, JOHN, John, Joshua, Annarita, Agnes and Winifred.

1775 SURMAN, PETER, Ann, Peter, Mary and Rachel.

1775 SWINDELL, JOHN, Isaac, Josiah, Jesse, Joseph, Rebeca, Job, John, Ruth, Prudence, Rachel and Jonathan.

1776 SATTERTHWAITE, ABRAHAM, Jonathan, Lydia, William, Abraham, Marmaduke and Elizabeth.

1781 SMITH, SAMUEL, John, William, Hannah, Mary, Samuel, Lucretia, Jude and Joseph.

1782 SLADE, HANNAH, Eeazer, Lydia, Mary and Keziah.

1782 SPRING, MOSES, Abner, John and Elizabeth.

1783 SPENCER, JOHN, Gibbs, Mary, John and Zilphia; Sanderson, Elizabeth and John.

1784 SMITH, MARY, Thomas, Betsy, John, Samuel and Lydia.

1787 SATTERTHWAITE, WILLIAM, Abraham, Sarah (wife), Isaac, William, Jemima, Hester and Sarah.

1787 SLADE, HEZEKIAH, Ann, John E., Susanna and Agnes.

1788 SELBY, WM., Ann and Nathan.

1788 SANDERSON, RICHARD, John, Benjamin, Richard, Thomas and Elizabeth.

1787 SELBY, JOHN, William, Talbert, Burrage, John, Jeremiah, Samuel, John, Sarah and Elizabeth.

1789 SWINDELL, JOSIAH, Sarah, Fred, Benjamin, Foster and Mary.

1790 SLADE, REUBEN, Ann and Reuben.

1790 SANDERSON, JOHN S., Richard, Sanders and Ives.

1791 SELBY, SAMUEL, Samuel; Spencer, Elizabeth; Gibbs, Mary and Jane.

1791 SWINDELL, CALEB, Elizabeth, Christopher and Cason.

1793 SPENCER, WM., Zachariah, Mary (wife), Thomas, William, Benjamin, Sarah, Cássandra, Mary, Sophia and Olivia.

1794 SLADE, ANN, John, Susanna and Agnes.

1795 SWINDELL, ZEDEKIAH, Benjamin, Valentine, Parker, Margaret and Phoebs.

1799 SWINDELL, ISAAC, Eleanor, Isaac, William, Joel, Silas, Josiah and Bethany.

1795 SPENCER, EDWARD, David, Tucker, Patty, Benjamin, Samuel, John, Sally, Nancy, Edward, Deidama, Peggy and James.

1799 SELBY, TALBERT, Elizabeth (wife), William, Brittana and Elizabeth.

T.

1771 THOROUGHGOOD, ARGENT, Esther, William and John.

1772 TOOLEY, JACOB, Catherine.

1776 TOOLEY, NATHANIEL, Ann, Cornelius, Ephraim, Levi, Mary, Sarah, Jeremiah and Sarah.
1781 TYSON, AARON, Mourning (wife), John.
1786 TYSON, DANIEL, Richard, Mary, Zachariah, Elizabeth, John, Levi, Hosea and Rebecca.
1794 TOOLEY, JOHN, John and Thomas.
1794 THORINTON, THOMAS, Joseph, Minnie, Mary, Susanna and Clark.
1798 TOOLEY, THOMAS, Alfred, Anson, Anthony, Clinton and Thomas.
1798 TOOLEY, LEWIS, Dinah, Nathaniel, Sarah and Sidney.
1798 TOOLEY, CORNELIUS, Anthony, James, Elizabeth, James and Levi.
1798 TOOLEY, JEREMIAH, Nathaniel, Laban and Agnes.

W.

1770 WINDLEY, JOHN, Samuel, Maple, Churchill, Smith and Moses.
1770 WINDLEY, ELIZABETH, Samuel, Churchill, Seth, Maple, Moses, Isaac and Dorcas.
1770 WILKINSON, WM., William R., Sabra, Dinah, Shadrack and Sarah.
1770 WEBSTER, WM., Katharine, William, John, James, Elizabeth and Pembroke.
1773 WILLIAMS, JOSEPH, Winnie, Lucretia, James, Judea, Hopkins, William, Elizabeth (wife), Elizabeth.
1774 WEBSTER, PEMBROKE, James, Elizabeth and John.
1780 WILKINSON, ISAIAH, Jacob, Elizabeth, Isaac, and Aaron.
1783 WILKINSON, JAMES, James, Charity, Fred, Jesse, John, Robert, Rebecca, Anna, Martha, Oden, Sarah D., Richard and Lydia.
1784 WILKINS, LITTLETON, John, Edmond, Patrick, Rotheus and Francis.
1784 WINFIELD, ROBERT, Wealthy (wife), Richard, Ann, Ohadiah, Elizabeth, John, Abigail, Hannah, William and James.
1785 WILKINS, FRANCIS, Patrick, John, Edmond, Respess, Margaret and Fanny.
1786 WILKINSON, JESSE, Fred, James, Oden, Richard, Sarah, Martha, Elizabeth, Rebecca, Ann, John and Robert.
1786 WRIGHT, WM., John, Elizabeth, Richard, Sally and Sarah.
1788 WORMINGTON, SAMUEL, Mary (wife), Edward, Rebecca, Mary, Britannia, Elizabeth, Dorcas and Nanny.
1788 WINFIELD, JOHN, Susanna; Children of Richard.
1789 WHITE, CALEB, Caleb, Joseph, Henry, Kader, Lydia, Sarah and Prudence.
1795 WINFIELD, JOHN, Richard, Jesse, Bryan, Robert, Davis, William and Winifred.
1796 WILKINS, BENJAMIN, Jacob, Mourning and Mary.
1796 WORMINGTON, BRITTANIA, Mary and Elizabeth.
1797 WRIGHT, THOMAS, Martha, Thomas and Nancy.

1799   WILKINS, THOMAS, Susanna, William, John
       and Elizabeth.
1799   WINFIELD, RICHARD, Patty, Lucretia, Rebec-
       ca, Margaret, Sally, Nancy, Richard   and
       Peggy.

JOHNSTON—WILLS

A.

1800 ADAMS, HOWELL, Elizabeth (wife); children (not named).

1787 AVERA, THOMAS, Mary (wife); William, Kedar, Anne, Edith, Mary, Winifred, Bathsheba, Zilpah and Thomas.

1761 AVERA, THOMAS, Judith (wife); Alex, Thomas John, Moses, William, Isaac and Mary.

1791 ATKIN, EPHRAIM, Mary (wife); James, Mary, Betsy, Sally, Thomas and Peter.

1795 AVERA, WM., Rachel (wife); Pheraba, Lewrany (Lorena), Sarah and Cynthia.

B.

1780 BRYAN, WM., Wife; Esther, Elizabeth and John.

1790 BOYKIN, SOLOMON, Judah (wife); William, Polly, Edea and Zilpha.

1787 BAILEY, HENRY, Tanice (wife); Phoebe, Milly and Hardy.

1794 BRADY, JOHN, Elisha (Eliza), (wife); Blake, Milly and Grace.

1788 BURCH, ROBERT, Mary (wife); Gideon and Senath.

1792 BALLINGER, JOHN, Elizabeth (wife); Polly, Readon and Sally.

1787 BULL, HENRY, Mary (wife); Barney, William, Elizabeth and Esther.

1797 BRIDGERS, BENJAMIN, Rebecca (wife); Elizabeth, Sally, Winifred, Joseph, Silas, Benjamin, William and Blake.

1796 BRIDGERS, ETHELDRED, Sally (wife).

C.

1793 CARTER, MATTHEW, Rachel (wife); Ervin, Zilphia, Lydia, Ada, William, Charlotte, and Kindred.

D.

1796 DUCK, JACOB, Sarah (wife); John, Lydia, Mary, Fanny, Milly and Elizabeth.

1794 DAVIS, ARTHUR, Elizabeth (wife); Betsy.

E.

1789 EDWARDS, WM., Elizabeth (wife), Sampson, Thomas, Micah, William, Stephen, Benjamin, Martha and Elizabeth.

F.

1793 FOLSOM, EDITH, Samuel, William, Barbara, Edith, Celia, Elizabeth, Esther and Ann.

1795 FISH, WM., Sarah (wife); Sally, Abby and James.

G.

1790 GILES, NATHANIEL, Charity (wife); John and other children (not named).

1795 GURLEY, EDWARD, wife; Jeremiah, Davis, Keziah, Alley.

1797 GODWIN, EDMOND, Edmond, Theophilus, Zilphia, Solomon, Mary, and Patience.

1792 GURLEY, MARY, William, Jacob, Tron, Rebecca, Lida, John and Polly.

1760 GURLEY, JOHN, Keziah (wife); Joseph, Nathan, Lucy, Rachel, Milea, Winea, Sunow and Esther.

1774 GURLEY, JOHN, Elizabeth (wife), Louis, Lazarus, Jeremiah, George, Joel and Edward.

H.

1791 HOLDER, JAMES, Elizabeth (wife); Jonathan, Josiah, Prudence, James, John.

1791 HOCUT, WM., Sapphira (wife); William B., Sarah and Elizabeth.

1793 HOWELL, ELISHA, Marion (wife); Elizabeth.

J.

1793 JERNIGAN, ANN, Lewis, Elizabeth, Belinda, Jemima and Jacob.

1791 JOHNSON, TRAVIS, wife; David, Keziah.

1787 JERNIGAN, JASPER, Martin.

L.

1800 LOCKHART, JAMES, Hannah (wife); Benjamin, Thomas, Cary, Elam, Joel, James, Britain, Stephen, Osborn, Patsy, Edey and Cary.

1774 LEE, ROBERT, Elizabeth (wife); Godfrey and Winifred.

1790 LYNCH, JAMES, Elizabeth (wife); Cornelius.

1768 LEE, JOHN, Mary (wife); Robert, John, Thomas, Fred, Mary, Sabra.

M.

1793 McCLENNY, JAMES, Patsy (wife); Samuel, Moses, James, William and John.

N.

1786 NOWELL, JOHN, Mara (wife); Eliza, John, James, Fetherboy and Elizabeth.

1792 NORRIS, JOHN, Sarah, Annie, Nabor, James, John and Naomi.

1790 NEWSOM, JOHN, Patience (wife); Zilpah, Elizabeth, Bethana, Joel and Sarah.

O.

1792 OLIVER, JOHN, Sarah (wife); Thomas, Henry, Mitchell, John, Elizabeth, Eleanor.

P.

1793 PEACOCK, SAMUEL, Cicily (wife); Moses, Samuel, John, Isham, Abraham.

1792 PEARCE, ARTHUR, Mary (wife); Theophilus, Winifred, Mourning, Jesse and Everett.

1790 PEARCE, RICHARD, Sarah (wife); Everett, Ephraim, Richard, John, Martha, Philip, Unity, Simon.

1789 PRICE, EDWARD, Samuel Price (grandson) son of daughter Winnie.

1792 MASON, MARK, Jenjamin and Mark.

1794 MANNING, RICHARD, James.

1792 MANN, THOMAS, Allen and Denton.

R.

1791 REAVES, FREDERICK, Betty (wife); Lydia, Cynthia.

S.

1793 STEPHENS, REBEKAH, Hayes, Samuel (brother), and Jernigan, Phebe (sister).

1795 SMITH, SAMUEL, Susanna (wife); John, Bryan, Esther, Elizabeth, Jane.

1794 STEVENSON, SOLOMON, Sarah (wife); Patty, James, David and John.

1783 SMITH, SAMUEL, John, David, Jonathan, Alexander, Jane, Edith, Samuel.

1793 SMITH, BRITAIN, William and Gideon (brothers).

1795 STANCILL, JOHN, wife; Randolph M., John D.

1793 STEVENS, REBEKAH, Samuel Mays, (brother).

T.

1799 TUCKER, WM., wife; William.

1791 TALTON, WM., Elizabeth (wife); Patience, Hardy, Rachel, James, Sally, William, John and Arthur.

W.

1780 WILLOUGHBY, RICHARD, Margaret (wife); Solomon, Edward, Anthony, Richard and Anna.

1792 WILKINSON, CHARLES, William, Benjamin, Reuben, Charles, Elkanah, Ann, Micajah, Nathan and Rowland.

Y.

1774 YOUNGBLOOD, HENRY, Mary Ann (wife); William, Aley, Mary and Ann.

JONES COUNTY—WILLS

A.

1795. February. AHAIR, JOHN, Pheraba (sister).

1797 May. AMYETT, VINCENT, Susanna (wife); Amos, John and Darius.

1798 May. ANDREWS, ADAM, Elizabeth (wife); Adam, Peter, John, Elizabeth and Daniel.

1789 December. ANDREWS, PETER, Samuel, Peter, Adonijah, John, David, Penina, Vicey and Lucy.

1780 April. AUSTIN, JOHN, Sarah (wife); Mary, John, Edmund and Abner.

1788 September. AMIET (Amyett), PETER, Mary (wife); Elizabeth, John, Vincent and Shadrach.

1808 February. ANTWINE (Antoine), ANDREW, Diana (wife); and 12 children (not named).

B.

1786 September. BLACKWELL, ALEXANDER, Agnes (wife); James, Elisha and Abraham; Eleanor Bailey and Sarah Clifton (daughters).

1788 December. BOGUE, ROBERT, Jesse, Josiah, Rhoda, Mark, Job and William; Lydia Draper (daughter).

1793 August. BLACKSHEAR, AGNES, Alexander (husband).

1794 May. BUSICK, JAMES, Margaret (wife); James.

1793 November. BUMP, ELIZABETH, William Griffith (son).

1793 November. BUMP, JABEZ, Elizabeth (wife).

1796 May. BARNETT, WILLIAM, Mary (wife); James, John, Jesse, Ann and Rachel.

1788 December. BLACKSHEAR, JAMES, Edward, David, Elijah, Penelope and Joseph; Betsy Bryan and Susan Bryan (daughters).

1791 April. BOGUE, MARK, Sarah (wife); Jonathan.

1794 May. BUSICK, MITCHELL, Mary, Penelope and Samuel.

1786 July. BLOUNT, FRANCIS, Hannah, Mary, James, Rachel and Susanna.

1797 August. BROWN, EDWARD, Aaron, Hardy, Moose, Daniel, Edward and John.

1798 August. BRYAN, NATHAN, Nathan, James R., John T., Needham and Winifred; Mary Croom and Nancy Lane (daughters).

1799 May. BECTON, MICHAEL, Mary (wife); William M., John B., Ann E., Polly, Fred and Bryan.

*1799 February. BUSH, WILLIAM, Penelope (wife); William L.; Levin, Hard, Penelope and Mary. ✗

1801 May. BRYAN, FREDERICK, Susanna (wife), Elizabeth, Council and Frederick.

1804 February. BROWN, JOHN, Rebecca (wife), Richard, Sally, John R. and Polly.

1804 May. BROWN, WILLIAM, Rhoda (wife), Samuel and Dempsey; Leroy Brown (grandson).

1808 February. BURNET, JOHN, Sally, Patty, Betsy and Bathsheba.

✗ also dau. Elizabeth & sons Lewis B & Nathan Bush.

1796 May. BRYAN, LEWIS, Mary (wife), Hardy, John, Lewis and William; Elizabeth Ventress (daughter); Lovick Ventress (grandson).

1809 August. BARRETT, THOMAS, Nancy (wife), Polly, Fanny and Aples.

1802 September. BECTON, MARY, John, Fred and William.

C.

1782 June. CIARK, GEORGE, Mary (wife), Elizabeth; Elisha (brother).

1783 March. CAHOON, JOHN, Appolonia (wife), Dudley, Susanna, Benjamin and Daniel.

1786 September. COX, ELISHA, Elizabeth (wife), Bryan, Marmaduke, John H., Abner and Hezekiah.

1782 March. COLVERT, JOHN, Tamar (wife), John, James, Isaac, William, Mary, Barbara, Winnifred and Charity; Nancy Mallard and Elizabeth Anderson (daughters).

1793 November. CHANCE, REBECCA, Thomas Dillahunty (friend).

1792 May. CLIFTON, EZEKIEL, Sarah (wife), Ezekiel; Nathan and Daniel.

1798 November. CORDEMAN, BARNARD, Margaret (wife), Fred, Eliza, John, George and Catherine.

1798 August. CONNER, JOHN, Rebecca (wife), John, Jesse, Silas and Daniel.

1812 July. COLLINS, BENJAMIN, Martha (wife), Elsie, Fanny, Martha, Hardy and Benjamin.

1805 February. CRUTCHFIELD, ANN, Richard, Philip and Eusebius; Mary Hazzard (daughter); James Hill (son).

D.

1788 June, DIAS. WILSON, Ann (wife), Children (not named).

1796 May. DIAS, WILSON, Ann (wife), Children (not named).

1794 May. DULIN, RICE, Mary (wife), Elizabeth, Mary, Nancy and Sarah.

1792 August. DULIN, THOMAS, Mary (wife), Reuben, Lod, Thomas and Asa.

1802 May. DUDLEY, ABRAHAM, Ruth (wife), Abraham, Betsy, Clarissá, Ruth and Jacob; Fanny Fisher (daughter).

1807 August. DUDLEY, THOMAS, Mary (wife), Elsie, Elizabeth, George N., Fanny, Thomas, Elijah; Cassie (Cassandra) Watson (daughter).

E.

1781 December. EDWARDS, SIMON, Sarah (wife), Asa, Winnifred, Zilpha and Frazer.

1776 July. EUBANKS, THOMAS, Rachel (wife), Thomas, Elijah and Daniel; Rachel Shepard and Rebecca Marker (daughters).

F.

1784 September. FIELDS, RICHARD, Mary (wife), James, Catherine and Nancy.

1786 March. FOY, JACOB, Elizabeth (wife), Fred.

1789 December. FOY, THOMAS, Elizabeth (wife), Fred and James (brothers); Fred Foy (nephew).

1797 May. FEARN, SARAH, Millicent; Travis Fearn (sister).

1789 August. FRAZAR, MICAJAH, Mary (wife), Urban, James, Lipsey, Lot, Lettice and Sarah; Nancy Sanderson and Aples Mattocks (daughters).

1791 December. FRANKS, WYCKLIFFE, Mary (wife), Mary and Betsy.

1790 September. FURR, THOMAS, Mary (wife), Penelope, Mary, Elizabeth, Ann and Sarah; Melissa Travers, (daugter).

1800 May. FOY, THOMAS, Lucy (wife), Thomas.

G.

1781 September. GILBERT, WILLIAM, Priscilla (wife), William and another son (not named).

1782 March. GILBERT, BENJAMIN, Mary (wife), John, Benjamin and Joseph.

1784 March. GUNTER, JOHN, Lucy (wife), Charles, Wiley, Nancy, John, Lucy, Isham, Thomas, Samuel, Mary and Joshua.

1784 June. GILBERT, JOSEPH, Mary (wife); Mary Ann Gregory (daughter); heirs of son Benjamin.

1796 May. GRAY, ISRAEL, William, Benjamin, Joab, Joseph and Thomas.

1791 May. GRANADE, JOHN, Ann (wife), John A., Anna and Huldah; Elizabeth Sanderson (daughter).

1791 May. GRIMES, ROBERT, Rebecca (wife), Nancy.

1781 September. GOODEN, (GOODWIN), AARON, Rebecca (wife), Fred, Daniel, James G. and Barden; Mary Adams and Elizabeth Cox (daughters).

1779 October. GRIFFITH, DANIEL, Esther, William, Barsheba, Sarah, Nancy, Ruth and John.

1779 November. GUNTER, RICHARD, Elizabeth (wife), William, John, Martin, Francis and Charles.

1778 February. GRAY, JOSEPH C., Zilpha (wife), Elizabeth and Israel.

1799 November. GRANADE, JOSEPH, SR, Margaret (wife), Stephen, Joseph, Nancy, John and Sally; Elizabeth McAlister, Barsheba Wood and Celia Wallace (daughters).

1801 May. GREEN, JAMES, Mary (wife), James, John, Joseph, Thomas and Nancy; Eleanor George and Hannah Lavender (daughters).

1803 May. GOODING, MOSES, Mary (wife), Francis, William and Council; Fred (brother).

1806 February. GRAY, WILLIAM G., Priscilla (wife).

1807 May. GILES, JOHN, Amy (wife); Nancy, Charity, William, Jacob and Richard; Polly Oliver (daughter).

H.

1783 December. HAMILTON, DAVID, Margaret, Anna, Martha and Hance.

1784 December. HUGGINS, LUKE, Nelly (wife), James, Luke, Isaac, Jacob, Esther, Hannah, Thomas, Charles and Temperance; Phoebe Shelfer, Sarah Standley and Nellie Littlejohn (daugters).

1790 December. HATCH, LEMUEL, Sarah (wife); Edmuhd, Sarah, Mary, Lemuel, Benjamin and Lucy.

1794 February. HALL, JOHN, Ann (wife), John.

1796 May. HOWARD, TITUS, Sarah (wife), Rhoda, Elizabeth, Salome, John, Titus, Sarah and Huldah; Ann Mundyne (daughter).

1796 May. HAY, THOMAS, Mary (wife), Elsa, William, Joseph, George, Charles, John, Thomas and Absalom.

1795 November. HARRISON, DANIEL, Celia (wife), Abner, William, Willis, Jones and May.

1793 November. HARRIS, JEREMIAH, Amelia (wife), Elijah, Mary, Anna and Joseph.

1789 March. HATCH, EDMUND, Mary (wife), Lucy, Hardy, Edward, Andrew and Polly.

1792 February. HARRISON, JAMES, Wife (not named) William, Edward, James, John, Stephen, Richard, Levi, Ephraim and Lurana; Anna Andrews (daughter).

1793 May. HARRISON, JOHN, Susanna (wife), John, Cyrene, Harmon and Elizabeth.

1778 April. HIGGINS, WILLIAM, Dorothy (wife), James, Michael, Edward, William, James, Curtis and Mary.

1797 November. HARGRETT, PETER, Ann (wife), William, Peter, Bryan, Barbara and Susanna; Hester Kornegay (daughter).

1797 September. HARRISON, WILLIAM, Elizabeth (wife), Joseph, Benjamin, Penelope, Ann and Simmons; Elizabeth Bryan, Sussanna Bryan, Mary Spight and Rebecca Isler (daughters).

1793 November. HATHAWAY, ISAAC, Eleanor (wife).

1799 February. HARBERT, WILLIAM, Priscilla (wife); Susanna Chance and Sarah Williams (daughters).

1802 August. HAY, CHARLES, Absalom; John and Thomas (brothers).

1788 April. HARRISON, JOHN, Susanna (wife); John, Thomas, Harmon, Cyrene and Elizabeth.

1772 March. HILL, SAMUEL, Mary (wife); Sarah (mother).

1793 November. HARRIS, ZEMERIAH, Amelia (wife), Elijah, Mary Anne and Joseph.

I.

1784 December. IPOCK, JACOB, Prudence (wife), William, Jacob, Phaltie and Christian.

1784 December. ISLER, FRED, Sarah (wife), John; William Isler (nephew).

1784 December. ISLER, WILLIAM, Hester (wife), Elizabeth, Pheraba and William; Anne Hargett (daughter).

1786 March. ISLER, SARAH, Lewis; William Bryan, Nathan Bryan and Isaac Bryan (sons); Mary Hatch (daughter); Ann and James Lewis (grandsons).

J.

1798 August. JACKSON, JOHN, Sarah (wife), James, John and Thomas; Sarah Gerator (daughter).

1796 February. JONES, JAMES, Ann (wife); Allen, Aretas, Rial, Ann, Aurelius, Sylva, Miranda Ellen and Elvira.

1795 February. JONES, WILLIAM, John James, Milly, Vines, Hardy, Fred and William; Nancy Smith and Jean Thomas (daughters).

1795 November. JOHNSON, COLLINSON, Leah (wife), Joseph, Robert and Edward; Margaret Warters, Mary Granade and Nanny Bootey (daughters).

1802 February. JONES, JAMES, Sarah (wife), Elizabeth, Fred, Sarah, Ezekiel, Mary, Elijah, Basil and Jacob.

1792 February. JONES, HARDY, Barbara (wife), Lavinia.

1794 May. JARMAN, HALL, Ann (wife), Mary and McClondal.

1808 May. JOHNSON, JAMES, Barbara (wife), Randal, Amos and Nathan; Lucy Williams and Mourning Doty (daughters).

K.

1782 September. KOONCE, MICHAEL, Elizabeth (wife), Richard, Emanuel, Alice and Mary.

1782 September. KING, MARY, Robert, Sarah and Elizabeth.

1784 June. KOONCE, JACOB, Martha (wife); Benjamin, Martha, Sarah, William and Abram.

1784 June. KORNEGAY, DAVID, Lettice (wife); Robert and Sarah.

1786 March. KORNEGAY, LETTICE, Robert and Sarah.

1791 May. KOONCE, JOHN, Catherine (wife); John, George, Rachel and Barbara; Ann Bender; Lishey (Melissa) Brown and Catherine Gilbert (daughters).

1795 May. KOONCE, CHRISTIAN, Philopena (wife); Fred.

1800 August. KORNEGAY, JOHN, Rachel (wife); Isaac, Abraham, Jacob and Susanna.

1802 November. KORNEGAY, DANIEL, Matilda (wife); Hepsibah and Dovey.

1801 August. KING, SAMUEL, Samuel, David, Nancy, Levarty, George, Rebecca and William.

L.

1785 June. LITTLETON, THOMAS, Siniah (wife).

1795 February. LIPSEY, ARTHUR, Barsheba (wife); Roscoe, Marmaduke, Barsheba, Huldah and Richardson.

1794 February. LIPSEY, JAMES Mary (wife); three children (not named).

1794 May. LIPSEY, TIMOTHY, Fanny (wife); Wealthy (daughter).

1792 May. LITTLETON, THOMAS, Mary (wife); William; Leah Johnson (daughter).

1780   May. LAVENDER, WILLIAM, William L., Melissa, Benjamin and Levin.

1792   February. LIPSEY, WILLIAM, John, James, Elijah, William, Elizabeth, Abigail, Isaac, William and Archbell.

1800   August. LEE, JOHN B. Rebecca (wife); Sally, Stephen, John and Pheraba.

1802   November. LAVENDER, WILLIAM, Hannah (wife); John and Levin.

M.

1783   March. McQUILLEN, ALEX, Sarah (wife); Philip.

1786   December. MORRIS, WILLIAM, Sarah (wife); William and Daniel; Sarah Dillahunty, Milly Smyth and Mary Gregory (daughters).

1788   March. MOORE, MATTHEW, Abigail and Wallace.

1796   February. MACKEY, ISAAC, Jean (wife); Samuel.

1794   August. MORRINSON, DANIEL, John Wilkinson, William Gardner and Lewis Bryan (friends).

1794   February. MEAD, THOMAS, Hannah (wife); Thomas, Tryphena, Barbara and Rachel; Hannah Collins (daughter).

1793   November. MESSER, BENJAMIN, Robert (brother).

1792   May. MUNDINE, JOHN, Sarah (wife).

1794   November. MEDDOR, ABSALOM, Fanny (wife); Sarah and John and two other sons (not named).

1797   February. MUNDINE, MAGDALEN, Mark, Buck and Berry; Rachel Jones and Pheraba Gibson (daughters).

1794   August. MORRISON, DANIEL, John Wilkin-George, Freezan, Fred, Nathan, Levin and Hardy.

1789   March. MILLER, TOBIAS, Mary (wife); Daniel, James, Martha and Lewis.

1792   May., MOORE, JOHN, Mary (wife); Sarah, Mary, Amelia, Judith and Gideon.

1791   November. MEW, PHILIP, John, Renny, Tabitha and Neamy (Nehemiah).

1791   August. MUNDINE, KITTRELL, Mary (wife); Charles, Sarah, James, Francis and Benjamin.

1798   February. MEAD, RACHEL, Hannah Mead (mother); Barbara Mead and Hannah Collins (sisters).

1799   May. MUNDINE, SARAH, Sarah, Mary and Cassandra; Clarissa Shine and Mary Lavender (daughters).

1801   August. MILLER, GEORGE, Elizabeth (wife); Stephen; Sarah Houston and Mary Houston (daughters).

1794   May. McCABINS, SAMUEL, Edward.

N.

1796   August. NELMS, JEREMIAH, Fanny (wife); Elsie and Sarah.

O.

1787   June. OLIVER, JOHN, Anne (wife); Rigsdon, Ann and William.

1799   March. ORME, ROBERT, William, Jane, Deborah and Lettice; Margaret Work (daughter); Betty Wickliff (granddaughter).

P.

1781   September. PRITCHARD, JEREMIAH, Mary (wife); Clement, Basil, Caleb and Sarah.

1782   June. PICKREN, MOSES, Sarah, (wife); William (son) and daughters (not named).

1782   September. PRITCHARD, CALEB, Basil, Clement and Sarah (brothers and sisters).

1786   December. PYBAS, HENRY, Mary (wife); John, Nancy, Catren (Catherine) and John.

1796   March. PARREY, WILLIAM, Ruth (wife); Benjamin.

1791   November. PRESCOTT, MOSES, Aaron (brother).

1789   November. PERKINS, REUBEN, Jemima (wfe); Daniel and Anna.

1780   April. PRESCOTT, THOMAS, Mary (wife); Mases and Aaron.

1800   February. PARREY, WAXIL, Sibyl (wife); Ailsa, Betsy, Catherine and Fred.

1800   May. PARREY, JOHN, SR. Sibyl (wife); John, Adonijah and Sibyl; Frances Smith and Zeruiah Koonce (daughters).

1779   April. PATE, EDMUND, Elizabeth (wife).

1799   December. PICKREN, RICHARD, Jemima (wife); Daniel, Annie and Naaman.

Q.

1785   September. QUILLING, DAVID, Eleanor (wife); Mary, Rachel, Daniel and John.

R.

1785   March. REYNOLDS, JAMES, Penelope (mother); Nancy (sister).

S.

1804   SHAW, CATHERINE, Daniel, John and Malcolm.

1803   STORM, USRY, Mary Sessoms and Margaret Purnell (daughters).

1795   SMITH, LUCY, Malcolm.

1780   STONE, BENJAMIN, William.

1792   SMITH, JOHN, Mother (not named); Margaret and Thomas (children).

1797   SALTER, SARAH, Brothers and sisters, George, John, William, and Jonathan Thomas; Elizabeth Purnell, Mary Crowson, Susanna Russ and Nancy McCullock (sisters).

1795   SALTER, RICHARD, Ann (wife); Mary Ann, Richard, John and James.

1796   SALTER, RICHARD, Ann (wife); William J. Mary and James.

1804   SMITH, SAMUEL, Mary (wife).

1797   SALTER, WILLIAM, Sarah (wife); Sarah, Ann and Margaret.

1786 SMITH, SAMUEL, Sophia (wife); Mary and John.

1765 SINGLETARY, BENJAMIN, Elizabeth (wife); Joseph, John, Richard, Benjamin and James.

1778 SANDERS, CHRISTOPHER, Sarah (wife); Thomas, Christopher, Sarah, Amelia, Elvira and Elizabeth.

1785 SINGLETARY, WILLIAM, Mary (wife); William and Council.

1783 SMITH, RICHARD, Lucy (wife); Elizabeth, Mary, Sarah, Tabitha, Tryon, Noble and Massey.

1771 STEWART, HUGH, Catherine (wife); Robert (brother).

1790 SINGLETARY, BREYTON, Mary (wife); Joseph, Deborah and Benjamin.

1792 SINGLETARY, JOSEPH, Mary (wife); Joseph, Sarah and Mary.

1792 SINGLETARY, RICHARD, William Singletary Cunningham (grandson).

1784 SMITH, STEPHEN, Joanna (wife); six children (not named).

1775 SAMREY, HENRY, John, Henry, Edward, Mildred, Ann, Elizabeth, Mary and Lucy.

1793 SEYMOUR, SARAH, Edward; John Hale and Duncan McCullock (friends).

1772 SHIPMAN, DANIEL, Eleanor (wife); James, Daniel, Elizabeth, Eleanor and Sarah.

1780 SHAW, DANIEL, Agnes, Duncan, Malcolm, Daniel, Ann and Jane.

1777 STEWART, PATRICK, Margaret and Ann (sisters); Duncan, James and Owen (brothers).

1773 SINGLETARY, RICHARD, Joyce (wife); Richard,

1773 SINGLETARY, ITHAMAR, Carolina (wife); Ithanat, Elizabeth, Deborah and Mary.
Benjamin, William and Mary.

1770 STAREN, WANDAL, John, Margaret and Mary.

1781 SMITH, JOHN, John, James, Thomas, Jonathan and Elizabeth.

1778 STEWART, WILLIAM, Wife (not named); Charles, Duncan, James, Catherine, Janoth, Anne and Elizabeth; Walter Stewart (grandson).

T.

1795 TEDDER, GEORGE, Mary (wife); Jesse and Thomas.

1796 TEDDER, GEORGE, SR. Sarah (wife); Sarah, George and William.

1796 THOMAS, GEORGE, Margaret (wife); Francis, Ann, Mary, John and Margaret.

1786 THOMAS, JOSEPH, Martha (wife); Jesse, Thomas, Joseph, William, John and Samuel.

V.

1760 VERNON, ANNE, Thomas and John Lucas (sons); Lillah Johnston (daughter).

W.

1797 WHITE, JOHN, Jonathan White (grandson).

1800 WILLIAM, DAVID, Mary and Martha.

1793 WHITE, MATTHEW R. Catherine (wife); David.

1795 WILKERSON, WILLIAM, Charity (wife); Charles and other children (not named).

1795 WILLIAM, LEWIS, Mary (wife); Rebecca, Richard, Joshua, Seth, Nancy and Peggy.

1787 WILLIS, ROBERT, Ann (wife).

1783 WHITE, WILLIAM, Mary (wife); children (not named).

1793 WEATHERSBEE, CADE, Elizabeth, Absalom, Oliver, Jane, Isham, Owen and Shadrach; Martha Hollingsworth; Mary Sikes and Lucy McLean, (daughters).

1792 WILLIS, BETTY, Jacob, Am, Sarah, Diana, Elizabeth, Daniel and John.

1766 WADDELL, MARY, Hugh, Haynes and John Burgwyn (sons); John Burgwyn (brother).

1770 WHITE, JOHN, Mary (wife); Griffith, John, William, David, Mary, Ann, Matthew and James Jane Kemp (daughter).

1785 WHITE, HENRIETTA, William; Lucy Brown (daughter).

1784 WILLIS, DANIEL, Elizabeth (wife); Daniel and John.

1772 WILSON, JOSIAH, Wife (not named); George, John and Ambrose.

1768 WHITE, THOMAS, Ann (wife); Joseph, Sarah and Mary.

1784 WHITE, JOSEPH, Henrietaa (wife); Sarah McRee (niece); William Jones (son-in-law); Mary Winslow (sister).

1772 WADDELL, HUGH, Mary (wife); John, Hugh and Burgwyn; John Burgwyn (brother-in-law and friend); Hannah Waddell (sister).

TRYON AND LINCOLN—WILLS

A.

1790 ABERNETHY, MILES, to wife and children. Robert, William, Charles, Julian, Miles, Sarah, Nathan, and Lucy Cox.

1772 ABERNATHY, ROBERT, to Miles.

1777 AKER, CHRISTIAN, to Eve, Peter, Christian and Daniel.

1779 ARMSTRONG, FRANCIS, to James and Matthew Leeper.

1784 ARNEY, JACOB, to Elizabeth and children.

1790 ABERNETHY, MILES, to wife and children.

1795 ASHABRANNON, URBAN, to children (not named).

1796 ARTHUR, SAMUEL, to Mary, John, Joseph, Samuel, Arthur.

1797 ANTHONY, PHILIP, to John, Paul, George, Daniel, Benjamin, Magdalena.

1769 ABERNETHY, DAVID, to wife Mary and children.

1790 AKER, PETER, to Mike.

1802 ALEXANDER, WILLIAM, to John and James.

1802 ALEXANDER, WALLACE, to Henderson, Lawson and Sallie Carolina.

1804 ATKINSON, JOSEPH, to Mary, William, Burrows, Harriet.

1807 ADERHOLT, FRED WM., to Mary Elizabeth, John C., John G., Jacob.

1807 ARENDS, JOHN GOTTFRIED, to Arends, John, Jacob, Frederick.

1813 ADAMS, JOHN, to William, Robert, Samuel, John.

1813 ALEXANDER, ROBERT, to Eliza, Evalina, Charity, Amanda.

1814 ABERNETHY, DAVID, to Ann, Miles.

1816 ABERNETHY, JOHN, to Jeremiah, Hurley, Bary, Clayton, Larkin and Polly.

1818 ALEXANDER, MARGARET, to Eliza, Evalina, Charity, Amanda.

1820 ARMSTRONG, ROBERT, to Hugh, Sarah.

1821 ALLEN, JOHN, to John, Phoebe.

1821 ABERNATHY, HERBERT, to Susanna, John, Turner, Miles.

B.

1770 BULLINGER, HENRY, to Elizabeth, Susanna, Magdaline, Sophia, George, Henry, David, Abraham, Joseph, Daniel.

1771 BOUNDS, GEORGE, to Adams, Francis.

1778 BRADLEY, JOHN, to Mary.

1780 BLACKWOOD, JOSEPH, to John, James, William.

1784 BAIRD, JOHN, to James, Adam, Witherspoon, Eleanor.

1786 BAKER, JACOB, to Susanna, Philip, Jacob, Michael, Henry, Conrad, John, Susanna, Catherine.

1786 BEATTY, THOMAS, to Margaret, John, Thomas.

1788 BRADSHAW, FIELD, to Judith, Benjamin, Charles, Joseph.

1788 BEATHY, JOHN, Elizabeth, William.

1789 BAIRD, FRANCIS, to eight children, no names.

1791 BRIDGERS, JOHN, to Margaret, Elisha.
1793 BORLAND, JOHN, to Christina, Mary, Elizabeth.
1794 BAKER, ENDYMION, to his children (not named).
1794 BARNES, JOHN, to John.
1794 BOLCH, ADAM, to Christina, Godfrey, Sebastian, Jasper, Adam, Elizabeth.
1794 BARNETT, SAMUEL, Thomas and James.
1797 BALLARD, LEWIS, to Elizabeth.
1800 BAKER, ABRAHAM, to Katie.
1806 BRADSHAW, CHARLES, to Pride.
1800 BORDERS, JOHN, to Catherine.
1802 BYNUM, SAMUEL, to Gray, William, Turner.
1803 BRADSHAW, FIELD, to Hannah, Annie and Isaac.
1803 BRIDGERS, ELISHA, to John, James, Elisha, Alfred.
1804 BEALK, JOHN, to Susannah, John, Lydia.

C.

1774 COLLINS, JOHN, to Phoebe and children.
1775 CLEGHORN, WILLIAM, to Lettice, Rebecca, Jane, Mary, William, James, and John.
1781 CATHEY, JAMES, to Martha.
1782 CARRUTH, ADAM, to wife and children (no names).
1784 CAMPBELL, THOMAS, to Rachel, Robert, Elizabeth.
1786 CHRONICLE, WILLIAM, to Dinah (Scott), William and John.
1787 CLUBB, PETER, to Peter and others.
1787 CHILDERS, ROBERT, to wife (no name).
1789 COOPER, ISAAC, to Dinah, Mary.
1789 CLARK, CORNELIUS, to William, Cornelius.
1789 CARSON, JOHN, to Catherine (wife), and child.
1790 COLLINS, SAMUEL, to wife and children.
1792 CLINE, BOSTIAN, to Elizabeth and children.
1794 COCHRAN, JOHN, to Rebecca and children.
1795 CLARK, JAMES, to Alex, James, John, Christopher, David.
1796 COOK, JOHN, to Catanira, George, Peter, Jacob.
1796 COBB, AMBROSE, to William, James.
1798 COUNTZ, NICHOLAS, to Elizabeth and John.
1799 COLLINS, JAMES, to Betsy, James B.
1799 CARSON, ANDREW, to James, Andrew, William, Samuel.
1800 CARPENTER, CHRISTIAN, to Frederick.
1800 CHERRY, DAVID, to David, Robert, William.
1800 CORNELIUS, WILLIAM, to Benjamin, Abner.
1802 CLUBB, PETER, to Anthony.
1800 COOPER, DINAH, to Isaac Bonn.
1803 CLAY, NICHOLAS, to Isaac.

D.

1794 DARR, LORENZ, to John, Andrew.
1794 DICKSON, JOHN, to William.
1804 DILLON, JOHN, to Henry.
1805 DYER, JANUAH, to Adiah, Elizabeth, Patsy, Hannah and Adrah, and Martin Collins.
1805 DECKER, CHRISTOPHER, to Christopher.
1808 DAVIS, ALLEN, to Susan and children.

E.

1781 EWART, ROBERT, to Margaret and children.
1803 ECKART, ADAM, to wife and children.
1803 EATON, WILLIAM, Sarah (wife); John, William, Rebecca, Phenix, Henry; also Brown, Bertha; Stowe, Sarah; Hunt, Elizabeth; Shaw, Ann; Williams, Milly and Elizabeth; Barrett, Thomas.
   John, Elisha, Millis, Ann, Mary and Diana.
1805 EWART, MARGARET, to children and grandchildren.

F.

1784 FAY, NICHOLAS. Elizabeth (wife); George, Jacob, Mary, Susanna.
1785 FISHER, STEPHEN, Elizabeth (wife); Stephen, Richard, Ezekiel, Samuel, John, Susanna, William; also to Barnes, Elizabeth; Morgan, Ann; Jones, Jemima; Allen, Mary.
1790 FRIDAY, NICHOLAS, to Mary, Andrew, Jonas; and Rudasill, Catherine.
1792 FINGER, PETER, to Daniel, Henry.
1792 FINLEY, ROBERT, to Alexander, Robert.
1795 FERGUSON, ROBERT, to Thomas, Andrew.
1798 FALLS, ANDREW, to Galbraith, William, John, George, James, Andrew.
1800 FOORDE, GEORGE, to Nathan.
1801 FEY, JACOB, to Mary and children.
1802 FINLEY, ISABEL, to James, Alexander, Robert.
1803 FELKER, MICHAEL, to Magdelena and children.
1803 FISHER, JOHN, to Joseph, George; and Barger, John.
1803 FISHER, JOHN, to Joseph, George.
1805 FRONEBARGER, WILLIAM, to William, Jacob, John.
1806 FORNEY, JACOB, to Jacob, Peter, Daniel.
1808 FULBRIGHT, WILLIAM, to Jacob.
1811 FERGUSON, ANDREW, to George and others.
1812 FRIDAY, JONAS, Elizabeth and children.
1814 FLANNAGAN, JOHN, to Susanna.
1815 FERGUSON, ROBERT, to James, Moses, John, Robert, Alexander; and Barr, Moses.

G.

1772 GREEN, JOSEPH, to Mary (wife), William, Anne, Abraham, Isaac, Mary, Jacob and Joseph.
1772 GRAY, SAMUEL, to John, James.
1776 GORDON, JAMES, to Henry, Hugh, James.
1790 GILLESPIE, JOHN, to John.
1794 GLENN, JOHN, to Blotsback, Daniel.
1795 GOLDEN, JAMES, to Margaret, Elizabeth, Hannah.
1795 GOODWIN, WILLIAM, to Abraham.
1796 GILLAND, ALEX., to John, Robert, William, Thomas.
1796 GORDIN, JEAN, to Wells, Mary and Hannah.
1799 GASTNER, JACOB, to Marelas, Robinson and James.
1803 GRAHAM, ARCHIBALD, to Archibald, Dillingham, John.
1805 GRAHAM, ARTHUR, John William, Lewis.

1805   GROVES, WILLIAM, to Samuel, Thomas.
1807   GILBERT, CONRAD, to Margaret, George, Andrew.
1813   GRAHAM, GEORGE, to McLeod, Margaret; Graham, Mary, James; Robison, Ann.

H.

1767   HUNTER, S., to Betty, Margaret and children.
1767   HANNAH, JOHN, to Mary (wife).
1774   HARMAN, JOHN, to Mary, John, Anthony and Davis.
1775   HEKER, WILLIAM, to Frederick, Simon, William and John.
1779   HENRY, JOHN, Joseph, William.
1781   HENDRY, MOSES, to John, William.
1782   HASLIP, ANDREW, to Thomas, Cherry and Mary.
1784   HILKER, GEORGE, to George, William, David, Jonathan and Simon.
1786   HENNON, JAMES, to Punch, Thomas.
1790   HAMILTON, JOHN, to Jane (wife).
1791   HOAT, MICHAEL, to Uley.
1793   HOYLE, MICHAEL, to Peter, John.
1793   HARM, JOHN, to Christian, Fred, Jacob, Utily, Sarah.
1794   HARBISON, WILLIAM, to Agnes.
1794   HARWELL, SAMUEL, to Samuel.
1795   HARMAN, PETER, to Lydia, Andrew.
1795   HENDERSON, JAMES, to Catrin, James, William, Logan; Patterson, James Henderson.
1797   HILL, JOHN, to Jean and children.
1800   HOMESLEY, JOSEPH, to John, Beryl, Polly.
1801   HAWN, JOHN, to John, Peter, Philip.
1801   HUGGINS, WILLIAM, to John and James.

I.

1785   ICARD, PETER, (Eiger, Peder), to Henry, Lawrence, Peter.
1800   IKER, HENRY, to Daniel, Henry.
1812   INGLE (ENGEL), MICHAEL, to Andrew, Henry.

J.

1786   JOHNSTON, PETER, to Duncan, John.
1796   JONAS, JOHN, to Nancy.
1805   JOHNSTON, JAMES, to Robert, James, William.
1805   JENKINS, ELIJAH, to Polly and children.
1806   JARRETT, SAMUEL, to Susanna, John, Joab, Margaret, Anne, Mary, Sarah.
1815   JOHNSTON, ROBERT, to Robert.

K.

1786   KIZER, LAWRENCE, to George, Adam.
1786   KOLE, WILLIAM, to Mary, Balzer.
1788   KILLIAN, ANDREW, to Daniel, Samuel.
1795   KILLIAN, LEONARD, to William, Mary, Margaret.
1800   KINCAID, THOMAS, to Jean.
1802   KILLIAN, ELIZABETH, to Jacob, and others.
1807   KEENER, JACOB, to John.

L.

1764 LANHAM, JOHN, to Comfort, William, Abel.
1772 LITTLE, WILLIAM, to Thomas, John, Archibald, Martha, James, Alexander.
1783 LITTLE, ALEXANDER, to John.
1791 LITTLE, THOMAS, to Lizzie, William.
1796 LEEPER, JOHN, to Elizabeth and children.
1799 LUCKEY, JAMES, to James, Hugh.
1799 LONGANIER, HENRY, to Christina, Henry, Jacob, John.
1803 LINEBARGER, PETER, to Susanna, Michael, Jacob, David, Daniel.

M.

1769 McAFFEE, JAMES, to Robert.
1770 McCORMACK, JOHN, to Agnes.
1771 MOORE, WILLIAM, to Joseph, John.
1777 McFADYEN, JOHN, to Hannah, Stephen, Alexander.
1779 MURPHY, WILLIAM, to Elizabeth, John.
1795 MURPHY, JAMES, to Elizabeth, William, Moses.
1788 MASSEY, JOHN, Winnie, Drury, William, Daniel.
1789 MORELAND, JOSEPH, to Isaac, Turner.
1790 McCURRY, WILLIAM, to Abraham.
1794 MYERS, PETER, to Daniel and Cline.
1795 MOSS, JOHN JOAB, to Polly, James, Johnson and John.
1795 McCORMICK, ANDREW, to Catharine, Joseph, Andrew.
1796 MILLER, MICHAEL, to Keener, John.
1789 McLEAN, ALEX., to Thomas.
1800 McCURRY, ABRAHAM, to Mary.
1804 McCASLAND, ROBERT, to Ramsey, Jean and others.
1805 MYERS, ELIAS, to Elizabeth.
1805 McGEE, DANIEL, to Catharine.
1806 McLEAN, MARGARET, to Charles.
1806 MAUNEY, VALENTINE, to George, Jacob, Peter.
1807 MARTIN, WILLIAM, to William, Richard, John and George.
1808 MILLER, JACOB, to Annie M. and children.
1809 McCULLOCK, MARY, to Elizabeth.
1809 MAUNEY, CATHARINE, to Adam and others.
1809 MINGES, CONRAD, to Conrad.
1812 MITCHELL, JACOB, to Mary and children.
1812 McCALL, JOHN, to Robert and William.
1813 MAUNEY, JACOB, to Nancy, Abraham, Isaac.
1814 MOSTELLER, PETER, to Maria, Daniel, Peter, John, Jonas, Magdalen, George, Jacob, Catharine, Christian and Joseph.

N.

1795 NEWMAN, MICHAEL, to Sarah.
1796 NIGH, CHRISTIAN, to Christian and others.
1801 NIXON, WILLIAM, to Elizabeth, Robert, William.
1808 NIXON, JOHN, to Sarah and children.
1800 NEFF, HENRY, to John, Adam; and Kistler, Jacob.

O.

1774 OAKS, JOHN, to Hannah and children.
1807 ORR, JOHN, to Elizabeth and John.
1811 OXFORD, SAMUEL, to James, Jacob, Isaac, and others.
1812 O'NEAL, CHRISTOPHER, to Honour (wife).
1816 O'NEAL, HONOUR, to Byrnes, Honour.

P.

1770 POTTS, JOHN, to Ezekiel, George.
1780 PATTERSON, JAMES, to Jean, John, Robert, Alexander.
1780 PLONCK, PETER, to Barbara (wife), John, Jacob, Mary, Elizabeth, Catherine, Susanna, Sarah, Barbara, Mary.
1799 PROPST, LEWIS, to Sophia (wife).
1803 PATTERSON, ARTHUR, to Elizabeth, James, Robert, Thomas.
1804 PERKINS, JOHN, to Catherine, Ephraim, John, Joseph, Alex., Eli; Miller, Mary; Snoddy, Sarah.
1806 PATTERSON, THOMAS, to Martha, James and others.
1806 POLK, HUGH, to Orr, Leah's heirs.
1806 POSTEN, DANIEL, to Sarah.
1807 PIERCE, PHILIP, to Betty (wife); Farewell, James, Jr.; Brin, Millie's children.

R.

1771 ROBINSON, DAVID, to Francis, Matthew, Molly, Israel, Isaac, Isham, James, David, Abner, Sally, John, George (nephew).
1779 RUTLEDGE, GEORGE, to Jean, James, John, George, Charles.
1784 ROBINSON, JOHN, to Elizabeth, William, John.
1786 RAMSOUR, DAVID, to Mary, John, Henry, Barbara, Daniel, David, Philip; and Shuford, Elizabeth.
1786 ROBINSON, JAMES, Catharine, Jesse, John.
1786 RUDISILL, JOHN, to Henry.
1790 RAMSAY, JOHN, to Jones, John.
1791 RATLEY, BENJAMIN, to Rebecca and others.
1792 REASE, GEORGE, to Eve, Hannah; and Scits, John, George and Henry.
1795 RUDISILL, PHILIP, to Elizabeth, Margaret.
1795 RIEL, GEORGE, to Daniel, Gottfried, Katharine.
1795 REIN, JACOB, to Elizabeth and others.
1797 RHYNE, PHILIP, to Hanna, John Michael, Jacob.
1800 REINHARDT, JACOB, to Conrad, Jacob.
1800 ROBINSON, DAVID, to Jean, James, Jesse, David, Henry.
1801 RUTLEDGE, JEAN, to Charles.
1805 RUSSELL, JAMES, to Duncan, Patrick.
1805 ROBINSON, ALEX., SR, to Joseph.
1805 RUTLEDGE, CHARLES, to George, John, William.
1808 ROBINSON, ISAAC, SR., to Catharine, Elijah, Isaac, Joshua, James, Joseph, Abraham, Jesse.
1809 REINHARDT, CONRAD, to George, Charles.
1809 RUTHERFORD, WILLIAM, to James and John.
1811 RINCK, FRANCIS, to Jacob, Andrew, John, David, Francis.
1812 RUDISILL, PHILIP, to Elijah.

S.

1771 SUMMEY, JOHN, to Moultland.
1787 SUMMEY, PETER, to Frederick, Jacob; Whitsel, Jacob.
1787 SHANNON, HUGH, to James.
1789 SPENCER, ZACHARIAH, to Ann, Elizabeth, Sarah, Zachariah, Charity, John, May, William, James, Joseph, George, Ezbal.
1790 SHUFORD, JOHN, to Daniel, David.
1791 SMITH, GEORGE, to Catherine; Potts, Michael.
1793 SHRUM, NICHOLAS, to Margaret, Henry, John, David.
1794 SEVITZ, GEORGE, to Rosnia.
1797 SEITZ, JOHN, to Sally and children.
1799 SHUTTEY, JACOB, to Adam and Andrew.
1800 SCOTT, ABRAHAM, to Margaret, Abraham, William, James.
1805 SUMNER, JOHN, to Margaret and her heirs.
1805 SPEAGLE, MARTHA, to Sarah, Daniel, John.
1805 STROUP, JACOB, to John.
1809 SCOTT, JAMES, to Mary, Abraham.
1811 SIGMON, JOHN, to Susanna.
1812 SETZER, WILLIAM, to Susanna and Anna.
1813 SHERRILL, MOSES, to Sarah, Thomas, Jr., William, Michael, Absalom.

T.

1775 TWITTY, WILLIAM, to Susanna.
1793 TRAVELSTREET, BARBARA, to William, Christian.
1794 TURNER, ANDREW, to Andrew, Daniel, Samuel.
1797 TRETT, BALLER, to Mary, Magdelene, Margaret, Samuel, Catharine, Henry, Molly.
1800 TUCKER, JOHN, to Ann, John, Samuel; and Cherry, Robert; McCaller, Robert.
1813 TORRENCE, HUGH, to John, Hugh, Matthew.

V.

1800 VENABLE, RICHARD, to Mary, John.
1811 VARNER, ELIZABETH, to Henry.

W.

1769 WELSH, JOHN, to Margaret, Rebecca, John, Margaret.
1769 WILFONG, JACOB, to Elizabeth, George, Catharine, Sarah.
1771 WATSON, JAMES, to Elee.
1774 WILLS, ALEX., to Thompson, Alexander.
1778 WATSON, WILLIAM, to Anna, Molly.
1778 WHITESIDES, WILLIAM, to Elizabeth, Francis, James.
1778 WILL, GERHARD, to Mary B., Conrad.
1784 WHISNANT, ADAM, to Barbara and children.
1787 WARD, CHARLES, to Catharine, Frederick, Melchoir, Balzer.
1788 WEARN, JACOB, to Margaret, Conrad, Jacob, Susanna, Eve, Mary, Christiana.
1791 WHISNANT, PHILIP, to Anna, Adam and others.
1792 WHITENER, HENRY, to Catherine; and also Dellinger, John, Joseph, Catherine, Barbara.

1793 WHITE, SAMUEL, to Eleanor, Francis, Samuel and Isaac.

1796 WILSON, JAMES, to Margaret (wife), Jane, James Sarah, Margaret, Elzabeth, John, Martha; also Patten, David; Hunter, Lewis; McKissick, Margaret.

1796 WHITENER, MICHAEL, to Elizabeth, Philip, Benjamin.

1796 WAGNER, CONRAD, to Eve, Nicholas.

1798 WHITLEY, GEORGE, to Margaret, Moses, Hannah.

1802 WILLOUGHBY, WILLIAM, to Mary, Catherine, David, William, and John, Jr.

1799 WILSON, JOHN, Mary, John, James, William, Samuel.

1802 WILLIAMS, CHARLES, to Richard and others.

1803 WOMACK, ABRAHAM, to James and others.

1803 WILSON, GEORGE, to John and others.

1804 WILSON, SAMUEL, to Thomas, Elizabeth, Margaret.

1804 WOODS, JOHN, to Sarah, Eleanor, Margaret.

1805 WILLIAMSON, ROBERT, to Robert and Thomas.

1807 WISE, FREDERICK, to David, John, Jacob, George, Henry.

1807 WILL, CONRAD, to Magdalen, David, Solomon, John.

1810 WEATHERS, JAMES, to Jennie, George, Elisha.

1811 WHEELER, THOMAS, to Susanna, Annie, Elizabeth, Sarah, Rachel.

1802 WILLENBERG, WILLIAM, Mary, Catharine, Daniel, William, John, Jr.

Y.

1807 YOUNT, HENRY, to Ann, John, Katie, Samuel, Susanna, Henry, Jacob, Ephraim, Sarah.

1790 YOUNT, JOHN, to Elizabeth, Henry, George, Andrew.

MARTIN—WILLS

A.

1790 ANDERSON, WILLIAM, Ann (wife), Ann, Elizabeth, William and Isham.
1793 ANDREWS, THOMAS, Henry, Thomas, Joseph.

B.

1775 BRYAN, WILLIAM, Elizabeth (wife).
1780 BLAND, THOMAS, Priscilla (wife).
1780 BOOTH, PHILIP, Elizabeth wife), Catherine.
1779 BROWN, WILLIAM, Abner.
1783 BONNER, JAMES, John, Stapleton and Miller.
1786 BRYAN, JESSE, Nathan, Sarah and Pheraba.
1789 BORDEN, ARTHUR, William and Asa.
1789 BORDEN, ELIAS, Elias, Jesse, Ann and Elizabeth.
1789 BIGGS, JAMES, Elizabeth (wife), Martha and Rhoda.
1791 BLAND, THOMAS, Thomas.
1791 BEST, THOMAS, Thomas, Henry and William.
1791 BIRD, WILLIAM, Fannie, Cottrell and Martin R.
1793 BAGGETT, THOMAS, Thomas and Uzziel.
1794 BUTERY, SYLVANUS, Thomas.
1794 BEACH, THOMAS, Elizabeth, Thomas and Hannah.
1790 BURNETT, MATTHEW, John.
1795 BENNETT, THOMAS, Silas.
1797 BRYAN, NEEDHAM, James.
1774 BRYAN, ROBERT, Elias and John.
1774 BROWN, HARDY, Elizabeth, Mary and Charity.
1774 BENTLEY. ISAAC, Sarah (wife).

C.

1780 COUNSELL, HARDY, James.
1780 CARVELL, SUSANNA, Thomas.
1781 CULPEPPER, HENRY, Jeremiah.
1781 COBB, CYNTHIA, Elizabeth and Susanna.
1783 COOPER, ELIZABETH, David.
1783 CRISP, WILLIAM, Jesse, Samuel, Benjamin and Ezekiel.
1779 COCKBURN, GEORGE, John and Frances.
1782 CONE, NOEL, Noel, Jesse, Levi and William.
1781 COKE, ROBERT, Martha, Cherry.
1785 COCKBURN, ELIZABETH, Francis.
1787 CURRELL, THOMAS, William, John and Thomas.
1787 CLAGHORN, SHUBAL, Shubal, Timothy, Thomas and Benjamin.
1788 COKE, MARY, Penelope (wife).
1788 CHERRY, FAITHFUL, James and Howell.
1789 CLAGHORN, TIMOTHY, House and Benjamin.
1789 CHERRY, ISAAC, Joel.
1792 COOK, WILLIAM, Courtney (wife), children (not named).
1793 CLEGHORN, SHUBAL, Hannah (wife).
1795 CONE, WILLIAM, Cloanna (wife), children (not named).
1795 CARNAL, THOMAS, Reuben and William.
1785 CHERRY, JAMES, John and James.
1798 COBURN, GEORGE, Frederick and Isaac.

D.

1781 DANIEL, ROBERT, James.
1786 DANIEL, ROBERT, James.
1797 DAVIS, WILLIAM, Henry, Sally and Thomas.
1795 DAY, JOHN, William.
1797 DUGGAN, AARON, John, James and Swain.

E.

1776 EVERETT, WILLIAM, SR, Saveah (wife), William, John and Samuel T.
1780 EASON, REUBEN, William and Thomas.
1780 EVERETT, JAMES T., James.
1790 EDMUNDSON, THOMAS, Pollard.
1792 EDMUNDSON, THOMAS, Nannie, Jesse and Sarah.
1794 EVERETT, JOHN, William and James.
1796 EVERETT, NATHANIEL, Miles.
1797 EDMUNDSON, REUBEN, James and Wiley.

F.

1792 FONES, JOHN, Robert and Thomas.

G.

1777 GARDNER, ELIZABETH, Hinson, William; John; Simpson, Mary; Cooper, Henry and Edward.
1778 GRIFFIN, MATTHEW, Matthew, John and Benjamin.
1781 GRIFFIN, JOHN, William, John and Ebenezer.
1780 GAINER, ARTHUR, Avery and Arthur.
1786 GAINER, JAMES, Mary (wife).
1785 GIBSON, WILLIAM, Mary, Winnie, Sarah, Pheraba and Howard.
1790 GRIFFIN, WILLIAM, William.
1790 GODWARD, GEORGE, George, Shadrach, Fred and Patience.
1791 GRIFFIN, EPINETUS, Ann, Joseph, Micajah and Asa.
1796 GRIFFIN, REUBEN, Reuben, Martin, Edward and Jesse.

H.

1778 HOOKS, JOHN, Ephraim.
1780 HARDISON, JOHN, William, Benjamin, John and Frances.
1784 HURST, WILLIAM, Asa, John, William, James and Hardy.
1784 HUDNALL, WILLIAM, Robert and William.
1785 HARDISON, BENJAMIN, Elizabeth, Ezekiel, Hardy, Seth, Samuel, Martha and Thomas.
1785 HUDSON, CHARLES, Mary, Abner and Joshua.
1787 HOOKS, EPHRAIM, Anna (wife), children (not named).
1788 HARDISON, JOSEPH, Millicent, Judith, Wiggins, Charles, William and Nancy.
1790 HOWELL, JETHRO, William, John, James, Asa, Roderick and Bethal.
1792 HYMAN, WILLIAM, Eleazar, John and Thomas.
1794 HOOTEN, WILLIAM, ·Henry.
1794 HUDSON, HARDY H., Celia (wife).
1795 HILL, JOSEPH B., Whitmel (father).

1797 HARDISON, WILLIAM, Benjamin and Cullen.
1798 HILL, WHITMEL, Winifred (wife), John and Thomas B.
1798 HOLLOWELL, LEVI, John.
1774 HYNES, JOHN, John.
1774 HYMAN, THOMAS, John, Thomas, Hugh and William.
1774 HASE, JOHN, Moore, William.

J.

1774 JACKSON, WILLIAM, William, Ann, Edward, Elizabeth, Pheraba and Sarah.
1789 JOYCE, JOHN, Elizabeth (wife).
1790 JOHNSON, ROBERT, Rachel (wife), James, Abraham, Elizabeth.
1790 JOYNER, THOMAS, Mary (wife), and children (not named).
1791 JENKINS, WILLIAM, John and Osborne.
1790 JONES, JOHN, John, William and Frederick.
1795 JOHNSON, JOSHUA, Joel, Joshua and Amos.
1774 JONES, WILLIAM, John.

K.

1786 KING, HIGASON, Robert and Higason.

L.

1775 LLEWELLYN, FRANCES, John, Amy, Chloe, Lydia and Abby.
1777 LONG, SAMUEL, Sarah (wife), Peggy.
1784 LILLY, JOSEPH, Kader, Simon and Josiah.
1785 LEGGITT, JAMES, Elisha and Llewellyn.
1788 LITTLE, BENJAMIN, Micajah.
1791 LEGGITT, JOHN, Elisha, Martin, John and Daniel.
1793 LANIER, JOHN R., John and Sarah.
1796 LAWRENCE, WILLIAMSON, Alrica (daughter), George (brother); children of brother Thomas.
1796 LILLY, JOSEPH, Daniel and Henry.
1797 LILLY, JOHN, Timothy.

M.

1776 MOORE, ANN, James.
1777 MATTHEWS, JAMES, Hill, John.
1780 MAYO, JAMES, Elizabeth (wife).
1780 MOORE, EZEKIEL, Rosanna, Celia and Elizabeth.
1778 McCASKEY, MARY, John.
1781 MORRIS, EDMUND, Edmund, William and James.
1784 McKENZIE, KENNETH, William, Ann.
1787 McCASKEY, JOHN, Edward, John, Martina and Eli.
1788 MITCHELL, RACHEL, Susanna, Henry and Penelope.
1789 MARTIN, THOMAS, John, Nancy, William, Polly and Thomas.
1792 MANNING, MARCOM, William, Reuben and Marcom.
1795 MOORE, HODGES, Jesse and James.

O.

1791 OUTERBRIDGE, MARY, Ann and Sarah (sisters).
1794 OUTERBRIDGE, WILLIAM, Catherine (wife), Stephen and Burr.

P.

1774 PRYOR, TEMPERANCE, Betty and Blanton.
1779 PIERCE, WILLIAM, John, William and Stewart.
1789 PRICE, JOSEPH, Jacob.
1789 PERRY, JOHN, Noah, Jacob and William.
1789 PHILPOTT, CHARLES, Samuel and John.
1794 PRICE, ELIJAH, Elijah.
1798 PURVIS, WILLIAM, Gason and Riddick.
1793 PIERCE, SUSANNA, Allen, Sherrod.

R.

1783 RIDDICK, THOMAS, Noah, Thomas, John and Mills.
1794 ROBASON, HENRY, Joshua.
1794 ROSS, JOHN, James, Henry and Luke.

S.

1777 SWANNER, WILLIAM, Thomas, William, Henry and Matthias.
1777 SWAIN, ELIZABETH, John, Sarah, Mary, William, Daniel and Ward.
1779 SHERROD, ROBERT, Lydia and John.
1779 SWAIN, JOHN, William and John.
1780 SHERROD, JOHN, James.
1781 SLADE, HENRY, William and Ebenezer.
1785 SMITH, MARY, John and Malachi.
1786 SAVIDGE, LOVELESS, William.
1787 SLADE, EBENEZER, Nancy, Ebenezer, Thomas, Henry, William and Edmund.
1789 SWANNER, THOMAS, William.
1789 SAVAGE, BRITTON, Silvia, Kinchen, Allen, Weathy and Asenath.
1790 SAVAGE, ROBERT, Warren.
1791 SLADE, WILLIAM, Ebenezer, Henry, William and Jeremiah.
1795 SMITH, JOHN, William and Richard.
1785 SWINSON, LEVI, Winnie and Millie.
1799 SWAIN, JOHN, John and William.
1784 SMITHWICK, EDMUND J., John, Samuel, Simon, Edmund, Hannah and Betsy.
1798 SMITH, JOHN, Samuel, Turner, Joel and John.
1774 SMITHWICK, EDMUND. John, Edmundson, Edward, Sarah.

T.

1795 TURLINGTON, WILLIAM, Kadar.

V.

1795 VIRGIN, SAMUEL, James and Samuel.

W.

1776 WATSON, THOMAS, Ann, Jacob, Thomas, David, Mary, Lydia and William.

1777 WYATT, SOLOMON, Ephraim, Solomon and
       William.
1799 WARREN, ROBERT, Pheraba (daughter), Joseph (brother).
1778 WILLIAMS, WILLIAM, Samuel, William.
1779 WIGGINS, THOMAS, John, Thomas and Jesse.
1784 WATSON, FRANCIS, Adson and Benjamin.
1784 WIGGINS, FANNY, Thomas, Catherine, Mary,
       Jesse and Robert.
1783 WIGGINS, JOHN, Samuel and Baker.
1779 WHITMELL, THOMAS, Thomas.
1790 WARREN, JOSEPH H., Robert.
1791 WHEATLEY, BENJAMIN, Henry and Benjamin.
1793 WARD, WILLIAM, Spellar (son).
1794 WHITNEY, SAMUEL, Mary Joyner.
1791 WATSON, JACOB, Thomas.
1798 WARD, FRANCES, Frances.
1774 WEATHERSBEE, THOMAS, Thomas.
1799 WATSON, WILLIAM, Rebecca and Sally.

MECKLENBURG COUNTY—WILLS

A.

1786 ALEXANDER, ABRAHAM, Dorcas, Joab, Cyrus, Isaac, Elizabeth, Abraham, Nathaniel, Ezra, Marcus.

1784 ALEXANDER, ZEBULON, Jane, wife; Phineas, Abel, Zebedee, Hannah McRee, Hannah Grier, Zenas, Mary Irvin, Ruth McRee.

1772 ALEXANDER, WILLIAM, Agnes, wife.

1779 ALEXANDER, JAMES, Rachel, wife, Moses.

1763 ALEXANDER, ARTHUR, Margaret, wife; Elias, Mary.

1771 ALEXANDER, AARON, David, Mary, Aaron, John B.

1776 ALEXANDER, JOSIAH, Elizabeth, wife; Josiah, Deborah, Mary, Elizabeth, Squire.

1776 ALEXANDER, DANIEL, Prudence, wife; Margaret, James, William, Stephen, Mother, Josiah, Hezekiah.

1798 ALEXANDER, EZRA, Eleazar, James, Dorcas, Abdon, Augustus, Polly, Ann, Paris, Redempta.

1775 ALEXANDER, CATHERINE, Sophia Sharpe, Araminta Sharpe, Joseph, Alexander.

1776 ALLEN, JOHN, Agnes, wife.

1784 ANDERSON, JAMES, James Givins.

1770 ALLEN, GEORGE, Sarah, wife.

1776 AYERS, THOMAS, Mary, wife.

1779 ARMSTRONG, MATTHEW, Lily, wife.

1792 ALGEA, FRANCES, wife.

1784 ALEXANDER, SAMUEL, Sarah, wife.

1782 ALEXANDER, ANDREW, Sarah, wife.

1796 ALEXANDER, DAVID, Elizabeth, wife.

1796 ALEXANDER, NATHANIEL, Jenny, wife.

B.

1772 BROWN, SAMUEL, Margaret, wife.

1772 BLACK, THOMAS, William, Thomas, John, William.

1775 BLACK, WILLIAM, Eleanor, Frances, William.

1775 BALDWIN, JOEL, Mary, Samuel, Jessie, Caleb.

1781 BERRYHILL, JOSEPH, Andrew, Joseph.

1764 BEATTY, CHARLES, Abel, John.

1775 BAXTER, ANDREW, Francis, Andrew, James, John.

1778 BRADLEY, JONAS, Winifred.

1764 BIGGERSTAFF, SAMUEL, Elizabeth, Eason, Benjamin, Samuel.

1778 BERRYHILL, SAMUEL, John and others.

1761 BEST, BOSTIAN, Wife and children.

1775 BOWMAN, ANDREW, Margaret.

1778 BARRETT, WILLIAM, Margaret, Abraham.

1763 BLACK, WILLIAM, William, John.

1769 BROWN, ROBERT, Wife and Richard.

1773 BEATTY, FRANCIS, Thomas, Wallace, James.

C.

1765 CRAIGHEAD, ALEXANDER, James, Margaret, Robert, Thomas.

1782 COWDEN, SAMUEL, Walter, John.

1782 CAMBELL, ARCHIBALD, Elizabeth and children.
1775 COWAN, JOHN, William.
1771 CARYL, SAMUEL, Samuel, Joseph, John.
1786 CATHEY, ANDREW, George, John, Andrew, Archibald.
1771 CUMMINS, CHARLES, John, Francis.
1792 CALDWELL, CHARLES, David, Charles, Martha.
1780 CALDWELL, DAVID, William, Ann.
1783 CAMPBELL, JAMES, Andrew.
1786 COCHRAN, THOMAS, John, William, Robert.
1776 CORZINE, JOHN, John, Samuel, George, William.
1775 CARRUTH, JAMES, John, Adam.
1769 CORZINE, NICHOLAS, Savoy, Nicholas, George.
1772 CLARK, WILLIAM, William, Joseph, Benjamin.
1782 CARUTHERS, HUGH, James, Hugh.

D.

1770 DAVIS, ROBERT, James, Robert, George, William.
1776 DONALDSON, ARTHUR, Arthur, Ruth, Hannah.
1778 DAVIDSON, JOHN, James, Samuel.
1780 DAVIDSON, WILLIAM, Isaac.
1787 DUYNE, DARBY, Hannah, wife.
1776 DAVIS, DAVID, William, George.
1776 DELLINGER, VALENTINE, Wife.
1790 DUNN, ANDREW, Andrew, James, Thomas.

E.

1764 EWART, ROBERT, Joseph.
1772 ELLIOTT, JAMES, Robert, Isabella.
1772 ELLIOTT, SOLOMON, John.
1775 EDWARDS, JOHN, John.
1779 ELIOTT, JOSEPH, Joseph.
1790 ERVIN, EDWARD, John, Robert.

F.

1769 FARRIOR, HENRY, John, Paul.
1764 FRANKLIN, JAMES, Wife, James, Joseph, William, Andrew.
1785 FLINN, NICHOLAS, Rebecca, Jane.
1786 FORD, HENRY, John.
1779 FLENNIKEN, JAMES, David.
1791 FESPERMAN, HENRY, John.
1784 FARR, EPHRAIM, Ephraim, James, Samuel,
1786 FERGUSON, SAMUEL, Alex, Agnes, Mattie.
1787 FRASER, JAMES, Wife, Mary, James, Samuel.
1794 FERGUSON, THOMAS, William.
1798 FOARD, JOHN, Zebulon.

G.

1771 GILES, JOHN, Susannah, Sarah, Mary.
1772 GILMER, JOHN, James.
1791 GIVENS, EDWARD, Michael, Jacob.
1777 GOODMAN, MICHAEL, George, John.
1776 GINGLES, SAMUEL, Samuel, James, Adlai.
1793 GREEN, JOHN, David.
1767 GRAHAM, WILLIAM, wife, Mary, Agnes, John.
1766 GABIE, ROBERT, John, Joseph.
1779 GIVENS, EDWARD, Samuel, Edward.
1781 GOLDMAN, HENRY, Henry, John.
1784 GARMON, GEORGE, George, Isaac.

H.

1766 HOGSTEAD, WALTER, Saumel, William, Walter.
1776 HARRLS, THOMAS, Rachel, wife, Jeremiah, Rachel.
1776 HARRIS, THOMAS, Thomas, James, William.
1779 HERRON, JAMES, Wife and children.
1778 HARRIS, JAMES, Robert, Samuel, John.
1785 HILL, ROBERT, John.
1782 HIPP, STEPHEN, Joseph, Jacob, Valentine.
1782 HEARNE, GEORGE, Jesse.
1790 HUDSON, RICHARD, Joseph, Richard, Thomas. and Edward.
1794 HARRIS, ROBERT, Samuel, Hannah, Margaret.
1777 HENDERSON, WILLIAM, Wife, Agnes.
1778 HAY, DAVID, John, Hugh.
1788 HENDERSON ROBERT, John and James.
1776 HARRIS, CHARLES, Robert, Samuel, Charles.
1776 HUTCHINSON, JOHN, Alex, James.
1776 HOUSTON, GEORGE, Margaret, wife.
1776 HOUSTON, AARON, David, James, John.
1782 HALL, HALBERT, Samuel, William.
1778 HENDERSON, ARCHIBALD, James, Rebecca.

I.

1783 IRWIN, WILLIAM, Mary, wife, Samuel.
1796 IRWIN, CHRISTOPHER, Jeannette, wife.

J.

1777 JULIAN, JACOB, George, Graham, James, and Decatur.
1780 JACK, PATRICK, Five granddaughters.
1795 JADESON, SHADRACK, Martha, Richard, Chloe, wife.
1800 JETTON, ABRAM, Isaac, John, Ephraim.

K.

1783 KRESS, NICHOLAS, Philip, Tobias, Henry, Jacob.
1776 KNIGHTON, THOMAS, John, Thomas and William.
1771 KERR, JOSEPH, Joseph, Elizabeth.
1772 KNOX, JOHN, SR., James, Samuel, Matthew, Joseph.
1777 KENNEDY, JOSEPH, Joseph, David, Samuel.
1784 KLINE, MICHAEL, George, Daniel, John.
1780 KISER, PETER, Peter.
1784 KERR, ROBERT, John, Robert, Samuel, Richard.
1789 KERR, JOHN, William.
1792 KNOX, JOHN, Robert.

L.

1780 LIGGETT, MICHAEL, Jackson.
1781 LUDWIG, NICHOLAS, Henry.
1791 LOVE, JOHN, David, Christopher.
1784 LEWIS, ALEXANDER, Benjamin.
1781 LIPPARD, WILLIAM, John.
1776 LINTON, EDWARD, Samuel.
1779 LINN, JAMES, William.
1777 LUSK, JOHN, John, Samuel.

M.

1771 MARTIN, CHARLES, Deborah.
1774 MASON, CHARLES, Richard, Gideon, Joseph.
1775 MOFFITT, JOHN, William.
1776 MILLER, ANDREW, William, Andrew, Matthew.
1776 MORGAN, REESE, William, Ramsay.
1778 MORTON, ROBERT, Samuel.
1778 MOFFITT, ROBERT, Martha.
1778 MOORE, DAVID, Joseph, Hugh.
1781 MORRISON, NEIL, William, Alexander, James.
1785 MAXWELL, ROBERT, Mary, wife.
1785 MOORE, MOSES, James, William, Abigail.
1765 MILLER, ROBERT, SR., James, John, Robert, Nathaniel.
1769 MOORE, JOSEPH, Josiah, Mary.
1777 MONTGOMERY, JOHN, John, Joseph.
1778 MOFFITT, DAVID, David, Elizabeth.
1778 MORRISON, JOHN, James, John, Elias.
1780 MITCHELL, JOSEPH, Alex Mitchell's children.
1782 MOFFITT, CHARLES, John.
1787 MARTIN, JAMES, James, Robert, William, John.
1740 MITCHELL, HARRY, Robert, Nathan, Jane.
1793 MURTLAND, ROBERT, William Still, Jr.
1793 MOORE, DAVID, C., Joseph and Jacob.

Mc.

1770 McDOWELL, ROBERT, Thomas.
1774 McHARRY, JAMES, John Campbell.
1774 McCALL, JAMES, William.
1774 McKINLEY, ROBERT, James, Elizabeth, Martha.
1775 McREE, ROBERT, Alexander, William.
1776 McKNIGHTON, THOMAS, John, Thomas, William.
1778 McLURE, JOHN, Joseph.
1778 McGOUGH, ROBERT, John, Robert.
1780 McDOWELL, WILLIAM, Dorothy.
1782 McCORMICK, DARIUS, Robert, John.
1782 McMURRAY, SARAH, James W. McCracken.
1786 McKINNIE, DANIEL, Daniel.
1767 McCLENAHAN, ROBERT, John, Elizabeth, Janet.
1770 McGUIRE, JAMES, Eliza, Thomas, John.
1779 McKEE, AMBROSE, Thomas, John, William, Ambrose.

N.

1766 NEIL, THOMAS, Joseph, Sarah.
1770 NORRIS, JAMES, James.
1787 NICHOLAS, THOMAS, Rachel, wife.
1787 NIXON, FRANCIS, Joseph, John, Allen, Mary.
1793 NEELY, THOMAS, John, Samuel, Thomas, Moses.

O.

1769 ORMOND, JAMES, John, Adam, Benjamin, Jacob.
1776 ORR, JAMES, James.
1788 OSBORNE, CHRISTOPHER, Jonathan, Christopher.
1790 ORR, ROBERT, Alex, John.
1792 ORR, GEORGE, George.
1779 ORR, NATHAN, James, Sample.

P.

1786 PATTERSON, JOHN, Robert, Alexander, Elizabeth, wife.
1761 PATTON, THOMAS, William— _w. Catharine_
*1775 PHIFER, JOHN, Paul, Margaret and Ann _Elizabeth c_
1775 PATTERSON, CHARLES, John, James D., Sarah.
1781 POTTS, JAMES, William, James.
1766 POVEY, CONRAD, Magdalena, Wife.
1783 POTTS, JOHN, Robert.
1791 PHILLIPS, JAMES, John.
1749 PRICE, JOHN, Wife and children.
1767 PARKER, THOMAS, Eleanor, wife.
1764 PRITCHART, DANIEL, Mary.
1781 PAXTON, JAMES, John.
1789 PHIFER, MARTIN, SR., Paul, Martin, Caleb.
1793 PINNIX, JOHN, Fanny and Mary.

R.

1764 RAMSOUR, JOHN, Jacob and David.
1789 ROSS, ANTHONY, John and Jean.
1785 ROBINSON, ALEX, Matthew.
1787 RESSE, DAVID, Solomon and George.
1785 ROGERS, JOHN, John N.
1795 ROGERS, BENJAMIN, James.
1798 RODDEN, BENJAMIN, Upton, Ben, Gabriel, Judy.
1764 RUDASILL, PHILIP, Mary, Michael, Elizabeth.
1763 RAMSOUR, HENRY, John, Jacob, David.
1765 REAMY, JOHN, Samuel, Benjamin.
1767 ROSS, NICKERSON, Hannah, James, Elizabeth.
1775 RAMSEY, JOHN, James, William and John.
1778 REID, HUGH, William and John.
1781 REID, AUGUSTINIUS, Elizabeth.
1785 RINEHARDT, ANDREW, John.
1787 RITCHIE, JOHN, William, John, David, Elizabeth, Jane.
1789 REYEN, ELIJAH, Joseph Maxwell.
1785 RUSSELL, JOHN, Joseph, Margaret, Eleanor.

S.

1780 STIKELEATHER, JOHN GEORGE, Margaret, wife; John George.
1762 SHUFORD, GEORGE, wife, Rhoda, and children.
1769 SAMPLE, WILLIAM, Wife, Esther, John, Joseph, William, Mary.
1771 SCOTT, JAMES, Three nephews.
1772 SLOAN, JAMES, David, James, Agnes.
1778 STEWART, THOMAS, John.
1779 STINSON, ANDREW, David, John, Andrew.   _Eleanore._
w. Isabel 1776✗SHELBY, MOSES, Moses, John, Thomas, Evan, William, daus.
1778 STINSON, HUGH, Hugh, Michael, Anna.
1777 STEWART, ROBERT, Jane, Isabel.
1783 SOSSAMAN, HENRY, Henry, Andrew, David, Jacob.
1787 SMILEY, WALTER, Mary.
1787 STELL, MOSES, John, Lavinia.
1781 SHORT, ABRAHAM, William.
1771 STELL, WILLIAM, Wife Jane.
1774 SMITH, JOHN, James, Margaret, Jane.

✱ See Grimes - Wills and Inventories, N.C- p 328 for will.
✗✗ See Springs Gen. pp. 52, 53. also McGuire's My Childrens Ancestors.
vol. 2, pp. 122, 123.

T.

1782 THOMAS, JOSEPH, Allen, Joseph, Lucy, Sarah.
1793 THOMAS, BENJAMIN, Rebecca.
1768 TORRENCE, ABRAHAM, Hugh, Paul, George, William.
1785 THOMPSON, JENNINGS, Joseph, Benjamin, Moses.
1777 TAYLOR, JOHN, Mary, Margaret.
1778 TAYLOR, ABRAHAM, Wife Mary.
1779 TANNER, JOSEPH, Wife Ann, John, James.
1781 THOMPSON, THOMAS, Wife Mary, John.

V.

1799 VANPELT, SIMON, Simon.
1778 VARNER, JAMES, Robert.
1784 VARNER, HENRY, Rebecca, John, Robert.
1797 VINSON, WILLIAM, Thomas, David, Penelope, Penina·

W.

1771 WYLIE, JAMES, John, Thomas, Martha, James, Robert.
1778 WILSON, SAMUEL, John, Robert, Margaret.
1777 WILLIAMS, DAVID, Phoebe, John, George, Robert.
1776 WALL, HENRY, Wife Rachael.
1782 WILSON, JOHN, Elizabeth.
1784 WYLIE, JOHN, John, Janet, Jane.
1781 WALKER, JAMES, Henry, Mary, James.
1781 WALLACE, JOSEPH, Wife Margaret, William, Edward, Samuel.
1763 WILKINS, SAMUEL, John.
1771 WADDINGTON, WILLIAM, John, Samuel, Robert, Frances.
1776 WILSON, JAMES, John.
1786 WILLIAMS, JOB, Ann, John, Joseph, Janet, Sarah.
1779 WILSON, JOHN, John, Andrew, Agnes.
1795 WAUGHUP, JAMES, Israel, William, Joseph.

MOORE—WILLS

B.

1794 BUIE, DANIEL, Gilbert, Alexander, **Angus,** Daniel, Mary and Margaret.

1795 BLUE, DANIEL, Rebecca, Alex, Effie, **Margaret,** William, Angus, Gilbert and Daniel.

C.

1799 CAMPBELL, CHARLES, Martha (wife), **Charles** and Catherine; John B. Campbell (grandson).

D.

1797 DYE, NANCY, William, Martin, Barbara and Nancy.

1799 DUNN, RUTH, William, Joseph and John; Pendleton, Sarah (daughter); McDonald, Nancy, (daughter); Lamb, Mary, (daughter); Atkinson, Hannah, (daughter).

F.

1799 FRAZER, JOSEPH, Elizabeth (wife), **George** and Ann.

G.

1800 GRAHAM, DONALD, McFarland, Malcolm (son-in-law), and the latter's wife, Nancy, and their daughter, Effie; Michael (brother).

H.

1797 HANCOCK, WILLIAM, Pattie (wife); John, William, Rhoda, Polly, Elizabeth Lydia and Pattie E.

K.

1799 KELLY, HUGH, Mary (wife), Joseph, **Thomas,** Spencer, John and Elizabeth.

1801 KENNEDY, ELENDER, (Eleanor), Robert, Annis and Esther.

L.

1800 LAWLER, JOHN, wife (not named), Eli, **Levi,** Evan, Ann and John.

M.

1794 McGEE, JOSEPH, Milly (wife), Absalom, Suckey, Tempe, Penny, Elizabeth, Charles, Judith, Joseph and Jacob.

1797 MERRITT, JAMES, Ann, (wife), Sylvanus, Obadiah, Liles, John, Mark, Molly, James, Lewis, Nancy, Sallie, Priscilla and Rhoda.

1799 McINTOSH, DUNCAN, Wife of Duncan Campbell (sister).

1800 MORGAN, JOHN, Joseph, Angeline, **Mary,** James, Lavinia, Natham; Smith, Delilah (daughter), Dunn, Elespa (daughter).

1800 McREYNOLDS, THOMAS, Lucy (wife); **Mary** B., John D., Elizabeth, James and Anna.

1801 McCALLUM, DUNCAN, children (not named).

N.

1795 NEWTON, NICHOLAS, Milony (wife); Sowel, Mary (daughter).

1796 NEWTON, CHARLES, John T. and William.

P.

1794 PATTERSON, DANIEL, Effie (wife), Mary and Isabel, Leach, Dugald (son-in-law); Johnston, Archibald (son-in-law(; Campbell, Duncan, (son-in-law); Johnston, John (grandson).

1795 PATTERSON, MALCOLM, Sarah (wife), John and Malcolm.

1799 PAIN, WILLIAM, Jerusha (wife); Moore, James and Nancy (grandchildren.)

1799 PHILLIPS, JOHN, Patience (wife), Lewis and John.

1801 PERSON, SAMUEL, Tabitha (wife), Thomas, Benjamin and Joseph S.

1793 PARRISH, SALLY, Wicker, Polly and Suckey.

R.

1801 ROBISON, ELIZABETH, John, Sarah, Eleanor, William and Mary.

1802 RIDDLE, JAMES, Temperance (wife); Mary and Sarah and two sons (not named).

1800 REYNOLDS, THOMAS, Lucy (wife), Mary, John, James, Dabney and Elizabeth.

S.

1796 SHEFFIELD, JOHN, Hannah (wife), Mark, John, Adam, Isham, Lydia, Milly, Averett, Dennis, Elizabeth, Sarah, David, and Mary; Dunn, Lucretia (daughter); Owby, Rebecca (daughter); Maingold, Hannah (daughter).

1796 STUBBS, JACOB, Elizabeth (wife), Jacob, John, Christian and Leonard; Furr, Mary and Elizabeth (daughters); Spivey, Susanna (daughter).

T.

1794 TYSON, CORNELIUS, Jane (wife) Richard, Benjamin, Aaron, Sarah, Rebecca, Jane and Thomas.

1797 TYSON, JANE, Tyson, Jane, (granddaughter); Hopson, Jane(granddaughter); Moore, Jane (granddaughter); Stevenson, Jane (granddaughter); Gilbert, Sabra (granddaughter); Myrick, Rebecca (daughter); Stinson, Sarah (daughter).

W.

1797 WILLIAMS, GEORGE, Ann (wife), Jeremiah, James, Thomas, William, Mary, Sally and Nelly.

1799 WATSON, WILLIAM, Matthew and William.

1799 WATSON, HUGH, Archibald, Robin, James, Hugh and Alexander.

NASH—WILLS

A.

1780 ADAMS, SACKFIELD, William, Robert and Susanna.
17,79 ATKINSON, JAMES, Margaret, Burwell and Ephraim.
1785 ALLEN, ARTHUR, Thomas, Arthur, Honor, Rhoda, Ease and Elizabeth.
1789 ADKINS, BENJAMIN, Rachel and Penelope.
1795 ARRINGTON, ARTHUR, Richard, Henry and Arthur.
1798 AVERETT, JEDUTHAN, Rebecca.
1800 AVENT, SALLIE, Ward, Francis.

B.

1791 BRYANT, SAMUEL, Robert, Samuel and Thomas.
1779 BELL, ARTHUR, Elizabeth (wife); Benjamin, William, James, Thomas, Green, Arthur; Beck, Sarah; Staller, Elvilah.
1779 BRASWELL, WILLIAM, Martha (wife); Robin, Dempsey, Mourning; Hunt, Alex, Nancy, Judah; Beckwith, Thomas; Powell, Rhoda.
1781 BAILEY, JOHN, Henry, Christiana, John, Ruth, Celia, Unity, Levy; O'Neal, Drusilla; Carter, Priscilla.
1788 BARNES, JACOB, John, Jacob, William, James, Elizabeth, Benjamin; Joyner, Sally; Jones, Ann; Whitley, Jonas B.
1785 BUNN, DAVID, Sarah, David, Seleter, Lucretia, Redmond, Mary, Benjamin, Ann, Elizabeth and Rachel.
1785 BROWN, JEREMIAH, Mary and Joseph.
1785 BRANTLEY, JOHN, Elizabeth and Jacob.
1789 BRADLEY, JAMES, Rogers, offspring of Robert.
1790 BARLOW, SAMUEL, Joyner and Milly.
1793 BARRON, BARNABY, Six Lees—Barnaby, Beed, Tarlton, William, Elizabeth and Nancy.
1794 BARNES, BENJAMIN, Dempsey, Edwin and Benjamin.
1795 BRASWELL, SAMUEL, Sampson and Wilson.
1795 BOTTOMS, SAMUEL L., Micajah, Alaminta and Allerene.
1796 BRASWELL, WILLIAM, John, William, Tappan and Cotney.
1796 BECKWITH, HENRY, Amos.
1798 BODDIE, NATHAN, Elijah, George and Bennett.
1800 BASS, ISAAC, Jethro, Isaac and Augustin.

C.

1779 CLINCH, EDWARD, wife; Hannah and Christopher (children).
1781 CHADWICK, NOAH, Martha (wife), Noah, Frances, Martha.
1785 COOPER, JOHN, Reuben, Carmen, Penelope, John and Joel.
1787 CROWELL, JOSEPH, John, James B., Edward and Betsy L.
1789 CULPEPPER, ELIZABETH, Whitehead, Rachel and Elizabeth; Manning, Martha.

1792 COCKRELL, JACOB, Jonathan, Nathan and William H.
1795 CLINCH, JOSEPH JR., Edward D., Lamon and Joseph J.
1798 COOPER, JOHN, Mack.
1799 CULPEPPER, JAMES, Jeremiah, Christopher and James.

D.

1780 DAVIS, LEWIS, Diocletian, Young, Priscilla, Lobycy and Tabitha.
1781 DENSON, BENJAMIN, Jethro, Joseph, Benjamin, John, Jesse, Mary, Isabella, Mollie, Ann, Huldah and Betty.
1785 DAVENPORT, DAVID, John and Elias.
1788 DEEMS, JEREMIAH, Molly and Sherrod.
1790 DORTCH, ANNA, Lewis.
1791 DEW, JOHN, Nancy and Duncan; Robbins, Betsy and Cole.
1796 DRAKE, HARTWELL, John H. and Benjamin.
1797 DEANS, THOMAS, John and William.
1782 DOZIER, WILLIAM, John, William, Sarah, Richard, Thomas, Martha, Peggy and Richmond.
1791 DRAKE, JAMES, Benjamin, Silas, John H. and Hartwell. Wid ɔ w/
1797 DAWSON, DEMPSEY, Dempsey.

E.

1778 EASON, DEMPSEY, Millie.
1794 EASON, SAMUEL, Nancy, Ellis, Eli, John S., and Margaret.
1783 EASON, WILLIAM, Samuel, Ann, Eunice, Edith and William.

F.

1782 FLOWERS, BENJAMIN SR., William, Dycia, Mary, Rachel and Martha.
1792 FLOWERS, HENRY, Nanny and John.

G.

1785 GRIFFIN, JOSEPH, Sarah, Micajah, Joseph and Pearce.
1795 GRIFFIN, JAMES, Five Drakes—Mary, Sion, Louisiana, Jesse and Isaac.

H.

1782 HORNE, THOMAS, William, Thomas, Catherine and Michael; Pridgen, Thomas; Futrell, William.
1788 HANEY, THOMAS, Frances (wife); Mary, Elizabeth and Frances.
1790 HILLIARD, ISAAC, James, Isaac, John, Robert C., Henry, William, and Leah; Davis, Elizabeth; Dortch, Isaac.
1782 HUNT, SARAH, Jesse and Decey; Long, Henry.
1793 HORNE, JOEL, Harriet, Hardy, Milberry and Rebecca.
1794 HART, THOMAS, Thomas.
1782 HORN, THOMAS, Joshua, Henry, Richard, William and Wilson.

1787 HACKNEY, WILLIAM, James, Jennings, Elizabeth and Penelope.
1788 HACKNEY, RACHEL, Betsy; Meals, Purity; Parker, Unity; Adkins, Penn.

J.

1785 JOYNER, WILLIAM W., Celia, Hard, Drewry, Burwell, Jordan and Cornelius.
1788 JONES, FRANCES A., Julia, Newsome and Cooper.
1795 JACKSON, GEORGE, Lewis and Mary.
1797 JONES, NEWSOM, Catap.
1799 JOLLY, JAMES I., Rachel.
1800 JONES, JULIAN, Margaret and Cooper.
1797 JONES, ALLEN, Willie and Tamerlane.

K.

1783 KNIGHT, JOHN, Ann, Elisha and Kiddy; Hart, Sarah.
1785 KNIGHT, GEORGE, Sarah and George.

L.

1778 LAFAYETTE, WILLIAM, wife; Powell, Willis; Whitehead, Burwell; Snipes, Martha.
1789 LEWIS, THOMAS, Lydia, Abner, Nicholson, Martha, John, Thomas, Nancy.

M.

1779 MERRITT, BENJAMIN, William, Henry, Benjamin and Sarah.
1781 MANN, JOHN, Thomas and William.
1788 MORGAN, JAMES, John, James, Peggy, Hardy, Elizabeth, Thomas and Belle C.
1783 MOORE, EDWARD, James, William, Elizabeth, Susanna and Edward.
1785 MASSENGALE, JAMES, SR., wife; Ann A. (daughter).
1789 MANNING, MATTHIAS, Margaret, Matthias and Pridgen; Richardson, Sarah; Pridgen, Mary.
1790 MORGAN, ELIZABETH C., James and William.
1792 MILTON, ZACHARIAH, John and Joshua.
1795 MANNING, LEVI, Joseph and Mourning.
1795 MILTON, JOHN, Thomas and Cooper.
1791 MANNING, WILLIAM, Mourning.

N.

1780 NICHOLSON, GEORGE, wife; Wright, David, George, Edward, Malachi, Joshua and Lydia; Lewis, Tressa and Lydia; Pitman, Chloe, Walker, Elizabeth.
1789 NICHOLSON, LYDIA, Jonah.

P.

1784 POLAND, JOHN, Elizabeth and William; Williams, Jean; Taylor, Mary.
1789 PEIRCE, JOSHUA, Elizabeth and Joshna.
1789 POPE, LAZARUS, Barbara.
1790 PURCELL, EDWARD E., Jeremiah, Hardy and James.
1795 PORTIS, GEORGE, William.

1797 PARKER, FRANCIS, John and William.
1789 POPE, HARDYMAN, Elisha, Dempsey, Joseph, Hardyman, Archibald and William.
1795 PARKER, ANN, William.

R.

1778 ROSE, ELIJA, Three Clinch—Edward, Joseph, Jr., and Elizabeth; Bellamy, Mary.
1786 ROGERS, THOMAS, James and Peleg.
1796 ROSE, FRANCIS, William, Benjamin, Tompkins, Martha and Ann.
1798 ROW, WILLIAM, Mary, Jane.
1791 ROGERS, ROBERT, Jacob, Jesse and Robert.
1790 RICKS, JOHN, Isaac, John, Richard, Mary, Gideon, Redmond, Larry, Jacob, Johannon and Delilah.
1789 RICKS, THOMAS, Priscilla, Alexander, Urban, and Milberry.

S.

1781 SMITH, MOURNING M., Chloe, Josiah and Micajah; Boddie, Nathan; Ricks, James, Mourning and Rhoda.
1788 STRICKLAND, JOSEPH, Jesse, David, Patience, Mary, Elizabeth and Burwell.
1783 SANDERS, ROBERT, Philander, Richard, Henry and Mary.
1783 SANDERFORD, TOMPKINS, Mary, Henry T. and Nathan.
1790 STRICKLAND, JACOB, Hardy.
1791 SORSBY, SAMUEL, William, Alexander and Frances.
1793 SCREWS, HENRY, William and Littleton.
1795 SELAH, JOSEPH, Benjamin and Richard.
1797 SIKES, JOHN, Joseph and John.
1799 SMITH, BENJAMIN, Samuel, Jordan and Bennett.

T.

1781 TUCKER, THOMAS T., Margaret, Thomas, Keziah, Betty and Willoughby.
1784 TURLINGTON, JOHN, Elizabeth, Mary, Timothy and Thomas.
1785 THOMAS, RICHARD R., Jethro, Rebecca, Mourning and Mary.
1788 TAYLOR, HENRY, Etheldred, John, Hardy and Boykin.
1788 THOMAS, MICAJAH, Boddie, Bennett and George; Jackson, Margaret T., Mourning T. and Temperance T.; Crudup, John and George; King, Julian; Cotton, Solomon.
1796 TURNER, JAMES, James.
1796 TAYLOR, JOHN, Dempsey, John, William and Willie.
1797 TUCKER, JAMES, Pheraba.

U.

1798 UNDERWOOD, JACOB, Levi.

V.

1790 VAUGHAN, DEMPSEY, Esther and Christopher.
1792 VIVERETT, THOMAS, Henry, Launcelot, Micajah and James.
1796 VICK, ROBERT, Jacob.
1797 VAUGHAN, EPHRAIM, Vinson.

W.

1779 WELLS, FREDERICK, Joshua and Solomon.
1779 WHITEHEAD, NATHAN, Nathan, Rachel, Benjamin, Theodore and Henry; Nicholson, Rhoda; Culpepper, Chloe; Beck, Isabel.
1780 WALL, JAMES, Sarah and Betty; Powell, Nathan.
1781 WILLIAMS, SAMUEL, Ann, Philander, Sarah, Zilpah, Cicely and Charity; Pope, Delilah; Cone, Betty.
1785 WHIDDON, LOT, Sarah, Maxwell, Elizabeth and James.
1790 WELLS, SOLOMON, John and Stephen and heirs of Redmond.
1792 WESTER, ARTHUR, William, Keziah and Mary; Joyner, Patience.
1794 WINSTEAD, JOSEPH, Susanna and Samuel.
1795 WHITE, JOSEPH, Sarah and Thomas.
1797 WILLIAMSON, JOSEPH, Thomas and Joseph.
1797 WILSON, JAMES, Richard C., James and Zachariah.
1798 WINBORNE, ABRAHAM, Sarah, John and David.
1800 WHELESS, AMOS, Milberry.
1800 WARD, FRANCIS, Francis, Fannie, Nathan and William. and children given below *
1781 WHITFIELD, THOMAS, Israel and Hardy.
1794 WHITEHEAD, BENJAMIN, James, Benjamin, William and Joseph.
1777 WILLIS, THOMAS, William and Wilson.
1796 WHITFIELD, ISAAC, Solomon.
1792 WHITFIELD, MARY, Elisha.
1794 WHITE, JOSEPH, Thomas, Joseph, Armiger and Gulielmus; Hall, Anne; Smith, Esther.
1799 WILSON, EDWARD, Elizabeth and Anne.
1794 WILLIAMS, PHILANDER, Samuel and Pride.

Y.

1798 YOUELL, HENRY, Turlington, Henry.

* additional names of children given in will of Francis Ward supplied by clerk of Superior Court of Nash Co. Aug. 29, 1932 as follows — Benjamin, Sally avent, John, nancy jones, Prisyla newsom, mary Southall — all mentioned in addition to ones above.

WILLS—NEW HANOVER

A

1801   ATKINSON, SAMUEL, Judah.
1797   AMALIO, NICHOLAS, Brother.
(No   ASHE, SAMUEL, Elizabeth, Samuel, Porter,
Date)   Paoli, Richard, Thomas, John Baptiste.
1772   ATKINSON, JOHN, Elisha, Anna.
(No   ASHE, JOHN, Rebecca, John, Samuel, William,
Date)   Algernon, Acourt, Rebecca; Swann, Samuel;
      Moore, George.
1779   ANCRUM, JOHN, Mary.
1792   ASHE, JOHN, Samuel.

B

1798   BOYD, MARY, DeRosset, Armand John; Turner,
      Mary Magdalen.
1798   BURTON, THOMAS, Charles, Watson, John,
      Straton.
1799   BLOODWORTH, JAMES, Ann, wife; Portevent,
      Susanna.
1777   BENSON, JOHN, James, Mary, Ann, Elizabeth.
1767   BARKER, JOHN, Mary.
1769   BORDEAUX, ANTHONY, Anthony, James, Peter,
      Duel, John, Israel, Isaac, Ann; Larkins, Pris-
      cilla.
1771   BONHAM, SAMUEL, Carter, Hezikiah, Nicholas,
      Tomlinson, Sarah.
1774   BLAND, JAMES, WM., James, Lettice, Mary,
      Anne; Wills, Elizabeth; Lober, Elizabeth;
      Annersey, Sarah.
1774   BARNES, GEORGE, Ross, Judith.
1779   BARWICK, WILLIAM, Priscilla, James, White,
      Elizabeth, Nancy.
1779   BARTHOLOMEW, SAMUEL, Jean.
1779   BANNERMAN, CHARLES, Charles, George,
      Robert.
1787   BISHOP, CHARLES, Nancy, Thomas.
1788   BROWN, ELIZABETH, Burton, William.
1788   BLOODWORTH, ROBERT, children (not named).
1780   BOWDEN, BACON, John, Richard.
1795   BELOAT, AUGUSTUS, Margaret.

C

1797   CUNNINGHAM, THOMAS, Kirkwood, Mary, Ann
      J., Robert; Robeson, Elizabeth.
1790   CLAYTON, FRANCES, Thomas; Harnett, Mary.
1793   CLAYTON, THOMAS, Rector, Isabella.
1795   CLAYPOLE, WILLIAM, Ann; Wright, Thomas,
      Joshua B.
1772   CHIVERS, EDWARD, Peggy.
1776   COLVIN, ALEXANDER, Margaret, John.
1776   COLVIN, JOHN, John, Mary, Jane.
1777   CRAY, JOHN, Joan, Anne.
1783   CORBIN, EDMUND, James, Mr. and Mrs. Fred.,
      Jr.,; Allen, Thomas; Craike, Thomas.
1788   COLSON, JAMES, Thomas.
1792   CODRAN, ROBERT, Walker, Jane.

D

1764   DUDLEY, CHRISTOPHER, Bishop.
(No   DUBOSE, ANTHONY, Ann, Mary Ann, William
Date)   P., Jacob; Riley, Jean.

1767 DUNBIDDEN, DANIEL, Ruth, Hannah, Jonathan; Ward, Jane.

1779 DEVANE ,THOMAS, John, Thomas: children of Portevent, James.

1780 DOTY, EDWARD, Hannah, James, Sarah, Edward, Mary, Hannah, Phoebe.

1789 DOYLE, MARGARET, Harnett, Elizabeth; Hooper, Elizabeth; Gike, Mary; DeRosset, Armand, John.

1785 DUNNING, MARGARET, McIlwaine, Thomas.

1785 DUNBIBBEN, JONATHAN, Hannah; Ward, Jane; Gough, Mary Ann.

1786 DeROSSET, LEWIS C., Armand, John, Magdalene, Mary, Margaret; Walker, James.

1789 DAVIS, JOHN, Jane, Thomas, George.

1796 DAVIS, THOMAS, Mary, Thomas.

E

1799 EASTIN, SAMUEL, Sherwood, Mary.

1769 EVANS, WILLIAM, Tabitha; Simmons, Elida.

1770 EVANS, JONATHAN, Eleanor, Rees, David.

1775 EZARD, WILLIAM, John; Rowell, Isaac; White, George.

1777 EARLE, RICHARD, Moses, David, Rachel, Mary, Ann.

1789 EAGAN, ELIZABETH, John G.

1790 ESSON, THOMAS, Janet, Archibald.

F

1799 FULLER, PLEU, Peggy.

1799 FERGUS, JOHN; John, McRee, Ann; Bruff, James.

1768 FORD, MARCUS, Jenkins, James.

1780 FORBES, DAVID, Hogg, Root; Turitty, Joseph, Gordon, John.

1782 FARIS, SARAH, McIlwaine, Thomas.

1782 FUTCH, ONESIMUS, wife; Carter, James, Jacob, John.

1789 FILLYAW, JOHN, Stephen, Cutting, Owen.

1782 FENNELL, NICHOLAS, Anthony, Lovely, Nicholas.

1797 FLOWERS, THOMAS, Patts, Joshua.

1798 FERGUSON, DANIEL, Margaret.

(No   FETZGERALD, THOMAS, John, Edward, Margaret, Henry, William.
Date)

G

1771 GURLEY, BENJAMIN, Mary, Elizabeth.

1779 GREGORY, WILLIAM, Abigail.

1783 GIBSON, WALTER, Margaret.

1788 GRAINGER, CALEB, Mary, William; Ancrum, Sarah, James H; Blount, Mary.

1787 GARDENER, JAMES, father, brothers and sisters.

1789 GUERRARD, JOHN, Rebecca, Huggins, Mary, Anthony, Elias.

1791 GORDON, MARSH, Sarah.

1793 GEIKIE, JAMES, Mary; Green, James; Moore, Mary.

H

1797 HAMILTON, MAHALIAH, Ann (wife), Eleanor, Margaret.

1771 HERN, BENJAMIN, Alice, Mary, Elizabeth, Frances, Charles.
1770 HAYNES, MARGARET, Waddell, Haynes.
1774 HERRING, JOHN, John.
1775 HARVEY, WILLIAM, Daniel, John.
1783 HILL, WILLIAM, John, Harvey.
1792 HARNETT, CORNELIUS, Mary Elizabeth.
1783 HILL, WILLIAM, Margaret, Nathaniel M., Thomas.
1784 HARVEY, FRANCIS, David, John.
1785 HASSELL, JAMES, SR. Ann, Sophia.
1785 HALLETT, JAMES R., Rebecca.
1787 HALL, JAMES, Ann.
1788 HENDERSON, THOMAS, Andrew, Isabella, Secia; Evans, Ann; Gotterson, Catherine; Cuvice, Jane.
1789 HERRING, BENJAMIN, Bright.
1797 HOPKINS, ISAAC, Sarah.

J

1795 JENKS, CHARLES, Wright, Joshua, Hallett, Peter.
1780 JONES, SARAH, Ann, William, W., Sarah, Evans; Price, James.
1799 JAMES, JOHN, Alice (wife), Hector, Mary, John, Alice, Elizabeth.
1799 JOHNSON, MATTHEW, Charity, Jennings, Matthew, Proudful.
1769 JOHNSTON, ANN, Harker, Henry.
1776 JONES, JOHN, Margaret, Ann.
1774 JONES, THOMAS, Fred, Florence, Maurice.
1782 JONES, WILLIAM, Samuel, William.
1787 JONES, MARGARET, Bloodworth, Timothy, James.
1787 JONES, PHILIP, Susanna, John, William, Elizabeth.
1788 JONES, MARMADUKE, Elizabeth.
1788 JACOBS, GEORGE, Fr'ont, Joseph, Ann.
1790 JONES, WILLIAM, S..rah (wife), Evan; Price, James, Sarah.
1792 JAMES, DAVID, Jane, John, Thomas, James, William.
1793 JAMES, DAVID, SR.; Rebecca, David and William.
1797 JONES, FRED., Jane; Swann, Lucy, John; Hill, Elizabeth; Cutler, Rebecca, Ann; Sampson, Jane.

K.

1799 KERR, DAVID, David.
1791 KINGSBURY, JOHN, Denellion, Gabriel.
1794 KINGSBURY, GABRIEL, Elizabeth, Jane H., Sarah; Dorsey, Laurens A.
1795 KIRKBY, J. H., Hannah.

L.

1798 LEGUIRE, MATTHEW, son, Matthew's children.
1782 LYON, JOHN, Mildred, Mary, Sidney, Jane; Swann, Samuel; McIlwaine, Archibald; Seaman, George.
1780 LORD, WILLIAM, SR., Sarah, William, Mary, John, James, Usher.

1786 LILLINGTON, ALEX., John, George, Sarah, Mary.
1788 LYON, MILDRED, Mary, Sidney, Jane.
1798 LAMBERT, ENOCH, Elizabeth, William.
1795 LILLINGTON, GEORGE, Sarah (wife), Sarah, Mary.
1785 LOWNES, WM. HAMILTON, Hogg, John, William C.
1785 LILLINGTON, JOHN, Mary.
1771 LOWERY, RICHARD, Macon, Caleb.

M.

1798 MOORE, THOMAS, Frederick, Augustus, Elizabeth.
1798 MOSELY, WILLIAM, Maria, Ann S., Margaret; Tucker, Mary.
1799 MEREDITH, WILLIAM, McVean, John; Jennett, Jesse; Asbury, Bishop.
1799 MESSICK, EVELIN, wife and children (not named).
1798 MOORE, PETTIGREW, Mary, James, William, Benjamin.
1776 McCRACKEN, ROBERT, James, Jane, Ann R.
1767 MORRIS, WILLIAM, James, William; Bishop, Thomas.
1767 MERRICK, THOMAS, George, Sarah, Dorothy, Elizabeth; Lillington, John; Jones, Maurice.
1771 MASON, CALEB, Lowery, Richard; Mason, Mary.
1772 McCLAMMY, RICHARD, Luke, William, Thomas.
1775 MONROE, JAMES, Gregg, Fred; Campbell, William; · Maclaine, Archibald; Moran, James Hurley.
1778 MABSON, ARTHUR, Arthur, Mary, Susanna, Samuel, William.
1778 MOORE, GEORGE, James, George, Thomas, William H., Fred, John B., Margaret, Martha, Sarah; Jones, Sarah.
1779 MUNRO, HUGH, Ann.
1782 McCLAMMY, PETER, Ann, Serena, Amelia.
1782 MOORE, ROGER, Mary.
1782 MORGAN, DANIEL, David, Daniel, Sarah.
1782 MUNFORD, WILLIAM, Ann.
1784 MORGAN, EZEKIEL, Aaron, James.
1785 McLORINAU, HENRY, James, Robert; Tompkins, Jonathan D.
1787 MOSELEY, THOMAS, Ross, Walter.
1789 McDONALD, WILLIAM, Johnson, Jacob, Joshua.
1790 MORGAN, DAVID, Jean.
1791 MACLAINE, ARCHIBALD, Hooper, George, Catherine.
1791 McLEOD, DANIEL, Rachel; Carney, John, Mary.
1792 McCLAMMY, LUKE, George, Elijah.
1795 McGUFFORD, SAMUEL, Samuel, Nathaniel, William.
1796 MOTT, BENJAMIN, Ruth, Benjamin, William, Amelia.

N.

1758 NIELSON, THOMAS, Jane, Ann.
1764 NEAL, JACOB, Simpson, John.
1774 NEWTON, MARY, Jane; Roots, Robert, Samuel; Maultsby, Samuel.

1775 NICHOLS, WILLIAM, Joseph; Riley, Elizabeth, John, Peggy.
1777 NIXON, ROBERT, Robert, Nicholas, George.
1785 NEWMAN, STEPHEN, Stephen P., Ann.
1788 NICHOLS, JOSEPH O., Ann.
1782 NIXON, THOMAS, James W., Richard.
1775 NICHOLS, ELIZABETH, Walter, James, Kinchin.

O.

1791 ORR, MATTHEW, Lewton, Samuel, John, Matthew, Julia.
1774 OLIVER, JOHN, Sarah, Francis.
1741 PORTEVENT, SAMUEL, Ruth, James, Joseph, Hester.
1776 PRICE, JAMES, Sarah, Richard.
1778 PLAYER, STEPHEN, Esther, Richard, Elizabeth, Mary, John, Jacob.
1782 PARKER, THOMAS, Jacob.
1783 PLAYER, WILLIAM, Ann, Richard.
1785 PLAYER, RICHARD, Mary, Stephen, Richard, Mary, Comfort, Mary (wife).
1791 PLAYER, MARY, Mary, Comfort, Stephen.
1791 PRICE, RICHARD, James.
1793 POINCEY, NATHANIEL, Martha.
1795 PLAYER, THOMAS, wife, John, Hester, Rebecca, Naomi, Hannah, Thomas, Ann.

Q.

1776 QUINCE, JOHN, Ann, Mary.
1778 QUINCE, RICHARD, Richard, Parker, Jane, Ann.

R.

1784 RILEY, WILLIAM, John, Edward, Mary.
1767 ROSS, ALEX, Elizabeth.
1777 ROSS, ANN, Walter, Susanna; Moseley, John, Sampson, James, William, Thomas.
1778 ROUSE, ALEX, Elizabeth, Sanders; McCulloch, Mary.
1782 RADCLIFF, JAMES, wife; Malpass, Rebecca.
1782 RONALDSON, ANDREW, Margaret, Mary, Alex.
1782 ROGERS, THOMAS, Thomas, James, Elizabeth.
1783 ROWE, JOHN, Casiah, Fred.
1784 ROTCHELL, JOHN, Etherington, Sarah.
1785 ROBINSON, JAMES, Tabitha, Benjamin.
1792 ROWAN, ESTHER, Richard, Elizabeth; Bland, Bathsheba.
1792 ROOK, HENRY, Hurst, Allay.
1795 ROSS, WALTER, Halsey, Susanna, William H., Ann, Henry; Mosely, William, Livingston, Ann.

S.

1798 ST. GEORGE, ELIZABETH, George W., John.
1799 SIMMONS, Hilary, Asa, James, Enoch.
1799 SIMMONS, THOMAS, Hilary, Asa, James, Enoch.
1799 SPALDING, PHILIP, Margaret (wife), Margaret.
1770 SCHAW, ALEX, Catherine.
1764 SQUIER, JOHN G., Devane, John, Thomas, Margaret; Thomas, Elizabeth; Corbett, Thomas.
1767 SPRINGS, JOHN, Christian.

1768 SLOAN, ALLEN, William.
1774 SWANN, SAMUEL, Jane; Ashe, Samuel; James, Jane, Fred, John S.
1777 STEWARD, CHARLES, sisters; Gordon, John, Allen.
1785 STEED, BEVRICE, Thomas; Bowen, Margaret.
1788 SCHAW, ANN, Alex; Howe, William T.; Vail, Sarah, Elizabeth.
1788 SPICER, JAMES, wife and daughter (not named).
1789 SIMPSON, JOHN, Charles.
1790 SELLARS, CATHERINE, Archibald; Robinson, Catherine.
1791 SIKES, JOHN, Martha.
1794 STAINER, GEORGE, George, William.
1793 STEWART, JOHN, Alex, Matthew, William, Agnes, Elizabeth.
1793 STANLEY, JOHN, Allither, Sperice, James.
1794 STRUDWICK, SAMUEL, Martha, William F.; Bourget, Margery.
1796 SUTTON, JOSHUA, Benjamin; Anthony, Joshua; Shepard, Tacob; Ashe, Samuel; Fentress, James.

T.

1795 TATE, JAMES, Lawson, George; Campbell, M. Hugh.
1799 TOOMER, HENRY, Anthony, John, Lewis H., Eliza.

V.

1795 VICKHEARS, THOMAS, Mary; Coxeder, James.
1797 VICKHEARS, MARY, Russell, Edward.

W.

1799 WOOD, EDWARD, Elizabeth; Bishop, David; Shephard, Edward.
1740 WALKER, ROBERT, Ann (wife); Allen, Eleazar; Rowan, Matthew; Blake, Thomas; James, Thomas.
1765 WAKELEY, GEORGE, Mary, Abigail, Elizabeth.
1769 WILLIAMS, JOHN, Rachel, Nehemiah, Stephen.
1769 WEBB, DANIEL, Samuel, Isaac.
1772 WRIGHT, THOMAS, Ann (wife), Thomas, Joshua.
1772 WILLIAMS, DAVID, Hester, David, Henry, Rebecca.
1772 WATSON, JONATHAN, Hannah, Hester, Elizabeth, Ann.
1774 WATSON, JOSEPH, William, John.
1779 WARD, ANTHONY, Jane (wife), Hannah, Jane, Catherine, Fred, Anthony; Dunbidden, Jonathan; Jones, Fred.
1780 WILLIAMSON, WILLIAM, William, John.
1784 WHITE, WILLIAM, Margaret.
1785 WILSON, JOHN, Simpson, Fred.
1787 WILLIAMS, JOHN, Francis.
1788 WARD, MARK, wife.
1788 WALKER, ANN, James; Quince, Ann.
1789 WILLIAMS, TABITHA, Elizabeth.
1796 WARD, NATHAN, Jane, Mary; Neill, Hannah.

Y.

1794 YOUNG, CATHERINE, Catherine, Henry.

NORTHAMPTON—WILLS

1787 ATHERTON, JESSE, Penelope, Temperance, Frances, Jesse, Betty (wife).

1761 AVENT, WM., John, Thomas, Joseph, Gilley, Sarah, Rebecca, William, and wife (not named).

1764 AMIS, JOHN, Thomas, William, Mary, Rachel, Margaret, Rebecca, Nancy, Mary (wife).

1764 ARNOLD, JOHN, Martha (wife), John, Aaron, Thomas, Mary and Susanna.

1764 AMIS, THOMAS, Thomas, John, Mary, and Lucy (wife).

1771 ANDREWS, WM., Gray, Abraham, William, Green, Averilla, Martha (wife).

1779 AVENT, PETER, William, Isham, Joseph, John, Thomas, Sarah, Eliza, Lucy, Mourning, Re- *Penelope Brown son* becca, Lucritia, Molly (wife).

1787 ATHERTON, JEPTHA, Temperance, Dorothy, *Dawson* Mary, Frances, Jesse, Betty (wife) *was 2nd wife*

Bynum 1784 ALLEN, RICHARD, Mary, William, Fanny, Mourning, Alice, Elizabeth (wife).

⚹ only child of 1st wife, the others - by 2nd wife Betty Taken from certified copy of will. B.

1765 BARRETT, THOMAS, Sarah, Mary, Martha and James.

1777 BRITTLE, JOHN, John.

1777 BRANTLEY, JOHN, James.

1761 BAILEY, JOHN, Katherine (wife), Mary,

1761 BADDIE, ELIJAH, Willis (brother).

1761 BOYKIN, FRANCIS, John and Mildred. Sarah, Henry, John, Charles and Elizabeth.

1761 BURK, WM., William, Mary and Mary (wife).

1761 BAGGET, NICHOLAS, Lewis, Martha (wife).

1761 BRADFORD, THOMAS, Mary (wife).

1763 BRADFORD, WM., William.

1764 BRADFORD, JOHN, Edwin.

1764 BRADFORD, RACHEL, William.

1800 BARRETT, THOMAS, Elizabeth, Martha, Mary, Sarah and James.

1768 BROOKS, WILLIAM, Hodges, Charles.

1765 BENNETT, WM., Grace (wife).

1765 BUFFALO, WM., Matthew.

1768 BRYAN, WM., Jane (wife).

1771 BROWNEN, RICHARD, Ellis, Elinder; Barker, Eliza.

1779 BEDDINGFIELD, THOMAS, Henry.

1780 BOYD, ROBERT, Pheraba, James.

1780 BRITTLE, JOHN, Jesse.

1781 BRYAN, ALSEY, Samuel.

1782 BRITTLE, BRITTAIN, Sarah (wife).

1783 BRIDGES, EDWIN, Mary (wife).

1796 BOON, THOMAS, William; children of Mary (daughter).

1777 BASS, JOHN, Jacob.

1777 BOYKIN, JOHN, Jesse.

1785 BRYANT, WM., Clarkey (wife), Joseph and John; Jane (mother).

1787 BITTLE, JOHN, Elizabeth (wife), Mary, Elizabeth, Sarah, Frances, Katherine and Eurydice.

1788 BRYANT, JOHN, John, Winnie and Polly.
1789 BULLOCK, JOHN, James, Thomas and Mary.
1789 BRYAN, BENJAMIN, Benjamin, Polly, Thomas, Samuel and wife (not named).
1790 BRANCH, JOHN, Mary (wife), Polly, Thomas, Norman, Bebecca and Bowen.
1790 BASS, SAMUEL, Sarah (wife), Harold, Anne, Susanna and Matthew.
1790 BOON, JACOB, Lucy (wife), Jesse, Sally, Lucy and Pattie.
1791 BRYANT, JOHN M., Fort, Charlotte (sister).
1791 BRITTLE, JESSE, Martha (wife), Jesse, Lucy, Nancy, Exum and John.
1788 BARKLEY, BENJAMIN, Rhodes.
1792 BENTHALL, SUSANNA, Mann, Thomas.
1793 BRYANT, CLARKEY, Pinner, Sarah (daughter).
1793 BURK, WM., John, Sally, Mary (wife).
1794 BURN, WM., Barnaby, William, James and Elizabeth (wife).
1774 BRYAN, THOMAS, Council, Barsheba and Mary.
1794 BASS, BURGESS, Charlotte (wife).
1790 BOON, JOSEPH, Savory (wife), William.
1795 BASS, JETHRO, Elizabeth (wife), Jethro, Burwell, Council and Merica.
1795 BOYKIN, BURWELL, John.
1795 BOON, WM., Anna (wife), Lemuel, Alice, William and John.
1795 BURN, OWEN, Sarah (wife), Etheldred, Henry and Milly.
1795 BRIGGS, HALCOTT, Jones, Allen.
1788 BOON, THOMAS, Ede (wife), John, Celia and Patience.
1796 BRYAN, BENJAMIN, Sarah (wife), John and Davis.
1798 BELL, JAMES, Elizabeth (wife), children (not named).
1798 BINFORD, JOHN, Martha (wife), Keziah and Judith.
1798 BENTHALL, JOSEPH, Joseph, Daniel, Laban, Babin, Mary, Clara, Tabitha and Rhoda.
1799 BURGESS, ROBERT, Tamar (wife), Malachi, John and Nathaniel.
1784 BARKLEY, GEORGE, Rhodes, Samuel, Elizabeth, Sally and wife (not named).

C.

1796 COBB, ABSALOM, Priscilla (wife), Polly, Sally, Deberry and Lucretia.
1760 CARROLL, JOHN, John, Sterling, Charles, Thomas, Agnes and wife (not named).
1761 COTTEN, JOHN, Faith (wife).
1763 COTTEN, CHARLES, William.
1764 CAPEL, THOMAS, Elizabeth (wife).
1764 CARTER, JANE, Knight, Catherine.
1767 COBB, ROBERT, Mary (wife).
1768 CATHCART. GABRIEL, William.
1794 COTTEN, WILLIAM, Harriet (wife).
1769 COLLIER, JOSEPH, Joshua; Tart; James Cotten (brother).
1771 CAMPBELL, ISRAEL, William.
1782 CLARK, JAMES, Silvia, Mary, Charity, Sarah, Angelina, Nancy, Patsy, Elizabeth and wife (not named).

1783   CRITTENDEN, HENRY, Henry.
1783   COTTEN, LYDIA, Roderick and Elizabeth.
1783   COTTEN, MARY, William.
1790   COTTEN, JOHN, Joab.
1790   COTTON, JOHN, Joab.
1795   COTTEN, ALLEN, Henry, Allen and John (bro-
       thers).
1795   CAPEL, EDWARD, Thomas, John, Judy, Polly,
       Seling and Charles.
1796   CARP, ALICE, John.
1795   CROW, ROBERT, Martha (wife).
1797   CLIFTON, BENJAMIN, Patsy (wife), Polly,
       Jonas and Cordal.
1797   COTTEN, JAMES, Elizabeth (wife), Polly and
       Dickinson.
1797   CHAPPEL, MARY, Benjamin, Robert, Elizabeth
       and Keziah.
1778   COKER, JOHN, John. *Also not Allen so given in his will and In Census*
1793   COLLIER, ALLEN, Susanna (wife); Nancy,
       Green, James, Sarah, Jane and Jonathan.

D.

1799   DELOACH, SOLOMON, Jesse and William.
1762   DAWSON, JOHN, Charity (wife).
1763   DEBERRY, JOHN, Henry.
1763   DAWSON, CHARITY, Alston, Solomon.
1767   DICKINSON, ISAAC, Priscilla (wife).
1763   DUKES, ROBERT, Isabel (wife).
1768   DAY, JOHN, Lucy (wife).
1770   DAVIS, BENJAMIN, wife (not named).
1770   DELOATCH, FRANCIS, William.
1789   DAUGHTARY, MANDEW, Joseph, Louis, Jack,
       Sarah, Willey and Celia.
1770   DAWSON, HENRY, John.
1783   DICKINSON, DAVID, David.
1784   DAUGHTRY, JOSHUA, Elizabeth (wife), Vina,
       Elijah, Elisha, Lucretia and Mary, Elizabeth
       (wife).
1784   DAY, EDMOND, Edmond, Thomas and Mary.
1787   DICKINSON, JOHN, Malachi, James, John and
       Mary.
1787   DICKINSON, JAMES, Elizabeth (wife).
1788   DEMPSEY, GEORGE, Rachel (wife).
1790   DUKE, JAMES, Milly (wife); Josiah (brother).
1790   DANCY, JAMES, Benjamin, John, James, Wil-
       liam, Elizabeth, Rebecca; wife (not named).
1791   DAVIS, JAMES, Mary, John, William, Eliza-
       beth and Arthur.
1787   DUKE, JOHN, Sarah (wife), Ann, Mary.
1788   DAFFIN, HENRY, Nancy (wife), Jemima
       (sister).
1788   DAUGHTRY, BRYAN, Bathsheba, Rachel, Mary,
       Bryan, Enos, Abigail, Ruth and Randolph.
1793   DAUGHTRY, MUNDEW, Lewis.
1794   DEBERRY, DREWRY, Hollomon, Charlotte,
       (daughter).
1795   DEBERRY, ABSALOM, Susanna (wife), Allen.
1796   DAUGHTREY, JESSE, Rhoda (wife), Henry,
       Temperance, Sarah.
1796   DEBERRY, PETER, Absalom, Peter and Sarah.

E.

1796   EARP, ALICE, William, John, Christian
       and Nancy (grandchildren).

1777 EDWARDS, WM., John.
1760 EDWARDS, JOHN, Josiah.
1765 EDWARDS, JOHN, Mary (wife), Thomas.
1767 EDWARDS, RICE, John.
1779 EWELL, SALLIE C., Roderick C.
1788 EXUM, WM. Charlotte (wife), Patsy.
1788 EDMUNDS, JOHN, Susanna (wife), Jane and Lucy.
1777 EXUM, MATTHEW, Mary (wife), Richard.
1788 EDWARDS, CHARITY, Parker, Samuel (cousin).
1788 ELLIS, JOHN, John, Mary (wife).
1789 EATON, WM., Thomas and Mary.
1790 EDWARDS, SAMUEL, Martha (wife), Samuel, John, William, Mary, James and Kinchin.
1790 EXUM, JOSEPH, Wife (not named), Harry, Matthew and Elizabeth.
1792 EXUM, ANN, James and Nancy.
1776 EATON, WM., Rebecca (wife), William.
1794 ELLIS, BARTHOLOMEW, Martha (wife), Bartholomew.
1796 EDMUNDS, NICHOLAS, Susanna (wife), Thomas (brother).
1798 EDMUNDS, JANE, Daughtrey, Susanna (mother); Lucy, Elizabeth and Martha (sisters).
1798 ENGLISH, NATHAN, Sarah (wife), Patience, and Rebecca.

F.

1775 FIGURES, BARTHOLOMEW, Richard.
1765 FIGURES, JOHN, Mary (wife).
1770 FUTRELL, THOMAS, Hannah.
1779 FLOYD, JOHN, Jessie.
1780 FUTRELL, JESSE, Lydia.
1781 FORSTER, MARGARET, Vincent, James.
1782 FENNEL, LEMUEL, John.
1778 FAISON, ELIZABETH, Henry.
1789 FLOWER, RANSFORD, Betsy, Ransford, Ann, Polly and Sarah.
1790 FUTRELL, BENJAMIN, Thomas, Elizabeth, Mary, Arthur, Fred, Etheldred, Moore, Milly, wife (not named).
1780 FUTRELL, JOHN, Thomas, John, Charity, Joel, Ephraim, John, Pheraba, Lawrence, Buckner, James, Charles, Granow and Allen.
1792 FLOYD, MORRIS, Mary (wife), Rosamund, Thomas, Edward, Andrew and Morris.
1795 FULKS, WM., Martha (wife), Benjamin, Edward, Miles, Mary and Martha.
1795 FUTRELL, THOMAS, Shadrack, John, Charity, Faith, Bathsheba, Patsy, Sarah (wife).
1799 FUTRELL, JOSEPH, Penelope (wife), Stephen, Rachel and Frea
1795 FUTRELL, DAVID, Anna (wife); David, Charity, Sarah, Elizabeth and Amy.

G.

1787 GRANBERY, WILLIAM, Mary (wife), Josiah, Thomas, John, William, James, Langley, David, Mary, Patsy, Peggy, Rebekah, Nancy.
1760 GREENE, THOMAS, Powell, Mary.
1763 GLOVER, MARY, Fred.
1764 GLOVER, BENJAMIN, Elizabeth (wife).
1767 GREGORY, CHARLES, Charles.

1767 GRANT, JAMES, Esther (wife).
1717 GRIFFIN, EDMUND, Martha (wife).
1771 GRIGGS, JOHN, William.
1782 GOODSON, EDWARD, Jesse, Celia, Edward and Amy; Julia (wife).
1782 GATLING, SARAH, Copeland, Wm. (cousin); Gatling, Anne, Edward and James.
1783 GREGORY, SYLVIA, Keziah.
1784 GAY, JOHN, Jesse and Martha; Prudence (wife).
1778 GRIFFITH, HANNAH, William.
1786 GEE, DRURY, Mary (wife), James T. and Boyce.
1788 GEE, HOWELL, Dupree, Jesse.
1789 GLOVER, THOMAS, John, Amy (wife).
1790 GLOVER, ALLEN, Jemima (wife).
1790 GLAUBERS, WM., Granbery, Mary.

H.

1777 HART, BENJAMIN, Mary (wife).
1777 HILL, HARMON, Henry.
1761 HART, MARY, Saunders, Mary.
1761 HART, THOMAS F., Anna (wife).
1761 HAYS, SAMUEL, Zilpha. ✓
1761 HUDSON, WM., Nicholas.
1762 HALL, MOSES, Wife (not named).
1762 HOWELL, NATHANIEL, Manner (wife).
1762 HACKNEY, SAMUEL, Jennings (son).
1762 HYDE, RICHARD, Lucas.
1764 HALL, JAMES, James.
1764 HILLIARD, JAMES, William L.
1767 HUGHLETT, JOHN, Minnie (wife).
1768 HOLLOWELL, JOSEPH, Silas.
1769 HILL, GREEN, Bennett.
1770 HOWELL, HOPKINS, Elizabeth (wife).
1771 HILLIARD, ANNE, Newsom, Isaac.
1780 HOLMES, SOLOMON, Wife (not named).
1781 HORN, MOSES, Millie.
1782 HART, MARY, Dawson, Nancy.
1783 HAYES, JOHN, Rachel (wife).
1784 HYDE, RICHARD, Averilla (wife).
1797 HAYS, MARY, Faison, Elias (brother).
1777 HORN, THOMAS, James.
1785 HYDE, DAVID, Mary, Deborah, Solomon and Stephen.
1785 HART, ARTHUR, Sarah (wife), Lucy and Mary.
1786 HARRISON, WM., Sarah (wife), Edmund, Isham, John, William, Henry, James, Mary and Betty.
1787 HOWELL, SARAH, Benjamin.
1787 HULME, WM., Wife (not named), Children (not named).
1789 HAYES, SAMPSON, Mary (wife), Temperance and Penelope.
1791 HATFIELD, BENJAMIN, Sally (wife), George, Polly, Patsy, Nancy, Sally and Esther.
1788 HART, ARTHUR, Martha (wife), Harry, Warren, Arthur, Wright, Robert and Isham.
1789 HART, WRIGHT, Boykin, Nancy.
1792 HILLIARD, HENRY, Hillard, Martha, Elizabeth and Mary Ann (sisters).
1793 HARRIS, EDWARD, Hartwell (brother).

1794 HOWELL, HENRY, Delilah (wife), Delilah, John, Celia, Elizabeth, Henry and Benjamin.
1794 HART, ELIZABETH, Parker, Moses (grandson).
1795 HAYES, JOHN, Sarah (wife), Elijah and Samuel.
1795 HAYES, SARAH, Meaner (daughter).
1796 HOUSE, DANIEL, Mary (wife), Children (not named).
1796 HILLIARD, JOHN, David and John; Priscilla (wife).
1796 HAYS, SAMUEL, Wife (not named), Jesse. John and Margaret.
1796 HOLLOMON, ARTHUR, Elizabeth (wife). Exum (son).
1779 HORTON, ROBERT, Martha (wife).

I.

1760 IRBY, JOHN, Jane (wfe).

J.

1765 JONES, THOMAS, Mary.
1766 JONES, WM., Harwood.
1766 JONES, ROBERT, Mary (wife).
1769 JORDAN, THOMAS, Elizabeth.
1769 JOINER, LUCY, William.
1771 JORDAN, OLIVER, Alsey.
1780 JORDAN, HENRY, John.
1783 JUDKINS, NICHOLAS, James, John, Joel, Carolus, Jesse, Faith.
1807 JONES, ALLEN, Mary (wife), Davie, Allen J. (grandson), Green, Allen J. (grandson); Long, Rebecca J. (granddaughter); Sitgreaves, John, Amerlla and Emily (grandchildren).
1797 JACOBS, JACOB, Susanna (wife), Jason, Joseph, John, Samuel, Jacob, William, Mary, Elizabeth, Winifred, Margaret, Sarah and Miriam.
1790 JOYNER, ABSALOM, Winifred, Thomas and Jesse.
1800 JEANES, WM., Millender (wife), James, Oliver and Polly.
1777 JOHNSTON, WILLIAM, John.
1784 JONES, FRANCES, Harwood and Tignal (brothers).
1783 JONES, NATHANIEL, Robert, George, Allen, Willie, Tamerlane and Elizabeth.
1784 JONES, WM., William.
1788 JOHNSTON, BENJAMIN, Wife (not named), Elizabeth, Sarah, Shadrack and Charity.
1791 JUSTICE, MARY, James, Mary, Sarah, Elizabeth and Lucy.
1789 JOHNSTON, JOSEPH, Joseph and Unity.
1789 JAQUES, WM., Dorothy E.
1789 JOHNSTON, SARAH, Elizabeth and Katie.
1789 JOHNSTON, ELIZABETH, Elijah (brother).
1789 JONES, HARWOOD, Nancy and John.
1792 JORDAN, GEORGE, Josiah, Hezekiah, Hanans, Olive and Sallie.
1793 JOYNER, ABRAHAM, Sarah (wife), Giles, Mary, Mildred, Elizabeth and Charity.
1793 JENKINS, WINBORNE, Emma (wife), Winborne and Benjamin.

1795 JOHNSON, JOHN, William (brother), Celia (sister).
1796 JONES, ROBERT, Priscilla (wife).
1797 JENKINS, EMMY, Winborne, Benjamin, Mary, Charity and William.
1798 JONES, HARWOOD, Jones, Harwood (son of John Jones).

K.

1786 KING, JOHN, Sarah (wife), Henry, Benjamin, John and Sarah.

L.

1795 LOVE, WM., Alex and Ann, wife (not named).
1761 LASSITER, JACOB, William.
1761 LOWE, JOHN, William.
1761 LEAK, WM., Jonas.
1769 LOW, JAMES, Sarah (wife).
1771 LAMON, MARTHA, John.
1780 LOW, SAMUEL, Mary (wife).
1782 LONG, JOHN, wife (not named).
1782 LAY, LITTLEBERRY, Anne (wife).
1785 LEWIS, ANGELICA, Griffin.
1783 LOWE, THOMAS, Lunsford.
1796 LEWIS, ELIPHAZ, Polly (wife), Benjamin, Patsy, Sally and Polly.
1778 LASHLEY, JOHN, Rebecca (wife).
1778 LASSITER, ROBERT, Dempsey.
1779 LONG, MARY, Littleberry.
1784 LASSITER, JESSE, May (wife), Tabitha, Lucretia, James, Jesse, Joseph, Miles, Aaron,Vina, Pheraba, Anne, Winifred May and Martha.
1785 LYNAM, CHARLES, Sally (wife), William.
1786 LILES, THOMAS, Elizabeth (wife), Benjamin, Jesse, Lucy, Elizabeth, Martha and Miller.
1787 LONG, NEHEMIAH, Sarah (wife), Henry, William and Bathsheba.
1790 LOVE, THOMAS, Eliza (wife), Pattie, Rhoda, Jenny, Sally; Sons (not named).
1792 LONG, BRITTAIN, Martha (wife).
1792 LASSITER, JOSEPH, Charity (wife), Joel and Bathsheba.
1794 LEWIS, JEAN, James, Benjamin, William and Celia.
1796 LAWRENCE, JOHN, Mary (wife), John, Ricks, Exum, Jonathan, Thomas D., Josephus and Nancy.
1797 LILES, BENJAMIN, Mary (wife), children (not named).

M.

1761 MASHBURN, MATTHEW, Sarah (wife).
1761 MERRELL, BENJAMIN, Mark.
1799 MORGAN, SIMPSON, Jesse, Polly and Patsy; Timothy Morgan (nephew), Timothy (brother).
1764 MORRIS, JOHN, Ann.
1765 MORGAN, WM., Joseph.
1765 MOORE, RICHARD, William.
1767 MONGER, NICHOLAS, John.
1770 MATTHEWS, THOMAS, Martha (wife).
1779 MALONE, ROBERT, Thomas.

1779 MELTON, ELIZABETH, Children (not named)

1781 MIZZELL, MOSES, James.

1783 MADDREY, JAMES, Nathaniel.

1777 MITCHELL, JOHN, William.

1784 MASON, HENRY, Mary (wife), Daniel; Mason, Jacob, William and Peyton (brothers).

1785 MERRIMON, JOHN, Francis and John.

1786 MADDREY, PETER, Randolph (brother), Lucy (sister) and Hannah (daughter).

1787 MOORE, RICHARD, James, Charles, Ann, Judith, Sarah, Anne, Tabitha and Judith.

1791 MURRILL, BARNABY, Amy (wife); Barnaby and Benjamin Hardy; Winifred, Amy, Martha, Mary Ann and Temperance.

1791 MARSHALL, ISAAC, George, Rhoda, Ichabod, Barbara, Susanna and Sarah.

1791 MALONE, ROBERT, Milly (wife), Ann, Elizabeth, John A., William and Charles.

1788 MOODY, JOSEPH, Solomon, Surrell, Lydia, Benjamin, Hinchey, Elizabeth, Dorcas and Sukey.

1792 MANN, THOMAS, wife (not named), Sylvia, Susanna and Theodoric.

1793 MARTINDALE, ABRAHAM, Benjamin, Henry, Delany, Pheraba, Claoditha, Angel and Lavinia.

1794 MECOM, SAMUEL, Matthew and Polly.

1794 MURRELL, BENJAMIN, Mary (wife), Winborne (son).

1795 MARYHON (Marion), WM., Milly (wife), John, Sally, Jesse, Fanny, Nathaniel, Mitchell and Edmond.

1796 MOODY, HINCHEY G., Rebecca (wife), John, Hinchey, Thomas and Rebecca.

1796 MELTON, JOHN, Mary (wife).

1797 MITCHELL, MARY, Webb, Rebecca and Nancy; Gee, Sarah.

1797 MONGER, WM., Patience (wife), Burwell, Martha and Dorcas.

N.

1765 NODEN, CHARLES, Woolfolk and Charles.

1780 NORSWORTHY, WM., Peggy (wife).

1781 NORSWORTHY, ISABELLA, Preston.

1789 NORSWORTHY, JOHN, John, Ann (wife), Samuel, Daffin (daughter), Pamela, Rutland, Keziah, Mary and Lydia.

1795 NORFLEET, MARMADUKE, Reuben.

O.

1781 O'QUIN, DANIEL, Mary (wife).

1789 OSBORNE, JAMES, Sarah (wife).

1791 ODOM, AARON, Elizabeth and Uriah.

1792 ODOM, MOSES, Moses, Josiah, Jacob, Ruth, Rachel, Rachel (wife).

P.

1799 PARKER, SAMUEL, Ann, Sarah, Elizabeth and Rachel.

1775 PACE, WM., Celia (wife).

1795 PEEBLES, RORERT, Robert.

1777 PRITCHARD, JOHN, Rebecca (wife).

1760 PEALE, JOHN, Richard.

1762 PURDY, WM , Catherine.
1762 PAUL, JOHN, Keziah.
1765 PACE, THOMAS, Amy (wife).
1765 PERKINS, SAMUEL, Mary.
1770 PRIDHAM, NASH, Brewer, Mary.
1780 PEELE, SAMUEL, Thomas.
1781 POPE, ELIJAH, Charity (wife).
1782 PEELE, ROBERT, Robert, Elizabeth, Mary, Sarah, Abla, David, Judith, Rachel and Celia.
1782 PATTERSON, BENJAMIN, Elizabeth (wife), Benjamin, William, Jonathan, Joseph and John.
1777 PRICE, THOMAS, Brittle, John.
1778 PHILIPS, MARK, Mourning (wife).
1778 PHILIPS, THOMAS, Mourning.
1784 PARKS, ISAAC, William.
1788 PEETE, WM., Angeline (wife), Edwin.
1790 PRITCHARD, SWAN, Mary (wife), Judah, Nancy and Augustin.
1790 PENRICE, FRANCIS, Joyner, Rebecca (daughter).
1791 POWELL, JACOB, Pheraba (wife), Mary, Elias, Bathesheba, Priscilla, Pheraba and Elizabeth.
1791 PARKS, JAMES, Sarah (wife), James, Peter, Andrew, Anne, Rebecca, Sarah and Agnes.
1791 PACE, WM., Solomon (brother).
1789 PACE, GEORGE, Collings, Mary and James.
1792 PACE, HARDY, William R., Thomas, Rebecca, Lucy (wife), Elizabeth.
1792 PARKER, JOSEPH, Sarah (wife), Jeremiah, Josiah, Alexander, Judith.
1793 PACE, WM., Faith (wife), Dorothy.
1793 PARKS, CHANEY, Aaron (brother), Angelia (sister).
1794 PEETE, MARY, Elliott, Nancy P., (granddaughter); Whitaker, Mary and Mary.
1795 PIPKIN, STEWART, Tabitha (wife).
1795 PRIDE, HALCOT B., Jones, Allen, Willie and wife of Cadwallader; Bradley, James; Pride, Halcot (son of May).
1795 PACE, SOLOMON, Beddingfield, Fanny (daughter); Stephen (brother).
1797 PARKER, THOMAS, Richard.
1798 PIERCE, JOHN, Jacob, Elisha, James, Rachel, Sarah and Nancy.
1799 PETERSON, KINCHEN, Anne (wife).
1799 PARKER, FRANCIS, Sarah (wife), Peggy, Priscilla, Martha, Susanna, William, Lewis, Robert and Lucy.
1784 PARKS, ROBERT, Elizabeth, William, Mary, Ann, Silvia, Catherine and Susanna.
1777 RUFFIN, ETHELDRED, Martha (wife),
1761 RAWLS, JESSE, Olivia.
1764 ROWELL, SAMUEL, Edward.
1767 RUFFIN, ROREBT, Anne.
1799 RANDOLPH, PENELOPE, mother (not named), Bryan (brother), Betsey (sister).
1771 RAGLAND, GEORGE, William.
1783 RAGLAND, WM., Neil, Sarah.
1783 ROOK, JOHN, John.

* From certified copy of Etheldred Ruffin's

1778   Ruffin, John, Millicent.
1785   Rogers, David, Sarah (wife), Anne and Sarah.
1784   Reavis, Wm., Mary (wife), William, Samuel and Isaac.
1786   Ruffin, Robert, Sarah (mother), Hannah, Sally and Rebecca (sisters).
1791   Richards, John, Mary (wife), William, John, Elizabeth, Sarah, Martha and Ann.
1792   Rutland, Martha, Sion, Mildred, Wilson and Winifred.
1792   Rogers, Joseph, Mark, Mary, Thomas, Michael and John.
1799   Reams, Jeremiah, Margaret (wife), William, John, Elijah, Jeremiah and Peter.
1792   Randolph, Giles, Barsheba (wife), William, John, Matticu, Penelope, Elizabeth, Bryant and Thomas.
1793   Rutland, Thomas, Abigail (wife), Elizabeth and Mary.
1793   Ricks, Wm., Jason, Sarah, Martha, William, Elizabeth, Dempsey and Susanna.
1794   Reams, Wm., Mary (wife).
1794   Roberts, Margaret, Delphia, Thomas, James, John, Mary, Faith, Christian, Phoebe, Hannah, Milla and Elizabeth.
1794   Roy, James, Elizabeth (wife), Samuel, Miles and Mary.
1795   Rutland, Wm., Sarah (wife), Sarah, Miles, Samuel, Rebecca, Mahala, Elizabeth and Abednego.
1799   Revill, Humphrey, Margaret (wife), Humphrey, Matthew, Lazarus, Sally, James, Shadrack, William, Nephaik and Randolph.
1799   Raney, Wm., Catherine (wife), Edmund, Thomas, Daniel and James.

S.

1775   Sikes, Thomas, Mary.
1760   Sherard, James, James.
1761   Stephenson, Wm. Charity (wife).
1764   Short, Wm., John.
1764   Sterling, Isaac, John.
1764   Squire, Sebastian, Jane (wife).
1765   Shorter, Benjamin, Drury.
1765   Stap, Joshua, Tomlinson, Thomas.
1769   Spawls, Thomas, Hilliard, John.
1770   Screws, John, Carter, Martha.
1770   Sikes, Joseph, James.
1771   Skinner, Wm., Susanna (wife).
1799   Sisson, James, Ann.
1779   Sowerby, John, Henry.
1780   Smith, Richard, Mary.
1781   Step, Joshua, Susanna.
1778   Stuart, Mary, Rachel (wife).
1778   Snipes, Joseph J., Mary.
1778   Sanders, Solomon, Christiana.
1785   Sumner, Richard, Sarah (wife), Richard, Mary, Elizabeth, Jennie, James and Sarah.
1786   Smith, Wm., Mary (wife), James and Turner.
1786   Seat, Billison, John, Lucy, Sarah and Mary.

1788 SHERROD, WM., Keziah (wife), Joel, Arthur and Benjamin.
1789 STRICKLAND, WM., Mary (wife), Nathan, Benjamin, William, Joseph, Martha and Nancy.
1790 STURDIVANT. WM., Robert, James, Margaret, Hannah, Frances, Elizabeth, Priscilla, Peter and Matthew.
1791 STEPHENSON, ABRAHAM, Winifred.
1792 SHORT, JOHN, John and Pattie.
1792 STEPHENSON, ARTHUR, Mary, Elizabeth, Martha, Mildred, Tabitha, Sukey, Abraham, wife (not named).
1794 STANSELL, NATHAN, John, Samuel, Savory, Lucy, wife (not named).
1795 SORET, THOMAS, Patterson, Joseph (friend).
1795 SKINNER, KINDRED, Judith (wife), Susanna, Sarah, Katherine, Mary and Martha.
1797 SHORT, JUDAH, William and Sarah.
1798 SMITH, FLOOD, Littleberry.
1798 SAVORY, JOHN, Savory, Mildred (sister).
1761 SMITH, WM., Mary (wife).

T.

1777 TARVER, JAMES, Harmon.
1776 THOMAS, ELIZABETH, Bryan, Samuel.
1777 TARVER, HARMON, Robert.
1762 TAYLOR, JOHN, Richard.
1768 TURNER, JAMES, Mary (wife).
1771 TURNER, JOHN, Mary (wife), Truelove, Lucy; Tomlinson, Lucretia.
1780 TARVER, ANDREW, Mary (wife).
1782 TYNER, ARTHUR, Elizabeth (wife).
1778 THOMPSON, JOHN, William.
1778 TARVER, SAMUEL, John.
1779 TYNER, WM., Ella (wife).
1785 TUCKER, CURLE, Haynes, Mary.
1785 TARVER, THOMAS, Thomas and Jacob.
1790 THOMPSON, CHARLES, Joanna (wife), Pamela, Washington, Etheldred, Nicholson and Clarissa.
1790 THRIFT, WM., Nathaniel (brother), Jenny (wife).
1788 TAYLOR, JOSEPH, Joseph, Peggy, Mary and John; Mary (wife).
1792 THOMPSON, WM., Hannah (wife), Thompson, Wm. (nephew).
1794 TART, WM. C., James C.
1794 TARVER, FRED, John, Benjamin and Andrew (brothers).
1795 TADLOCK, THOMAS, Sally (wife), Joel, Thomas and Lucy.

U.

1791 UNDERWOOD, JOHN, · Sarah (wife), Jesse, Eleanor, John, Sarah.
1795 UNDERWOOD, JESSE, Elizabeth (wife); Sarah (mother); Ezekiel and Jonathan (nephews).

V.

1764 VINSON, THOMAS, John.
1765 VAUGHAN, VINSON, Vinson.
1766 VEAL, MORRIS, Melbra (wife).

1790 VAUGHAN, WM., Irene (wife).
1781 VEAL, RICHARD, John.
1794 VAUGHAN, WM., Sarah (wife), Mary, Elizabeth, Thomas, Miley, Wm., Nancy, Calhoun and James.
1796 VALENTINE, ALEXANDER, Mary (sister); John (brother).
1796 VASSER, JOSEPH, Tabitha (wife), James, Joseph, Josiah, Lemuel, Susanna, Patty, Sally, Rebecca.
1797 VAUGHAN, THOMAS, Martha (wife), John.
1798 VINSON, JAMES, Unity (wife), Henry, James, Abner, Silas, David, Lydia, Samuel and Elizabeth.

W.

1776 WADDELL, TURNER, Angelina C. (wife).
1761 WINBORNE, WM., William.
1766 WASHINGTON, JAMES, Robert.
1777 WINBORNE, PHILIP, Anne (wife).
1800 WEAVER, PETER, Sarah (wife), Richard H. and Edwin.
1768 WASHINGTON, ETHELDRED, John.
1768 WASHINGTON, JOHN, Sarah (wife).
1768 WASHINGTON, ROBERT, Agnes.
1779 WINBORNE, DAVID, Elizabeth (wife).
1778 WHEELER, HENRY, Henry.
1780 WILLIAMSON, LEWIS, Priscilla (wife).
1782 WILLIAMS, JESSE, John.
1784 WILLIAMS, REBECCA, Jane, Nathan, Thomas and Lucy.
1778 WALDEN, WM, David.
1778 WEBB, JOHN, Mary (wife).
1785 WEBB, THOMAS, John, Thomas, Mary, Rebecca, Margaret, Nancy.
1786 WILLIAMS, CHRISTOPHER, Elizabeth (wife), Thomas, Samuel, Sarah, Jane, Christopher and Gray.
1784 WOOD, JAMES, Sarah (wife); Wood, Mary and Elizabeth (granddaughters).
1786 WARREN, JESSE, Elizabeth (wife), Sarah and Elizabeth.
1789 WARR, JOYCE, William.
1792 WALTHROP, MICHAEL, Wife (not named), Mary, John and Grafton.
1790 WOOD, JONAS, James.
1791 WOOD, JOSEPH, Nellie (wife).
1791 WOODARD, JOSEPH, SR., Joseph, Benjamin, Mary, Elizabeth, Ann and Sally.
1791 WALTHROP, MITCHELL, Floyd, Mary.
1792 WOOD, CULLEN, Sarah (wife), James and Lawrence (brothers).
1793 WALL, JOHN, John.
1793 WESTBROOK, THOMAS, John, Penina and James; Wife (not named).
1795 WALTHROP, JOHN, Nancy (wife), Sarah.
1795 WARREN, ROBERT, Joshua; Warren, Elizabeth (granddaughter), Deberry, Susan.
1796 WOOD, HENRY A., Elizabeth (wife), Dawson. Peyton, Henry, James, Elisha A.
1796 WARR, JAMES, Lemuel and Milley; Milly (wife).

1796 WHITE, POLLY, White, Peggy and Catherine, (sisters).

1797 WOOD, JAMES, Celia (wife), Mary, Celia, Freeman, Elizabeth and John.

1797 WEBB, JOHN, Thomas (brother), Rebecca, Margaret and Nancy (sisters).

1797 WEBB, THOMAS, Mitchell (son), Mary (mother), Rebecca, Margaret and Nancy (sisters).

1797 WEBB, HENRY, Jesse (brother).

1798 WASHINGTON, JAMES, Lucy (wife), Telemachus (brother).

1799 WHEELER, JOHN, Celia (wife), Hezekiah, Bryant, John, Dirden, Sally, Thomas B., Polly and Milly.

Y.

1796 YOUNG, GERRARD, Edwards, Rebecca.

ORANGE—WILLS

A.

1760 ALSTON, JAMES, John, James, Christian, Joseph, Mary, Charity, Sarah; Glenn, Worsham; Summers, Josiah.

1767 ASTEN, WILLIAM, Mary, Downey, Peter and William; McLeroy, Thomas; McBryde, William.

1767 AKIN, JOSEPH, Thomas, Joseph, Mary, Luella; Jefferson, George.

1770 ALLEN, JOSEPH, John, William, Daniel.

1772 ALLEN, ISAAC, Mary (wife).

1779 ABERCROMBIE, ROBERT, Charles, Robert.

1779 ASPEN, THOMAS, Sarah (wife); Paschal, William.

1790 ALLISON, JOSEPH, Elizabeth, Daniel, Joseph, Margaret, Mary, Sarah, Nancy.

1790 ALLEN, ZACHARIAH, wife; George, Elizabeth, William, James, John, Mary, Sarah, Robert, Ruth, Joseph, Zachariah.

1790 ALBRIGHT, JOHN, Hester, John C. and Elizabeth.

1790 ARMSTRONG, JOHN, Margaret (wife); William, Elizabeth, Mary, Margaret, Rachel.

1791 ALBRIGHT, JACOB, Catherine (wife); George, John, Jacob, Joseph, Henry, Daniel, Sophia, Catherine.

1793 ANDREW, ROBERT, Robert, David, Thomas, Sarah (wife); William, Ann, Sarah, James.

1796 ALLISON, JOHN, Joseph, James, John, Charles, Hamilton, Grisel, Agnes, Martha, Elizabeth.

1796 ARMSTRONG, JAMES, William, Thomas, James.

B.

1760 BOHANNON, DUNCAN, Susanna, John, Mary, Betty, Benjamin, Richard.

1761 BRASWELL, RICHARD, Valentine, Jr., Richard, William, Mary, Tabitha, Joyce.

1761 BERRY, THOMAS, Elizabeth (wife); Thomas, Elizabeth, Nancy, William, Jane, Bryan.

1761 BOOKER, JOHN, Patience (wife), James, Patience.

1761 BOSNEY, JOHN, William, Richard, Simon, David, John.

1764 BROWN, WILLIAM, Ray, Margaret.

1764 BROOKS, JACK, Mary (wife), John, Mary, Elizabeth, James.

1767 BASKETT, WILLIAM, Ruth (wife), Mary, Elizabeth, Ruth, Thomas, William.

1768 BORING, WILLIAM, Charles, Joseph.

1769 BOMER, GEORGE, Margaret (wife), children (not named).

1770 BLACKWOOD, WILLIAM, Elizabeth (wife), James, John, Martha, Mary, Janet, Elizabeth, Ann, William, Margaret.

1771 BASKETT, JOHN, Ann, William, Thomas.

1774 BURTON, PRISCILLA, Sarah, Priscilla, Robert.

1773 BARNETT, JOSEPH, Rachel, Samuel, Mary, Sarah.

1774 BISHIND, JACOB, Catherine, Hannah, Judah.

1775 BURGESS, JOHN, Elizabeth (wife).

1776 BORING, WILLIAM, Elizabeth, Rebecca, Nicey, Mary.
1776 BUMPAS, WILLIAM, Robert, Mary.
1782 BERRY, MICHAEL, Dunnikin, John.
1782 BUTLER, JOHN, Anne (wife).
1775 BOWIN, JOSEPH, Susanna, John, James, William, Isaac, Joseph, David, Susan, Becky, Phoebe, Sue, Patty.
1783 BLAKE, BENJAMIN, Benjamin, Penelope, Ann, Bethana, James.
1784 BRAZIER, THOMAS, Thomas, John, Aquilla, James, Samuel, Hannah, Mary, Cossa, Jean, Rachel.
1784 BURKE, THOMAS, wife; Mary.
1791 BENTON, JESSE, Nancy (wife).
1792 BARBEE, CHRISTOPHER, Dicey (wife).
1784 BREECE, THOMAS, Martha (wife); Richard, John, William, James, Robert, Martha, Thomas, Robeson, Rachel.
1785 BOWLING, JEAN, Archibald, Abraham, Alexander, Andrew, Elizabeth.
1795 BURCH, JAMES, Mary, John, George, Sarah, James, Johnston, Agnes, William.
1795 BUCKINGHAM, JOSEPH, Margery, William, Joshua.
1796 BOYLE, JOHN, John, William, Martha.
1797 BELVIN, WILLIAM, Magdalen (wife).
1797 BARNHILL, ROBERT, James, John, Sarah, Margaret.
1797 BYRN, JAMES K., Mary (wife), Thomas, Elizabeth, James, Abraham, Resin, Mary.
1799 BARBEE, JOHN, Sarah (wife), Mack, Young, William, Joseph, Pat, John, Slyvia, Edie, Sally, Elizabeth, Rosanna, Theina.

C.

1759 CURRIE, MARY ANN, Margaret, Mary, John, James.
1762 COLLINS, JAMES, James, John, William.
1766 COLLINS, JOHN, William, Catherine.
1766 CALDWELL, ANDREW, Janet, Mary, Elizabeth, Samuel, William.
1767 COX, WILLIAM, William, John, Thomas.
1767 CATE, ROBERT, Elizabeth, Richard, Sarah, Ann, Thomas, Joseph.
1774 CRABTREE, THOMAS, William, John, Mary, Elizabeth, James, Thomas.
1775 CAMPBELL, JOHN, Margaret, Joseph, David, John.
1776 COHARON, ALEX., Esther (wife), John, James. Elex., Samuel, Jean, Esther, Isabel.
1778 CLAPP, LODOVICK, wife, John.
1779 CAIN, JACOB, Joanna (wife).
1780 CAPPER, THOMAS, Ann, Nancy.
1781 CLARK, THOMAS, Susanna, Sarah, Mary, Catherine, Thomas, William.
1781 CAIN, WILLIAM, William, Hugh, James, Allen, Ann, John, Fanny, Margaret, Elizabeth.
1782 CLARK, WILLIAM, William, James, Susanna, John, Hannah, Mary.
1782 CORRIGAN, WILLIAM, wife, John, Joseph, Eli, Mary.
1782 CLARKE, WILLIAM, Daniel, George.

1783 CORRIGAN, EDWARD, Margaret, John, James.
1783 CHRISTIAN, JOHN, Thomas, John, Mary (wife), Elizabeth, Henrietta, Mary, James. Charles, Richard, William, Nathaniel, Blount.
1785 CRAIG, WILLIAM, Abigail (wife).
1785 CRAIG, DAVID, wife, William, David.
1790 CANTRELL, JACOB, Martha, Jane, Hannah, Sarah, Susanna, Mary, Zebedee, Thomas, Joseph.
1792 CONNER, JOHN, Elizabeth (wife), Margaret, James, Wilson.
1791 CRAIG, SAMUEL, Mary, William, David, Samuel, Martha, Margaret, Jenny, Elizabeth, Isabel.
1791 CARSON, ALEX., wife, Robert, Alex., Elizabeth, Mary, Samuel.
1791 COMBS, WILLIAM, Ann, James, Mary, Nancy, John.
1792 CHILDS, FRANCIS, Samuel, Wilson, Francis.
1793 COBLE, GEORGE, Henry, David.
1794 CATE, RICHARD, Emilia (wife); James, Jesse, Richard, Thomas, John, Emilia, Susanna. Benjamin.
1795 CLENCY, SAMUEL, William, Samuel, Jonathan.
1796 CATE, JOSEPH, Ann, Steven, Charles, Solomon, Elizabeth.
1796 CLARK, JAMES, Elizabeth, James, Thomas, William, Jesse, Eleanor, James, Katrina.
1796 CHISENHALL, ALEX., Celia, Samuel, Robeson, John.
1799 CARSON, DAVID, James.
1799 CATE, BENJAMIN, John, Jesse, William, James, Mary.

D.

1767 DEBOW, SOLOMON, John, Fred, Benjamin, Hannah, Jane, Ann, Mary, Sarah, Elizabeth, Hannah.
1770 DONALDSON, ROBERT, Thomas, Mary, Hannah (wife), Robert, Hannah, Elizabeth, Jean, Sarah.
1770 DEASON, JOSEPH, Mary, Nathan, Stephen, Solomon, Jesse, Eli, Joseph.
1774 DOBBIN, THOMAS, Hugh, John, Thomas, Rachel, Margaret, Elizabeth, Nancy.
1783 DEBOW, JOHN, John, Stephen, Lucy, John.
1784 DOSSETT, PHILIP, Celia, Siney, Susanna, William.
1784 DIXON, JAMES, Nancy, James, Stewart, Robert, William, Thomas, Polly, Margaret. Mary, Fanny.
1792 DAVIS, ENOCH, Abraham, John.
1793 DOHERTY, GEORGE, Mary, Francis.
1795 DUNWIDDIE, HENRY, Elizabeth, Abraham, James, John.
1796 DURHAM, MATTHEW, Susanna, Mark.
1799 DONNEGAN, WILLIAM, Sarah, William, Sherwood, Ashley, Peggy.
1791 DIBLEY, JACOB, Margery, Jacob, James, John,
1799 DURHAM, SUSANNA, Matthew, Lysias, Mark, Mary.

E.

1757 ELLETT, MICHAEL, Phillips, William.
1784 EDWARDS, WILLIAM, wife and children (not named).
1793 EFLAND, PETER, Catherine (wife), David,
1799 ESTES, JOHN, Elizabeth (wife).

F.

1757 FOUSHEE, CHARLES, Susanna, William, Charles.
1757 FOUSHEE, JOSEPH, wife, Jonathan, Mary, Richard, Joseph, Benjamin, Hannah.
1764 FORBES, WILLIAM, Margaret (wife), William, Hugh, George.
1759 FOUSHEE, CHARLES, Susanna, William, Charles.
1776 FARLEY, MOSES, John, Sarah, Josiah, Elizabeth.
1778 FOREST, WILLIAM, Joel, Gresham, William, Shadrach, Jesse, Lavinia.
1780 FOGLEMAN, GEORGE, Catherine, Henry, John, Peter, Eve, George A.
1785 FAUCETT, WILLIAM F., Margaret, William, Eliza.
1766 FIELDS, JOHN, John, Roger.
1775 FAUCETT, ROBERT, wife, George, Robert, Thomas, Edmund, Fanny, Elizabeth.
1786 FARMER, JOHN, wife, Nathaniel, James, Anna, Priscilla.
1790 FARMER, TOBIAS, wife, Nathaniel, Anne, Drusilla, James.
1791 FEW, JAMES, Frances, Elizabeth, Bethiah, James.
1791 FOREST, JOHN, Philip, John, Jonah, Christian, George, Barbara, Peter, Daniel, Judith.
1797 FAUCETT, JOHN, Thomas, Polly, Pheraba.
1798 FORREST, JACOB, Silvia, Willis, Mary, Sarah, Milly.
1798 FANN, JOHN, Rebecca, Patsy, Anne, Betsy, Elijah, William, Rawley, Elizabeth, Machias,
1800 FRUTH, JAMES, Grizzel, John, Eleanor, Hannah, Nancy.

G.

1768 GREASON, ISAAC, Margaret, Jacob, Nicholas.
1770 GEER, JOHN, wife, David, Fred, Tabitha, John, Lucy, Sarah, William.
1775 GEORGE, JOSEPH, Peggy, Ambrose, Jesse, William, Isaac, Eleanor, Janet.
1775 GRAY, JOHN, Hart, Thomas.
1776 GIBSON, GEORGE, Mary (wife) and children (not named).
1782 GWINN, MOSES, Elizabeth (wife), Jane, Mary, Elizabeth, Moses.
1783 GANT, EDWARD, Elizabeth, John, Thomas, Cary, Sarah.
1784 GRADY, CHRISTIAN, Hogg, James; Gattis, Isaac.
1785 GWIN, MORDECAI, Edward, John, Mordecai, Mary, Sarah, Elizabeth.

1799   GAINES, EDWARD, Susanna, Thomas, Joseph, Francis, Solomon, Moses, Nancy, Wilson and Broaddus.

H.

1760   HADLEY, JOSHUA, Patience, Joseph, Lydia, Joshua, Jeremiah, Thomas, Deborah, Hannah, Katharine.

1767   HOLDING, ISAAC, Thomas, Sarah, Isaac.

1767   HALLIBURTON, DAVID, wife, Charles, Thomas, David, John, William.

1768   HAYGOOD, JAMES, George, Benjamin, Elizabeth, James, William, Rebecca.

1767   HOLT, MICHAEL, Elizabeth, Peter.

1770   HARDEN, EDMUND, Mary (wife) and children (not named).

1774   HARRISON, NATHANIEL, Ellender (Eleanor), Nathaniel, Arthur, Edward, Mary, Charles, Unity.

1774   HARRISON, ANDREW, Jane (wife), Elizabeth, Ninian, Molly, Jane, Andrew, Nancy, William, Thomas.

1776   HARRISON, BURGESS, Elijah, Elisheba, Drusilla, Ezekiel, Penina, Jemima, Elizabeth, John.

1778   HOLLOWAY, ROBERT, Martha, Samuel, Bridget, Priscilla, Susanna, Ann, Stephen, Rachel, Ruth, Jane, Selice, Stephen.

1780   HALL, GEORGE, wife, Henry.

1785   HALL, JOHN, Jean, Rebekah, William, Robert, Mary, Sarah, John, Thomas, Rachel.

1785   HARRIS, JAMES, John, Mary, James, Richmond, Elizabeth, Sarah, Susanna.

1785   HOGAN, DANIEL, wife.

1785   HOBSON, RICHARD, Elizabeth, Martin, Daniel, Sarah, Mary, Younger.

1785   HOLT, NICHOLAS, wife, Michael, Francis, John, Nicholas, James, Rachel.

1785   HAMILTON, ARCHIBALD, Joseph.

1785   HENDRICKS, PETER, Amy, Isaac, William, Aholen, Ann, Mary, Elizabeth, Balander.

1790   HUFFMAN, CHRISTIAN, Peter, Elizabeth; Aycock, Joshua.

1790   HOTSLEIN, JOHN, Mary, Susanna, Barbara.

1793   HAMILTON, WILLIAM, Elizabeth, Jean, Margaret, Nancy.

1792   HALL, JEAN, William, John, Robert, Sarah, Rachel, Thomas.

1792   HORN, THOMAS, Henry, Thomas, Nelly, Margery, James, Joshua, William, John.

1792   HUNTER, JAMES, Christian, Richard, Andrew.

1794   HANLEY, DANIEL, wife, William, Esther, Susanna, Catherine, Elizabeth, Ruth.

1794   HULGAN, THOMAS, Fanny, Robert, Stephen, Rosanna, Mary.

1795   HOOPER, ANNE, William, Thomas.

1796   HUTCHINSON, JAMES, Margaret, James, Ross.

1796   HALL, JAMES, Mary, Levi, Elizabeth, John.

1796   HERNDON, GEORGE, Sarah, James, George, Zachariah, Reuben, Edmund, Lewis.

1798   HOLT, GEORGE, Cissie-(wife).

1799   HILL, JONATHAN, Rezzie, Elzey.

1799   HOLT, MICHAEL, Jean, Joseph, Joshua, Isaac, Michael, William, Cashion.

J.

1790 JOHNSTON, WILLIAM, Isabel, Amelia; Hogg, James; Bennehan, Richard.

1790 JOHNSTON, CHARLES, Martha, George; Strayhorn, Charles; Freeland, John; McCauley, Matthew.

1790 JENKINS, SANFORD, Sanford, Mary, John, Thomas, Betsy, Polly, Patience, Catherine.

1793 JAMIESON, WILLIAM, Rachel (wife), John, Ellis, Rachel, William, John.

K.

1782 KING, JOHN, Hannah (wife), Thomas, William, Nanny, Elizabeth, Obedience, Rebecca, Hannah.

1797 KING, THOMAS, Thomas, Edward, Armona, William, John.

L.

1765 LAUGHLIN, HUGH B., Mary (wife), Elizabeth, Mary, Rebecca, Charity, Joanna, Susanna, William.

1766 LINON, HUGH, Welsh, William; Lindsay, Thomas, William and Ruth.

1767 LITMAN, SAMUEL, Zerubbabel, Priscilla.

1767 LUKY, ALEX., Mary (wife), Margaret, Sarah, Thomas, William, Mary.

1774 LEA, HENRY, Elizabeth, Francis.

1779 LAY, MARTIN, Catherine, George.

1782 LINDLEY, THOMAS, Ruth (wife), Katharine, Thomas, John, Jonathan, Ruth.

1784 LEAK, RICHARD, Richard.

1784 LINDLEY, WILLIAM, Mary (wife), Thomas, Ruth, Mary, Jonathan, Samuel, William, John, Thomas.

1784 LEWIS, NATHANIEL, John, William, Elizabeth, Lydia, Sarah, Rebecca, Mary.

1784 LYTLE, ARCHIBALD, William, Sarah.

1786 LACKEY, JOHN, Elizabeth (wife).

1799 LOWRY, JOHN, Henderson, Thupiah.

1792 LLOYD, THOMAS, Thomas, Fred, Stephen.

1792 LOCKHART, CATHERINE, William; Micklejohn, Elizabeth; Merriwether, Jane.

1794 LINDSAY, JOHN, Mary, John, Caleb, Dille.

1797 LONG, CONRAD, Jacob, Conrad, Mary, Elizabeth, Katie, Caspar, Henry.

1799 LEWIS, ENOCH, Moore, John; Massey, Abner. Gwin, Thomas, Enoch, Ann, Daniel.

1799 LAY, GEORGE, William, John, Jacob, George, Henry, Sally.

M.

1760 MAYNER, HENRY, wife, Rachel, Mary, Elizabeth, Susanna, Ann, Betty.

1763 MASON, ADAM, Anthony, Fannie, Adam, Elizabeth, Ann, Tobias, Jacob.

1766 MILES, THOMAS, Hannah, Aquilla, Misie, Abraham, John, Thomas, Peter, Jacob and Poteat.

1768   MORROW, CHARLES, Adam.

1768   MONTGOMERY, ALEX., wife, Alex., William, John, Elizabeth, Anne, Mary.

1768   McALLISTER, JOHN, James, Joseph, Sarah, Mary, Martha, Rosanna, Jeals, Elizabeth.

1768   McCAY, JOHN, wife; Francis, Isabel, Elizabeth.

1769   McCOMB, JOHN, Rachel, John, William, Jesse, Mary, Jane, Dorcas, Hannah, Sarah, Margaret, Elizabeth.

1770   MOTHEREL, ROBERT, wife, John, Samuel, Joseph, Robert.

1770   McGOWAN, JAMES, wife, William, James, Mary, Susanna, Etta.

1770   MILES, JOHN, Mary, William, Charles, Thomas, John.

1775   MIER, CHRISTOPHER, wife, George.

1779   McBRIDE, ANDREW, Jane.

1779   MORDAGH, JOHN, Elizabeth, James, Catherine, Agnes, Janet, David, John, Elizabeth.

1780   McDANIEL, MELCHOIR, Margaret (wife).

1782   MORDACK, JOHN, Mary, Robert.

1782   MULLINS, JAMES, Ross, James.

1783   MORROW, HUGH, Sarah, James, Mary.

1784   McBROON. ANDREW, Mary, Andrew, William, Jane, Rebecca, Mary.

1784   McCANLESS, JAMES, Jane, John C., Robert L., Elizabeth, James, David, William.

1784   McCULLOCK, JOHN, Mary, Robert, James, John.

1784   MORGAN, SARAH, Hardy, John.

1784   McDANIEL, ELI, Margaret, William, John, James, Elizabeth, Susanna.

1784   MARLEY, ADAM, Rosanna, Robert, Adam, Sarah.

1784   McADAM, SAMUEL, Catherine (wife), Mary, James, William, Sarah, Ellender, John, Joseph.

1784   MANGUM, ARTHUR, Lucy, William, Holley, Clara, Chaney, Arthur, William, Willie.

1793   MEBANE, ALEX., wife; William, Alex., James, John.

1794   MOORE, JOHN, wife, Asabel, Elizabeth.

1795   MITCHELL, ANDREW, James.

1795   MILLER, GEORGE, Joseph, Jesse, George, James.

1794   MORTISE, THOMAS, Mary (wife).

1794   McALLISTER, GRIZELL, Allison, David, John, Margaret, Jane, Elizabeth, Sarah.

1793   MEBANE, ALEX., wife, William, Alex., James, William, Susanna, Elizabeth, Robert, Nancy, John, David, Jennett, Margaret, Mary.

1794   MOORE, JOHN, Elizabeth, Asabel, Martha, James, Henry, Elizabeth, Martha.

1795   McCRCKEAN, ALEX., Abigail, Samuel, Thomas, John, William, Robert, Alex.

1795   MASSEY, TENTS, Ruth, Mary, James.

1796   MULHOLLAND, THOMAS, Martha, Mary, Hugh, John, Thomas, Henry, Elizabeth.

1796   MURDOCH, JOHN, Ann, John, William, Prudence.

1797   MORGAN, HARDY, Sarah, Lemuel, Allen.

1798   MERCY, ABIGAIL, Jemima.

1799   MASSEY, ABRAHAM, Gwinn, Anne, Abner, Daniel, Enoch, Thomas, Mary.

wife. Mary. Will pro. July court, 1793 - other Ch - named in will were David, Margaret and Mary. No Robert and only one William

1799 MORDACK, JAMES, Elizabeth, James, Catrin, Ann, William.
1799 MOORE, JOHN, James, John, Nathan, Alfred, Ephraim, Martha, Sarah, Mary.

N.

1765 NORRIS, DANIEL, Martha (wife), Beale, Thomas; Jones, Evan.
1768 NALL, FRED, Martelenor (wife.
1774 NORTON, STEPHEN, Jane, John, William, Anne, Richard, Margaret, Elizabeth.
1782 NOE, PETER, Hannah, John, Joseph.
1786 NELSON, WILLIAM, Rachel ,Rebecca, Ruth, Elinor, Ann, Hannah, Samuel.
1790 NELSON, ROBERT, James, Robert, Mary, Jean, John.
1799 NELSON, JAMES, John, Abraham, Sarah, Nelly and Archer; Rencher, James.

O.

1769 OWEN, THOMAS, Mary, Hester, Joanna, Lewis, Jonathan, John, Elizabeth, James, William, George, Michael.
1797 O'NEAL, WILLIAM, Elizabeth (wife); Perkins, William, Thomas and Mary.

P.

1768 POOR, PETER, Peter, Mary Ann, Ann P., Eve, Elizabeth.
1770 PIGGOTT, WILLIAM, John, William, Samuel, Jeremiah, Sarah, Abigail, Sarah, Mary Ann, Elizabeth, Rachel, Margery.
1770 POINDEXTER, JOHN, Elizabeth, William, Sibyl, Thomas, Frances.
1772 PRYOR, JOHN, Robert, Elizabeth, John, Betty, Dorothy, Horitha, Abner, Margaret.
1781 PATTERSON, JOHN T., Sarah, Milly and Page.
1772 PINKERTON, DAVID, Margaret, John, William, David, Martha, Mary.
1774 PIKE, JOHN, John, Samuel, Abigail, Nathan.
1775 PARKER, JOSEPH, Rebecca, Richard, Stephen, David, Francis, Abner, Winny, Sally, Betty.
1785 PEACOCK, ABEL, Temperance, Nancy, James.
1785 PRATT, THOMAS, James, Lucy, George, Peggy.
1796 PATTERSON, MARY, Mary, Letitia, Judy, Elinor, Elizabeth and Conner.
1790 PARKS, SAMUEL, Mary, Thomas, Nancy, Samuel, Alex., John, James, Tiney.
1790 PAULL, JAMES, Elizabeth, William, John, James, Rachel.
1790 PATTON, ANDREW, Robert, Thomas, Andrew, Margaret.
1791 PATTERSON, JOHN, Margaret, David, Isaac, Jean, William, Agnes, James, John, Mary.
1791 PATTERSON, NATHANIEL, Isaiah, William, Mary.
1798 PHILLIPS, RAINEY, Nanny, Polly, Rachel, Benjaminfi, Lucretia, Leander.
1792 PAUL, ELIZABETH, James, Elizabeth.
1798 PIPER, JOHN, John.
1799 PATTON, JOHN, William, John, Jean, Mary.
1799 PARRISH, HENRY, Henry, William, Mary.

x Ch. of Peter Noe and wife Hannah, John, Joseph, Katherine Righterhour, Susannah Ridge, Elizabeth Coon and Elizabeth Ragan (as given in will)

R.

1765 ROONEY, JAMES, Elizabeth, Benjamin, James, Ann.
1767 ROGAR, ADAM, wife, Mary, William, John.
1769 RUORD, JOHN, David, Mary, John, Sion, Comfort.
1769 REED, SAMUEL, Mary (wife).
1774 ROBISON, ALEX, Elinor (wife).
1774 REA, WILLIAM, Catherine, William, David.
1772 RUSSELL, ALEX., Jane, James, Margaret, Elinor, Alex., Elizabeth, Jane.
1783 RUE, JOHN, Catrin.
1782 RIGGS, WILLIAM, Mary, George, Ann, Thomas, James, Henry, Jane, Samuel.
1782 RANTHALL, ANDREW, Catherine, Mary.
1782 REED, JOHN, Lydia, Rebecca and Jamieson.
1791 RHODES, WILLIAM, Mary, Hannah, Elizabeth, Alex.
1791 RIELY, JOHN, Mary, William, Nancy, Elizabeth, Robert, Samuel.
1792 ROACH, JAMES, Ann, Absalom.
1793 RAY, ROBERT, Hannah, Cassie, Matthew.
1793 ROSS, JAMES, Margaret (wife).
1795 ROBERTSON, ATHANASIUS, Nathaniel, Dilley.
1797 ROGERS, WILLIAM, Absalom, Theophilus, Nathan, Elizabeth, Leazy, Launey.
1798 RIGGS, GEORGE, Sarah, James, Margaret, Agnes, Rachel.

S.

1761 SHEPHEARD, MARY, Slater, Jacob.
1764 SAWNEY, WILLIAM, Catrin (Katharine), George, Margaret, Janet.
1766 SINKLER, CHARLES, Ann, Catherine and Chandler.
1767 STUART, ALEX., Elizabeth, Robert, John, Abigail.
1768 SERJANT, WILLIAM, Sarah, Thomas, Joseph, James, Elizabeth, Stephen.
1768 SMITH, ROBERT, Mary (wife), Robert, Elizabeth, Mary, Isabel, William. *William Saunders*
1768 SUTTON, JOSEPH, Hughes, Daniel. wit
2-245 *11-12* 1776 * SANDERS, JAMES, SR., James, Fanny, Richard, William, Cassandra. *Susanna, Sarah*
1776 STEPHENS, ARTHUR, Sarah, Lavinia, Elizabeth.
1781 SYNNOTT, MICHAEL, Richard.
1782 SHARP, ISAAC, Phillippina, John, Bostron, Peter, Christian, Elizabeth.
1782 SCOBY, MATTHEW, Janet, David, Robert.
1783 SMITH, WILLIAM, Mary, Margaret, Samuel, Robert, William, Jonathan, Annie and Cunningham.
1784 SCOTT, ROBERT, Mary, Jesse, William, Richard, Molly, John, Henry.
1784 SHEELS, JOHN, Cummings, Mary.
1784 STROUD, WILLIAM, Elizabeth (wife), William, Thomas, John, Elizabeth.
1784 SEARS, THOMAS, Elizabeth (wife), William, Joseph, Mary. Thomas, Henry, Elizabeth, John.

* dau. Susanna m. Robert Terry and dau. Sarah m. Wm. Twigg. From attested copy

1790 STANFORD, ANTHONY, Elizabeth (wife), Charles, Robert, Agnes, Jean, Martha, Elizabeth, James, William, Mary, Margaret.

1792 SULLIVAN, DANIEL, Margaret (wife), Joseph, Daniel, Edmond, Mary, Sarah, John, Isaac, Margaret.

1792 STAGG, JUDITH, Charles, Celia.

1792 SURBASTEN (Sebastian), ISAAC, Sarah.

1793 STEEL, JOHN, Mary (wife), Agnes, Elizabeth, Mary, Sarah, Joseph.

1793 SNOTERLY, PHILIP, John, Henry, Elizabeth, Jacob, Susanna, Rachel, Catherine.

1794 STANTIFER, ISRAEL, Cavander, Ephraim, Joshua, Israel, Mary, Elizabeth, Benjamin.

1795 SHANNON, WILLIAM, Mary, Thomas, Robert.

1795 SMATHERS, THOMAS, Susanna, William, John, James, Thomas, Sarah, Mary.

1795 SHY, JOHN, Martha.

1796 SEARLES, THOMAS, wife, Henry, Ephraim, Francis, Edward, Betty, Winnie and Corenton.

1798 SMITH, THOMAS, Sarah, Abraham, Elizabeth, Mary, Hannah.

1799 SMITH, CONRAD M., Leonard, Stephen, Mary.

T.

1763 TERRELL, TIMOTHY, Jemima (wife), Ruth, Willie, Solomon, Micajah, Nimrod, Simon, Moses, Mary, Betty, Keziah, Daniel, Richard.

1766 THOMAS, JOHN, John, James, Elizabeth, Mary.

1767 THEDFORD, WALTER, Rebecca, Josias, William, Simon, Deborah.

1770 TALBERT, JAMES, Mary, John, Benjamin.

1770 TAPLEY, HOSEA, JR., John P., Hosea.

1774 TATE, GEORGE, wife, James, George, Ketturah, Agnes, Mary, Elizabeth, Lettice, Janet, Margaret.

1781 TRICE, JAMES, James, Sarah, Charles, Joseph, John.

1782 THOMPSON, AMOS, Martha, Charles and Littleton.

1784 ✱TRUESDALE, JOHN, Elizabeth, William, John, James, Margaret, Mary.

1785 TELFORD, THOMAS, Elizabeth (wife), Hugh, Robert, Thomas, Rosanna, Elizabeth, William, Samuel.

1791 TOLBEY, SAMUEL, Elizabeth, William, and Hitchcock.

1794 THOMPSON, JAMES, James, John, Elinor, Martha, Joseph.

1795 THOMPSON, BRYAN, Sarah, Frances, Robert, Richard, Stephen, Samuel.

1796 THOMPSON, THOMAS, Samuel, Abraham, Ann, John.

1798 TINNEN, JAMES, Elizabeth, Robert, James and Cearns.

1798 TATE, ZACCHEUS, John, Jean, Lydia, Eudoxia, Zaccheus, Valentine, Uriah, Zephaniah, Uzziah, Zeus, Sampson.

1799 THOMPSON, FRANCES, Margaret and Anderson.

✱ Trousdale

U.

1774 UNDERWOOD, SAMUEL, Anna (wife), Henry, Alex., Samuel, Benjamin, James, Anna, Jane, Ruth, Sarah, Elizabeth.

V.

1760 VANBROOK, AARON, Katharine, David and Lawrence.

1760 VAUGHAN, JAMES, Catrin.

W.

1767 WADE, JOSEPH, John, James, Sarah.

1769 WALKER, WILLIAM, William, James, John, Abraham, Alexander.

1769 WALTON, NATHANIEL, Mary (wife), Mary, Jemima, Keziah, Peter.

1774 WRIGHT, ISAAC,, Mary (wife), Zaccheus, Isaac, Prudence, Mary.

1774 WEST, JONATHAN, Elinor and Jonathan.

1777 WATSON, JAMES, Helen, Rebecca, James.

1781 WILSON, WILLIAM, Mary (wife), Samuel, Gregory, Mary.

1795 WATTS, JOSIAH, Susanna (wife), Susanna.

1781 WAGNER, GEORGE, Mary, Elizabeth, Ann, Henry.

1785 WAGONER, HENRY, Mary (wife), Katrina, John, Henry, Jacob, Mary, Judith, Uli, Agnes.

1785 WATSON, WILLIAM, Elinor (wife).

1785 WILLIAMS, WILLIAM, William, Elizabeth, Samuel.

1792 WOODY, JAMES, Joseph, Lewis, Robina.

1792 WOODS, JOHN, Margaret (wife), Matthew, John, Richard, Margaret, Nancy, Sarah.

1792 WALTON, MARY, Jemima, Keziah.

1795 WALKER, PHILIP, wife.

1793 WALKER, JAMES, Elizabeth, James, Jeremiah, William, Lydia and Sanders.

1799 WYATT, JOSHUA, Elizabeth (wife), Joshua, Fred, Elizabeth.

Y.

1770 YARBOROUGH, SAMUEL, Sarah (wife), Samuel, John, William, Elizabeth, Sarah, Louisa.

1781 YOUNG, JOSEPH, wife, John.

ONSLOW COUNTY—WILLS

A.

1772 ANDERSON, ELENDER, Sons (illegible).

1790 ALEXANDER, ESTHER, Anna and Katherine; Hannah Pickett and Mary James (daughters); John James (son).

1795 AVIRETT, ARTHUR, Anne (wife); John, Richard, Ancrum, Betsy and Peggy.

1786 ALEXANDER, EZEKIEL, Esther (wife); Katherine, Ann and Joseph.

1793 AMAN, JACOB, Mary (wife); Esther, Nancy and Robert.

1785 AVIRRETT, JOHN, Mary (wife).; Arthur and Nathaniel; Elizabeth Simmons (daughter); Esther Walton (daughter); Alse Cooper (daughter); Susanna Howard (daughter). ter).

1764 AMBROSE, WM., John Ambrose (grandson).

1789 ALEXANDER, JOSEPH, Sarah (wife); James and Sarah.

1798 AVIRETT, ANNE, Amerum. sallie and Peggy Ann.

1784 AVIRETT, NATHANIEL, Father (not named).

1784 AMBROSE, JOHN, Mary Ann (wife).

1785 ALLHINS, JAMES, Jacob, Moses and Aaron Field (friends).

1798 AVIRETT, BENJAMIN, Amy (wife); Hannah, Spooner, Aaron, Joseph and Pheraba (children).

B.

1777 BATES, DANIEL, Deborah (wife).

1766 BARBER, MICHAEL, Susanna (wife); John and Michael.

1792 BURNS, FRANCIS, Elizabeth (wife); Otway; Susanna Spooner (daughter).

1792 BARNES, HEZEKIAH, Alinder (wife); Joseph and Sally and other children not named.

1790 BURNS, JAMES, Fred and James; Desdemona Rose (daughter).

1790 BIDDLE, JACOB, Mary (wife); Gabriel and David Waters (nephews).

1784 BEST, THOMAS, Deborah (wife); Ann.

1780 BROWN, JEREMIAH, Mary (wife); Nancy, Benjamin, Wm, Sarah, James and Martha.

1769 BRINSON, ADAM, Adam, Matthew, John, Isaac, Nancy, Phereba, Apsila, Sarah, Stirring.

1793 BENNETT, WM., Esther (wife); Wm. B. Creff (grandson).

1799 BARROW, ABRAHAM, Sarah (wife); Elizabeth, Zachariah. Abraham and John; Sarah Oliver (daughter).

1792 BLANKS, WM. N. Mrs. Ann Young (friend).

1788 BATTLE, THOMAS, Ann (wife); Benjamin.

1798 BATTLE, EPHRAIM, Lot, Abner, Wm., Mary, Thomas, Fred, Jane; Sarah Williams (daughter).

1778 BAISDEN, HUGH, Holland, Joseph, Cordell and Jesse.

1799 BURNAP, ISAAC, Peggy (wife); John; Peggy Burnap (granddaughter).
1799 BROWN, RACHAEL, Hester; Ruth Goffone and Susannah Harper (daughters).
1763 BIDELL, ISAAC, Honor (wife); Elisha.
1779 BRYAN, THOMAS, Elizabeth (wife); Jonathan.
1793 BERRYMAN, JOSEPH, Priscilla (wife); John and daughters, (not named).
1769 BATTLE, THOMAS, Mary (wife); Ephraim and Thomas; James Dunn (son-in-law).
1798 BARRON, ABRAHAM, Wife (not named); Jesse and James.
1785 BALL, STEPHEN, Nancy (wife); James, Phereba, Elizabeth and Nancy.
1799 BRINSON, GEORGE, Rachel (wife); John, Sarah and Penelope.
1777 BATES, DANIEL, Deborah (wife); Keziah.
1761 BARROW, THOMAS, Elizabeth (wife); Thomas, Jacob, James, Hosea and Moses.
1785 BRADY, JOSHUA, Jemima (wife); Samuel, Joshua and Anastatia; Mary Strange (daughter).
1790 BARBEE, RICHARD, Hannah (wife); Thomas, Ann and Mary.
1792 BOARDMAN, JONATHAN, Wife (not named) and six children (not named).
1776 BRACK, WM., Elizabeth (wife); John.
1774 BRANNARD, ANN, George; Bethelia Evans (daughter); Jonathan Brannard (grandson).
1800 BARBER, THOMAS, Elizabeth wife); Absalom and other children not named.
1778 BRINSON, STIRRING, Anna wife); Sarah, George, Moses, David, Jerusha, Pheraba and Anna.
1780 BRYAN, ELIZABETH, Rachel and Zilphia Lester (neices); John Brinson and Banister Lester (brothers).

C.

1791 CARNOTT, JOHN, Christian (wife); Alexander, Margaret, Mary, Jennie and Robert.
1771 COX, CHARLES, Rebecca (wife); Charles, Jasper, Susanna, Sarah, Moses and Aaron.
1792 CRAFT, STEPHEN, C. Esther (wife); Benjamin, Archibald, Micaih, Rebecca and Betsy; Isaac Craft (brother).
1799 CONWAY, JOHN, Leah (wife); Elizah and Cine.
1767 CAREY, MATTHEW, Sarah Parker (his mistress; Cora (wife).
1778 CRAY, WM., Mary (wife); Wm., Joseph S. Henrietta and Charlotte; Joseph Cray (grandson).
1794 COLLINS, RICHARD, Sarah (wife); Bishop (son).
1776 COX, MARY, Wm., Eli. Celia and Henrietta.
1777 CLARK, DAVID, Wealthyann, Jemima, Keziah, Wm, Amy, Sarah and Mager.
1761 CUMMINS, THOMAS, Sarah (wife); George, Robert, Mary and Susanna.
1789 CLANDONALD, MARYANN, Hanah; George Farr, (grandson).

1770 CARTER, ANN, Mary Cleasy and Abraham Daws (friends).

1785 COSTEN, MATTHIAS, Phoebe (wife); Francis and John Casten (brothers).

1780 COFTON, JOHN, Mary (wife).

1794 COX, ELIZABETH, Wm and Josiah Cox (brothers).

1796 COSTEN, FRANCIS, Dorrity (wife); Matthew and Stephen; Comfort Justice (daughter); heirs of John Costen and Sarah Sinclair (daughter).

1791 COOPER, JOHN, John; Frances Huggins, Mary Simmons and Esther Simson (daughters).

1791 CRAFT, ANTHONY, Hannah (wife); Jacob, John, Stephen and Isaac; Ann Cooper and Rachael Johnston (daughters).

1793 CARY, MATTHEW, Mary (wife); Thomas, Matthew, Mary and Fanny.

1787 CASON, JAMES, Elizabeth (wife); James, Isham, Elisha, Rebecca, Rachael and Nancy.

1771 CATHOLIC, DANIEL, Christina (wife); Sarah, Mary and John K.

1785 CRAWFORD, JOHN, Mary (wife); John; Ann Cheson, Mary Williams, Sedwell Lane, Rachael Costen and Sarah Dixon (daughters).

1774 CUMMINS, ROBT. Sarah (mother); Thomas (brother).

1779 CHATWIN, JOSEPH, Frances (wife); Thomas, Frances, Mary and Louisa; Margaret Jones (daughter). Elizabeth Dolly (daughter).

1785 COX, MOSES, Elizabeth (wife); Celia, Henrietta, Wm, Eli, Josiah, Matilda and Hannah.

1781 CHANDLER, JOHN, Sarah (wife); Mary Wheeler (daughter); Ann and Barbara.

1787 CLANDONALD, GEORGE, Mary (wife).

1778 COSTEN, JOHN, Thomas and John; Elizabeth Marchant (daughter).

D.

1772 DEVANE, WM., Jemima (wife); Wm, George, Christopher, Joshua and Daniel.

1770 DUDLEY, ELIZABETH, Wm, John and David; Sarah Cahoon, (daughter).

1787 DUDLEY, BISHOP, Rebecca (wife); Guilford, Creed. Anne, Margaret, Bishop, Edward, John and Christopher.

1776 DUDLEY, DAVID, Nancy (wife); David and Nancy.

1769 DIXON, THOMAS, John.

1784 DASSON, JEAN, Mercy, Jean, Reuben, Meloy, Mary, Cruiez and Johnston.

1780 DOTY, BENAJAH, Elizabeth (wife); Nancy, Lemuel, Benajah, James; Hester Brock (daughter).

1786 DAWSON, ROBT. Robt. and Jeremiah.

1774 DAVIS, THOMAS, Lucy (wife); Samuel and Thomas.

1798 DAVIS, THOMAS, Susanna (wife); Samuel (brother).

1772 DUDLEY, WM., Elizabeth (wife); Edward, Thomas, Stephen, Katherine and Rebecca.

E.

1779   EVANS, CALEB, Ann.

1781   EVANS, JOHN, Bethelia (wife); David, Zaccheus, Samuel and John Evans (nephews).

1792   EDWARDS, ELIZABETH, Josiah.

1769   EDMUNDSON, BRYANT, Sarah (wife); James, Richard, William, Mary, and Elizabeth.

1774   EVANS, JAMES, Sarah (wife); Zaccheus, David, James, Samuel, John, Frances, Mary, Jeremiah.

1789   EVANS, JAMES, Elizabeth (wife); Lot.

F.

1783   FRAZER, JAMES, Sally (wife); Micajah, Benjamin, Sally, Mary, James, George, Cornelia and Penny.

1796   FIELDS, ZACHARIAH, Anna, Samuel, Zachariah, Lenna, Abigail and Nathan.

1793   FREEMAN, ELISHA, Betty (wife); Isaac, James, Mark, John, Betty.

1782   FIELDS, SAMUEL, Catherine (wife); Richard, Nancy, Samuel, David and John; Sarah Fonville and Ellen Berry (daughters).

1758   FARR, RICHARD, Hannah (wife); Richard, Titus, James and Wm.

1781   FREE, CHRISTIAN, Polly (wife); Jacob (brother).

1771   FOYLE, JANE, James, John, Charity and Elizabeth.

1774   FRENCH, JOSEPH, Abigail (wife); Joseph.

1779   FRENCH, ABIGAIL, Wm. and Joseph French (grandsons).

1788   FULLWOOD, WM. Wife and child (not named).

1789   FOX, MOSES, Purify (wife); Moses.

1757   FARR, TITUS, MaryAnn (wife); John, Elizabeth, Richard and Hannah.

1796   FULLWOOD, ANDREW, Katherine, John, James and Thomas; Sarah Russell (daughter); Andrew Fullwood (grandson).

1780   FOX, AARON, Aaron, Jemima, Susanna, Solomon and Margaret.

1775   FONVILLE, STEPHEN, Lucy (wife); Frederick, Hatchell and Brice.

G.

1784   GIBSON, WM. Mary (wife); Isaac, Wm. and Thomas; Rebecca Field, Ann Lipsey and Hannah Simson (daughters).

1767   GRANT, ALEX., Solomon, Stephen, Alex., Seth, Baptist, Mary and Ruth (daughters).

1790   GREGORY, HARDY, Wife (not named); Celia, Arthur and Hardy.

1792   GODFREY, WM., Francis, Enoch, Wm. and Bonetta.

1779   GIDDENS, ISAAC, Abraham (brother); Nancy Shephard (sister).

1776   GLENN, HUGH, Susanna (wife); Jones and Sarah (children); John and Thomas (brothers).

1778   GRANT, STEPHEN, Miriam (wife); two children (not named).

1793 GREGORY, JESSE, Mary (wife); children (not named).

1770 GIDDENS, JACOB, Nancy (sister); Isaac and Abraham (brothers).

1771 GRANT, SOLOMON, Sarah (wife); Reuben, Rachel and Experience.

1766 GRAY, WM. Mary (wife); Whittington (son); John and James (brothers).

1791 GIBSON, RACHEL, Sarah Noble (daughter).

1757 GRANT, JANE, Mary Pitts and Ann Pitts (daughters).

1779 GAGE, PETER, Catherine (wife); Johnson.

1784 GILLET, ANDERSON, Philany (wife); John, Thomas, Alex., Seth, Elizabeth, Mary, Sarah, Eleanor and Anne.

1790 GIBSON, ISAAC, Rachel (wife); Abram, Isaac, Ann, Archelaus; Fanny Ferrell (daughter).

1791 GLENN, MARGARET, Sarah, Mary and Nathan (children); Thomas Glenn (brother).

H.

1781 HUSSEY, SIMEON, Ann (wife); Betsy, Edward and Shields.

1786 HICKS, MOSES, David (brother).

1791 HUMPHREY, JACOB, Jacob, Ezekiel and Alse.

1788 HOWARD, JOSEPH, Joseph, Molly, Wm. and Philip.

1765 HOWARD, WM. Jean (wife); Mary, Wm., Shadrack. Joseph, Ann and Amy; Alse, Heartt, Hannah Lupton and Pithany Costen (daughters).

1799 HOWARD, WM Shadrack and Hannon.

1790 HOWARD, JAMES, Elizabeth (wife); Fanny, Harriet, Joseph and Carsey.

1791 HAWKINS, JOSEPH, Dorothy (wife); Gideon, Lesbia, Janet, Rebecca, Whitehurst, Lydia, Joseph and Rhoda; Rachel Bryan and Esther Hammond, (daughter).

1788 HEIDELBERG, JOHN, Wife (not named); Samuel, John, Bathsheba, Miriam, Thomas and Catherine; Sabra Brinson (daughter).

1780 HUSSEY, SIMEON, Ann (wife); Edward, Betsy, Charity, Peggy and Shields.

1777 HIGGINS, MICHAEL, Wife (not named); Sarah Dudley (daughter).

1765 HAY, CHARLES, Hannah (wife); Thomas.

1786 HOUSE, JAMES, Mary (wife); Charles, Sarah, James, Polly, Nancy, Lorance and Buckner.

1778 HICKS, DAVID, Martha (wife); Solomon. Alex., Moses, Fred, Fanny, David and Martha.

1786 HADNOT, WM. Obedience (wife); West and Whitehurst (sons).

1781 HAWS, JOHN, Elizabeth (wife); Mary and Susanna.

1799 HAWKINS, STEPHEN, Helen (wife); Peter and Elizabeth, Naomi Burns (daughter).

1791 HUMPHREY, HUSTRESS, Martha (wife); David and Hustress.

1789 HADNOT, WEST, Sarah (wife); Children (not named).

1780 HUMPHREY, THOMAS, Mary (wife); Francis.

1772 HADASH, ROBERT, Weston (son); Sarah Hunter (daughter).

1790 HART, ABRAHAM, Anne (wife); John and Hobart.

1773 HUNTER, EZEKIEL, Rachel (wife); Mary, Asa, Ezekiel and Sena.

1777 HEWITT, JOHN, Wife (not named); John and Thomas; Sarah Weeks (daughter).

1761 HADNOT, WM. Sarah, Wm. and Case.

1794 HAWS, JOSEPH, Celia (wife); Matilda and Elizabeth.

1772 HADNOT, RACHEL, Eleanor Gillet (granddaughter).

1762 HICKS, DANIEL, Comfort (wife); John, Robt, Sarah, Elizabeth, Lucy and Argless; Betty Jenkins (daughter).

1791 HALL, SHADRACK, Winifred (wife); Shadrack, Hester, Mary and Elizabeth.

1760 HOLMES, JOHN, Sisters and brothers, Barbara Andrews, Lida Horner, Ebenezer Holmes and Lewis Holmes.

1773 HAMMOND, ORCHELANS, Elizabeth (wife); Judah, Ameziath, Archelans, Charles and Hildah; Margaret West (daughter).

1777 HEWITT, JOHN, Wife (not named), John and Goldsmith.

1794 HOPKINS, NEAL, Nancy (wife).

1784 HAYNIE, BENJAMIN, Rebecca (wife); Jesse. Benjamin, Abraham, Jacob, Sarah, Hezekiah and Henry.

1800 HANCOCK, NATHANIEL, Wife (not named); Gabriel, Enoch, Magdelen and Zebedee.

1785 HARDISON, JOHN, Ann (wife); Elizabeth, Jesse, Hardy and Nancy.

J.

1784 JARMAN, MARY, Lawrence; Sarah Parker, Mary Foils and Nancy Humphrey (daughters); Mary Jarman and Thomas Malbury (grandchildren).

1772 JOHNSTON, WM. Mary (wife); John, Wm, Sarah, Mary, Thomas, Elizabeth and Tamar.

1771 JAMESON, WM. Elizabeth (wife); Thomas, Wm, and Elizabeth.

1789 JARROTT, ELIZABETH, Alex., Elizabeth, Thomas, Margaret and Ming; Nancy Lee and Mary Shawn (daughters).

1763 JENKINS, LEWIS, Elizabeth, Lewis and Henry.

1791 JENKINS. GEORGE, Sarah (wife); Heater.

1780 JONES, WM. Verlinda (wife); Jacob and Wm.

1777 JONES, LLOYD, Elizabeth (wife); Peter; Mary Cragg and Elizabeth Ruark (daughters).

1791 JOHNSTON, JOHN, Miriam (wife); John, Nathan and Elizabeth; Hannah Trott and Jemima Farr (daughters).

1785 JARROTT, ABRAHAM, Elizabeth (wife); Thomas Alex and Margaret; Nancy Lee and Mary Shiver (daughters).

1783 JENKINS, JONATHAN, Allender (wife); children (not named).

1771 JOHNSTON, GARRETT, Mary (wife); Thomas, Charles, Rebecca, Rachel and Nellie.

1785 JAMESON, WM. Elizabeth (sister).

1789 JONES, EMANUEL, Keziah (wife); Wm, Richard and Kilby.

1796 JENKINS, SARAH, Jonathan Ericson (brother).

1768 JARROTT, JOHN, Margaret, Esther, Richard and John; Sabra Howard (daughter).

1779 JOHNSTON, BENJAMIN, Mary (wife); Benjamin, Sarah, Pamela, John and Thomas; Phereba Hearn, Hester Thompson, Fillany Hearn and Christie Johnston (daughters).

1771 JETER, JAMES, Eleanor (wife); Jane; Edward and John (brothers).

1796 JONES, HALL, Mary (wife); Owen, Dempsey and Redding 13 other children (not named).

K.

1775 KING, WM. Elizabeth (wife); John, Esther, Elizabeth and Mary; John (brother).

1797 KING, ELIZABETH, Hester Willey and Elizabeth May (daughters).

1790 KING, JOHN, Priscilla (wife); Zilpha, John, Benajah and Mary.

1778 KAY, JONATHAN, Susanna (wife); Polly, Nancy and Betsy.

1772 KIBBLE, EDITH, James; Lucy Fonville and Mary Williams (daughters); Esther Williams (granddaughter).

1781 KENNEDY, JAMES, Sukey (wife); Elizabeth; Wm. F. Godfrey (father-in-law); Wm. E. Godfrey (brother-in-law).

1787 KIBBLE, JAMES, Elizabeth (wife); Matilda Dudley (daughter).

1771 KOONCE, TOBIAS, Anne (wife); Mary, Rebecca, Nancy and Jesse; Wm. Gibson (father-in-law).

1784 KELPIN, ISAAC, Sarah, Charlotte and Sophia.

L.

1788 LEE, JOHN, Rachel (wife); Abigail, Sarah, Mary, Henry and Jacob; Penelope Marshburn (daughter).

1764 LEE, STEPHEN, Mary (wife); Margaret (mother); Mary and Melburne Baldridge (aunt and uncle); Hopkins (son).

1777 LLOYD, WILLIAM, Elizabeth (wife); Peter, George; Mary, Cray and Elizabeth Branch (daughters).

1794 LLOYD, JOSEPH, Mother; Joseph, Wm., John and Daniel Fisher (nephews).

1792 LESTER, BANISTER, Mary, Banister, Elizabeth and Rhoda.

1798 LOVE, PATMOS, Mary (wife); Amos, John, Charles, Winifred, Elephi (daughter); Mary, Hannah and Penelope.

1787 LLOYD, WM. SR. Ann (wife); Wm and Celia; Nancy Thompson and Mary Gurganus (daughters).

1746 LUTEN, ADAM, Eliza (wife); Mary.

M.

1760   MURRILL, TIMOTHY, Mary (wife); John, Kent, Mildred, Patty, Anna and Keziah; Elizabeth Brack and Sarah Johnson (daughters).

1765   MUMFORD, JOSEPH, (illegible).

1798   MASON, RICHARD, Anna (wife); Children (not named).

1780   MELTON, WM. Sarah (wife); Edward, John, James, Richard and Josephia; Sarah Bryant (daughter).

1780   MCKOY, WM. Robt. Dawson (friend).

1796   MILLER, LEWIS, Achilla (wife); Ann; Benjamin Williams (father-in-law and his 3 sons, Iphetus, Lot, and Julius).

1790   MUMFORD, JAMES, Penelope (wife); Bryan, James, Elizabeth and Rebecca.

1769   MELTON, RICHARD, Mary (wife); Samuel, Elizabeth, Sarah, Keziah and Mary.

1783   MARSHBURN, EDWARD, Elizbeth (wife); Joseph, Sarah, Martha and Rebecca.

1760   MORRIS, PHILEMON, Amy (wife); Ludowic, Philemon, Wm, James and Thomas.

1793   MORRIS, THOMAS, Mary (wife); John, James, Mary and Sarah.

1772   MCGRAIN, JOHN, Hannah (wife); Rebecca.

1770   MUMFORD, JOHN, Winifred (wife); John and Esedack; Mary Salter (daughter).

1784   MELTON, ROBT. Mary (wife); Jesse, Solomon, Reuben and Thomas.

1796   MCADAMSON, GEO. Mary (wife); George and Celia.

1785   MCKOY, JANE, Ward McKoy (brother).

1799   MCCULLOUGH, JOHN, Mary, Phoebe and James.

1791   MUMFORD, LOUIS, Elizabeth (wife); Joseph, Edward and Charlotte.

1791   MANNING, MOSES, Wife (not named); Moses and Martin; Sarah McCoy (daughter).

1796   MORTON, PETER, Anna (wife); Micajah, Asa, Anna, Esther, Benjamin and Peter; Susanna Morris and Elian Ball (daughters).

1780   MELVIN, SOLOMON, Sarah (wife); David and John.

1792   MUMFORD, LOUIS, Elizabeth (wife); Charlotte, Joseph and Edward.

1762   MALTSBY, THOMAS, Sarah (wife); Mary and Susanna.

N.

1794   NIXON, ROBT. Sarah (wife); Charles, Robt, Nathan, Daniel and Rebecca; Sarah Fields and Mary Cox (daughters).

1777   NUNTON, JOHN, Elizabeth (wife); Elijah, Daniel, Marmaduke and Benjamin; Ann Morton and Helen Dulany (daughters).

1778   NICHOLS, MATTHEW G. Elizabeth.

1794   NETHERCUTT, WM. George, Loftin, Wm. and Reuben.

1794   NEWTON, ELIJAH, Elizabeth (wife); Nancy, Sarah, Anne and Hardy.

1778   NELMS, WM Martha (wife); Jeremiah and William.

1789 NORMAN, JOHN, Mourning (wife); Wm,
Sarah, Milly, Polly, Betsy and Patty; Anne
Williams (daughter).

1794 NEWTON, BENJAMIN, Nancy; Daniel (brother); Thomas Dulaney (brother-in-law).

1778 NICHOLS, MATTHEW G. Elizabeth and Anne.

1780 NEWTON, JOHN, Elizabeth (wife); Elijah,
Daniel, Marmaduke, Benjamin, Daniel and
Ann; Helen Dulany (daughter).

O.

1781 OLIVER, JAMES, Ann (wife); John, Thomas,
Frances and Benjamin; Lucretia and Rebec-
ca Brown (daughters); Mary House and Anr.
Smith (daughters).

1776 OGDEN, ISAAC, Tabitha (wife); Isaac Ogden
(nephew).

1784 OGDEN, TABITHA, Elizabeth Wood (daughter); John Jones and Rhoda Simmons (grandchildren).

1773 OLPHIN, WM. Elizabeth (wife); Delilah, David, William, Jesse, Mary and Thomas.

P.

1770 PENNY, JOHN, James, Wm, John, Sukey,
Jane, Mary, Nancy and Sarah.

1780 POUND, MARY, Ann Harrison (daughter);
Mary Wilson, MaryAnn Clendening and Hannah Ford (daughters); John Farr (son by
former marriage).

1792 PORCUPINE, JOHN, Hannah Walker (sister).

1792 PARRY, JOHN, Betty, Esther, Thomas and
Winnie; Sally Barlowe (daughter).

1777 PIERSON, SALISBURY, Mary (wife); Elizabeth,
Anna and Rebecca.

1796 PADRICK, PETER, Magrel (wife); Jonathan,
Benjamin, Susanna and Peggy.

1780 PEARSON, JAMES, Samuel and Asia (sons).

1770 POUND, JOHN, Mary (wife); Eunice; Temperance Harris and Esther Player (daughters); Betty Bray (granddaughter).

1796 PERRY, WM. Elizabeth (wife); Katron
(daughter); Mary Cahoon (daughter); John
Abbott (stepson).

1782 PARROTT, JOHN, Jenny (wife); Phereba Dona-
ho (daughter).

1795 PANIL, STEPHEN, Daniel, Stephen, Hezekiah,
Hosea, Samuel and Nathan (brothers).

R.

1786 ROSE, JOHN, Dedemiah (wife); Johnson,
Harmon and Archibald.

1778 RHODES, JAMES, Wm. Johnson (uncle); Mary,
Mercy and Elizabeth Rhodes (sisters).

1793 ROBERTS, HOUSTON, Margaret (wife); Richard
and other children (not named).

1772 ROYALL, SAMUEL, Mary (wife); Mary, Isaac,
Nancy, Esther and Nice.

1786 RHODES, JOHN, Elizabeth (wife); Anna and
Wm. Rhodes (grandchildren).

1780 ROSE, HARMON, Martha (wife).

1776 ROBERTS, EDWARD, Ann Reaves (sister); Edward Simmons (brother-in-law).

1786 RHODES, HENRY, Elizabeth (wife); Henry and Woodhouse (sons); Sarah Ward and Elizabeth Fonville (daughters); Henrietta, Mary and Abiff (daughters).

1780 RIELES, JOHN, Wife (not named); Mary.

1786 RICHARDSON, JOHN, George Ward (friend).

1789 RAN, (Wran) WM. Catherine (wife).

1768 RAMSEY, SAMUEL, Wm, Elizabeth and Subrieg.

1788 ROTCH, BRIDGET, Stephen, Celia, Wm, John, Bryan, Simon, Nancy and Spire (children).

S.

1799 SCOTT, ADAM, Elizabeth (wife); Joshua; Allefair Carmalt and Pamela Hinson (daughters).

1787 STOKES, WM. Patsy (wife); Elizabeth.

1794 SKIPPER, JOSEPH, Jemima (wife); Priscilla, Nathan and Milly.

1771 SPEARMAN, ELIZABETH, John.

1760 SKIBBONS, HENRY, Sarah (wife); Lewis and Elizabeth; Ann Fenter (daughter).

1791 SAUNDERS, ROBT. Rachel (wife); Margaret and Wm.

1798 SINCLAIR, ROBT., Sarah (wife); Elizabeth, Samuel and Fanny.

1788 SIMSON, HANNAH, Fanny and Alma; Solomon, Thomas and Elisha Biddle (sons by a former marriage).

1778 SHACKLEFORD, JOHN, Ann (wife); Wm, Francis, John, Stephen and George; Ann Williams (daughter).

1780 SCOTT, WM. Eleanor (wife); Sarah, John, Wm, Samuel, Edmond, James, Benjamin and Eleanor.

1775 SIMSON, JOHN, Ann (wife); Abraham and Simon.

1780 SIMPSON, EDWARD, Wife (not named); Hannah.

1798 SCREWS, JOSEPH, Wife (not named); Benjamin, John, Wm, Joseph, Mary, Frances, Henry, Martha and Elizabeth.

1789 SPICER, JOHN, Milliah Hatch (daughter).

1789 STYLES, JOHN, Sarah (wife); John, Wm, and Becton.

1795 SHEPARD, WM. Nancy (wife).

1784 SUMNER, JOSEPH, Wife (not named); Richard, Joseph, Christian, Ruth and Mary.

1777 SCOTT, WM. Lurana (wife); Wm, John, Elvin, Lurana and Ann.

1780 STOUT, CHARLES, Constance (wife); Jacob and John.

1766 STARKEY, WM. Sarah (mother); John and Peter (brothers).

1795 SIMMONS, BENJAMIN, Mary (wife); James, Elijah and Richard.

1769 SLOAN, WM. Esther (wife); children (not named).

1791 SHEPHARD, BENJAMIN, Sarah (wife); Daniel, Joseph, Benjamin, Stephen and Mary; Susanna Brinson (daughter).

1770 SHEPHARD, GEORGE, Wife (not named); Wm. George and Smith; Mary Prescott and Ann Prescott (daughters).

1796 SAUNDERS, JOHN, Jesse, John, Isaac and Ruth; Abigail Wood, Frances Walker and Ann Boardman (daughters).

1790 STARKY, PETER, Sarah (wife); John, Edward. Peter and Wm.

1781 STARKEY, EDWARD, John Starkey (brother); Hasten Starkey (sister); Wm. and Edward Starkey (nephews).

T.

1786 THOMPSON, JAMES, John, Priscilla, Nancy, Rebecca, Joanna, Mary and Richard.

1794 THOMPSON, RICHARD, Rebecca (wife); James and Frederick.

1798 THOMPSON, JOHN, Sarah (wife); Martha and James.

1760 THOMPSON, EDWARD, Eleanor (wife); Ruth.

1792 THOMPSON, JAMES, Mother; Enoch (brother); Thomas Johnston (nephew).

1790 THOMPSON, RICHARD, Elizabeth Sanders and Maggie Gibbs (sisters); James (brother); Alfred and Alsey Thompson (nephews).

W.

1767 WARD, ELIZABETH, Benjamin, Enoch, Seth and Dorothy; Martha Simmons, Ann Granade, Mary Williams, Elizabeth Hadnot, Ruth Strange and Obedience Hadnot (daughters).

1774 WARD, RICHARD, Dorothy (wife); Ruth and Huldah; Magdelen Jarrott and Dorothy Edwards (daughters); Elizabeth Foy (granddaughter); Richard Thompson (nephew).

1781 WILDER, HOPKINS, Jonathan and Joel; Keziah Brown (daughter).

1776 WOODHAM, JOHN, Numerous cousins.

1774 WALLACE, RICHARD, Ann (wife); Sarah, Mary, Frances and Margaret; Elizabeth Holt (daughter).

1785 WILLIAMS, OBED. Milly (wife).

1793 WILLEY, JOHN A., Nancy and John; Priscilla Sill, Katy Farnal and Sarah Hadnot (daughters); Willie and Edward St. George (grandchildren); John and Arella Farr (grandchildren).

1789 WALDRON, JOHN, Polly (wife); John, Aretus, Chloe, Sally, Belony and Polly.

1788 WILLIAMS, STEPHEN, Martha (wife); Stephen, Pearl, David, Hezekiah and Hosea.

1760 WARD, JAMES, Wife (not named); children (not named).

1767 WALTON, JAMES, Wife (not named); Thomas.

1780 WILLS, JOSEPH, David, William and Joseph.

1791 WILLARD, GABRIEL, Peter Thompson (friend); brother and sister (not named).

1765 WHITEHURST, RICHARD, John, Richard, Mary and Margaret; Rachel Hadnot (daughter).

1785 WHARTON, JOSEPH, Miriam (wife); Watson, William, John, Absalom, Isaac and Edward.

1790 WILLIAMS, BRYAN, Ann (mother); Bryan (brother); Penelope Williams (sister).

1786 WARD, SETH, Cora (wife); George and Seth; daughters (not named).

1784 WILDER, JONATHAN, Fanny (wife); Hosea and Hezekiah; Sally Askew, Amity Gregory, Nancy Cosland and Betty Gregory (daughters).

1778 WILLIAMS, BENJAMIN, Nicola (wife); Benjamin and James; Ann Battle (daughter).

1792 WILLIAMS, ANN. Bonita and Benjamin.

1783 WILLIAMS, LEWIS, Ann (wife); Bryan; Sirene Hicks (daughter).

1797 WALKER, SAMUEL, Frances (wife); John, Elizabeth and Frances.

1799 WARD, DAVID, Abigail (wife); Benjamin, Ruth and Josiah; Asenath Williams and Obiah Russell (daughters).

1776 WOODHOUSE, JOHN, Sarah Ward (cousin).

1777 WHITEHURST, RICHARD, Wife (not named); Thomas, James, Nelson, Richard, Nancy and Nellie.

1787 WEST, LEVI, George, Andrew, Levi, John, Francis, Jacob and Jeptha; Prudence Hickman, Mary Milton and Sarah Milton (daughters).

1784 WILLIAMS, JOSEPH, Margaret (wife); Christian, Samuel, Laban, Thomas and William.

1777 WILSON, SAMUEL, Eleanor, Elizabeth, Tabitha, Mary and Deborah.

1782 WESTON, DORCAS, Mary Ann, Elizabeth, Samuel, Benjamin and Dorcas.

1770 WOOD, WILLIAM, Rebecca (wife); Mark.

1761 WARD, BENJAMIN, Mary (wife); Abigail, Benjamin, Richard, Edward and Joseph.

1797 WILLIAMS, JANE, William (husband); George (son).

1769 WEBB, WILLIAM, Elizabeth (wife); Thomas and William.

1790 WILKING, ROSEMOND, Titus, Rosanna and Gilliam (daughters).

1792 WILLIAMS, JOHN, Clowey (wife); Dolly, Serena, Richard and Hopkins.

1773 WHITEHURST, MARY, Nelson, James, Thomas, Eleanor, Richard and Nancy; Mary Fuller, (daughter).

1781 WARD, ENOCH, Elizabeth (wife); Eli, Elijah, Elizabeth and Zilphia.

1790 WILLIAMS, SAMUEL, Penelope (wife); Hill, Ebenezer and John (brothers); Martin and Nillissa (sisters).

1788 WARD, JOSEPH, wife (not named); David, James, Mary and Maurice.

Y

1795 YATES, DAHIEL, Peneolpe (wife); Elizabeth, Benjamin, Louisa, Sarah, Daniel, Nancy and Leah.

PASQUOTANK—WILLS

A.

1784 ADAMS, PETER, Mary (wife).
1765 ALBERTSON, JOHN, Lydia, Albert, Mary (wife).
1766 ALBERTSON, JOSHUA, Eliza (wife); John, Arthur, Solomon, Jane.
1765 ANDRUS, WILLIAM, Martha (wife); Bailey, son.
1784 ARMOUR, JOSEPH, Sarah (wife); children (not named).
1792 ARMOUR, MARTHA, Markham, Joshua (son).
1762 ARMOUR, ROBERT, Eliza (wife); Joshua, William.
1764 ARMOUR, THOMAS, Thomas (brother); Blackstock, John (grandson).

B.

1764 BAILEY, BENJAMIN, wife (not named); Benjamin, Joseph, David, Elizabeth, Mary, Sarah.
1785 BAILEY, BENJAMIN, Bailey, Joseph (brother); Whedbee, Benjamin (cousin).
1782 BAILEY, HENRY, Ann (wife); Patrick, Henry, Jesse, James, Josiah.
1774 BAILEY, JOHN, John, Henry, Mary.
1784 BAILEY, JOHN, Jean (wife), John, Gabriel, Elizabeth, Thomas, Benjamin, Jean.
1784 BAILEY, JOSEPH, wife (not named), Benjamin.
1764 BAILEY, PATRICK, John, David, Elizabeth.
1793 BAILEY, ROBERT, John, (son); Warner, Tamar (daughter); Spruill, Polly (daughter); Warner, Samuel.
1790 BANKS, JONATHAN, Ann (wife); Thomas, William, Jonathan, Mary, Rebecca, Ann.
1774 BANKS, SARAH, James, Joseph.
1785 BAPTIST, EDMUND, Ann (wife); Mary, Elizabeth, Ann.
1792 BARCLIFT, WINIFRED, Keaton, Joseph (son); Gordon, Sally (daughter); Keaton, Charles (son); Davis, William (son).
1769 BARNARD, HULDAH, James, Nancy (a friend); Barnard, Elizabeth (cousin).
1774 BARNES, WILLIAM, (Tyrrell), Thomas, Stephen, James, Millicent, Ann, Elizabeth (wife); Mary, Catherine, Elizabeth.
1765 BELL, BENJAMIN, Harrison, Mary Lou (daughter), Nathan, Lyda, Benjamin, Joab, Josiah.
1781 BELL, LAUNCELOT, John, Margaret, Caroline, Miriam, Sarah (children).
1776 BELL, LEVI, Joseph (father), Ann (mother)
1773 BELL, MARY, Sarah, Linner, Mary, Barbara, Rhoda.
1771 BELL, WILLIAM, JR., William, Mary, Jane, Sarah, Susanna, Ann, Grace, Barbara, Mary (wife).
1787 BLACKSTOCK, JOHN, Mary (wife).
1761 BOOMER, JOHN, Mary (wife), Joseph.
1769 BORDEN, JOSEPH, Hannah (wife); Theophilus, Mary, Josiah, John.

1782 BOYD, THOMAS, Ann (wife); John, Grizzell.
1771 BOYD, WILLIAM, Anne, John, Joshua, Roger, William, Elizabeth (wife).
1762 BRAY, CHRISTOPHER, Christopher, Joseph, Susanna (wife).
1774 BRAY, WM., William, Abigail, Sarah.
1793 BRITE, RICHARD, Anne (wife); Asa, Richard, John, Fanny, Lovey, Courtney, Edey, Clark.
1762 BROTHERS, JOHN, Ann (wife); Malachi, Mary, Drew, William, Pheraba, Sarah, Miles.
1774 BROTHERS, JOHN, Thomas, John, Joseph (sons).
1783 BROTHERS, JOHN, Ann (wife); John, Jonathan, Thomas, Ann, Tamar, Mabel.
1765 BROTHERS, WILLIAM, Robert, William, Joseph, Benjamin, Thomas, Coverton; Dorcas (wife).
1785 BUNDY, CALEB, Miriam (wife); Dempsey, Benjamin, John, Caleb, Moses.
1762 BUNDY, JOSEPH, 'Elizabeth (mother); Sarah (wife); Joseph, Josiah.
1768 BUNTING, SAMUEL, Esther (wife); Charles, Philip.
1764 BURGESS, ELIZABETH, Dorothy, Jemima, Mary, Miriam.
1763 BURGESS, JOHN, John, Freelove, Dempsey, William, Zephaniah.
1761 BURGESS, WM., John, William, Jesse, Bevorie, Elizabeth, Mary; Elizabeth (wife).
1762 BURNHAM, BENJAMIN, Gabriel, Benjamin, Mary (wife); Thomas, Ann, Mary.
1765 BURNHAM, JOHN, John, Joshua, David, Elizabeth.

C.

1775 CANADY, ALEXANDER, Miriam (wife); Joshua, John, Arthur, Elizabeth, Chloe, Mary.
1763 CARTWRIGHT, ABRAM, Ezekiel, Abram, Elizabeth (wife).
1760 CARTWRIGHT, CHRISTOPHER, Ann (wife); Joseph, Ann.
1776 CARTWRIGHT, ISAAC, Caleb, Jesse, Isaac, Asa, Elizabeth, Mary, Lydia, Dinah, Elizabeth (wife).
1777 CARTWRIGHT, JESSE, Jesse (son), Eliza (wife).
1776 CARTWRIGHT, JOB, Martha (wife); Miriam,
1762 LOW, THOMAS, Sarah (wife); William (son), Ann, Elizabeth.
1790 CARTWRIGHT, JOHN, Elizabeth (wife); John,
1762 CARTWRIGHT, THOMAS, Robert, Sarah, Tamar, William.
1778 CARTWRIGHT, JOHN, wife (not named); Caleb, Barnaby and John (brothers).
1784 CAPPER, BENJAMIN, Benjamin. Malachi, Caleb, Joel, Mary, Susanna, Dorcas, Sarah, Keziah.
1778 CASSE, JAMES, Dorcas (wife); two sons (not named).
1790 CASSE, JOHN, Dorcas (wife); William, Arthur, Page.
1780 CASSE, THOMAS, Ruth, Charity, John, Dorcas (Scott), Mary .(Barrett), Elizabeth (children).
1765 CHAMBERLAIN, ROBERT, Samuel, George, Charles; Elizabeth (wife).

1778 CHANCEY, EDMUND, Elizabeth (wife); Micajah, Edmund, Mary.

1790 CLARK, ICHABOD, Childs, Elizabeth (sister); Clark, Trustun (nephew).

1783 CLARK, MARY, Joseph, James, John.

1789 CLARK, SYLVANUS, Ruth (wife); James, Cornelius, Reuben, Sabah, Sarah, Joseph, Mary.

1769 COLLIER, ZACHARIAH, Mary (wife).

1774 COMMANDER, JOHN, John, Thomas, Miriam, Sarah (wife); Ann, Elizabeth.

1763 COMMANDER, JOSEPH, Elizabeth (wife); Elinor, James, William.

1785 CONNER, CADER, wife (not named); William, John, Crawford.

1790 CONNOR, DEMPSEY, Ann (wife); George, Fanny, Polly, Jack.

1774 CONNER, JOHN, Love (wife); Aletia and Mary (daughters).

1779 CRAWFORD, JOHN, Lily, Laurat, William.

D.

1774 DALEY, JOHN, Joshua, Zadock, John, Enoch, (sons); Chamberlain, John (friend).

1784 DAVIS, JOHN, Priscilla (wife).

1772 DAVIS, JOSEPH, Elizabeth (wife); Jackson, Mary, (daughter); Ann, Elizabeth.

1778 DAVIS, JOSEPH, David, Fred (cousin).

1787 DAVIS, JOSHUA, Mary Ann (wife); Dedrick and Frederick.

1789 DAVIS, NANCY, Nancy, Lovey, Lydia.

1769 DAVIS, SAMUEL, Joseph, William, John, Ann (wife).

1788 DAVIS SAMUEL, Ann (wife); Elizabeth, Ann, Lovey, Lydia.

1781 DAVIS, THOMAS, Lydia (wife); Caleb, Thomas, Nathan, Sarah, Mary, Miriam.

1791 DAVIS, THOMAS, Rebecca (wife).

1781 DAVIS, WM., Lydia (wife).

1788 DRIVER, MATTHEW, Rhoda (wife); John, Edward.

E.

1786 EVENTON, WILLIAM, Rhoda (wife); James, John, Thomas.

F.

1774 FORBES, BALE, John, Bale, Caleb, Henry, Elizabeth, Mary; wife (not named).

G.

1766 GALLUP, ABEL, Robert, Abel, Josiah, Mary (wife).

1764 GARRITT, JONATHAN, Mary (wife); John, James, Sampson.

1762 GILBERT, HENRY, Sarah (wife); Mary, Eliza.

1774 GILBERT, THOMAS, Elizabeth (wife); Josiah, Sarah.

1778 GORDAN, WM., Sarah (wife); Joseph, William.

1761 GRANDY, THOMAS, Ann (wife); Mabel, Davis, Letitia, Effiah, Mary, Thomas, Ann (wife).

1765 GRAY, GRIFFITH, Charity (wife); Dorothy, Lochlenneh (daughters).

1770 GRAY, THOMAS, Priscilla (wife); Joseph, Lemuel, John, Nancy (Sanderson).

1776 GRAY, THORNTON, Elizabeth (wife); Judah, Catherine, Julia, Barthema, Thornton.

1765 GREENE, JAMES, Jane (wife); James, Fanny.

1777 GREGORY, JAMES, Ruth (wife); Richard, James, Arthur, Noah, Caleb, Lemuel, Mary, Tamar, Ruth, Elizabeth, Margaret.

1761 GREGORY, SARAH, Swann, Charlotte (granddaughter); Winslow, Ann (granddaughter).

1763 GRIFFITH, ISAAC, Wilson, Nathaniel (his partner).

H.

1770 HALL, CLEMENT, Robert (brother); Sarah (sister).

1788 HALL, ELIZABETH, Caleb (son); Overman, Sarah (sister).

1783 HALL, ROBERT, Robert, Deborah.

1762 HALL, STEPHEN, Elizabeth (wife); Ann, Elizabeth, Sarah, Benjamin.

1783 HALSTEAD, DUN, Edward, Thomas, Samuel, Simon, Latimore, and John (brothers); Sawyer, Lovey (sister); Miles, Jane (sister).

1791 HALSTEAD, JOHN, Millicent (wife); John, Benjamin, Thomas, Charlotte, Love, Mary.

1778 HARRIS, ESTHER, Sexton, James, David and Obadiah (sons).

1762 HARRIS, JOHN, Hezekiah, Joseph, Anne, John, Mary; wife (not named).

1775 HAUGHTON, HENRY, Elizabeth (wife), Malachi, Margaret, Martha.

1761 HIGH, JAMES, Elizabeth (wife), Meeds, Nancy, Sarah, Elizabeth.

1781 HIXON, TIMOTHY, John (son); McPhannon, Joshua.

1792 HOSEA, JOHN, Mary (wife); John.

1781 HOSEA, ROBERT, Elizabeth (wife); Henry, Thomas, Lovey, Abraham, Millicent.

1762 HUNTER, REBECCA, Samuel and William Swann (sons).

1760 HUNTER, THOMAS, Rebecca (wife).

I.

1771 IVEY, JOHN, Elizabeth (wife); Hannah and James.

J.

1762 JACKSON, DANIEL, Bailey, Moses, John.

1774 JACKSON, MATTHIAS, Mother (not named); Douglas, Mary (niece); Mary (sister).

1785 JACKSON, SAMUEL, Miriam (wife); James, Lashel, William, Courtney, Ann.

1774 JACKSON. SIMON PETER: Jackson, Joab (wife).

1774 JACKSON, SIMON PETER, Jackson, Joab (cousin).

1778 JACKSON, WM., Courtney (wife); Jacob, Joab, Samuel, William.

1765 JAMES, JACOB, Willis, Noah, Eliza; wife (not named).

1772 JAMES, JANE, Noah, Willis, Elizabeth.

1778 JAMES, WILLIAM, JR., Ann (wife).
1761 JENNINGS, CALEB, Mary (wife); Sarah, Miriam, Dorcas.
1774 JENNINGS, BENJAMIN, Jabez, Jesse, Benjamin, Elizabeth, Miriam, Susanna, Hannah.
1768 JENNINGS, DAVID, Dewey and Lemuel (brothers).
1791 JENNINGS, ARTHUR, Susanna (wife); Malachi, James, Parthenia, Love, Nannie, Miriam.
1791 JENNINGS, JESSE, Jesse, Peggy, Dolly, Mary.
1777 JONES, GRIFFITH, Miles.
1776 JONES, ISAAC, Mary (wife); Timothy, John, Joseph, Mary, Dempsey, Anna.
1772 JONES, WILLIAM, John, Jarvis, Caleb; wife (not named).
1762 JORDAN, JOSEPH, Robert and Nevil (sons).
1768 JORDAN, MARY, John Duke, of Northampton (friend); Micajah (son).
1762 JORDAN, MATTHIAS, Miriam (wife); Thomas, Josiah, Matthew, Samuel.
1769 JORDAN, MICAJAH, Nicholson, Mary (niece); Henley, John (nephew).
1779 JORDAN, NEVIL, Jordan, Robert and John A. (nephews); Conner, Dempsey, Jordan and William (cousins).
1765 JORDAN, ROBERT, Elizabeth (wife); Micajah (brother).

K.

1781 KEATON, JOSEPH, Stephen, William, Miriam, Ann, Henry, Joseph, John, Patrick, Clarky.
1785 KEETON, ZACHARIAH, Joseph, Zachariah.
1768 KEITE, CHARLES, Ann (wife); Ann, John, Amos, Charles, Elisha.
1785 KENNON, BENJAMIN, wife (not named); Joseph, Levi, Elizabeth.
1774 KNIBLOE, PETER, Keziah (wife).

L.

1786 LANCASTER, JOHN, Mary (wife).
1791 LANCASTER, MARY, George, John, Mary and Frances Conner (grandchildren).
1761 LANE, WILLIAM, John, William.
1763 LEAK, FRANCIS, John, Jeola, Mary, Keziah; wife (not named).
1781 LEAK, JEREMIAH, Sarah (wife); Jeremiah, Isaac, Maxcy, Lydia, Elizabeth, Keziah, Nannie.
1785 LEAK, MARY, Sarah (mother); Jeremiah (brother).
1770 LOW, ELIZABETH, George, son.
1786 LOW, GEORGE, Tamar (wife); Thomas, Jesse. Jesse. Robert, Darius, Charlotte, Jonathan, Peleg.
1779 LOWRY, JOHN, Robert, John, Benjamin, William.
1788 LOW, WILLIAM, Mary (wife).

M.

1778 MABIN, JAMES, McMorine, Robert (friend).
1766 McBRIDE, JOHN, Josiah, Elisha, Sarah, Rhoda, Sarah (wife).
1786 McCLEAN, ELIZABETH, John, Ann.

1789 McCLAIN, ALEXANDER, Ann, John.
1780 McDANIEL, JAMES, Rachel (wife); Temple,
Susanna and Rhoda (daughters).
1770 MADREN, JACOB, Thomas, Matthias.
1786 MADREN, JOSEPH, Dorcas (wife); Samuel.
1783 MANN, JOSEPH, Ann (wife); William.
1761 MARKHAM, ANTHONY, Charles, Elizabeth,
Joshua, Sarah, Anthony, Martha.
1775 MEEDS, JOSEPH, Tamar (wife); Timothy,
John, Sarah, Benjamin, Nancy.
1785 MEEDS, THOMAS, Mary (wife); three children (not named).
1759 MEEDS, TIMOTHY, Davis, Wm.; Pendleton,
Henry; Jamison, James; High, Nancy;
Meeds, Sally and Eliza.
1776 MOORE, JONATHAN, Moore, Aaron, and John
brothers); Arnold, Sarah, sister.
1775 MORGAN, ANN, Lemuel, Seth, Benjamin, Hannah, Charles, James
1758 MORGAN, BENNETT, Robert, Lidie, Bennett,
Grace; Dorothy (wife);
1771 MORGAN, JAMES, James, Lemuel, Ann (wife),
Seth, Charles, Benjamin.
1777 MORGAN, JOSEPH, Cartright, Peter and wife,
Jean (daughter) and their children.
1774 MORGAN, ROBERT, Jane (daughter), Nancy
(wife).
1770 MORRIS, AARON, SR., Joshua, Joseph, Mary
(wife), John, Aaron, Miriam.
1777 MORRIS, JOHN, Ruth (wife); Margaret, Susanna.
1778 MORRIS, JOHN, Aaron, Keziah.
1759 MURDEN, ROBERT, wife, Jeremiah, Caleb,
Elizabeth, Robert.

N.

1771 NASH, JOSIAH, Caleb, Solly, John, Mary
(wife).
1779 NEWBY, BENJAMIN, wife (not named), Mary,
Sarah, Lydia.
1778 NEWBY, THOMAS, Sarah (wife); James,
Naomi, Sarah.
1779 NICHOLS, DAVID, James, Ann, Benjamin,
Elizabeth, Miriam.
1775 NICHOLS, HENRY, David, Willis, Anthony,
William; Jeremiah, Thomas, Aggie (wife).
1792 NICHOLS, JABEZ, Mitchi (wife); Enoch, Sarah.
1778 NICHOLS, JEREMIAH, Keziah (wife); Abner.
1769 NICHOLS, WILLIAM, Sarah (wife); William,
Susanna, Caleb (sons); Jonathan Nichols
(grandson).
1783 NICHOLS, WM., Elizabeth (wife); Olley, Polly.
1771 NICHOLSON, JOSEPH, Rebecca (wife); Zachariah, Christopher.
1777 NIGHTS, EMANUEL, Lucy, John, Emanuel,
Thomas, Ann; wife (not named).
1774 NIXON, TIMOTHY, McCarson, Courtney
(daughter); Timothy (son), Courtney
(wife).
1774 NORRIS, WM., Ann (wife); Susanna, Mary.

O.

1771 OGGS, JOHN, Alice, Jesse, Prudence, Charles.
1774 OGILVEY, WM., Children of James (brother) in Scotland.
1763 OVERMAN, ANN, Samuel, Benjamin, Enoch, Ann, Mary, Elizabeth.
1762 OVERMAN, CHRISTOPHER, Sarah (wife).
1773 OVERMAN, ENOCH, Ruth (wife).
1792 OVERMAN, ENOCH, Tamar (wife).
1785 OVERMAN, EPHRAIM, Jacob and Ephraim (sons); Bowles, Keziah and Clark, Martha, (daughters); Tamar and Abigail (daughters).
1784 OVERMAN, ISAAC, wife (not named).
1779 OVERMAN, NATHAN, Sarah (wife); Thomas, Nathan, Ann.
1785 OVERMAN, REUBEN, Tamar (wife); Ann, Sarah, Samuel.
1761 OVERMAN, THOMAS, Christopher, Benjamin, Joseph, John, Hannah, Thomas.
1784 OVERMAN, THOMAS, Sarah (wife); Joseph, Peninah.
1789 OVERMAN, THOMAS, Sarah (wife).
1789 OVERMAN, THOMAS, Charity (wife); Charles, Rhoda, Thomas, Hannah, Samuel, Enoch.
1774 OVERMAN, WM., Ann, Mary (daughter).

P.

1789 PAINTER, MATTHEW, John, William, Joseph, Thomas.
1768 PALIN, HENRY, Thomas, John, Joseph, Miriam.
1788 PALIN, HENRY, Thomas, Miriam, Elizabeth.
1784 PALIN, JOHN, Lemuel, Polly, Nancy, Mary.
1784 PALMER, ROBERT, Millicent, Nancy.
1791 PAVEY, SARAH, John.
1770 PELL, JOHN, Joseph, Elizabeth, Sarah, Assiah, Mary (wife).
1774 PENDLETON, GEORGE, Pendleton, Lemuel and George Jr. (nephews).
1784 PENDLETON, HENRY, Ann (wife).
1778 PENDLETON, JOHN, Timothy, Samuel, Hiram, Anne, Abijah.
1791 PENDLETON, JOSEPH, Ann (wife); Frederick, Joseph, Thomas, Caleb, John.
1763 PENDLETON, SARAH, Thomas, Joseph, Tamar, Nancy, Elizabeth.
1781 PENDLETON, THOMAS, Joseph (brother); Palin, Tamar (sister).
1774 PENDLETON, TIMOTHY, Mary (wife); Zachariah, Joshua, George.
1774 PHILLIPS, BENJAMIN, Daniel, Benjamin. Mitchell, Caleb, Mary, Margaret; Betty (wife); Sarah, Grace.
1782 PHILLIPS, JEMIMA, Benjamin, Miriam, Jemima, Mary.
1785 PIKE, BENJAMIN, Jean (wife); Benjamin, John.
1790 POOL, ELIZABETH, Rebecca, Malachi, Elizabeth.
1774 POOL, JOHN, Robert, James, Sarah, Elizabeth, Joshua, John, Joseph.
1771 POOL, JOSEPH, Richard, William, Elizabeth (wife).

1782   POOL, RICHARD, Sarah (wife); John, Patrick, Samuel, Joseph, Thomas.

1761   POOL, SOLOMON, John, William, Barnaby, Patrick, Elizabeth, Sarah; Ann (wife).

1781   POOL, WM., SR., Clarky (wife); Joshua, John,

1774   POINTER, JOHN SR., Elizabeth (wife); Mary, Sarah, Samuel, John, Martha, Elizabeth.

1784   POYNTER, SAMUEL, Hepsibah (wife); John, William, Joseph, Thomas.

1791   PRITCHARD, BENJAMIN, Martha (wife); Susanna.

1772   PRITCHARD, BENNONI, Miriam (wife) Elizabeth, Mary, John, Joseph.

1762   PRITCHARD, JOSEPH, Sarah, Mary, Eliza, Benjamin, Miriam; Sarah wife).

1777   PRITCHARD, MARY, Thomas (husband); Elizabeth, Joseph, Thomas, John, Ricks (children).

1760   PRITCHARD, THOMAS, Thomas, Joseph; Elizabeth (wife).

1772   PRICHARD, THOMAS, James, John, Dolly, Jesse; Rowe, Ann (daughter); Jackson, Elizabeth (daughter); Pethiar, (wife).

1791   PRITCHARD, THOMAS, Elizabeth (wife) Elizabeth, Polly, Thomas, John, Nancy.

1781   PUFFIN, ISAAC, To the Poor of the Parish.

1761   PURSLEY, NATHAN P., Caleb, Levi, Nathan, Garrott, Cornelius, Elizabeth.

R.

1762   RAPER, JOSIAH, Mary (wife); Cornelius, Penelope, Benjamin, Margaret.

1780   READING, BENJAMIN, Millicent, Ann, Clarky (sisters).

1761   REDING, JEREMIAH, Samuel (brother).

1766   REDING, JONATHAN, Thomas, Joseph, Ann (wife), Sarah.

1762   REDING, SAMUEL, Trimagin (brother).

1775   READING, SARAH, Trimagin, Ann, Millicent, Benjamin, Cleartha.

1762   REDING, THOMAS, Joseph, Sarah; wife (not named).

1778   READING, TRIMAGIN, Clarky, Ann, and Millicent (sisters).

1772   REEFE, THOMAS, Thomas, Enoch, Elizabeth, John, Penelope.

1774   REEFE, WM., Dorcas (wife); Robert, William, Joseph, Rebekah, Sarah, Nathan.

1790   RICHARDSON, BENJAMIN, Ann.

1761   RICHARDSON, JOHN, John, Ede, Elizabeth, Catherine (wife).

1780   RICHARDSON, JOSEPH, Evan, Richard, David, Daniel, Joseph, Dorothy, Rhoda.

1774   RICHARDSON, JOSIAH, Ruth (wife); James and Jacob (sons); Benjamin and Stephen (brothers).

1778   RICHARDSON, LEBBEUS, Abigail (wife); Stephen, Lebbeus, Thomas.

1791   RICHARDSON, WM, Isaac, Elijah, Priscilla, Catherine, Fanny.

1791   RUSSELL, THOMAS, Elizabeth (wife); John, Mary.

S.

1788 SANDERS, HENRY, Lovey (wife); Joseph, Evan, Richard, Elizabeth, Sarah, Hosea, Deborah.

1765 SANDERLIN, MARY, James, Joseph, Ezekiel, Maximilian, Devotion.

1781 SANDERLIN, MAXIMILIAN, Dorcas (wife); Mabel, Sidna (daughters).

1781 SAWYER, DAVID, Tamar (wife); Isaac, Charity.

1762 SAWYER, JOHN, Jabez, Miriam, Mary, Cornelius, children; wife (not named).

1772 SAWYER, JOHN, John, Lemuel, Arthur, Miller, Huldah, Sophia.

1777 SAWYER, JOSEPH, Jane (wife); Delby, Betsy, Joseph, Benjamin, Peggy and Frederick.

1765 SAWYER, ROBERT, Absalom, Laben, Rachel.

1768 SAWYER, SAMUEL, Thomas, Samuel, Betty, Mary (wife).

1765 SAWYER, THOMAS, Thomas, Caleb, Elizabeth; Margaret (wife).

1784 SAWYER, WILLIAM, Pheraba (wife); Miriam, Keziah, Samuel, Caleb, Malachi.

1781 SCARFE, JOHN, James, John, Joseph, Elizabeth, Susanna, Ann.

1762 SCOTT, EDWARD, Mary (wife); Stephen, Samuel, Joshua.

1770 SCOTT, SAMUEL, Stephen, Joseph, Sarah, Mary.

1774 SCOTT, WM., Mourning Scott (half sister); Elliott and Joseph Scott (brothers); Thomas, Elizabeth (sister).

1781 SEXTON, WM., Pethiar (Pritchard) Miriam, Malachi, Rhoda, Nancy (children).

1771 SIKES, JAMES, John, Polly, Elizabeth, Rachel, Mary (wife).

1787 SIMSON, ROBERT, Elizabeth (wife); Joab, Susanna, Dorcas.

1768 SIMPSON, WILLIAM, Joel, Robert, Joab, Ruth (wife).

1788 SMALL, OBADIAH, Sarah (wife); Joshua, Nathan, Elizabeth, Jesse, John, Obadiah, and six younger children.

1770 SMITH, JAMES, wife (not named); James, Elizabeth, Martha, Dorcas, Rhoda, Hannah, Jane.

1792 SMITHSON, THOMAS, Sarah (sister).

1763 SOLLEY, JOSEPH, Sarah (wife); John, Sarah.

1785 SPENCE, ESTHER, Miriam, Nancy, Elizabeth, Mary.

1785 SPENCE, WILLIAM, Judah (wife); Thornton, Joseph, Sarah, Elisha.

1783 SPENCER, JOSEPH, Sarah (wife); Sawyer, Sarah (daughter); Samuel, Mark, (sons).

1772 SQUIRES, JOHN, Thomas, John, Miriam (children); Wright, Ann (daughter); Mary (wife).

1775 SQUIRES, MIRIAM, Thomas (brother); Elizabeth (sister).

1783 SQUIRES, ROGER, wife (not named); Elizabeth, Hannah, Roger, Sarah, Mary, Benjamin, Margot.

1774 STAFFORD, SAMUEL, Josiah, Sarah, Samuel, Mary, Joseph, wife (not named).

1781 STAMP, DEBORAH, Stamp, Miriam (sister); Stamp, Richard (brother).

1789 SWANN, JOHN, Margaret (wife); Rebecca.

1781 SWANN, JOSEPH, John (brother).

1768 SWANN, SAMUEL, Samuel, John, Stephen; wife (not named).

1772 SWANN, SAMUEL, John and Joseph (brothers); Rebecca (sister).

1787 SWANN, SAMUEL, John, Thomas, William.

1766 SWANN, WM., Samuel, William, Wilson, Martha (wife); Rebecca.

1789 SYMONS, ABRAHAM, Abraham, Benjamin, Elizabeth, Ann, Mary. Martha, Sarah, Penelope, Elizabeth (wife).

1776 SYMONS, BENJAMIN, Grissell Edwards (mother).

1768 SYMONS, JEHOSAPHAT, John, Nathan, Jesse, Sarah, Mary Ann, Lydia, Penelope, Millicent, Elizabeth (wife).

1788 SYMONS, JOHN, Elizabeth (wife); Thomas, Matthew, Abraham.

1777 SYMONS SAMUEL, Elizabeth (wife); William, Mary, Elizabeth.

1769 SYMONS, THOMAS, Elizabeth, Jane (wife).

1761 SYMONS, WILLIAM, Cornwell, Mary; Saunders, Eliza; Samuel, William (all children); John Symons (grandson).

T.

1762 TADLOCK, EDWARD, James, Edward; Mary (wife).

1792 TADLOCK, JOHN, Keziah (wife); Elizabeth, Absalom, Simeon, Penina, James, Millicent.

1771 TAYLOR, WILLIAM, Mary (wife), Maccabeus, Garland.

1791 TEMPLE, THOMAS, James, Susanna, Peggy, Thomas.

1771 THACKERAY, JOHN, Ann (wife); John, Mary, Jane, Joseph.

1775 THACKERAY, JOSEPH, Taylor, Robert and William (nephews).

1775 TILLET, WILLIAM, Lydia (wife); Lemuel (son).

1775 TOMLINSON, ELIZABETH, Carver, Job; Albertson, Elias (sons).

1776 TORKSEY, BENJAMIN, Benjamin, Caleb, Ellet, Annas, Joseph, Elizabeth (wife).

1765 TORKSEY, THOMAS, Thomas, Philip, John.

1759 TRUEBLOOD, AMOS, Thomas, Josiah, Joshua, Caleb, Abel.

1762 TRUEBLOOD, JOSHUA, Aaron, Thomas, Mary, Susanna, Miriam (wife).

1776 TUMBLIN, SAMUEL, John.

U.

1767 UPTON, JOSEPH, Anne (wife); Joseph, Absalom.

W.

1762 WARDSWORTH, EDWARD, Ann (wife); Mary, Willie, Lewis, Thomas, Barnaby, Caleb.

1765 WAYMAN, WM., William, Calvin, Thomas, Lydia, Tamar, Charity (wife).

1788 WAYMAN, WILLIAM, Ann (wife); Amos, John.

1785 WEST, CHARLES, Tamar (wife); Charles, Joshua.

1787 WHARTON, ABEY, Catherine, Parthenia, Mary, Luca.

1771 WHARTON, EDWARD E., Caleb, Willis, Sarah (wife); Isaac, Elizabeth, Edward, Timothy, Robert, Lydia.

1785 WHITE, BENJAMIN, Miriam (wife); James, Samuel.

1790 WHITE, BENJAMIN, Rachel (wife); Benjamin, Josiah, Jesse, Joshua, Parthenia, Ann, Elizabeth, Abigail, Rachel, Ruth.

1779 WHITE, JOSHUA, Hulda (wife); Nehemiah, Robert, Benjamin.

1790 WILLIAMS, DANIEL, Tamar (wife); David, Tamar, Mary, Lydia, Ann.

1790 WILLIAMS, EDWARD, Daniel, Owen, Rhoda.

1770 WILLIAMS, LODOWICK, Lodowick, John, Elijah, Lydia, Dorothy (wife).

1777 WILLIAMS, TULLER, Lemuel, Elizabeth.

1778 WILSON, JOHN, Rachel (wife); Joseph (son), Chamberlain, Mary (daughter).

1763 WILSON, JOSEPH, Mary (wife); James, Mary.

1767 WILLSON, NATHANIEL, Surrey, Thomas and William (sons-in-law); Miriam (wife).

1772 WILSON, WILLIAM, John, William, Dempsey, Lemuel, Willis, Samuel, Sarah, Ann, Mary, Rosamond.

1788 WINBERRY, JOHN, Elizabeth (wife).

1785 WINSLOW, JOSIAH, Elizabeth (wife); James, Sarah, Mary, James, John.

1774 WINSLOW, SAMUEL, Ruth (wife); Mary.

1790 WOOD, EVAN, Margaret (wife); Thomas, Miriam.

1778 WOOD, GEORGE, Elizabeth (wife); Thomas, Evan, Ann, Betsy, Miriam.

1753 WOODLEY, THOMAS, Taylor, Thomas (grandson).

1767 WOOTEN, WILLIAM, Mary (wife).

1772 WRIGHT, CHARLES, Anne (wife); Augustin; Cartright, Elizabeth (daughter); Levi.

1772 WRIGHT, JOHN, John, Cornelius, Barnaby, William, Peter, James, Matthias, Gamaliel (sons).

WILLS—PERQUIMANS COUNTY

A.

1763 ASHLEY, WM., Elizabeth (wife).
1774 ARNOLD, WM., William, Benjamin, Mary, Thomas, Joseph.
1762 ALBERTSON, AARON, Bryan.
1784 ALBERTSON, WM., Benjamin, Chalkley, William, Sarah.
1785 ALBERTSON, NATHANIEL, Joseph, Jesse.
1785 ALBERTSON, ELIHU, Josiah, John, Joshua, Miriam.
1793 ANDERSON, JOSEPH, Benjamin, John, William, Isaac.
1794 ARNOLD, WM., William, Jonathan, Miriam, Mary.

B.

1763 BAGLEY, THOMAS, Thomas.
1763 BOSWELL, JOSHUA, Mary (wife).
1768 BOND, SAMUEL, William, Samuel, Job, Pritlow.
1772 BRINKLEY, PETER, Mary, Peter, John.
1773 BATEMAN, WM., Benjamin, Joseph, Betty.
1777 BARCLIFT, JAMES, William (brother), William (son).
1777 BARCLIFT, WM., William, Sarah, Elizabeth, Nancy.
1779 BARBER, JOSEPH, wife, Joseph.
1777 BRAINER, MICH'AEL, Sarah, Millicent.
1784 BRATTEN, JOHN, Nathaniel, Benjamin.
1784 BARCLIFT, NOAH, William B., Noah, Asa, Millicent, Mary C.
1784 BLOUNT, CHARLES, Edmund, John, Elizabeth, Mary.
1778 BARCLIFT, SAMUEL, Samuel.
1785 BARCLIFT, ASA, Asa.
1786 BULLOCK, MARY, Martha.
1787 BULLOCK, MARTHA, Harrell, Obed, Hannah, Sarah, Rachel.
1788 BOGUE, JOB, Elizabeth, Jesse.
1791 BOND, WM., Abigail, Josiah, John, Job.
1792 BRINKLEY, JAMES, Sarah, Eli, Miles, Mary.
1793 BARCLIFT, JOSEPH, Joseph, Denson, Thomas, Mary, Lanera.
1761 BUNDY, JOSIAH, Joseph, Elizabeth, Ellis, Joshua, Josiah, Caleb.
1761 BOSWELL, ICHABOD, Peter, Lydia.
1796 BUNCH, JOSHUA, David, Sarah.
1797 BARCLIFT, NOAH, Sanderson, John.

C.

1765 CROXTON, ARTHUR, Pearson, Elizabeth, John, Sarah, Mary, Joseph, Eliza, Job.
1768 COCKS, ROBERT, Anne, Joseph, John, Robert, Seth.
1771 CHARLES, WILLIAM, wife, William, Joshua, Aaron.
1772 CALLAWAY. JOHN, Zebulon, Joseph.
1774 CHAPPELL, ROBERT, Malachi, John, Robert, Job, Elizabeth, Mark, Miriam, Rhoda, Hannah.
1774 CHARLES, SAMUEL, John, Samuel, Sylvanus, Joseph, Sarah, Benjamin, Mary.

1777 CHAPPELL, MALACHI, Jesse, Malachi, wife.
1777 COLLINS, ANDREW, Samuel, Jeremiah, Joshua, John, Anne, Elizabeth, Sarah.
1777 CREECY, JOHN, Catherine, Levi, Thomas, John, Deborah, Rhoda.
1779 CHOCKE, GEORGE, Sarah, William, Sibyl.
1781 CLAYTON, RICHARD, Askew, Richard, Elizabeth, Anne, Sarah, wife.
1787 COLSON, JOHN, Rebecca.
1791 CALLAWAY, ZEBULON, John, Elizabeth.
1788 CHARLES, JOHN, Elizabeth, Daniel.
1793 COSAND, AARON, Benjamin.
1795 COLLINS, CHRISTOPHER, Elizabeth, James.
1795 COLE, RICHARD, Nathaniel, Hannah.

D.

1764 DOCTOR, JACOB, Sarah, wife.
1764 DRAPER, PETER, Joseph, Silas,
1768 DONALDSON, ANDREW, Sarah, James, Margaret, Charity, Andrew, John, Spencer, William.
1774 DELANO, ICHABOD, Sarah, Mary.
1794 DRAPER, SILAS, Joseph, Lemuel, Chalkley, Jesse, Mary, David, Dick, Benjamin.
1795 DONALDSON, JOHN, James.
1795 DEERAW, SARAH, Sarah, Elizabeth.
1796 DIGLEY, JAMES, James, Dorothy.
1799 DAVIS, ROBERT, Margaret, James, Mary.

E.

1774 ELLIOTT, BENJAMIN, Sarah, Josiah, Benjamin, Seth, Exum.
1774 EASON, GEORGE, Sarah, Seth, Jesse, Abner.
1787 ELLIOTT, PRITLOW, Mary, William, Pritlow, Job, Thomas, Jesse, John, Huldah, Rachel, Mary.
1788 ELLIOTT, JOSEPH, Mordecai, Caleb, Hannah.
1789 ELLIOTT, ISAAC, Joshua, Isaac, Jacob, Nathan, Margaret, Rebecca, Sarah, Miriam.
1791 ELLIOTT, JAMES, Martha, Nathan, Gabriel.
1797 EVANS, ROBERT, John, Thomas, William, Benjamin, Joseph.

F.

1763 FOSTER, FRANCIS, William.
1784 FOREHAND, SAMUEL, Sarah, wife.
1785 FLETCHER, RALPH, Joshua, Jesse, Margaret, Miriam.
1761 FOSTER, FRANCIS, William; Barclift, Elizabeth.

G.

1768 GIBSON, JAMES, John.
1772 GRIFFIN, JOHN, Elizabeth, Eliab, John, Josiah.
1774 GODFREY, THOMAS, Joseph, Thomas, Tully.
1774 GRIFFIN, JOHN, Josiah, Eliab, Lydia, Ruth, Huldah, Elizabeth.
1790 GUYER, JOSEPH, Miriam, Nathan, William, Joseph.

H.

1763   HARRELL, RICHARD, Dempsey, James, John.
1768   HENBY, SILVANUS, John, Margaret; Outlaw, Joseph.
1772   HUDSON, JOHN, Uriah, Duke, Peter, Dick.
1772   HOLLOWELL, THOMAS, Sarah, Thomas, Silas, John.
1773   HASKET, WM., Mary, Thomas.
1774   HOLLWELL, JOEL, Abner, Thomas, Ezekiel, Joel, James, Miriam, Cortney.
1775   HALSEY, THOMAS, Catherine, Martha, William, Margaret, Penelope, Deborah.
1775   HARVEY, JOHN, Mary, Joseph, Thomas, John, James, Miles.
1766   HASKITT, JOSHUA, Joseph, Joshua, Ails, William.
1777   HARVEY, MILES, Elizabeth, Augustus, Miles, Albridgedon.
1784   HOLLWELL, JOHN, Henry, William, wife.
1785   HARVEY, MILES, Mary, James, Miles E.
1785   HALL, JACOB, Elizabeth, Nancy, Sarah.
1788   HOSEA, JOSEPH, Samuel, Joseph.
1788   HARVEY, THOMAS, Mary, Charles, Thomas, Edward B., Sarah, Mary, Margaret, Martha B.
1788   HENDRICKS, JOB, Solomon, Sarah, Nathan, Joseph, Dempsey, Seth, Penniah.
1790   HALL, EDWARD, Edward.
1791   HOLLOWELL, THOMAS, Miriam, Riddick, Fred, Abraham, Millicent, Joel, William, Willis.
1792   HALL, MARY, Henry, Sarah, John.
1792   HALL, HENRY, John.
1794   HOLLOWELL, EZEKIEL, Christian.
1797   HASKITT, ALICE, Joseph, Joshua, William, Rachel.

J.

1764   JONES, EVAN, Samuel.
1772   JACKSON, AARON, Moses, Samuel, Joseph, Parthenia, Charles, Priscilla, William.
1774   JACKSON, JOHN, Rebecca, wife.
1777   JONES, MALACHI, Mary, Joshua.
1788   JONES, THOMAS, Margaret, Thomas, William, Zachariah, Mary, Sarah.
1789   JORDAN, JOSIAH, Elizabeth, Thomas, Josiah, Matthew, Miriam, Sarah, Dorothy, Mary.
1791   JONES, FRANCIS, Jeremiah, Rachel; White, Theophilus.
1793   JONES, JOSEPH, Aquilla.
1793   JACKSON, MOSES, William, Elizabeth, Sallie.
1794   JACKSON, WM., Joseph, Moses, Mary.
1794   JONES, WM., Anne, Sarah, Mary, Margaret, Josiah, Thomas.

K.

1776   KNOX, ANDREW, Christian, wife; Hugh, Andrew, Christian.
1777   KENYON, ROGER, Wife; Roger, Josiah, Duke, Benjamin, Sarah, Thomas, William.
1797   KENYON, JOAB, Mawood, Josiah, Joab, Elizabeth.

L.

1781 LONG, THOMAS, Edward, Nathan, Charlotte.
1786 LACY, JOHN, Maudlin, Jane, Tarlton, Joshua.
1786 LAYDEN, ISAAC, Elizabeth (wife).
1791 LONG, JOSHUA, Joshua, Thomas, Miriam, Sarah.
1793 LEIGH, GILBERT, Elizabeth, Francis, Richard, Thomas, James, Benjamin.
1795 LONG, REUBEN, Mary, Lemuel, William, Josiah.
1797 LUNCEFORD, JOHN, Creecy, Levi, Wingate, Sarah, Mary.
1798 LACEY, NATHAN, Mary, Henry, Isaac, Joseph.

M.

1763 MOORE, GIDEON, Cornelius.
1768 MURDAUGH, JOSEPH, Millicent, John;   Smith, Mary; Scott, Joseph.
1769 MOORE, JESSE, William, Thomas, Samuel.
1775 MORRIS, JOHN, Cornelius, Sarah, Joseph, John.
1775 McMULLAN, JAMES, William, Bridget, James.
1775 MAUDLIN, GIDEON, Zebred, Nathan, Samuel, Gideon, Mary, Deborah, John, Margaret, Mills.
1777 MORRIS, JOSHUA, Rebecca, Mary, John, Nathan, Benjamin, Joseph, Zachariah.
1786 MULLEN, THOMAS, Levi.
1790 MOORE, CHARLES, Charles, John, Edward S.
1791 MOORE, JOSHUA, Hannah, Joseph, Robert, Martha, Sarah, Mary.
1791 MULLEN, JOSEPH, Isaac, John, Josiah, Elizabeth; Whedbee, Mary; Williams, Tully.
1760 MUNDIN, BENJAMIN, Betty, Elisha.
1795 McCOY, WM., Josiah, Julia, Joshua.
1796 MORRIS, JONATHAN, Jehosaphat, Jonathan.
1796 MULLEN, JAMES, Calloway, Elizabeth.

N.

1763 NEWBY, NATHAN, Keziah (wife), Francis, Thomas.
1763 NIXON, JOHN, Zach, John, Ezra, Fred.
1766 NEWBY, JESSE, Francis, Robert, Mark; Fletcher, Ralph.
1768 NEWBY, JOSIAH, Galvile, Josiah, Benjamin, Phenice.
1769 NIXON, ELIZABETH, Nicholson, Zachariah.
1772 NIXON, PHINEAS, Peliver, Barnbay, Phineas, Nathan, Ezra, John, Mary.
1773 NIXON, FRANCIS, John, James, Samuel, Thomas.
1777 NEWBY, SAMUEL, Joseph, Gabriel, Gideon, Samuel, Jesse, Elizabeth.
1776 NIXON, ZACKARIAH, Mary, Joseph, Zachariah.
1784 NEWBY, WM., Dempsey; Josepha, William, John, Mary; Maudlin, Anne; Bryan, Elizabeth; Moore, Isabella; Albertson, Sarah.
1785 NEWBY, MARK, Zachariah, Jonathan, Mary, Mourning, Elizabeth; Arrington, Margaret.
1785 NIXON, JOHN, James, Samuel, Thomas.
1787 NICHOLSON, SARAH, Thomas, Nathan, Phineas.
1789 NIXON, JOSEPH, Zachariah.

1790 NEWBY, ROBERT, Thomas, Robert, Wyke, Huldah, Willis; Paker, Cain; Walton, Mary; Cosand, Sarah; Cannon, Jeremiah.
1793 NEWBY, THOMAS, Exum; Jordan, Elizabeth; White, Josiah, Sarah; Albertson, Elias, Mary.
1793 NEWBY, ZACHARIAH, Mark, Nathan, Exum.
1797 NEWBY, THOMAS, Mary, John, William, Josiah, Jacob, Robert.

O.

1775 OVERMAN, CHARLES, Joshua, Anne, Charles.
1786 OVERMAN, JACOB, Charles, Rachel, Mary; Outland, Sarah, Martha.
1790 OVERMAN, JOHN, wife, Reuben, Jacob.

P.

1762 PEARCE, RICHARD, John, Christopher, Elizabeth (wife), Moses.
1763 PIERCE, JAMES, Fen, Miles.
1764 PERISHO, JOSEPH, Elizabeth, Miriam, Benjamin, Joseph, Sarah.
1766 PRITCHETT, MARY, Benjamin.
1772 PRATT, JEREMIAH, Joseph, Penniah.
1773 PEARCE, THOMAS, Joseph, John, Davy, Abner, Nathan, William, James.
1779 PERRY, ISRAEL, Josiah, Israel, John, Cader, Jacob, Mary.
1777 PERRY, JACOB, Jacob, Israel, Reubin; Dempsey, John, Anne.
1784 PERISHO, JOSEPH, Benjamin.
1785 PEARSON, JOSEPH, Elliott, Heliah.
1785 PERISHO, ELIZABETH, Josiah; Saunders, Richard.
1785 PHELPS, BENJAMIN, Sarah (wife); Dorothy, Margaret, Sarah, Mary.
1789 PORTLOCK, THOMAS, Colson.
1790 PERRY, JACOB, Mary, Miles, Lawrence, Hepsibah, Leah, Mary, Maria.
1760 POWELL, LEMUEL, Judith, Esther, John.
1795 PEARSON, ELEAZAR, Barsheba.
1796 PARK, NATHAN, Humphrey, Josiah.

R.

1763 ROGERSON, DANIEL, David, Daniel, Solomon, Edith, Milderson, Hezekiah.
1763 ROBINSON, THOMAS, Roland.
1764 ROBINSON, JOHN, John, Thomas, Jemima.
1765 REED, JOSEPH, Joseph, John, Christian, Thomas, Benjamin.
1768 REED, DURANT, Whedbee, Benjamin.
1774 REED, JOSEPH, Elizabeth.
1777 REDDICK, MILLS, Henry, Mills, Nathaniel, Daniel.
1785 ROBINSON, WM., Joseph, William, Josiah.
1780 ROBERTS, MARY, Joshua, Charles.
1787 ROGERS, EZEKIEL, Mary.
1787 ROBINSON, THOMAS, Elizabeth, David.
1787 RATLIFF, JOSEPH, Sarah, Elizabeth, Mary, Penniah, Catherine.
1789 RAPER, ENOCH, Luke, Robinson, Fanny.
1791 ROPER, JOHN, Margaret. Henry, John, Priscilla, Penelope, Grace.

1792   ROBINS, JOHN, John G., Jane, John, Rachel, Mary; Trapier, Elizabeth; Gardin, Mary; Booth, Margaret.
1761   RIGGS, ABRAHAM, Jane, Abraham.
1795   REED, BENJAMIN, Mary, Benjamin.
1798   RIDDICK, JACOB, Willis, Sarah; White, Absolah, Christian.

S.

1763   SUTTON, JOSEPH, George, Joseph.
1764   SUTTON, SAMUEL, Sarah, Samuel, George, John.
1765   SHEARWOOD, JONATHAN, Jonathan; Anderson, Leah.
1768   STANDIN, EDWARD, Samuel, William, Penelope.
1768   STALLINGS, NICHOLAS, Nicholas, John, Christian.
1768   SITTERSON, JAMES, Isaac, Mary (wife), Hannah, Mary, Anne, Rachel, Sarah.
1769   SHEROD, JONATHAN, Anderson, Penniah.
1770   SANDERS, RICHARD, John, Elizabeth.
1771   SANDERS, ISAAC, Mary Anne, Skinner, John.
1772   SUTTON, JOSEPH, Joseph, Benjamin, Sarah, Ashbury, Samuel, Elsbury.
1772   SAINT, DANIEL, Daniel.
1773   SUTTON, JOSEPH, Mary, Nathaniel, Thomas.
1774   STEVENSON, THOMAS, Thomas, Parthenia.
1775   SAUNDERS, BENJAMIN, William, Josiah, Margaret, Joshua.
1777   SUTTON, SARAH, Sarah.
1777   SAUNDERS, JOHN, John.
1778   SKINNER, JOSHUA, Joshua, John, Mary.
1779   STANDIN, SAMUEL, wife; Sarah, Samuel.
1784   STANTON, THOMAS, Tonison.
1784   STAFFORD, JOHN, Anne, William, John, Alex, Mary.
1785   STALLINGS, ELIAS, Elias, John, Reuben, Job, Luke, Priscilla, Penniah, Jesse, Cader; Webb, Elizabeth; Colley, Mary; Forehand, Sarah; Lee, Zilphia.
1781   SKINNER, SAMUEL, Richard, James, Evan, Jonathan, Nathan, Miriam.
1786   SKINNER, JAMES, Joseph, Joshua, Benjamin, Anne, Lydia.
1787   SUMMER, SETH, James, Thomas, Mary.
1788   STALLINGS, SIMON, Mary, Daniel.
1789   STALLINGS, WM., Anne, Sarah.
1789   SANDERS, THOMAS, Richard, Anne, Hannah, John, Benjamin.
1789   SMITH, SAMUEL, Job, Josiah, Millicent, Leah; Parker, Sarah; Morris, Lydia; Elliott, Leah, Rachel.
1791   STONE, MOSES, Lydia, Moses, Jonathan.
1792   SKINNER, RICHARD, Rachel, James, Josiah, Sarah, Elizabeth, Mary, Rachel,
1793   SUTTON, ASHBURY, Joseph, William R., Benjamin, Anne (wife), Penelope, Elizabeth, Anne.
1793   SAINT, DANIEL, Margaret, Thomas, Mary.
1795   SUTTON, QUEENSBURY, Martha.
1795   SAUNDERS, BENJAMIN, Abraham, Thomas, John, Benjamin, Penelope, Mary.
1798   SMITH, JOHN, Hosea, Sarah, John, Mary, Betsy, Polly, Maxmilian; Lamb, Lovey, Sarah.

1799   STALLINGS, LUKE, Jesse, Mills, Priscilla, Solomon, Reuben, Job, Penniah.
1799   STANTON, JOHN, John, Thomas, Miriam.

T.

1767   TOWNSON, WM., William, Rachel, Betty.
1770   TURNER, JOHN, Joshua, Timothy, John, Sarah.
1771   TOWNS, FRANCIS, Zachariah, Caleb.
1774   TOWNS, ZACHARIAH, Francis. Margaret, Winifred, Rebecca, Margaret, Elizabeth.
1775   TURNER, ABSALOM, William, Benjamin, Ezekiel, Miriam.
1777   THOMPTON, MARY, Joseph.
1779   TOMS, FOSTER, Joshua, John, Gosby, Foster, Martha.
1784   THATCH, GREEN, Elizabeth, Joseph, Spencer, Leaven.
1784   TURNER, DEMPSEY, George, Dempsey.
1784   TURNER, JOHN, Abraham, Pleasant.
1785   TOWNSEND, WM., Josiah, William, Charles, Elizabeth.
1791   TAYLOR, JOHN, Wife; William.
1792   THACH, THOMAS, Henderson, Steven, Thomas, Joshua.
1794   TOMS, FOSTER, Joseph, Samuel.
1795   TURNER, JOSHUA, Mary.

W.

1762   WHITE, THOMAS, Benjamin.
1763   WEEKS, THOMAS, Elizabeth.
1762   WINSLOW, ISRAEL, Elizabeth, Benjamin.
1763   WEEKS, THOMAS, John, Thomas, Benjamin, Samuel, James. Wilson.
1768   WINSLOW, JOSEPH, Thomas, Joseph, Mary.
1768   WEEKS, JOHN, Sarah (wife), John, Thomas, Shadrack, Sarah, Irene.
1771   WINSLOW, JESSE, William, Martha, Jesse.
1772   WHITE, JOHN, Silas, Benjamin, Charles, Rachel.
1772   WHITE, WM., Joseph, William, Josiah.
1774   WILLIAMS, JOHN, James.
1774   WINGATE, WM., Edward, John, Mary, Hannah, Ephriam; Creecy, Elizabeth; Stafford, Sarah.
1774   WINSLOW, JACOB, Elizabeth, William, Mary, Millicent.
1775   WHITE, JOHN, Francis, John, Lydia, Samuel.
1775   WINSLOW, OBED, Caleb, Sylvanus, Jesse, Mary; White, Rachel; Townsend, William; Cannon, Betty.
1776   WILLIAMS, NATHANIEL, Mary (wife), Nathaniel, Mary, William, Charles.
1777   WILLIAMS, JOSEPH, James, Joseph, William, Francis, Nathaniel, Elizabeth, Anne, John, Mary.
1777   WILLIAMS, JAMES, Mary (wife), Miriam, John, Sarah, Thomas, Mary.
1779   WHITE, SAMUEL, Gabriel, Joshua, Henry, Benjamin, Hepzibah.
1779   WEEKS, JAMES, Wilson.
1784   WHEDBRE, JOHN, William, Thomas, George.
1784   WHEDBRE, GEORGE, James, Lemuel, William, Wife.
1784   WHITE, JOSHUA, Zachariah, Joshua, Mary, Mourning, Elizabeth, Mary (wife).

1785 WHEDBEE, RICHARD, Thomas, Samuel, John.
1785 WILLIAMS, RICHARD, Tully.
1785 WILSON, THOMAS, Elizabeth, Thomas, Samuel, William.
1788 WHITE, MILES, Orpah, Elizabeth, Miriam.
1788 WHITE, MATTHEW, Benjamin, Nathan, Mary, Stephen, George.
1788 WYATT, JACOB, William, James.
1789 WELCH, NATHANIEL, Sarah, Richard.
1789 WILLIAMS, NATHANIEL, Nathaniel, William; Creecy, Isaac.
1790 WILSON, JOSEPH, Samuel, Lydia, John, Miriam, Joseph, Elizabeth, Nathan.
1790 WRIGHT, THOMAS, John, Winifred, Joseph, Phineas, Chloritdum and Thomas.
1790 WILLIAMS, SAMUEL, William, Nancy (wife), Samuel, Richard, Mary, Penina, Anne.
1793 WILSON, JOSIAH,, Jonathan; Symons, Absola; Elliott, Miriam, Juliana.
1760 WILLSON, JOHN, Joseph, Elizabeth (wife), John, Mourning, Joseph, Elizabeth, Lydia, Keziah.
1794 WINSLOW, BENJAMIN, Joseph, John, Jordan, Benjamin, Sarah, Rachel.
1794 WILSON, REUBEN, Rebecca, Jacob, Robert, Mary.
1795 WILSON, ABRAHAM, Lydia; Elliott, Miles, Abraham, Penniah and Dorton.
1795 WHITE, WM., Jesse, William, Joseph, Thomas, Elizabeth; Newby, Pleasant.
1795 WHITE, CALEB, Francis, Caleb, James, Josiah, Rebecca, Mary, Betty, Elisha.
1796 WHITE, WM., Townsend, Charlton.
1797 WILLIAMS, LOCKHART, James L., Richard.
1797 WRIGHT, JOHN, Thomas.

PERSON COUNTY—WILLS

A.

1792 September. ATKINSON, JOHN, Frances (wife), Carter, John, Thomas, Richard and Henry (sons); Isabella Pelham and Elizabeth Person (daughters).

1798 March. ATKINSON, EDWARD, William and Thomas Atkinson (nephews); Henry Atkinson (brother).

B.

1792 June. BAUGHN, ZACHARIAH, Drusilla (wife), Granville, Dicey, Dorcas, Carwell, Milly and Avis.

1792 September. BOSTICK, WILLIAM, Micha (wife); Obadiah Bostick (grandson).

1793 December. BLACK, THOMAS, Elizabeth (mother); George (brother); Elizabeth Harrelson (niece); John Black (nephew).

1795 December. BLACK, JOHN. Mary (wife); Samuel, Robert, John, Martha, Margaret and Nancy.

1796 June. BARRET, HUGH. Margaret (wife), Hugh, Mary, Harris, Martha, Margaret and Nancy.

1797 September. BARRETT, HUGH. Elizabeth (wife); John, Hugh, William, Margaret, James, Elizabeth and Mary.

1797 December. BURTON, CHARLES H., Sarah Ann (wife); Thomas.

1800 June. BARRET, THOMAS, Mary (wife); John, William and Thomas, (sons); Margaret Douglas (daughter).

1801 March. BLACK, GEORGE, Robert, Nancy, Mary, Margaret and William (children); Elizabeth Hamilton and Sarah Curry (daughters).

C.

1801 March. CHAMBERS, WILLIAM, Elizabeth (wife); William, Abner, Elijah, Henry, Davidson, Benjamin, John, Francis and Josias (children; Jane Rogers, Elizabeth Barrett, Lucy McFarland and Ann Patterson (daughters).

D.

1792 June. DAVEY, GABRIEL, Elizabeth (wife), Edmund B. and Ashburn and William.

1796 September. DUNCAN, MARY, Abner, Martin and Nathaniel (sons); Polly Merritt (granddaughter).

1797 March. DAVEY, JAMES; Betty (wife); children (not named).

E.

1798 December. EUBANKS, GEORGE, Betty (wife), George, Thomas, Cartherine and Betty (children); Frances Wyatt and Mary Carlton, (daughters).

F.

1796   March. FULLER, PETER, (Wife) (not named); Reaty (daughter) and six other children (not named).

G.

1796   September. GUNN, THOMAS, (Wife) (not named), Gabriel.

H.

1792   December. HENDY, EDWARD, Letitia (wife); Edmund Hendley, (nephew).

1799   June. HOLLSWAY, JOHN, Ann (wife); James, John and William (sons); Ann Parker (daughter).

1800   June. HARGIS, RICHARD, William, Joseph, Sarah, Adam and Dennis.

1800   September. HATCHER, BENJAMIN, Elizabeth (wife), Charles and Thomas.

J.

1794   September. JOHNSTON, JOSEPH, Ann (wife); Martha Scogger, Mary Leak and Elizabeth Lewis (daughters.)

1795   June. JOHNSTON, JOSHUA, Kiddy (wife); Mary, Ehoda, Anne and James, (children); Sarah Smith (daughter).

1797   December. JONES, RICHARD, Nancy (wife); James, Richard, Benjamin and Samuel (sons); Mary Lumpkin, Nancy Van Hook and Elizabeth Bowen (daughters).

L.

1792   September. LEWIS, EDMUND, Mary (wife); Hiram, Ware, Warner, Elizabeth, Francis, Fielden and Burwell.

M.

1795   June. MESKELL, DAVID, Elizabeth (wife); William and David (sons), Mary McReynolds (daughter).

1800   March. MOORE, STEPHEN, Grizzell (wife); Robert, Philip, Ann, Mary, Portius, Samuel and Sidney, (Children); Francis Dickens (daughter).

1800   December. McKISSOCK, JOHN, Rebecca (wife); John, Thomas and William.

P.

1799   September. PULLIAM, JAMES, Elizabeth (wife) and children (not named).

R.

1797   September. ROGERS, JOHN, Elizabeth, John, Bird and littleton.

S.

1798   March. STONE, HEZEKIAH, Mary (wife); Anderson, John, William, Nancy, Elizabeth, Susanna and Ketturah.

T.

1794 December. TALBERT, JOHN, Margaret (wife).

1797 June.   TAYLOR,   CHARLES,   (wife)   (not named) ; Esther, Critcher and Elizabeth Tiddy (daughters).

V.

1795 December. VANHOCK, DAVID, Victory (wife) ; Robert, William, Lucia and Elizabeth.

1797 March. VASS, KATIE, Vincent Vass (brother).

W.

1793 June. WILLIAMS, THOMAS N., Mary (wife) ; John W.

1793 September. WOODS, SAMUEL, Mary (wife) ; Andrew, William, John, Samuel, Thomas and James.

1795 March. WARREN, JOHN, Mary (wife) ; James, Heckley, William, Samuel and Elizabeth.

1795 December WALKER, JOHN, Ann (wife) ; Susanna Moore (daughter) ; Elizabeth Moore, Mary William and John Williams and John Walker (grandchildren).

1795 December. WHITEHEAD, SAMUEL, Ursula (wife) ; Elizabeth, Nancy, Ursula, Samuel. Susanna and Ebenexer.

RANDOLPH—WILLS

A.

1785 ANDREWS, REUBEN, Henrietta (wife).
1789 ALDRIDGE, WILLIAM, Wife, daughter Mary, sons William, Ezekiel.
1792 ANDREWS, ADAM, Peggy wife, Conrad son, Susanna, Catherine, daughters.
1792 ALLRED, JOHN, John, Joseph, sons.

B.

1785 BOILE, CONRAD, Frederick, son.
1787 BARTON, WILLIAM, wife, three sons, (none named).
1784 BECK, JEFFREY, Susannah (wife), Abraham, Jesse, sons.
1775 BEESON, RICHARD, Benjamin, Isaac, sons.
1789 BROWN, DANIEL, Henry, Daniel, sons.
1791 BRYAN, JOHN, Mary, Peter, children.

C.

1783 CLARK, SAMUEL, Thomas, George, William, Joseph, children.
1787 CRAWFORD, JAMES, Wife; Catherine, Mary, daughters.
1787 CLARK, THOMAS, Samuel, Thomas, Catherine, Hannah, Jane, Sarah, children.
1782 CANNADY, JOHN, Wife; Shurrard, William,

D.

1790 DUFFY, WILLIAM, John, Moses, Elizabeth, Harriet, children.

F.

1784 FRANCIS, DANIEL, wife, Sarah, Thomas, children.

G.

1783 GRAY, MICHAEL, John, William, Edward, sons.
1789 GIBBONS, WILLIAM, William, son.
1792 GRAVES, WILLIAM, Leonard (brother).
1792 GRAY, JOHN, Wife Janet; six children, not named.
1782 GREEN, ROBERT, Elinor, Charles, James, John, children.

H.

1786 HENSON, JOSEPH, wife.
1787 HARMAN, GEORGE, Philip, Martha, Cutliffe, Alice, George, children.
1787 HENDCOCK, JOHN, Vachel, Jethro, sons.

K.

1779 KERR, JOSEPH, John, William, sons; Mary Dugan, daughter.
1790 LAMB, ESAU, wife Elizabeth; Joseph, Miriam, Ruth, children.
1791 LEWIS, STEPHEN, Stephen, David, Susanna, Priscilla, children.

M.

1793 MILLSAPS, ROBERT, wife; Alex, Moses, Robert, William, sons.

1781 McCALLUM, DUNCAN, wife Esther; James, Isaac, Jonathan, Ben, Stephen, sons.

P.

1788 PENNINGTON, LEVI, Wife Martha; Levi, Rachel, children.

R.

1788 ROBERTS, JOSEPH, wife, William, John, children.

1789 ROBERTSON, WILLIAM, Mother, Ann.

1790 RAINS, ISHMAEL, Wife, Sarah, John, George, children.

1790 RIDGE, GODFREY, Wife Ann; Thornburg, William, sons.

S.

1783 SMITH, FRED, Fred, son.

1789 SHARD, EDWARD, Michael, son.

1790 THORNBURY, EDWARD, wife Ann; William, son.

1784 THORNBURY, WILLIAM, Elizabeth, Martha, Sarah, children.

1787 TAYLOR, ISAAC, wife Rachel.

V.

1785 VICKERY, MARMADUKE, wife Elizabeth; Sampson, Marmaduke, sons.

W.

1773 WALKER, SAMUEL, William, son.

1784 WALLINGSWORTH, ENOCH, Joseph, son.

1790 WARREN, WILLIAM, wife Ann; Rachel, Henry, children.

1793 WOOD, THOMAS, wife Jean; Isabel, Mary, daughters.

Y.

1792 YORK, JOHN, wife Margaret; John, William, children.

1782 YORK, SIMON, wife; Jeremiah, Sarah, children.

1784 YORK, THOMAS, Lettice, Elinor, daughters.

RICHMOND—WILLS

A.

1782 ADAMS, RICHARD, Amy, Mary, Betsy, Prudence, James, William, Thomas, Richard.
1793 ALMOND, WILLIAM, Elizabeth, Rebecca, Patsy, Sally, John, Mary, Hannah, Betsy.

B.

1790 BRICE, FRANCIS, Sarah (wife), Francis, Mary.
1795 BENNETT, WM., William, Nevil, Sarah, Silas, John, James.
1795 BILLINGSLEY, HEZEKIAH, Rebecca, John, Sophia, Hezekiah, Elizabeth.
1799 BOSTICK, JOHN, Elizabeth, Patience, Patience, (wife), Ezra.

C.

1781 COLE, JOHN, John, Francis, Peter, Edward, David, Elizabeth, Nancy, Rachel, Sarah.
1788 CURRY, MARY, Sarah, Duncan.
1789 CRAWFORD, THOMAS, Rebecca, Mastin, John, William, Thomas, Ann.
1789 CLARK, THOMAS, Robert.
1794 COVINGTON, WILLIAM, Elizabeth, Sarah, Nathaniel, William, John, Rachel, Phoebe, Peter, James, Benjamin, Asa.
1786 CHILDS, JOHN, Micajah, James, Elizabeth, Lydia, Thomas.
1793 CHAVIS, NATHAN, Sarah, Samuel, Nathaniel.
1799 CAIRN, DANIEL, MC., Catharine, Neill, Archibald, Christian, John, Sarah, Hugh, Flora, Catherine (wife).
1799 CURRY, DONALD, Flora (wife) and children.

D.

1781 DONALDSON, JOHN, Sarah, John, Peter, William.
1782 DAVIS, SAMUEL, Mary Jane Williams Davis, (one name).
1795 DONALD, ZACHARIAH, Leysdia (wife) and children.
1800 DOUGHERTY, GEORGE, Guinea Pigg and Dr. Coke.

E.

1800 EVERETT, LAWRENCE, Mary, William, Lawrence, Elizabeth, Hannah, Edward; Meacham, Nancy.

F.

1783 FREEMAN, GEORGE, wife; Elizabeth.
1788 FREEMAN, ABRAHAM, wife.

G.

1796 GREEN, NICHOLAS, Ellandry (wife).
1799 GORDON, THOMAS, Mary (wife) and children.

H.

1779 HUNTER, SAMUEL, Elizabeth, Rachel, Samuel;
White, Elizabeth.

1782 HALLEY, WM., Isham, Randolph, Silas, William, Lucy M.

1783 HURLEY, TIMOTHY, Sarah, Thomas, Moses;
Cole Mary; Clark, Rachel.

J.

1780 JEFFERSON, GEORGE, wife, Peter, George,
John, Garland, Samuel, Robinson, Francis.

1790 JOHNSON, ZACHARIAH, Courd, Joyer; Wallace,
Charles, Henry; Jones, Benjamin, William.

1795 JAMES, ROBERT, Mary, James, John, Nancy,
William, Champ, Israel, Martin.

1795 JAMES, JOHN, Mary, Philip, John, Robert,
Nancy, William, Israel, Martin, Champ.

1795 JOHNSTON, THOMAS, Susanna, Elizabeth,
Anna, Josiah, Luke; Griffin, Patience.

L.

1789 LEAK, FRANCIS, Walter, Judith, Sallie H.

1784 LEATON, HUGH, Mary, Lucy, William.

M.

1789 McNAIR, EDWARD, Mary (wife), Neil, John,
Barbara, Catherine, Mary.

1781 MASK, JOHN, John, Dudley, Mary, John, Jr.,
Pleasant M.

1782 MOORMAN, THOMAS, wife; Sarah, Millie, Rachel, Agnes, Fanny, Archelaus, Thomas,
John.

1796 McNAIR, ROGER, Mary, Alex.

1782 MOORMAN, BENJAMIN, wife; Andrew, Benjamin, William.

1790 McGUIRE, WILLIAM, Ann, Lucy, William,
Owen, Nathan; Pembroke, Mary.

1788 MIMS, BENJAMIN, wife and children.

1790 McCALL, CHRISTIAN, Catherine, Carmichael,
Claiborne, Macy, Neil.

1799 McAIRN, DANIEL, Catherine, Neil, Archibald,
Christian, John, Sarah, Hugh, Flora, Catherine (wife).

N.

1793 NEWBERRY, JOHN, Susannah, Mary, Sarah.

1793 NEWBERRY, WM., William, Jonathan, John,
Joseph; Rye, Mary.

1798 NICHOLSON, RODERICK, Catharine, Peter, Daniel, Roderick; McQuaig, Flora.

O.

1800 O'BRIAN, DENNIS, Naomi, Mial, Martha.

P.

1788 PHILLIPS, JAMES, Mary, James, Joel, Solomon, Lambin, Sarah, Priscilla, Esther; Gosford, Ann; Bulla, Mary; Almond, Elizabeth;
Huse, Rebecca.

R.

1783 ROE, JOHN, John E., Rachel, Samuel, Jane, Susannah; Phillips, Sarah R.; Ussery, Marika.

1799 ROBINSON, WM., Mary, Charles, Jane, Lydia.

1797 RODGERS, WM., Rachel, Benjamin, John.

S.

1787 STRICKLIN, BURRELL, Urisey (wife) and children.

1787 SNEAD, DAVID, Nanny.

1788 SNEAD, ISRAEL, Hanly, Samuel; Watkins, Keziah; Diggs, Ann; Husbands; Francis; Hicks, Martha, Francis; Cole, Martha, William, Snead, Joanna.

1795 STROTHER, SOLOMON, Nancy (wife) and children.

1791 SMITH, JAMES, Sarah (wife), John, Sarah; Ward, Mary.

1791 SMITH, CATHERINE, McAirn, Catherine; McAlpin, Alexander.

1795 SNEAD, NANCY, Polly, Nancy; Rye, Elizabeth.

1795 SNEAD, DAVID, Mary (wife), Brooks, Lucy; Sexton, William.

1796 SMITH, MALCOLM, wife, John, Malcolm, Archibald, Duncan, Sarah, Mary, **Margaret**, Catherine, Anne.

T.

1780 THOMPSON, RICHARD, wife, William, Theophilus; Tate, Abiah, Sprall, Morgan; Jackson, Phoebe.

1797 THOMAS, PHILEMON, Elizabeth, Elijah, Eli, James, Nathan, Elizabeth (wife).

W

1785 WALTERS, JOHN, George, Nancy, Eunice, John; Shepherd, Pamela; Mingquison, Thomas.

1790 WATKINS, WM., Thomas, John, William, Israel, Samuel, David, Keziah; James, Sarah; Cole, Agatha, Elizabeth; Long, Francis; Watkins, Alex.

1794 WEBB, JOHN, Robert, Hundley, William, Turner.

1794 WILLIAMSON, SHADRACH, Isaac, John, Thomas; Smith, Esther.

1794 WEBB, GEORGE, Margaret, Samuel, Rachel, Thomas, Henry, Elizabeth, Susanna, Mary, George, William, Ann, Luevessey.

1799 WILLIAMS, EDWARD, Susannah, Thomas, Edward, William, Polly, Winifred; Blewitt, Edward W., Betsey, Rebecca.

1799 WILLIAMS, NILES, Benjamin, Joseph, William; Baggot, Lucy; Lloyd, Sarah; Chaplin, Phoebe.

ROBESON—WILLS

A.

1785 ARD, JAMES, Thomas, Reuben, James.
1794 ALFORD, JACOB, Mary (wife), Warren, Elias, Sion, James, Mary, Wiley, Charity.

B.

1788 BELL, JOHN, Mary (wife).
1782 BULLARD, JOHN, Elizabeth (wife), John.
1789 BAGGETT, JOSEPH, Barton, Reddin, Leah, Sarah (wife).
1789 BROWN, HUGH, William, Neill, John, Anna, Mary.
1790 BLOUNT, JOHN, Jacob, Philip; Stogner, John.
1794 BROWN, JOHN, Hugh, Mary, John, Catharine; Bennett, William and Mary.
1794 BARNES, ABRAHAM, Josiah, Elias, Asenath; *w* *Sm*Bridgers, Mary.*wife of John Wills.* *(S.P.)*
1795 BRITT, SAMUEL, Alex., Nathan, Nancy, Britain, Mary, Charity, Betsy, Polly.
1795 BYRD, ARCHIBALD, Esther, John; Chloe Rigsby's children.
1797 BROWN, DUNCAN, Catherine, Nelly.
1800 BYRD, WILLIAM, Mary (wife), Henry, Elizabeth, William, Mary, Nancy.

C.

1788 CADE, JOHN, Elizabeth, Stephen, James, Washington, Robert, Ayres, Elizabeth; Kennedy, William, Mary.
1790 CAMPBELL, DUNCAN, Christian, Hugh.
1797 CAIN, OLIVE, Olive, Samuel, John, James.
1799 COPELAND, JOHN, Mary, James; Sizemore, Elizabeth; Colwen, Christian; Upton, Anna; Holmes, Abigail; Watson, Ruth; Wiggins, Moorning; Humphrey, Rachel.

F.

1797 FORT, JOSEPH, Elizabeth, Anne, Abraham, Pheraba, John, James; Hand, Elisha; Brown, Catherine, Elias F.; Muse, Humphrey, James, Thomas, Joseph, Elias.

G.

1789 GRICE, MOSES, Mary, Benjamin, Patty, Tabby, Fathey, John, Jonathan.
1794 GLARE, STEPHEN, Mary (wife), Bencaler; Smith, Esther; Pitman, Betsy; Britt, Celia; Phillips, Mary Ann; Little, Wren.

H.

1787 HUNT, BRASWELL, wife.
1788 HUMPHREY, JOHN, William, John, Thomas, James, Lucy, Samuel.
1799 HINSON, JOSEPH, Raney, Charity, Rachel.

I.

1794 INMAN, HARDY, Charity; Flowers, William; Barfield, Patsy P., Mary, Betsy, Nannie, Dicey, Eunice.

1799 INMAN, ELIZABETH, Barfield, Mary; Flowers, Elizabeth, William; Wishart, Susan.

L.

1784 LOCKERLER, JOHN, wife, Samuel.
1792 LEE, JOHN, Shadrach, Rebecca; Jackson, Jemima; Cinlaw, Rebecca; Razor, Rebecca; Bullard, Elizabeth, Shadrach.
1797 LAMM, JOHN, wife; Kenneth, Daniel, Murdoch.
1797 LITTLE, ARCHIBALD, wife, Katharine.

M.

1788 MERCER, SOLOMON, Sarah, Malachi, Solomon, Christopher; Biggs, Uthany; Taylor, Sarah; Campbell, Nancy; Glover, Constant.
1791 MESSER, HENRY, Hannah, Peter, William, Dorothy, Elizabeth; Malloy, Nancy; Willis, Margaret.
1793 MOORE, JOHN, William, Mary (wife), Morris.
1787 McKAY, DONALD, wife; Nancy, Catherine, Barham, Flora, Mary, Betty, Janet.
1787 McSWAIN, DONALD, Peggy, Malcolm, James; McMillan, Kitty.
1788 McCRANIE, HUGH, Murdoch, Neil, Elizabeth, Catherine.
1783 McPHAIL, MRS. MARIAN, Mary, Neil; McCranie, Christian; Leech, Mary.
1790 McNEILL, MARY, Neil, Daniel, Janet, Catherine; McPherson, Marian.
1792 McNEILL, DONALD, Janet, Donald, Daniel, Piegri, Polly, Hector, Neil.
1792 McNEILL, TURQUIL, Lauchlan, Duncan, wife, Margaret, Turquil; McNair, Mary; Ferguson, Marian.
1794 McLEAN, ARCHIBALD, Nancy, Mary, Chatererine, John, Lauthen.
1798 McARTHUR, PETER, Peter, John, Nancy, Jean, Peggy, Neil, Duncan

P.

1787 PITMAN, NEWIT, Hardy, James; Speir, Ann; Thompson, Lamb.
1798 PARNELL, JOHN, John.
1799 PITMAN, NATHAN, Sampson, Levi, Noel, Newit, James, Robert, Jesse, Samuel, Temperance, Elizabeth.

R.

1795 REGAN, RALPH, Joseph, Samuel, Daniel, Millie, Richard, Sarah, Nancy, Martha; Powers, Olive.
1796 REGAN, ANN, Richard, Sarah, Nancy, Martha, Mary, Elizabeth; Spann, William, John, Jr., Ralph, John, Sr.; Hawthorne, Sarah; Powers, Olive; Ezzell, Olivia; Andrews, Nancy.
1798 ROZAR, REUBEN, William M., Charles, Robert, Martha, Shadrach.

S.

1789 STRICKLAND, JOSEPH, Levi, Annie.
1798 SPIVEY, EDMUND, Elizabeth; Hammons, John, Sr., Jacob, Samuel, Enoch, John, Harvey.

T.

1792 THOMAS, RICHARD, Mary (wife).
1792 THOMPSON, CADOR, Peacock, Sapphira; Taylor, Posey, Axey, Dicey, Mary, Olive, Nancy, Ammons.

W.

1790 WISHART, ELIZABETH, Jonathan; Harrison, Sarah, Ann.
1799 WILKSON, ROBERT, wife, Neil, Donald, John, Margaret.

ROWAN COUNTY—WILLS, 1753-1800

A.

1761 ANDERSON, ROBERT, Wife, Samuel, Robert.
1760 ALLISON, JAMES, Allison, Mary.
1758 AKINDER, JOHN, ———.
1764 ARCHIBALD, WILLIAM, Elizabeth (wife); John, William, Thomas, Robert, Jean, Elizabeth.
1777 ANDREWS, DAVID, John, Henry, David.
1777 ARCHIBALD, WILLIAM, Martha, Alex, William, Margaret, Agnes, Elizabeth.
1779 ADDERTON, JEREMIAH, Joseph, James, Jeremiah, John, William, Rebecca; also Neal, Nancy; Carney, Elizabeth; Dawan, Sarah.
1783 ALLISON, SARAH, John; also Oliphant, Elizabeth.
1781 ADAMS, MATTHEW, George, Nancy, Chloe, Frances, Walter, Rachel, Elizabeth, Diana, Luke.
1780 ALLISON, THOMAS, Martha, Richard, Thomas, Naomi, Ann.
1792 ARMSTRONG, MARGARET, Abel, Elizabeth, Mary, Margaret.
1792 AGINDER, HENRY, Henry, Jr., David, Catherine, Mary.
1780 ARMSTRONG, WILLIAM, Margaret, Elizabeth, Mary.
1780 ALLISON, ANDREW, Adam, Elizabeth, Sarah, Theophilus, Oliphant, Andrew.
1795 ARNHART, JOHN, Catharine.
1789 ALLEN, ERASMUS, William, Thomas, Rachel, Rowe, Hannah, Esther; also Chapman, Allen, Erasmus, Patty, Strushly, and Sally; Dewitt, Francis, Sally, William, Jane, Thomas; White, Milly; Terrell, Sally.

B.

1765 BRALY, THOMAS, William, Peggy.
1759 BUIS, THOMAS, Wife, William, Thomas.
1772 BRANDON, GEORGE, Marion, John, George, Abraham, Christopher, Eleanor; also Barton, Martha, Silvia, James; McGuire, Mary; Witherspoon, Sidney.
1767 BRINNIGER, ADAM, John, Adam, Elizabeth. Jacob, Katrina, Barbara.
1762 BEST, JAMES, Elizabeth, Martha.
1767 BARR, WILLIAM, Catharine, Mary, Sarah, Elizabeth, William; Catherine (wife).
1762 BONDGER, BENJAMIN, Ridge, Gotterg.
1763 BUIS, WILLIAM, Wife, Joshua, James, John, Grizelle, Susannah, Rebecca, Ann, Thomas.
1765 BATES, DANIEL, John, Daniel, Jesse, Hannah and wife.
1763 BRYAN, MORGAN, Joseph, Samuel, James, John, Morgan, William, Thomas; Linville, Elinor; Forbis, Mary.
1770 BRUNER, HENRY, Anna, Catharine (wife), George, Sophy, Catharine, Henry, Jr., Jacob, Anna, Mary, Rosanna, Grissan, Margaret.
1771 BARTHOLOMEW, WILLIAM, Walls, William.

1772 BROWN, WILLIAM, Margaret (wife), William, John, James, Susannah, Elizabeth, Margaret; also Robeson, Charity; Elliott, Constant; Wynn, Constant.

1758 BAKER, SAMUEL, Robert, John, Eliza (wife), Margaret, Mary.

1774 BRITTAIN, JOSEPH, James, Phoebe, Jemima, Philip, William, Joseph, Benjamin, Aaron, Samuel.

1775 BAILEY, JOHN, Isabella, Margaret, Thomas, William, Mary, Alexander, John, David, Robert, Jean, Rebecca.

1777 BAKER, ABSALOM, Wife, John, Christopher, Joshua, Benjamin, Samuel, Greenbury.

1777 BECK, JACOB, Cartharine, Jacob, Ludwig; also James, Catharine.

1777 BALLINGER, HENRY, Elizabeth, Henry, Fred, Joseph, John, Daniel, Philip, Peter, Jacob, David.

1777 BUFLE, PAUL, Catharine, Margaret, Adam, Valentine, Martin; also Passinger, John; Wallace, Oliver; Eller, Christain.

1778 BOWACKER, MICHAEL, Mary, Arthur.

1778 BROWN, JAMES, John, George, Nancy.

1781 BUTNER, THOMAS, Sarah (wife).

1782 BRYAN, WILLIAM, Mary, Samuel, Daniel, Phoebe, Hannah, Sarah, Elizabeth, Mary.

1790 BRANDON, JAMES, William, Benjamin, John, Abel, Armstrong, Rebecca; also Wilson, James.

1785 BEARD, DAVID, William, James, David, Thomas.

1785 BELL, ROBERT, Isabel, Andrew, William, Jean, Hannah, Agnes; also Beard, Thomas,

1777 BULLINGER, HENRY, Elizabeth, Henry, Matthias, Fred, Joseph, John, Daniel, Philip, Peter, Jacob, David.

1784 BRANDON, THOMAS, Smith, Thomas; Crage, Isaac.

1791 BRICE, JOHN, Mary (wife); Green, John.

1791 BEATTY, JOHN, Margaret, John.

1791 BAGLEY, SAMUEL, Tabitha, Daniel, William, Samuel, Kerr, Johanna, Richard, Judith, Sarah, John.

1791 BEAN, MICHAEL, Adam, Thomas, Daniel, Jacob.

1790 BRANDON, RICHARD, John, Mary, Elizabeth, Matthew.

1790 BONER, WILLIAM, Joseph, Joshua, Isaac, Alpha.

1790 BUNBLOSSOM, CHRISTIAN, Wife; Abraham, Jacob.

1788 BARR, JAMES, Wife, and children (not named).

1788 BARTLEY, ROBERT, Leah, Samuel, David, John, Margaret, Elizabeth, Catharine, Mary, Rachel, Robert, William, Walter.

1789 BEARD, JOHN LEWIS, Christina (wife); Valentine, Lewis, Michael, John, Christina, Catharine, Salina.

C.

1765 COVE, MICHAEL, Catharine (wife), Christian, Eve, Michael, Southey, Valentine, Margaret, Mary.

1759 CARMICHAEL, JOHN, Ruth (wife).

1766 CATHEY, ALEX, Elizabeth (wife), James, Richard, John, William, Margaret.

1762 CUNNINGHAM, JOHN, Isabel (wife), Margaret, Jane.

1765 CARTER, JAMES, Brown, Mary and Susanna; Camilla (grandchild).

1770 CURRY, NATHANIEL, Elizabeth (wife), Samuel, Joseph.

1769 CARRUTH, WALTER, James, John, Agnes.

1759 CARSON, WILLIAM, Muron, Susanna, Robert, William.

1772 CRESWELL, ISAAC, Margaret, David, Isabella, James, Robert.

1757 CATHEY, JAMES, Ann (wife), Margaret, Ann, John, George, Andrew.

1764 CATHEY, JOHN, Jean, (wife), James, Hugh, Agnes, Jean, Ann, John, William.

1774 CARSON, JAMES, Wife; John, Thomas, James, Henry, William, Hugh, Prudence, Horner.

1777 COLES, WILLIAM T., Sarah (wife), Henrietta, William.

1777 COCHRAN, SAMUEL, Sarah (wife), Sarah, Margaret, William, John, Andrew, James, Samuel.

1777 COCHRAN, SARAH, James, William, Samuel, Margaret, Andrew, John, Sarah.

1777 CLEMENTS, JOHN, Elizabeth, William, Roger, David.

*1777 CAWDEN, JOHN, _wife_ Jean, Matthew, John, William, _dau._ Elizabeth, Martha.

1778 COX, MOSES, John, Charles, Moses, Sarah.

1781 CAMPBELL, DANIEL, Bowes, William.

1785 COOPER, SAMUEL, Agnes, William, Samuel, Thomas, Jane, James, Isaac, David.

1784 CONGER, JOHN, Jonathan, John.

1778 COX, ISRAEL, Mary, David.

1791 CLOYN, PETER, Peter, Daniel, Mary.

1791 COWAN, WILLIAM, Jane, William, Sarah, Isaac, George, William, Benjamin.

1791 COVEY, NOBLE, Mary (wife).

1785 CLIFFORD, MICHAEL, Elizabeth, Michael, Jacob, John.

1786 CLAYTON, GEORGE, Sarah, George, Lambert, Rachel, Hannah, Henrietta, Ann, Margaret.

1786 CLEAVOR, JACOB, Wife, John.

1786 CASPER, PETER, Ann, Henry, Adam, John, Eve.

1786 CARRUTH, ALEX., Alexander.

1784 CALL, WILLIAM, John, Henry, Adam, Daniel, Margaret, Christiana, Dorothy, Eve, Catharine, Ann.

1784 CARSON, JAMES, Hannah, John, Thomas, James, Henry, William, Hugh, Prudence, Mary.

1785 CAPE, NICHOLAS, Catharine, Elizabeth, Philip, John, Dorothy.

1789 COWAN, JOHN, Mary, John, William, Thomas, Moses, David.

* Cowden, John - Will made in Paxtang Twnchp Lancaster Cs. Pa. 29 of
May, 1777, states he was of Rocky D. Creek Settlement, Rowan Co. N.C. Names
Wife, Jean, Sons Matthew, John & William, dau- Elizabeth &
Martha.

1766 DICKS, NATHAN, Zachariah, Joshua, William, Hannah, Deborah, Grace, Mary (wife).

1770 DENNY, WILLIAM, Ann (wife), James, William, Hannah, Agnes, Jane, Catharine, Margaret.

1765 DAVIS, JAMES, James, Elinor (wife), Samuel, Evan, Ruth.

1760 DAVISON, GEORGE, Margaret (wife), George, William, Samuel.

1774 DENNITT, JAMES, Barbara (wife), James, Barbara, William, John.

1775 DOUGLAS, WILLIAM, Mary, David, Solomon, John, William, Mary.

1777 DAVIS, JOHN, Mary, Benjamin, David, Elizabeth, Sarah, Rachel.

1872 DAVIDSON, WILLIAM, Mary, George, John, Ephraim, Jean, Nanela, Margaret.

1779 DOUGLAS, JAMES, George.

1784 DOUGLAS, DAVID, Hannah, Elizabeth, Rebecca.

1791 DANIEL, PETER, Wife; Paul.

1791 DOBBIN, JAMES, John, Anna, Alexander, Hugh, Elizabeth, Margaret, Rebecca, Catherine.

1784 DOUTHIT, JOHN, Mary (wife); Abraham, Elizabeth, John, Mary, William, Thomas, Isaac, Sarah, William.

1799 DOERNER, PAUL, Sophia, John, Jacob, Paul, William, Katharine, Barbara, Elizabeth.

1799 DAVENPORT, AUGUSTIN, Mary (wife); Sarah, Augustin, James, David, Anna, Joel, Jesse, Mary, Susanna.

1789 DAVIS, THOMAS, Jean, Peggy, Lucy, John, William, Thomas, Henry, Edward, Benjamin, Ephraim.

1796 DAVIS, JACOB, Henry, Jacob, John, Mary, Sarah, Samuel, Benjamin.

E.

1769 EDWARDS, HANNEL, David, Joshua, Isaac, Elinor (wife), Elinor, Martha, James.

1765 ENOCHS, JOHN, David, Gabriel, Margaret (wife), Isaac.

1770 ERWIN, JAMES, Agnes (wife), Alex, William, James, Joseph, Isaac, John, Agnes, Mary, Isabella, Jane.

1762 ESHEVEN, WILLIAM, Isabel (wife), Robert, William.

1782 ENOCHS, DAVID, Mary (wife); Thomas, David, Susanna, Rebekah, Elinor, Ann.

1782 ELLER, JACOB, Jacob, Barbara, Elizabeth.

1783 ERWIN, GEORGE, George, James, Deborah, William, Mary, Sarah, Elizabeth, Edwin and wife.

1791 ELLIOTT, WILLIAM, Jean, William.

1793 ERWIN, CHRISTOPHER, Sarah, William, Andrew, Christopher, Mary, George, James, Thomas.

1789 EATON, JOHN, Elizabeth, Samuel, Daniel.

1785 ELROD, CHRISTOPHER, Adam, Sarah, Catharine, Margaret, May, Christopher, Oldsby, Lydia, Robert, John.

1788 EVENHART, HENRY, Christina, Henry, Abraham, John, Eve, Barbara.

1793 ERVIN, JOSEPH, Agnes (wife); Mary, William, Grisel, Agnes, Peggy, Joseph.

F.

1763 FLEMAN, PETER, Elizabeth, John, Jean.

1765 FRASER, NICHOLAS, John, Peter, Christian, Margaret, George, Susanna, Philip.

1770 FORGEY, SAMUEL, Sarah (wife), James, Samuel, Rachel, Elizabeth, Mary, Jonathan.

1769 FORBIS, GEORGE, Olif (wife), Robert, Janet, George, John.

1777 FOY, MARK, Barbara, John, William.

1777 FENEY, JANET, Thomas, Jean, Mary, Rebekah.

1781 FOSTER, THOMAS, Lucy, Ann, Mary, Edith, Elizabeth, Rebecca, Lucy.

1786 FOY, THOMAS, Elizabeth (wife).

1784 FLEMING, GEORGE, Margaret, Henry, Allison, Mitchel, John, Milford, Ann.

1784 FROHOCK, JOHN, William, Thomas.

1794 FELPS, THOMAS, Jane, Abington, John, Thomas, Samuel, Britton, William, Keeling, Ezekiel.

1794 FROHOCK, THOMAS, Hewett, Elizabeth, Sally and Thomas.

1787 FISHER, MARTIN, Margaret (wife).

1796 FRACK, CONRAD, wife, Henry.

1797 FERGUSON, ANDREW, Elizabeth, Thomas, Hugh, Rebecca.

1796 FISHER, JAMES, Esther (wife), John, Jane, Esther, Margaret.

1794 FRASER, JAMES, Janet, John, Abigail, James, Peter, Margaret.

1796 FOX, PETER, Jacob, Philip, John.

1796 FISHER, FRED, Ann, Mary, Barbara, Milly, Marion, Christina, Charles, Rosanna.

G.

1796 GLANDON, STEPHEN, Mary, Ann, James, Elizabeth, George, Jeremiah, Sarah, Rachel, Isaac, Jacob, Martha.

1765 GIBSON, HUGH, Bickerstaff, John.

1789 GRAHAM, JAMES, Richard, James, John, Jane.

1757 GARRETT, JOHN, David.

1795 GRAHAM, JOHN, Sarah, James, Richard, Moses, William, John, Samuel.

1774 GITCHLY, JOHN, Christina, Jacob, John, Fred, Mary, Eve, Ellen, Catharine, Seigel.

1775 GIBSON, ALEX., John, James, Samuel, Alex, Isaac.

1777 GOSS, JOSEPH, Margaret (wife), Margaret, Mary, Barbara, Nancy.

1781 GREEN, JOHN, Mary, Elizabeth, Robert.

1779 GRAHAM, RICHARD, Agnes, Eleanor, Joseph, James, William, Richard, Jane, Mary, Calsane, John, Richard.

1779 GRAHAM, JAMES, Mary, Jane, Elizabeth, William, John, Hause, Grizzell, Margaret, Sarah, John.

1785 GRAHAM, HUGH, Mary (wife), Frances, Susanna.

1790 GLASCOCK, JOSEPH, Harmon, Henry, Mary, Sarah.

1791 GRAHAM, JOHN, Elizabeth, Jean, Sarah, Margaret, Samuel.

1788   GAITHER, BENJAMIN, Rachel, John, Jeremiah, Zachariah, Basil, Edward, Riason, Rachel, Ann.

1784   GLASCOCK, PETER, Mary, Spencer, Charles, Moses, William, Wharton, Elijah, Margaret, Gregory.

1797   GILLESPIE, THOMAS, Naomi, George, Thomas, Isaac, John, David, Alex, Robert, James, Thomas, Jacob,

1787   GILBERT, WILLIAM, Eleazer, Huldah, Mary.

H.

1765   HALLUM, JOHN, Mary (wife), John, William, Dorenst, Mary, Sarah, Rachel, Martha.

1758   HAMPTON, DAVID, Hannah, John, William.

1762   HOUSTON, DAVID, Mary (wife), Aaron, Archibald, William, John, David, Ann, Mary, Jane, Agnes.

1763   HUNT, THOMAS, Abner, Thomas, Ann (wife), Jacob, William, Isham.

1766   HALE, JOHN, Ann, Arminda.

1775   HOLMES, JOHN, William, Richard, Mary, Janet, Jean, Katrina.

1775   HILL, DAVID, Isabella, Jean, Margaret.

1775   HAINLINE, JOHN, Catharine, Jacob, Henry, John, George, Christopher, Abraham.

1775   HINKLE, PETER, Salome, Anthony, Mary.

1783   HAIRSTON, MARY, William, Elizabeth, David.

1778   HULL, MOSES, Moses, Joseph, Daniel.

1783   HUNT, JONATHAN, wife, Andrew, Charles, John, Wilson, Levi, George, Gresham, Enoch, Noah.

1783   HILLHOUSE, SAMUEL, wife, Sampson, Robert, Ann, Elizabeth, Martha.

1792   HUGHEY, JACOB, Margaret, Henry.

1792   HUGHES, TIMOTHY, John, Samuel, Thomas, Joseph, Jean, Timothy.

1792   HUGHEY, HENRY, Robert, Henry, Jacob, Isaac, Rachel.

1788   HAMMOND, PETER, Elijah, William, Peter.

1786   HAZLETT, JOHN, John.

1789   HARTMAN, GEORGE, Mary (wife).

1781   HOWARD, JOHN, Gideon, Mary, Matthew.

1786   HEMPHILL, JAMES, Andrew, John, William, Samuel, Thomas, James, Anna, Susanna.

1786   HARDEN, ROBERT, Jean, Margaret, William, Mary, Phoebe, Priscilla, Rebecca.

1783   HENDERSON, JOHN, Mary (wife).

1782   HOUSTON, JAMES, Samuel, Peter, Robert, Martha.

1790   HUGHEY, SAMUEL, Mary, James, Henry, Samuel.

1790   HADEN, WILLIAM, Unity, Douglas, Jenny.

1795   HUDGINS, WILLIAM, Elizabeth, William, Pleasant.

1793   HARPER,, WILLIAM, Zephaniah, Mary (wife), William, Rhoda, Elizabeth, Zilpah.

1787   HUNTER, JOHN, Andrew, Richard, Sarah, John, Alex, Mary, James.

1797   HANNAH, JOSEPH, Mary, Thomas, Anna, Sally.

1789   HUNT, DANIEL, John, Gershem, Arthur, Owen, Jonathan, Abel.

I.

1783 IRVIN, GEORGE, Archibald, wife, James, Deborah, William, George, Mary, Sarah, Elizabeth.

1797 INGLISH, ALEX, Jean, Andrew, Samuel, Alexander, Josiah.

J.

1757 JOHNSON, ROBERT, Lily, John, Thomas, Robert, Martha, Sarah, Mary, Phoebe.

1767 JOHNSTON, THOMAS, Mary (wife).

1774 JAMES, SAMUEL, Sarah, Rowland, Matthew.

1778 JAMISON, JAMES, Isabel, Eleanor, William, David.

1792 JOHNSON, WILLIAM, Judith, Samuel, Manoah, Christian, Elizabeth, Margaret, Amy.

1779 JOHNSTON, ROBERT, Elizabeth (wife); William, John, Anna, Jean, Margaret, Mary, Robert, Catherine, Elizabeth.

1787 JACKS, RICHARD, Ann, Elizabeth, Thomas, Richard, John, William, Barbara, Ann, Rachel.

1786 JETTON, ABRAHAM, Nancy, Benedict, John, Joel.

1784 JACOBS, JEREMIAH, Edgar, Ruth, Jeremiah, Joseph, Zachariah.

1784 JOHNSTON, THOMAS, Amos, Margaret, John, Hester.

1796 JOHNSTON, WILLIAM, Rachel, John, Robert, William, Samuel, Jesse, Polly, Elizabeth.

1797 JOHNSTON, JOHN, Joel, Ganaway, Obedience, John, Fanny, Rachel.

1795 JAMES, DAVID, Sarah, Ezra, Elizabeth.

1787 JOB, THOMAS, Thomas, John, Samuel, Mary.

K.

1772 KNOX, JEAN, Benjamin, Joseph, Samuel, James.

1763 KING, PETER, Benajah, Peter, Nicholas.

1782 KING, RICHARD, Thomas, Robert, James, Andrew, John, Ann, Elizabeth, Margaret.

1782 KING, PETER, Peter, Nicholas.

1782 KERR, ANDREW, Mary, Ann, Joseph, Samuel.

1782 KIMBROUGH, MARMADUKE, John, Orman, Mary, George, Golman, Ann.

1785 KINDAR, COOPER, Anna, Betsy, John, Jacob, George.

1794 KARN, JOHN, Esther, Mary, Susanna, Daniel, Peter.

L.

1772 LAWRENCE, PETER, wife and children (not named).

1772 LUCKIE, ROBERT, Mary (wife), Margaret, Mary, Rachel, Janet, Hannah, Martha, Lydia.

1766 LIMLEY, GEORGE, Catherine, Joseph, Jacob, Philip, Henry, John, George, Elizabeth.

1761 LAMBE, HENRY, Elizabeth, Isham, Jacob, Joseph, Elizabeth.

1768 LOWRANCE, PETER, Mary (wife), Peter, William, Christian, Eve, Ritick, Mary.

1772 LITTLE, JOHN, Thomas, George, Martha, Mary, Jean, Elizabeth.

1767 LIKENS, JACOB, Rachel, Elinor, Rebekah, Drewzikah, Ann.

1772 LAWSON, HUGH, Roger, Mary, Hugh.

1773 LUSK, SAMUEL, William, John, Carolina.

1777 LITTLE, DANIEL, Daniel, John, Peter, Henry, James, Lewis, Mary.

1782 LEONARD, VALENTINE, Elizabeth (wife), Phelps, Jacob, Peter, Barbara, Elizabeth, Catharine.

1782 LYALL, THOMAS, Mary (wife), Margaret, Elizabeth.

1785 LYONS, JOHN, Eliza, Jonathan, Josiah.

1779 LAWRENCE, JOSEPH, John.

1781 LAWRENCE, JOHN, Ann, Jacob, Alex, Abraham, Andrew, Joshua, Margaret, Mary, Elizabeth, Agnes.

1782 LATTA, ROBERT, Jane (wife), James, Samuel, Jane, Agnes.

1789 LINN, WILLIAM, Israel, William, Sarah, Hannah, Henry, Mary.

1792 LOPP, JACOB, Peter, Jacob, John.

1789 LUCKY, JOHN, James, Robert, George, Mary, Isabella. Jean.

1785 LYBERRY, CHRISTIAN, Troy.

1783 LEATHMAN, NICHOLAS, Elizabeth, Christian, John, James, Daniel, Martha, Rachel, Laya, Susanna.

1789 LAWRENCE, JOSEPH, John, Elizabeth, Abraham, Andrew.

1786 LINN, HUGH, Susanna, Robert.

1786 LAYRLE, CHRISTOPHER, Christopher.

1798 LUCKIE, SAMUEL, Ann, Samuel, Robert.

1782 LYALL, THOMAS, Mary, Margaret, Elizabeth.

1794 LOWASSER, JOHN, Elizabeth.

1796 LEDFORD, WILLIAM, Elizabeth, Sally, John, Jacob, Lequire, Thomas, William, Phoebe.

1799 LANG, THOMAS, Catharina (wife), Thomas, Daniel, Mary, Catharina, Rose, Christiana, Sarah, Molly.

1795 LITTLE, JAMES, Job, James, Nancy, Samuel, William, Margaret.

1795 LINN, JOHN, Katy (wife).

1796 LOCKE, FRANCIS, Anna (wife), Francis, Matthew, Anne, Mary, Penny, Elizabeth, Armstrong.

1799 LOCKE, MATTHEW, Eliza, James, Robert, Richard, Matthew, Moses, Francis.

M.

1772 MADEN, ANDREW, Eleanor, Hannah, John, Andrew, Larous, James.

1772 MILLER, SAMUEL, Jane, Samuel, Thomas,

1772 MORGAN, WILLIAM, John.

1770 MORISON, ANDREW, Mary, Sarah, John, Martha, David, Andrew, William.

1769 MORRISON, ARCHIBALD, Mary (wife), Archibald, William, Sarah, Ann, Mary, Margaret, Jane, Alexander.

1770 McBROOM, ELIZABETH, John, James.

1771 McDOWELL, JOSEPH, Margaret, Hugh, Charles, John, Joseph.

1771 MABRY, GEORGE, Martha, John, James.
1771 McPHEETERS, JOHN, Mary (wife), Margaret, Mary.
1771 McHENRY, HENRY, Eleanor, Henry, John, Jason, Agnes, Margaret, Janet.
1771 MORRISON, WILLIAM, Hugh, Andrew, William, Patrick.
1772 McKANN, JOHN, Mary Ann, Joseph, John, James, Martha.
1760 McCONNELL, ANDREW, Jane (wife), John, Andrew, Mary, Jane, Margaret.
1768 McMACKIN, ANDREW, wife, Margaret, Jane, Elizabeth, Ann, Andrew, John.
1768 MYERS, MICHAEL, Mary (wife), Barbara, Mary, Michael, Hannah, Susanna.
1766 McCUISTON, ROBERT, Ann, Walter, James, Margery, John, Jean, Sarah, Mary.
1758 McCULLOCH, JAMES, Elizabeth, Samuel, Alex, John, Matthew.
1760 McKNIGHT, WILLIAM, Charles, Thomas, William, James, Hugh, John, David.
1757 MURRAY, MARY, Robert, James, John.
1761 MULL, CONRAD, Mollana (wife) ; John.
1757 MILIKAN, JOSEPH, William, Mary, Catherine.
1769 McDONALD, GEORGE, Mary, Peter, Jane, Isabel.
1766 McCUISTON, JAMES, Janet, Sarah, Mary, Dorcas, Gustavus, Thomas, James.
1762 McGUIRE, JOHN, Edward, John, Anna, Sarah.
1761 MILLS, JOHN, Rebecca, Thomas, John, Hur, Henry.
1762 MILLS, HUR, Micajah, Amos, Charity, Jeremiah, Elizabeth, Rachel.
1767 McNEELY, ADAM, Thomas, David, Adam, Sarah, Rebecca, Ann, Margaret.
1774 McCALLUM, JOHN, Elizabeth, Andrew, James.
1775 MORDAH, JAMES, Agnes, John, William, Robert, James, Jean, Elinor.
1775 McNEELY, ISAAC, Andrew, James, Hugh, Jean.
1777 McNEELY, DAVID, Margaret, Adam, Thomas, Jean, Rebecca, Ann.
1777 McMAHON, JOHN, James, Samuel, William.
1777 McCLELLAND, NICHOLAS, William, John, Jean, Martha, Agnes, Mary.
1777 McPHERSON, WILLIAM, Joseph, Mary, Ann.
1778 McCLELLAND, WILLIAM, Mary, William, Rachel, John, Mary, Agnes, Elizabeth, Jean, Rebecca, Sarah.
1776 MILLER, ANDREW, Sarah (wife), David, Margaret, Sarah.
1785 McCREARY, HUGH, Susanna, Lydia, Ann, Boyd, Hugh, Elizabeth, Margaret.
1776 McHARGUE, JOHN, Margaret, Alexander, John, James.
1784 MORRISON, ELIZABETH, Andrew, William, Thomas, James.
1776 McCOLLUM, ELIZABETH, James, Charles, Elizabeth, Agnes, Andrew.
1779 McLAUGHLAN, JAMES, Mary, Eleanor, John, Samuel, James, Elizabeth, Margaret.
1779 MOORE, ROBERT, Martha, William, Robert, Eugene, Josiah, Mary, Elizabeth, Martha.
1780 MOORE, MICHAEL, Susanna, George.
1780 MILLER, JOHN, Henry, Michael, John.

1780 MYERS, MARY, Michael, Barbara, Mary, Elizabeth.
1791 McCONNELL, JOHN, Daniel, Montgomery, Margaret, Mary, Rebecca, John.
1793 McHENRY, ELINOR, John, Samuel, Nancy, Isaac, Janet, Henry.
1786 McCRACKEN, JOHN, Jean (wife).
1791 MOTZINGER, FELIX, Elizabeth, John, Jacob, Daniel, Elizabeth.
1782 MILLER, GEORGE, George, John, Jacob, Frederick, David.
1782 MILLER, JANE, Samuel, Jane, Agnes, Willie, Samuel, James.
1785 McGUIRE, EDWARD, Isabel, Henry, Edward, Anderson, Anne, Hannah, Elinor, Sarah, Rachel.
1785 McCARTNEY, THOMAS, Margaret, Lewis, Thomas.
1790 MORRISON, JOHN, Frances, Andrew, Mary, Margaret, Robert, James.
1799 McBROWN, JAMES, John, Henry, James, Abel, Ann, Isaac, Jenny, Alexander.
1789 MOYERS, PHILIP, Barbara, Jacob.
1794 McPHEETERS, DANIEL, Martha (wife), Charles, Mary, Jane, Martha.
1799 McMACKIN, JAMES, Susanna, Samuel, William, John, Thomas, James, Elizabeth, Mary.
1780 MONTGOMERY, HUGH, Hugh, Jane.
1798 MOCK, DIEWALT, Daniel, Phoebe, John, Mary.
1787 McCONNAUGHY, JOSEPH, Martha, Joseph, James, Hugh, Sampson, Samuel.
1798 MOORE, NATHANIEL, Nathan, Eli, Susanna.
1795 MOORE, JOHN, John, Charles, Edward, Casin, Anne, Susanna, Sarah, Mary, Priscilla, Elizabeth.

N.

1769 NICHOLS, JOSHUA, wife and children (not named).
1770 NEWBERRY, ALEX, Annas, William, James, Alex, Andrew, Jean, Mary.
1771 NELSON, MOSES, Janet, Thomas, James.
1757 NESBIT, JOHN, James, David, William, John, Thomas, Elizabeth.
1765 NELSON, SAMUEL, Margaret (wife), John, Margaret, David.
1775 NEWFONG, MARTIN, Anna, Martin.
1775 NOLAND, STEPHEN, Mary, Stephen, Lindston, James.
1775 NESBIT, MOSES, Elizabeth, William, Ross, Esther, Thomas, Stephenson, John, Samuel.
1775 NESBIT, JOHN, James, David, Thomas, Elizabeth, Sarah.

O.

1768 OGBURN, WILLIAM, Rebecca, Abraham, Richard.
1777 OSBORNE, ALEXANDER, James, Adlai.
1777 ORTON, JAMES, James, Joseph, Jane, Rachel, Rebecca, John.
1783 OLIPHANT, JOHN, Elizabeth, Etor, Andrew, William, Robert, John, Martha, Ann, Jean.

1777 OWEN, JOHN, Elizabeth, Thomas.
1785 OWEN, HENRY, Henry, Ralph, Judy, Arentstill.
1794 OWEN, HENRY, Benjamin. Edward, Stephen, William.

P.

1761 PORTER, WILLIAM, Robert, Mary, Janet, Ann.
1770 PIDGEON, WILLIAM, Sarah (wife).
1772 PAGE, HUMPHREY, Sarah, Mary.
1774 PASINGER, JOHN, Magdalen, Christian, Paul, Frederick.
1775 POTTS, HENRY, Margaret (wife), William, Henry, Margaret, Mary, Susanna, James.
1785 PARKS, NATHAN, Mary, Richard, Joseph, Charles.
1785 POSTON, JOHN. Mary, Jean, Margaret, Elizabeth, Robert, John.
1785 PINKSTON, RICHARD, Jane, Thomas, Sarah, Patty, Mary, William, John, Edward.
1784 PAIN, JOHN, Margaret, Benjamin, Bever, Mary, Sarah.
1782 PARKS, GEORGE, John, Joshua, Jacob, Agnes,
1785 PAWLAS, WILLIAM, Anna, Hanadaus.
1781 PARKER, HUGH, Margaret, John, Hugh. Elizabeth, Mary, Huldah.
1789 PEARSON, RICHARD, Jean, Jehannah, Asa.
1789 PORTER, JAMES, William, James, Susanna, Ann, Jane, Keziah, Margaret.
1788 PARKS, MARGARET, John, Hugh, Jean, Margaret.
1788 PICKETT, RALPH, William, Charles.
1790 PATTERSON, WILLIAM, Jane (wife).
1796 PARKS, JOHN, Jean (wife), Margaret, Mary, Jean, Hugh.
1797 PENDRY, JAMES, Eli, Jemima, Dinah, Sarah.

R.

1766 ROTHERA, DAVID, David, Rachel, Rebecca, James.
1760 RANKIN, GEORGE, Lydia, John, Robert.
1772 REES, JACOB, Martin, Ann, Valentine.
1757 ROBISON, WILLIAM, John, William, Hugh.
1774 ROBY, THOMAS, Elinor, Ann, Verlinda, Charlotte, Prior.
1775 ROSEBROUGH, SAMUEL, Jean, Samuel.
1775 RUTLEDGE, JOHN, Elinor, John, James, Susanna, Joseph.
1777 ROBY, ELEANOR, Charles, Isaac, William, Elias, Luke.
1777 REED, ALEXANDER, Alex, Margaret, Samuel, Andrew, John, George.
1777 ROSEBROUGH, JOHN, Mary, Margaret, Robert, James, John, Samuel.
1782 RHODES, JACOB, Jacob, Mary.
1785 REED, GEORGE, Abigail, Aventon, George, Philip, Thomas, William, Amos, Edathe, Elizabeth.
1791 ROBISON, BENJAMIN, Moses, Alice, Benjamin, Sarah.
1793 RAIBLEN, MARTIN, Anna (wife), Martin, Jacob, Ann, Elizabeth, Sarah, Susanna, Rachel.

1788 ROBEY, NATHAN, Nancy, Elizabeth, Charlotte.
1785 ROSEBROUGH, MARGARET, James, Samuel, John.
1785 RAMSEY, ROBERT, Jean, James, William, David, John, Robert, Henry.
1786 ROBISON, GEORGE, Hugh, Margaret, Elinor, Janet, Ann, Elizabeth, Mary, Anna, Henry.
1786 ROSS, JAMES, Jean (wife), Joseph, Benjamin,
1799 ROBISON, RICHARD, Margaret, Huy, Rosanna. George, Henry, William, Richard.
1796 RICHARD, JACOB, John, Casper, Leonard.
!787 RICH, ISAAC, Margaret, John, Sarah, Anne.
1793 RICH, HENRY, Anne (wife), John, Sarah, Ann.
1793 RUMBLY, EDGAR, James, Thomas, Louise, Ann.
1794 RICHER, HENRY, Catharine, Henry.
1794 ROBERTS, STEPHEN, Phoebe, Warren, Joshua, Nancy, Betty.

S.

1762 SHINN, SAMUEL, Abigail (wife), Thomas, Samuel, Mary, Macey, Sillos, Rachel, Sarah, Hannah, Benjamin.
1767 SIMONTON, MARY, Adam, Theophilus, Alexander.
1760 SCOTT, JOHN, James, John.
1762 STORY, JAMES, Martha, Samuel, William, James, Isabella, Jean.
1767 SMITH, PETER, Peter, John, Margaret, Mary, Susanna, Elizabeth, George, Magdalen.
1770 STEWART, SAMUEL, Joseph, Bejamin.
1770 SCHORR, JOHNANNES, Magdalen, Johannes, Peter, Henry.
1771 SNAP, LAWRENCE, Elizabeth, Christian.
1757 SIMONTON, THEOPHLILUS, Mary (wife), Robert, Ann, Magdalen, Mary, John, Nathan.
1774 STEEL, WILLIAM, Elizabeth, John.
1774 STILLWELL, THOMAS, Margaret, David, Thom-Susannah, Jean.
1775 SNODDY, JOHN, Andrew.
      as, Elizabeth, Giles, Mary, Isaac, Phoebe,
1775 SMITH, ANDREW, Cornelius, Thomas, Anna,
1796 MORRIS, JONATHAN, Jehosaphet, Nathan. Catherine, Andrew.
1775 SMITH, JAMES, Ann, Janet, Mary, James, Samuel, William.
1777 SMITH, MICHAEL, Fred, Rosanna, John, Lisey, Michael, Barbara.
1777 STAGNOR, JOHN B., Elizabeth, Basnet, John, Sarah, Christian, Elizabeth, Barbara, Dorothy.
1782 STRANGE, JOHN, Robert, Gideon, and wife.
1781 SWINK, MICHAEL, Leonard, Michael, Henry, Mary.
1781 STEELE, ROBERT, Jean, Ninian, Henry, Robert.
1784 SMITH, GASPER, Margaret (wife), Philip, Gasper, George, Margaret, Barbara, Christian, Mary.
1778 SALT, ANTHONY, Rosanna.
1781 STEVENS, SAMUEL, John, Jean
1781 SAWER, PHILIP, Wife.
1780 SHARP, WALTER, Elizabeth, Thomas, Adlai.
1791 SHAFE, HENRY, Christina.
1791 STEELE, ELIZBETH, John.

1791 SMITH, MICHAEL, Elizabeth, Jacob, Isaac, Michael.
1788 SLOAN, ARCHIBALD, Margaret.
1786 SHELLY, JOSEPH, Elizabeth (wife), Benjamin, James, Richard, Thomas, Joseph, Elizabeth.
1781 STEWART, WILLIAM, Elizabeth, William, Thomas.
1779 STEWART, JAMES, Elizabeth.
1780 SLOAN, JOHN, Mary, Archibald, John, Jeremiah, Margaret, Mary.
1794 SCUDDER, MATTHIAS, Abner, Isaac, Elizabeth.
1795 STEGERWALT, PETER, Wife, Peter.
1796 SWAN, THOMAS, William, Elizabeth, Thomas, Isaac, Catherine, Matthew, James, Catharine, Mary, Margaret.
1787 SMITH, DAVID, Ann, Leonard, David, Fred, Casper, Peter, John.
1790 STEEL, SAMUEL, Agnes, Robert, James, Duncan, Samuel, William, Elizabeth.
1790 SHIELDS, ANDREW, Joseph, Anna, Isabella, Margaret.

T.

1760 THOMPSON, JOHN, Margaret, John, Joseph, James, Moses, Jane.
1774 THOMPSON, JOHN, Martha, Alex, Thompson, William, John, Joseph, Margaret.
1777 TODD, THOMAS, Elizabeth (wife), Joseph, Thomas, Elizabeth, Sarah, Jemima.
1779 TATE, ROBERT, Rebecca, John.
1783 TRENTHAM, MARTIN, Jeptha, Martin, Margery, Ann, Mary.
1778 THOMAS, JACOB, John, James, Henry, Jacob, William, Elizabeth, Anne, Margaret.
1792 THOMPSON, GEORGE, Mary (wife), Lande, Zachariah, William, Mary.
1786 TOMLIN, HUGH, Sarah, Archibald, Perry, Hugh, Samuel.
1796 TODD, CALEB, Margaret (wife), Caleb.
1794 THOMPSON, THOMAS, James, Elizabeth, Pamela, Alex, Elinor, John.
1799 TROUTMAN, PETER, Ann, Adam, Melchoir, Peter, Elizabeth, Jacob.
1794 TEAGUE, MOSES, Ann, Ruth, Moses, Aaron, Elizabeth, Miriam, Abraham, Martha.

V.

1788 VERBLE, DANIEL, Braylor, Leonard.
1786 VAN ETTEN, JOHN, Samuel, John, Abraham, Isaac, Elizabeth, Christian, Rayannah, Sarah.
1795 VAN POOL, JACOB, Elizabeth, Jacob, John, Lydia.

W.

1772 WEISNER, MICHAEL, Ruth (wife), Micajah, John, William, Abigail, Ruth.
1760 WOODS, OLIVER, Martha, William.
1766 WOODS, ROBERT, Samuel, Sarah, Elizabeth, Ruth, Margaret, Mary, Benjamin, Jean.
1759 WINSLEY, BENJAMIN, Mary, Benjamin, Moses, Samuel.

1775 WOODS, MATTHEW, Robert, David, Elizabeth, Joseph, Samuel.

1775 WILSON, THOMAS, Jean, George, John.

1777 WORK, ALEXANDER, Isabel, John, Rebecca, Jean, Sarah, Esther, Ann, Alexander.

1778 WOODS, SAMUEL, Ann, Andrew, Isabel, Rebekah, Samuel, Elizabeth, Margaret, Jane, Martha, Alexander.

1782 WHITE, JAMES. Sarah (wife).

1783 WILLIAMS, WILLIAM, Harry.

1785 WARLOW, PETER, Elizabeth (wife).

1785 WEISNER, MICHAEL, Ruth (wife), Micajah, John, William, Abigail, Ruth.

1791 WISEMAN, MARY, James, Ann, Elizabeth.

1793 WILSON, SAMUEL, William, John, George.

1781 WOODS, JAMES, Samuel, Andrew, Alex, Margaret.

1791 WAGNER, JOSEPH, Joseph, Catherine, Susanna.

1793 WILKERSON, THOMAS, Thomas, Rachel.

1791 WALCK, MARTIN, Elizabeth (wife).

1785 WASSAN, ARCHIBALD, Ann, Joseph.

1786 WILCOXSON, GEORGE, David, George, John. Mary, Elizabeth, Isaac, James.

1786 WHITE, MOSES, Eleanor, David, William, John, James.

1779 WISEMAN, ISAAC, William, James.)

1785 WRIGHT, RICHARD, Benjamin, Peter, Richard, William, Amos, John and wife.

1787 WILDY, ABRAHAM, Mary (wife)

1793 WILKERSON, SAMUEL, William, John, Samuel, George.

1795 WOOD, GARRET, William, Archibald, Jeram, James, John, Daniel, Joshua, Leah, Ann, Elizabeth, Mary, Martha, Garret.

1795 WILKINSON, THOMAS, Rachel (wife).

1795 WEIGHTMAN, GEORGE, Mary (wife), Jacob, Mary, Elizabeth, Rachel.

1799 WINKLER, ADAM, Catherine, Daniel, Adam.

1799 WINKLER, LEWIS, Henry, Francis.

1790 WENZEL, HENRY, Barbara (wife), Jacob, Henry, Anna, Barbara.

1794 WILLIS, THOMAS, Thomas, George, James, Adam, Rachel, Hannah.

Y.

1770 YOUNG, ALEXANDER, Jean, Ann, Alex, James, Samuel, Martha.

1793 YOUNG, SAMUEL, William, Janet, Samuel, James, Margaret, John, Joseph, Samuel.

Z.

1793 ZIMMERMAN, CHRISTIAN, Catherine (wife), John, Christian, Benjamin, David, Martin, Samuel, Joseph, Daniel, Margaret, Susanna, Regina, Elizabeth, Catharina, Sarah, Christiana.

RUTHERFORD—WILLS

B.

1776 Dec. 5, BATTLE, JOHN, Sarah (wife); John, Mary, William, Angelica (children).

1796 January 22, BLANTON, GEORGE, Susanna (wife); Burrell, William, Frances, John, Mary, Peggy, Richard (children); Bridgers, Ann, Catherine and Betsy.

D.

1802 March 9, DANIEL, JOHN, William, Harden, sons; Abigail (wife).

1786 Dec. 18, DILLS, PETER, Giles, Molly; Thomas (brother); Elizabeth Dills (sister).

G.

1798 July 16, GOODE, EDWARD, Mary (wife); Watson, Sarah; John, Thomas, Elizabeth, Richard, Benjamin, Agnes, Lusby, Priscilla, (children).

H.

1797 Dec., HARRIS, JOHN, Frances (wife); Peter, John, Reuben (children).
Fanny (granddaughter); Philip (son), Patty (wife); William, Martha, Judah, Fanny (children).

1786 Aug. 18, HUDDLESTONE, DAVID, Hannah (wife); Mary, David, James, William, John, mrs Jane Smart, ~~Jane~~ (children); David (grandson). of Son William From certified copy- 1909 Will

K.

1801 May 1, KEETER, JAMES, James, John, Joshua, Benjamin, (children); Lucy (wife).

L.

1779 Oct. 20, LEWIS, JOHN, Susanna (wife); Rowland, Mildred (daughter); Rhodes, Frances (daughter); Julius C. (son); David J. (son).

1801 March 13, LONG, GLOUD, Jane (wife); Patrick, Gloud, James, Isabel, Peggy, Jane, Polly, John (children).

M.

1801 Sept. 10, McDONALD, MARY, Colla, Susanna McDonald and Elizabeth Moses (children).

1797 April 14, McMINNISH, ROBERT, Jane (wife).

1780 March 1, MOORE, AARON, wife (not named); children, Moses, Elisha, Sarah, Mary, Margaret, Rachel, John, Ann; Harman, Elizabeth (daughter).

P.

1783 January 5, PAIN, JOHN, Betty (wife); Benjamin, Mary (children).

1801 January 19, PETTY, GEORGE, Sarah Ann (wife); Mary, James, Lettice, Fania, Elizabeth, Clara, Orasha, Joseph (children).

R.

1802 Sept. 20, REED, SAMUEL, Sarah (wife); John, James, Rachel, (children).

S.

1802 Sept. 6, SCOTT, JOHN, Lettice (wife).

T.

1798 March 17, THOMPSON, DAVID, Eleanor (wife); Eleanor (daughter).

W.

1784 Feb. 11, WALKER, JESSE, Sarah, Jane, Ann, Rhoda, William, Elizabeth (children).

1798 May 25, WALKER, THOMAS, Ursula, Sarah, James (children).

1800 May 23, WATKINS, DANIEL, Elizabeth (wife); Evan and Daniel (sons).

1802 March 2, WATSON, JOHN, Jenny, Sawney, John, Joseph, William, David (children); Ann (wife).

1801 May 31, WATKINS, PETER, Hannah (wife); David, William, Evan, children; Capishaw, Esther; McKinney, Nancy; Philips, Ellenda.

1782 April 14, WILLIS, JOHN, Elizabeth (wife); Buchanan, Arthur (grandson); Willis, William (son); Jacob (son); Hill, Elizabeth.

SAMPSON—WILLS

A.

1762 June 15. AMMONDS, THOMAS, Elizabeth, Vaughn, Howell, Joshua.

B.

1792 May 10. BULLARD, JEREMIAH, G. S., James, Jason, Simmons, John.

1797 June 13. BAREFOOT, ISABEL, Porter, William, Sarah; Brown, Sallie, John.

1786 August 18. BASS, CHARLES, Elizabeth, William, Burell.

1791 September 23. BUCHANAN, SAMUEL, Rachel.

C.

1791 October 31. COOPER, JOHN, Scott, Jonathan, Raphael, Hester, Betsey, Zylphia, Patience, Elizabeth.

1782 February 7. CRUMPLER, JOHN, Jacob, John, Rachel, Nancy, Elizabeth, Micajah.

1795 July 2. COOPER, FLEET, John, Coroph, William; Wiggins, Elizabeth; Peterson, Mary; Holmes, Grace, Polly.

1798 March 22. CARR, THOMAS, Mary, Reddin, Theophilus, Betsy, Joseph, Moat, Enoch, Jonathan, Thomas, William, Patrick, Tamar.

1797 February 12. COGGIN, THOMAS, Martha, Mary.

1786 June 3. COOK, JAMES, John, Cornelius, Jean; Watkins, Ann.

F.

1785 June 6. FRYAR, JACOB, Winifred.

G.

1791 March 11. GAINEY, EDMUND, Edney, Beatty, Martha, Elias, Abram, Noel, William, Reddick; West, Willis; Westbrook, Lee.

H.

1796 September 13. HERRING, JACOB, Stephen, Mary, Sarah.

1795 April 9. HOLLINGSWORTH, HENRY, SR., Mary (wife), James, Elizabeth, Sarah; Faison, Mary, Charity; Powell, Lydia.

1800 December 21. HILL, FRANCIS, Hill, B. H.; Thornton, Martha, John; Westbrook, Aley, William; Hobbs, Hester, Simon.

1770 June 27. HOLDER, JOHN, Jesse, Nathan, Mary, Sallie, Emma, Martha, Glada, Lettice, Lilla, Ann (wife).

1770 July 4. HERRING, ABRAHAM, Abraham, Martha (wife).

1799 August 25. HOLDER, GEORGE, Mary (wife); Hodge, Rachel; Bell, Mary.

1784 HAY, CHARLES, Sarah (wife); Peter, Solomon and Winnie.

K.

1795 January 6. KELLY, JOSEPH, Mary, Jemima, William, Jacob, Elizabeth (wife).

M.

1797   February 27. McQUINN, NORMAN, Catherine (wife).

1778   August 20. McLENDON, LEWIS, Shadrach, James, Zilpha, Dennis, Sallie, Patsy, Surrell.

1792   March 14. McILWIN, JOHN, Fannie (wife); Stewart, Elizabeth.

O.

1787   April 24. ODOM, SARAH, Jacob, Richard, William; Lockamy, Sarah; Harris, Bathany; Smith, Charity.

P.

1792   January 11. PRICE, JOSIAH, Jeremiah, Dorothy, Richard, Joseph, Susanna, Judith.

1796   June 27. PORTER, JOHN, Alsalom, John, Samuel, William, Sapphire; Butler, Elizabeth; Hairr, Delilah; Hinson, Ann; Cole, Jeremiah.

1798   April 14. PORTIVENT, SAMUEL, Mary (wife), John, Isaac, James; Larkins, Susanna; Bloodworth, Ann.

R.

1794   November 15. ROYALL, WILLIAM, Young, Betsey, Hardy, Mary; Ander, Edna; Carroll, Lucy.

S.

1780   October 30, SELLARS, SAMUEL, Hannah (wife), Abraham, Zilpha; Cooke, Unity, Rhoda; Pridgen, Elizabeth; Register, Alice, Sarah, Pearl.

1788   February 25, SCOTT, JONATHAN, Mary, Asha; Chestnut, Jenny; Murphy, Jerusha; Ader, Peggy.

1787   December 6, SAMPSON, JAMES, Mary (wife), John L.

1800   September 16. STEVENS, BARNABAS, Lydia (wife), William, Oates, Susanna, Elizabeth, Nancy, Arachsah.

T.

1795   February 25, TART, JOHN, Patty (wife), Mason, Charlotte, Sarah, Janet, John, Turner, Mildred.

1785   March 5, TOOLE, EDWARD, Jeralus, Judith (wife), Elizabeth Ann, Matilda, Unity.

1797   February 18, TUBERVILLE, SAMPSON, (Turbyville, properly D'Urbeville), Alfred, Tempe (wife).

1794   September 16, TUBERVILLE, JOSEPH, Mary (wife), Joseph, Sampson, Samuel, Rhoda, Milley; Bunt, William.

W.

1797   August 20, WILLIAMSON, WILLIAM, Timothy, Esther (wife), Nathaniel, James, William, Stephen, Mary, Anthony, Samuel, Nathan, Winnie, Elsie.

1795   October 19. WILLIAMSON, JACOB, Mary, Theophilus, Elias, Rachel, Lucy, Patience, Elizabeth.

Y.

1793 November 24, YOUNGER, DAVID LEE, Jessie
       Lee, Joel Lee, Aaron Lee, Nancy, Farby,
       (Pheraba).

STOKES—WILLS

A.

1792 ADAMAN, THOMAS, Mealy (Amelia(wife; Forrester, Elizabeth, Nancy and John.

1799 AUST, MARY, Ladd, Constantine; Stauber. Francis and Ann; Mickey, John, Magdalen and Lewis; Hauser, Mary.

1802 AUST, JOHN G., Leonard, Fred, Maria, and William.

B.

1790 BANNER, HENRY, Charity (wife), Joseph, Ephraim, Benjamin and Eleanor.

1793 BINKLEY, PETER, Margaretta (wife); John Peter, Fred, Joseph, Jacob, and Christian.

1794 BOWMAN, EDWARD, Margaret (wife), William, Richard, George' and Archibald.

1796 BAYER, HENRY, Catherine (wife); Margaret, Adam, John, Jacob, Henry, Joseph, Isaac and Robert.

1796 BINKLEY, CHRISTIAN, John S.

1800 BAGGE, FRANGAT, Johann L. and Charles F.; Stotts, Samuel; Hertil, Cariter; Vierling, Maria R.; Spach, Hannah.

C.

1793 CROOK, JAMES, Elizabeth (wife), Regnal Jennie, Jeremiah and William.

1795 CHANDLER, WILLIAM, Delisha (wife).

1797 CALAER, JOANNA, E. Ephraim.

1797 CHRISTMAN, BALTHAZAR, Elizabeth (wife), Jacob and Benigna.

1799 CLAYTON, BRITA'N, Lucy (wife), George, Warren, Gasper, P.ly, Charles and Katy.

1801 CARSON, WILL'AM, Martha (wife); Samuel.

D.

1799 DEANGE, MICHAEL, Catherine (wife); Michael and Elizabeth.

1802 DUTTON, JOHN, John (son) and the latter's wife.

E.

1790 EVANS, THOMAS, Elizabeth (wife).

1792 EBERT, MARTIN, Eva B. (wife); Martin and John G.

1798 ESTERLINE, MATTHEW, Anne M. (wife); Daniel.

1799 ESTERLINE, ANNA M., Daniel.

1800 EVANS, EDWARD, Martin, Margaret, Mary, John and Hampton.

F.

1790 FOLK, ANDREW, Mary M. (wife); Andrew and John.

1795 FARE, JOHN, Alice (wife); John.

1798 FRY, VALENTINE, Michael, Valentine, Henry, John and Peter.

1801 FRENCH, PETER. Joseph, William, Samuel and John.

G.

1794 GAMAWELL, JAMES, Lucretia (wife); William, Andrew, James, Betsy, Peggy, Joseph and Samuel.

1798 GEOFFERT, GEORGE, Baumgartner (son).

1800 GWINN, ALMOND, Mary (wife), Thornton.

H.

1793 HUPP, DANIEL, Ann (wife), John Daniel, Keziah, Mary, Jesse, Ann and Rebecca.

1795 HAM, JOSEPH, Arth, Ezekiel, Daniel, Thomas, John and Jacob.

1795 HURST, JAMES, Mary (wife); The Single Brothers Diacony; The Single Sisters Diacony.

1795 HINE, JOHN, Jacob N., John and Fred.

1796 HILL, ISAAC, Mary (wife); Joshua.

1797 HOENS, JOHN M., Anna E. (wife); John, Philip, Christian, Martin and Rosina.

1799 HILSABECK, FRED, Catherine (wife); Jacob, Henry, Mary Magdaline and Susan.

J.

1796 JOINER, WILLIAM, David, Mary, Peggy, Sallie, Atkinson, Betsy and Joseph.

1797 JACKSON, JAMES, SR., Francis; children of James (son).

1798 JOHNSON, DAVID, Mary (wife); Nancy, Miriam, Rhoda, John, Elizabeth and Sarah.

K.

1790 KERLEY, HENRY, Susanna (wife); Jesse, Pleasant, Edmund and Samuel.

1802 KRIENZELL, FRED, Salome (wife).

L.

1791 LINEBACH, ABRAHAM, Ann (wife); Daniel and Fred; children of Abraham (son).

1793 LEWIS, WILLIAM, Ansley, Obey, James, William, Mary, John Washington and Samuel.

1796 LADD, WILLIAM, Doshea (wife); William, Maser and Noble.

1797 LADD, THEODDIA, Thomas, Hannal and Hampton.

1800 LOVE, JAMES, SR., James; children of John (son).

1800 LEINBACH, LEWIS, Barbara (wife); Christian, Joseph, John, Peter and Mary.

M.

1792 MILLWOOD, JAMES, Nancy (wife); James and other children (not named).

1793 MARTIN, MASON, Mary (wife); Jesse, Jonathan, William, Zachariah, James, John and George.

1796 MARKLAND, MATTHEW, Ancyble (wife); Nathaniel and Matthias, children.

1798 MIDLER, JACOB, John, Joseph, Fred and Jacob.

1801 MAYER, JACOB, Phillip, Henry, Samuel and Dorathea.

N.

1799 NEELY, JOHN, Katie, Polly and Richard.

P.

1791 PEDDYCOURT, SARAH, John, William, Basil, Barlow, Thomas, Greenberry, Eleonora, Sarah and Lucy.
1795 PENNEGAR, PETER, Mary (wife); Matthia.
1799 PATTISON, ANDREW, James H. and David.

R.

1798 REDDICK, HARDY, Mourning (wife), Hardy, John, Abraham, Thomas, Mourning, Sarah, Elizabeth and Margaret.

S.

1791 SMITH, GEORGE, Christian and Mary.
1794 SOUTHERN, WILLIAM, Judith (wife); Magdalena and John, children of (son) William.
1795 SAUNDERS, NATHAN, Susanna, Ardea, Mary A., Jesse, Richard and Benjamin.
1800 SMITH, CHRISTIAN, Ann (wife); Catherine, John, Peter, Christian and Margaret.

T.

1793 TRANSON, PHILIP, Magdalena (wife); John, Abraham, Philip, Mary, Rosina, Elizabeth and Catherine.
1797 TATE, RACHEL, Samuel, Elizabeth, Owen, Robert and Rachel.
1802 TAYLOR, WILLIAM, Isaac.

V.

1789 VANHOY, JOHN, SR., Jemima (wife); John, Jr., Edward, James, Thomas, William, Abraham, Nancy, Susanna, Clayton and Rachel.

W.

1798 WARNOCK, SAMUEL, John and James.
1799 WOODS, JOHN, Neeley.
1800 WEBB, WILLIAM, Henrietta (wife); children son William.

Y.

1800. YARREL, PETER, Nancy (wife); Thomas, Anna and Mary.

SURRY COUNTY—WILLS

A.

1796 ANGEL, CHARLES, Sybilla (wife); Lawrence and Charles.

1782 ARMSTRONG, WILLIAM, Catherine (wife); William, John, Hugh and James.

1789 AUST, GOTTFRIED, Mary (wife).

1801 ALLEN, JOHN, Jane (wife).

B.

1782 BAKER, CHRISTIAN, Baker, Elizabeth (cousin).

1783 BLAIR, HUGH, John, Hugh and Elizabeth.

1783 BURKE, JAMES, Lucretia (wife); Burke, Thomas (grandson).

1774 BOND, CHARLES, Mary (wife); John and Jesse.

1774 BOHANNON, JAMES, Jeremiah, Ann and Isabel.

1772 BLACKBURN, NEWMAN, Elizabeth (wife); John, Younger, William, Mary and Reuben.

1777 BAKER, MICHAEL, Wife (not named), Mosses and John.

1780 BOWLES, BENJAMIN, Thomas and John (brothers); Ford, Mary (sister).

1785 BOHANNON, JOHN, Neal.

1785 BRADLEY, TERRY, Wife (not named), Leonard K., John and George.

1787 BOONE, RATCLIFF, Ruth (wife); Joseph, Ruth, Ratcliff, James Hester, Mary, Rachel and Daniel.

1792 BAKER, HENRY, Franky (wife); Caleb and Patty.

1796 BARR, JOHN, Barr, William (a friend).

1800 BOWEN, THOMAS, Sarah (wife); Whitlock, Bowen (a friend).

1801 BURCH, JOHN, Lucretia (wife), Charity and Thomas C.

C.

1780 COOK, ROBERT, Mary (wife); John, Abel, William, Mary, Thomas, Elizabeth, Israel and John.

1781 CHARLES, JAMES, Sarah (wife); Oliver, Mary, Frances, Joel, Martha, Sarah and Nancy.

1782 CLAYTON, PHILIP, Mary (wife); Elizabeth and Nancy.

1783 CONWAY, EDWARD, Margaret (wife); Charles, Elizabeth, James, Rachel, Roger and Susan.

1791 CRESON, ABRAM, Mary (wife); Joshua, Steelman, Jane (daughter).

1797 CHANDLER, ISAAC, Kerenhappuch (wife); George.

1801 COOK, WILLIAM, Samuel, Elizabeth and Frances.

D.

1778 DUNLAP, SAMUEL, James and Mary.

1795 DAVIS, WILLIAM, Nancy (wife); William, Anne, Sarah, Luckett, Samuel, Thomas, Leonard Chiloe and Louisa.

1777 DUNCAN, MARSHALL, Mary Ann (wife); John Mary Ann, William, Anna, Marshall, Thomas, Rice, Charles, Joseph, Robert and James.
1798 DOOLING, JOHN, Jemima (wife); Nancy, John, Milly and William.
1777 DONAHU, HENRY, Thomas and Ann.
1783 DAVIS, DAVID, Eizabeth (wife); Daniel.
1784 DUGAN, THOMAS, John G.
1787 DEAN, REZIA, John.
1789 DENNUM, HUGH, Clayton, John, Clemmons Hugh (nephew).
1788 DICKERSON, GRIFFITH, Ann (wife); William, Nathaniel and Matthew.
1798 DOBBIN, JACOB, Ann (wife); William, Jacob, Thomas and Joshua.

E.

1774 EVINS, NICHOLAS, Eulie (wife); Thomas.
1777 ELLIOTT, ANN, Thomas, John and Mary.
1789 EDELMAN, PETER, Margaret (wife); Lyon, Sarah (daughter).

F.

1772 FISHCUS, FRED, Eve (wife); Fred.
1778 FORRESTER, THOMAS, Mildred (wife); Hezekiah, James, John and William.
1779 FISHER, THOMAS, James (son); James (father).
1786 FULPS, GEORGE, Mary (wife); Peter and Valentine.
1787 FAIR, BARNABAS, Elizabeth (wife); *John,* Barnabas, Michael, Barbara, Dorothy, Margaret and Mary Ann.
1794 FLEMING, JOHN, Jane (wife); Martha, Sarah, Nancy, William, Mordecai, John M. and Edward.
1796 FREEMAN, SAMUEL, Elizabeth (wife); Joshua, James. Aaron and Rachel.
1800 FENDER, CHRISTIAN, Mary (wife); Gabriel Nimrod, Michael, John, Henry, Sarah and Catherine.

G.

1801 GITTENS, RICHARD, Margaretta (wife .
1774 GRAVES, JOSEPH, Sarah (wife); John Absalom and Cleveland.
1775 GLENN, TYREE, Wife (not named; Thomas, Sukey, Jeremiah, Aggie and Jenny.
1781 GLENN, JAMES, Wife (not named); Lucy, Susanna, Elizabeth, Nancy, Martha and Thompson.
1783 GERBER, MICHAEL, Magdalena (wife); Christian and John G.
1801 GITTENS, JOHN, Margaret (wife).
1785 GREEN, SAMUEL, Deborah (wife); Samuel, Nathaniel, Foster, Andrew, Susanna, Jean, William, Rebecca, Margaret and Isabella.
1789 GROEBER, JACOB, Mary C. (wife); Jacob.
1789 GOODE, THOMAS, Mary (wife); Edward Richard, George, William and Nelly.

X Given in copy of Will of Barnabas Fair in Library Files.

1800 GREGORY, THOMAS, Phoebe (wife); Elizabeth, Susanna, James, Gabriel and Thomas.

H.

1781 HOWARD, WILLIAM, Children (not named).
1777 HUDSPETH, RALPH, Catherine (wife); David, Carter, Ralph and Giles.
1777 HUDSPETH, WILLIAM, Benjamin and Charles.
1780 HUDSPETH, JOHN, Mercy (wife); Ralph, David, Lucy and Catherine.
1781 HOLCOME, JOHN, Elizabeth (wife); Thomas John Grimes, Philemon, Lawrence and George.
1783 HOWELL, THOMAS, Elsie (wife); Catherine, Hannah and Ruth.
1784 HOUZER, JOHN, Hannah (wife); children of son William (not named).
1787 HILL, WILLIAM, William, Daniel H., Thomas, Robert, Uel, Jesse, James, Joshua, Joel and Eliza H.
1789 HAUSER, MICHAEL, Lena (wife), Michael, Peter, Christian, Daniel and John.
1789 HAUN, Margaret B. Snyder, Philip (brother).
1792 HUTCHINGS, STRANGEMAN, Benjamin; Stanly, John, Brooks, Mary.
1792 HUDSPETH, BENJAMIN, Milly (wife); Giles, Morgan, Johnson and Sarah.
1794 HANNA, JOHN, Wife (not named), James, William, Samuel, Roderick and Robert.
1795 HANNA, SAMEUL, Mother (not named).
1797 HUDSPETH, GILES, Elizabeth (wife), Rachel, John, Charles, Martha, Hannah and Mary.
1799 HUDSON, HALL, William and Richahrd.
1799 HERRING, HENRY, Wife (not named).

J.

1777 JONES, ABRAHAM, Hannah (wife), Abraham, Elizabeth, Mary, Anna, Joseph, Jonathan and Lewis.
      muwl, Eunice, Elizabeth, Ruth and Sarah.
1793 JAYNE, NATHANIEL, Stephen and Henry; daughter of son William (not named).
1796 JESSUP, JOSEPH, Priscilla (wife); Caleb, Eli, Elijah, Joab, Sarah, Mary, Joseph, William, John, Rachel and Hannah.

K.

1799 KENNEDY, JOHN, Alexnder (son); Welch, John (a friend).

L.

1778 LANKFORD, JAMES, James, Richard and Susanna.
1782 LADD, NOBLE, Wife (not named); Constantine, Judith, Elizabeth, Joseph, William, Ed and Noble; Ladd, Amos (grandson).
1783 LASH, JACOB, Anna (wife); John C., Anna R. and Susanna.
1786 LANIER, ROBERT, Jane (wife); Thomas and Elizabeth.

1787 LINVILLE, DAVID, Worlley and Thomas (sons).
1790 LOGAN, PATRICK, Mary (wife); George, John, Hugh and James.
1791 LAYNE, WILLIAM, John Taylor, William Connex, Susanna, Sarah and Betsy.
1796 LONGINS, JOHN T. Sarah (wife); James Hugh, Bartholomew, John, Thomas, Lodosica (Laodicea); Elizabeth and Amelia.

M.

1796 MEREDITH, MILDRED, Mary, Daniel and William.
1800 MEERS, THOMAS, Amy (wife); Moses, Mary and John C.
1780 McCARRAL, NATHANIEL, Elizabeth (wife); Thomas, Mary and John.
1781 MASTERS, JOSEPH, Nicholas and James (brothers).
1782 MOSES, LEONARD, Sarah (wife); John Peter, Jacob, Michael, Frances, Christian, Henry, Sarah, Mary and Christina.
1787 MELTON, DAVID, Connie (Cornelia) (wife): David and John.
1787 MOSBY, SAMUEL, Susanna (wife); Nancy, Elizabeth, Sally, Ketturah, Sebretta and Thomas.
1790 MEREDITH, JAMES, Mildred (wife); John and Mary.
1793 MASTERS, WILLIAM, Mary (wife); Nicholas and James.
1795 MILLER, CHRISTIAN, Jacob, Mary and Elizabeth.
1799 McLEMORE, EPHRAIM, Hannah (wife); John, Gilliam, Sterling, Hannah and Martha.
1799 MILLER, JOHN, Nancy (wife).

N.

1786 NELSON, SOLOMON, Margaret (wife).
      named).
1791 NOBLET, JOHN, Rebecca (wife); sons (not

P.

1790 POLLY, HENRY, John T. Lazarus and Edward.
1777 PHILLIPS, BENNETT, Children (not named).
1788 PENIEL, BENJAMIN, Susanna (wife); William, Thomas, Betty and Mary.
1786 PETTIT, THOMAS, Judith (wife); Thomas and George.
1786 PETTIT, BENJAMIN, Elizabeth (wife); Thomas and Benjamin.
1889 PETTIT, THOMAS, Sr., Rachel (wife); Thomas, Jr. and Benjamin.

R.

1771 ROMINGER, DAVID, Jacobina (daughter): Lorenty; Rev. Bagge (a minister).
1777 ROBERTS, WILLIAM, Rosanna (wife); John, Anne, Sarah, Ruth, Elizabeth and Esther.
1777 RAINWATER, JOHN, Mary (wife); William, John and James.

1794 RENAGAR, GEORGE, Barbara (wife); Herman, Joseph and George.
1785 ROBERTSON, GEORGE, Wife (not named); Lyon, Sarah (daughter).
1800 RIGGS, SAMUEL, Elizabeth (wife); Silas and Lot.

S.

1774 SHORE, FRED, Henry, Fred and Margaret; Shore, Henry, Johannes, Peter and Jacob (grandchildren).
1772 STEWART, LYDIA, David and Samuel.
1782 SHILLER, EDWARD, Wife (not named).
1791 SOUTHARD, ISAAC, Wife (not named), Phoebe and Micajah.
1792 SESSIONS, ISAAC, Wheaton, Daniel and Calvin (friends).
1796 SIMS, MATTHEW, Mary (wife); James and Jemima.
1781 SHEPPERD, JAMES, Lucy (wife); John and Henry.
1775 SKIDMORE, HENRY, John, Thomas and Abraham.
1781 SMITH, WILLIAM, Elizabeth (wife); Samuel, William, Thomas, John, Mary, Betty, Susanna, Martha, Nancy and Sally.
1782 SEIDEL, NATHANIEL, Marschall, Frederick (a friend).
1783 SMITH, JOSEPH, Wife (not named); 8 children (not named).
1784 SHELTON, EDWARD, Mary (wife).
1785 SHELTON, WILLIAM, Mary (wife).
1785 SUMMERS, ROBERT, Thomas, Robert, Coleb, Joshua, Pheraba, Prudence Abigail and Sarah.
1786 SHOEMAKER, ADAM, Anna M. (wife).
1787 SPAINHOUR, WERNER, Elizabeth (wife); Peter, Henry, Elizaneth, Jacob, Michael and Erevil.
1788 SPAINHOUR, HENRY, Elizabeth (wife); Henry, Houser, Elizabeth (daughter).
1789 STREET, JOHN, Elizabeth (wife); Adam and Samuel.
1793 STEELMAN, MATTHIAS, Ruth (wife); James, Charles and George.
1794 SHERMAN, PETER, Peter, Margaret, Molly and Catherine.
1795 STANLY, JOHN, Edith (wife); John H.; Hutchins, Elizabeth (daughter).
1796 SPEAR, JACOB, Catherine (wife); Thomas and Jacob.
1797 SPEAR, THOMAS, Rebecca (wife); Robert, William, Drury and Reuben.
1799 SHERMAN, MARGARET, John.
1800 STONEMAN, GEORGE, Elizabeth (wife); Charles and James.

T.

1792 THOMPSON, SAMUEL, Jane (wife); John, William and Daniel.
1788 TURNER, ROGER, Elias, Robert and Elizabeth.
1785 TURNER, ELIAS, Robert (brother).

1786 THOMPSON, JOHN, Wife (not named) ; Tobias and William.

1796 TILLEY, HENRY, John and Lazarus.

1807 TRUETT, SAMUEL, Mary (wife) ; Joseph, Jane and Saxagatha.

V.

1780 VARNELL, RICHARD, Wife (not named) ; mother (not named).

1789 VANCE, SAMUEL, Ailey (wife) ; David, Nathaniel, Samuel, Als, Elizabeth, John, Joseph and James.

1793 VESTAL, JAMES, Thomas, Jesse and Davis.

1795 VENABLE, WILLIAM, Ursula (wife).

1795 VANDERFORD, ABRAHAM, Wife (not named) ; Josiah, Hezekiah and John.

1773 VANDERMERK, JACOBUS, Christiana (wife).

W.

1778 WARD, ROBERT, Mary (wife) ; John, Ann, Elizabeth, Mary Sarah, William, Henry, Robert and John.

1796 WOOTEN, THOMAS, John, Richard, Abraham, Caleb, Rachel and Thomas.

1780 WARD, CHARLES, Wife (not named).

1781 WALKER, WARREN, Betty (wife), Mourning, Pattie, Judea and Betty.

1782 WAGGONER, PHILIP, Elizabeth (wife) ; Adam, Elizabeth, Catherine, Christian and Eve.

1786 WALKER, ROBERT, Mary (wife) ; James, David, Polly, Robert, John and Betsy.

1787 WHITAKER, THOMAS, Mary (wife) ; Mark and Joshua.

1790 WRIGHT, JOHN, John, William, James, Anna, Sallie, Peggy, Polly, Rosey and Patsy.

1798 WILLIAMS, JOHN, Joan (wife) ; Jean, Rachel and Margaret.

1801 WEATHERMAN, CHRISTIAN, Margaret, Christian, Samuel, John, Simon, Susan and Margaret.

Y.

1791 YOUNG, EDWARD, Lucy (wife) ; Isham, Katie and Priscilla.

1794 YORK, C. E. L. C. (son) ; Blackwood, E. L. (a friend).

Z.

ZINN, MARGARETTA, Sarah, Valentine, Hieronymus and Christina.

TYRRELL—WILLS

1758 ALEXANDER, ANTHONY, Anthony, Elizabeth, Sarah.
1760 ALEXANDER, CHRISTIAN, Martha, Sarah, Ludford, Isaac, Thomas, Joshua, William, Michael, Benjamin, Joseph.
1763 ALEXANDER, WILLIAM, Joseph, Susanna and Thomas.
1763 ALEXANDER, JOSEPH, Sidney, Martha, Samuel.
1770 ALEXANDER, LUDFORD, Abram, Nancy, Ludford, Elizabeth.
1777 ALEXANDER, ISAAC, Anthony, Sarah, John, Joshua, Joseph.
1780 ALEXANDER, ISAAC, Ezekiel, Benjamin, Mary.
1781 ALEXANDER, JOSEPH, John, Abner, Jesse, Zilphia.
1776 AIRS, JOHN, Martha, David, John.
1780 ALEXANDER, ISAAC, Lilphia (wife), John, Joseph, Abner, Jesse, Mary, Ann, Sarah, Jemima, Lilphia, Milly, Clarca.
1781 ALEXANDER, MICHAEL, Christian, Michael, William, Abram, Martha and Mary.
1784 ALEXANDER, ANTHONY, Mary A., Joshua, Zephaniah, Joanna, Ann, Milly.
1784 ALEXANDER, BENJAMIN, Martha and Ludford.

B.

1761 BATEMAN, JONATHAN, James, Jonathan, Stephen, wife (not named).
1761 BRICKHOUSE, PETER, Elizabeth, Caleb, Hannah, Matthew, William and Major.
1765 BUTLER, JAMES, Willson, William; Rhodes, John.
1765 BLOUNT, JACOB, Hannah, Jacob, William, Samuel, James and Thomas.
1759 BONNER, WM., James, William, John, Ann, Stapleton and Catherine.
1764 BLOUNT, JOHN, Thomas, John, Jerusha and Deborah.
1772 BROOME, JOHN, Williams, Ann; Draper, Richard.
1787 BAKER HILARY, Ann (wife).
1769 BALLARD, JOSEPH, Joseph, John, Elizabeth, Robert, Ann, James, Silas and Elisha.
1778 BLOUNT, SAMUEL, William, Long, Joanna.
1783 BATEMAN, JOHN, Henry, Sarah.
1786 BUFFET, JOSIAH, Jesse, Rachel.
1786 BEST, JAMES, Elizabeth (wife), Michael, Mary, Joseph and Elizabeth.
1786 BLOUNT, BENJAMIN, Africa, Edmund, Benjamin, Levi.
1790 BATEMAN, NATHAN, Isaac, Henry, Jonathan, Andrew, Jane.
1753 COOMBS, THOMAS, May, William, Thomas, Jeremiah, John, Elizabeth, Judath.
1761 CONNER, JAMES, Charity, Louis, Penelope, Rosanna, Hugh, Michael, Peter, Catherine, Rose and Mary.
1766 CHERRY, JOHN, Mary, Elizabeth, Martha, Jesse, Daniel and John.
1763 CARRON, JAMES, George, Elizabeth, Ann, Miriam, Sarah and Patience.

1766 CHESSON, JOHN, John, William, Samuel, Joanna, Mary and Ann.
1770 CURRELLS, WM., George.
1778 CHAPMAN, JASPER, Ann and Elinor.
1770 CASWELL, MATHEW, Absalom, Isaac, John, Patty, Lovey and Elizabeth.
1772 COMBS, WM., Alice, Mary and Thomas.
1780 COMBS, THOMAS, Martha, Jesse, David and Jonathan.
1783 CORPREW, MATHEW, Esther, Mary, Elizabeth.

D.

1750 DAVIS, JONATHAN, William, Jonathan, Anne, Elizabeth.
1763 DUGAN, JOHN, Aaron, William, Elizabeth, Milly, Rhoda, Josiah, Higman.
1763 DUGAN, LANIER, Elizabeth, William, Aaron, Josiah.
1762 DAVIS, THOMAS, Elizabeth, John, Elizabeth (wife), Robert and Daniel.
1763 DUGAN, JOHN, John, William, Lanier, Aaron, Elizabeth, Millicent.
1773 DAVENPORT, RICHARD, John, Jacob, Benjamin, Ezra, Sarah.
1779 DAVIS, JONATHAN, William, Arthur, Edward B., Gresille, Matilda.
1780 DOWNING, HENRY, Richard, Stephen.
1782 DAVENPORT, WM., Elizabeth, James, Daniel and David.
1790 DAVENPORT, JAMES, Joanna, Susanna, Elkana, Moses, Isaiah, Ann, Leah and Uriah.

E.

1765 EVERETT, JOSHUA, Sarah, Benjamin, Nathaniel, Elizabeth, Jerusha, Hannah.
1782 EVERETT, NATHANIEL, Elizabeth, Joshua, John, James, Joshua, Edmond, Thomas, Jeremiah, Nathaniel, John.
1781 EVERETT, NATHAN, Elizabeth, John, James, Charlotte, Sarah.

F.

1770 FLEMING, PHILIP, Rebecca, William, Zachariah, Sarah B.
1772 FAGAN, RICHARD, Sally, Enoch.
1777 FAGAN, BEDFORD, Fred, Thomas, Mary, William, Stephen, Shadrack, Joshua, Enoch, Richard.
1777 FAGAN, THOMAS, Blount, Judith and James; Rhodes, Arthur, Sarah, Jordan.

G.

1758 GARRETT, DANIEL, Thomas, Daniel, James, John, William.
1762 GRAY, HENRY, Henry, Godfrey, Mary, Sarah, Ann, Lydia, Frances.
1779 GREENE, ELISHA, Bateman, Nathan.

H.

1762 HASSELL, JABEZ, Jane, William, Agnes.
1766 HARRISON, JOHN, Elizabeth, Thomas, Mary, Drusilla, Susan, John.

1766 HASSELL, ISAAC, Joseph, Rachel (wife), Rachel (mother, John.
1772 HASSELL, EDWARD, Edward, Solomon, John, Elisha.
1734 HASSELL, JOHN, Jesse, Ann.
1778 HASSELL, RACHEL, Benjamin, Joseph.
1781 HASSELL, BENJAMIN, Susanna (wife).
1783 HOPKINS, JOHN, Samuel, Philip, John, Elizabeth, Thomas, Marian.
1783 HASSELL, JOSEPH, Joseph, Ann, James, Silby, Isaac, Susanna.
1783 HASSELL, WM., Ann (wife), William, Hannah, Polly, Penelope, Jesse, Joshua, Jeremiah.
1788 HOWARD, BENJAMIN, Sarah (wife).
1790 HOOKER, JOHN, Stephen, Ann, Nathan, William, Sarah, John, Ann (wife).

J.

1772 JONES, BENJAMIN, Frily.
1783 JONES, CHARLOTTE, James, Frily, Sarah.

K.

1759 KING, HIGASON, Elizabeth, Higason, William. Robert, Mary, Elizabeth (wife), Chloe, Martha, Sarah.
1761 KENNEDY, WM., Benjamin, Cahen (wife).

L.

1757 LONG, JOHN, Robin, Susanna, Thomas, Francis, Ware, Sarah, John, Richard and Shadrack.
1761 LEGGETT, ELIAS, William, Elias, Jeremiah.
1762 LINTON, THOMAS, Jeremiah, Elizabeth.
1762 LUDFORD, THOMAS, Frances, Enoch, William.
1752 LONG, JAMES, Ann, Jeremiah, Sarah, Mary, James, Stephen, Levi, Isaac.
1771 LEE, FRANCIS, Black, Elizabeth; West, Elizabeth; Burtonshell, Richard.
1775 LARY, JAMES, James, Joseph, Salathiel, Sarah, Martha.
1779 LEE, STEPHEN, Mary (wife), Thomas, Mary, Elizabeth.
1780 LEARY, THOMAS, Thomas, Joshua.
1783 LIVERMAN, JOHN W., John, Thomas, William.
1785 LONG, ANDREW, Ann, Jeremiah, James, William, Elizabeth, Mary.
1782 LONG, GILES, Nehemiah, Thomas, James.
1787 LONG, JAMES, James, Rebecca, Daniel, Simon, James, Jesse, Levi.
1790 LONG, JOHN, John.
1790 MANN, THOMAS, Christian (wife), Mary, John, Thomas, Patsy, Dorothy, Sarah.
1785 MACKEY, WM., Mary, Thomas, William, Eleanor.
1767 MIDDLETON, JAMES, Sarah, Thomas.
1771 MARINER, JOHN, Peter, Elizabeth, Tabitha, John.
1773 MARINER, ROBINSON, Ann.
1770 MARRETT, JOHN, Hezekiah, Zachariah, Jesse, Isaac, Keziah, Jonathan.
1790 MILLER, JAMES, Ann (wife).
1760 McCASKY, JOHN, John, Susanna, Mary Cassandra, Drannah, Ann, John, Susanna.

1772   MEHOON, JAMES, Hezekiah, James, William, (wife), Penelope, John, Mary.

1775   McGOWAN, WM., Joseph, John, William, Thomas, Mary, Frances, James.

1786   McDOWELL, THOMAS, Fred, Thomas, James, Simeon, Nancy.

N.

1780   NORMAN, NEHEMIAH, Rachel (wife), Henry, Elizabeth, Sarah, Mary, Nehemiah, Amelia, Rachel, Nathan, Charles.

1787   NORMAN, MARY, Keziah, Susanna, Joel, James, Simeon, Priscilla, Jeremiah.

O.

1779   OVERTON, RACHEL, Spicer, Roger.

1781   OLIVER, ALEXANDER, Alex, John, Mary (wife), Mary.

P.

1758   PHELPS, JOSEPH, Joshua, John, Mary (wife).

1772   POWELL, ROBERT, William, Mary, Sarah (wife), Martin, Benjamin, Milly, Sarah.

1776   PERISHO, JAMES, James, Devotion, Willy, Rufus, Armistead, Mourning, Joseph and Mary.

1778   PHILIPS, JOHN, Joseph, Vijiah, Joanna.

1778   PARSONS, SAMUEL, Sarah, Samuel, Susanna.

1784   POWERS, JOHN, Ephraim, Benjamin, John, Salak, Ann.

1787   PHELPS, EDMUND, Benjamin, Jeremiah, John, Susanna, Rosanna, Ann (wife), Ann.

1787   PHELPS, JOSEPH, Ann (wife), Joseph, Benjamin, Simeon, Hannah, Ann, Rachel, Amelia.

R

1760   ROBASON, MARMADUKE, Mary, Ann.

1765   RHODES, WM., Parthenia, Charles, Judith, Arthur.

1765   RHODES, JOHN, Elizabeth, Stephen.

1763   ROUTON, JOHN, Richard, Edward, Daniel, Elizabeth, Gina, Agnes.

1782   RONGHAM, WM., Elizabeth.

1781   RAY, MARY, Mourning.

1781   ROUSHAM, JOSEPH, Barbara, Joseph.

1787   ROUSSOM, EDWARD, Hannah, John, Isaac, Joseph, Job.

1789   ROGERS, THOMAS, Ann (wife), Airs, Nathan, Stephen, Mary, Esther, Ann.

S.

1758   SWINSON, WM., Harrison, Elizabeth; Duance, Francis; Bengall, Mary.

1760   SPRUILL, SAMUEL, John, Evan, Mary, Jeremiah, Nehemiah.

1760   SPRUILL, JOSEPH, Mary, Godfrey, Thomas, Joshua, Hezekiah, Benjamin, Lilpha and Talitha.

1766   SLADE, HENRY, Ann, Willy, Joshua, Barbara, John G.

1765   SNELL, ROGER, Elizabeth, Roger, Holt, Rebecca, John.

1763 SMITH, THOMAS, Alice and Riddick.
1759 SPRUILL, JOHN, John, Evan, Mary, Elizabeth, Jemina, Deborah.
1763 SWAIN, JAMES, Elizabeth, Susanna, Elizabeth.
1769 SNELL, HOLT, Carson J. and Roger.
1765 SPRUILL, SAMUEL, Elizabeth, John, Joseph, Stephen, Simeon, Samuel.
1765 SWAIN, JOHN, John, Jemina, Priscella, Hannah, Joshua.
1771 SWAIN, MARY, Jeremiah, Samuel, James, Ann, Stephen.
1772 SNELL, ROGER, Susanna, Holt, John.
1783 SMITH, JAMES, Rachel, John and Hinds.
1780 SWAIN, WM., Mary, Zilphia, Ann, William, Joseph.
1781 SPRUILL, JEREMIAH, Sarah, Jesse.
1785 SEDGEX, ANN, Jennett, Joseph; Spruill, Ann and Hezekiah; Hassell, Benjamin.
1787 SPRUILL, BENJAMIN, Grace, Joseph, Jack, James, Jackson, Ann.
1787 SWAIN, JOHN, Ebanezer, John, Cornelius, Simeon, Mary, Keziah, Penelope, Sarah, Priscilla.
1791 SPRUILL, BENJAMIN, Anne (wife), Rosinah, Ann.
1789 SAWYER, EPHRAIM, Josiah, Keziah, Sarah, Frances.
1788 SLUBBS, JOHN, Thomas, James, Nancy, Fanny, Richard, William.
1790 SWAIN, JOHN, Jeremiah, Nathaniel, James, George, John, Spencer, Joshua, Jesse, Timothy, Titus, Ann, Joanna, Betsy and Sarah.

T.

1764 TURNER, JOSHUA, Lewis, Jesse.
1755 THORP, PAUL, Paul, James, Hannah, Job, Mary, Sarah.
1759 TATUM, WM., Elizabeth (wife).

W.

1798 WARRINGTON, JOHN, Thomas, Cally and Rally.
1755 WYNNE, THOMAS, John, Anna, Jeremiah and Peter.
1761 WHITFIELD, WM., Martha, William, Jesse, John, Winnie and Stephen.
1765 WOODLAND, MARY, Wheatly, Ann.
1765 WILLIAMS, EDWARD, Thomas, Stephen, Eleveth, Ann, James, Elizabeth and Ann (wife).
1771 WEBB, ROBERT, John.
1771 WARD, FRANCIS, Rachel (wife), Sarah, Francis and Robert.
1777 WOODLAND, SAMUEL, Stephen, John and Samuel.
1782 WYNNE, PETER, Andrew, Robert, Jesse, Benjamin, Willie and Susanna.
1766 WALKER, JOHN, Thomas, Stewart, Parthenia, John, Susanna and Margaret.
1776 WHEDBEE, JOSEPH.
1776 WEEB, NATHANIEL, John and Harmom.
1778 WHITSON, MICHAEL, John, Margaret.

Y.

1772 YOUNG, JOSEPH, Anna (wife), Jesse, William, Margaret ,Ann, Hezekiah.

WAKE COUNTY—WILLS

A.

1774 ALLEN, YOUNG, Martha (wife); William, Josiah, Coleman, Robin, Drury and David.

1777 ABBOTT, WILLIAM, Agnes (wife); Abraham, Isaac, Jacob, William and John.

1781 ATKINS, JOHN JR., John Sr. (father).

1792 AMBROSE, WILLIAM, SR., William Jr., Mial, Betsy and Agnes.

1792 ATKINS, JOHN, Elizabeth (wife); Lewis, Ica, Hutchins, Sally and Betsy.

1798 AYCOCK, JOHN, Fielding and Tyrece.

1800 AMBROSE, WILLIAM, Sarah (wife); Warren, Michael, Wilson, Benny, Bryan and Betsy. children.

1803 ATKINS, THOMAS, Penny (wife); Polly and John.

1803 ATKINS, ELIZABETH, Ica, Isaac, Lewis, Joseph, William and Nicholas; (sons); Nancy Myatt and Sally Hutchins (daughters); Polly Pearson (daughter); Betsy Mills ·(daughter).

B.

1788 BLACK, JOSIAH, Eleanor Cox (friend).

1771 BUNCH, PAUL, Ann (wife); David, Pheraba and Thompson; Mary McNatt, Anne Pace and Elizabeth Farrell (daughter).

1775 BEDDINGFIELD, WILLIAM.   ?

1777 BARBEE CHRISTOPHER, Margaret (wife); Christopher, Beneldge. Thomas, Ann, Joseph and Rosey; Martha Wimberly and Sarah. Ann Bewgley (daughters).

1779 BARKER, JOEL, Lewis, Edward and Julius; otho Huff (grandson).

1780 BABB, WILLIAM, Tabitha (wife); Jethro and Benjamin.

1781 BIRD, EDMUND, Wife (not named); Joel and Lydia.

1782 BELVIN, ROBERT, Priscilla (wife); John, James, Abraham, Nancy and Susanna.

1782 BIRD, JOAB, Jane (wife); Benjamin, William, Colby and Drury.

1788 BEANFIELD, JOHN, Elizabeth (wife); Elijah, Wyatt, William, Jesse, Elizabeth, John and Susanna.

1792 BUTLER, JAMES, Judith (wife).

1784 BOHANNON, ROBERT, Celia (wife); William, Edmund, Kinchin and Gideon.

1802 BARKER, WILLIAM, William, Lewis, Elijah, Bartlett, Cillent, Elizabeth and Polly.

1803 BUNCH, THOMPSON, Willis.

1803 BROWN, THOMAS, Wife (not named); John, Thomas, James and Hinson.

1800 BAUCOM, JOHN, Rachel (wife); John, Cader, Lewis, Britain, ~~Reuce~~, Asa and Joseph (sons); Jemima Branch (daughter); Rachel Scott (daughter). many Beddingfield

1775 BEDDINGFIELD, WILLIAM, Thomas, Robert, Charles, Solomon and Lewis (sons).

1794 BEASLY, JOHN, Sarah (wife); Fred, William
and James (sons); Rebecca Jenkins (daughter); Silvia Jones (daughter); Esther Lewis (daughter).

1794 BRASWELL, VALENTINE, Patience (wife).

1795 BROWN, WILLIAM, Mary (wife); Benjamin, James and John (sons); Penny (daughter); Anna Nichols, Betty Holderfield and Polly Hill (daughters).

1790 BRASFIELD, ELIJAH, Rebekah (wife).

1795 BENTON, JOHN, Robert and Mary.

1796 BRASFIELD, WILLIAM, Sukey (wife); Cynthia, Middy and Sukey.

1798 BUTLER, JAMES, Elizabeth (wife).

1800 BROWN, JOSIAH, Esther (wife); Stephen, Pearson, Rachel, Charlotte, Betsy, Pheraba and Winnie.

1800 BAUCOM, JOHN, John, Lewis and Cader.

1804 BRADLEY, GEORGE, Sarah (daughter).

C.

1791 COLLINS, ANDREW, Martha (wife); Lewis, Riddick and Ulrich (sons); Charlotte Stephens (daughter).

1790 COLE, HENRY, MaryAnn (wife); George, Martin, Henry, Shadrack, Mary Ann and Thursday.

1785 COLLINS, DENNIS, Margaret (wife).

1786 CURTIS, MICHAEL, Dorcas (wife); John.

1794 COOK, ARTHUR, Martha (wife); Martha (daughter); Mary Utley (daughter); Winnie Darnold (daughter); Celia Gordon (daughter); Burwell and Reddin Sims (grandsons).

1772 CHEVES, THOMAS, Mary (wife); John, Thomas, Sarah and William (children); Elizabeth Pulliam and Tabitha Mobley (daughters); Susanna Lee and Mary Ledbetter (daughters).

1784 CANNON, JOHN, Sarah (wife).

D.

1783 DEMPSTER, JOHN, Prudence (wife); Clement, Lewis, Winnie and Betsy.

1787 DAWSON, ISAAC, William, Mary, Nancy and Agnes.

1790 DAVIS, JOSEPH, Wife (not named); Edward C. John S., Jesse, Charity, Polly, Sally, Obedience and Jeffrey (children); Betty Hall (daughter).

1790 DAVIS, HUMPHREY, William and Rebecca; Ann Pittard (daughter); Frances Landis (daughter).

1791 DANIEL, WOODSON, Nancy (wife); James, John, David, Franky, Polly and William.

1793 DOCKERY, WILLIAM, Elizabeth (wife); Benjamin, Polly, Hastings, Hiram, William, Ceial, Balaam and Elizabeth.

1794 DENNIS, WILLIAM, Dredy (wife); Henrietta, Jeremiah, Dorothy, Anna, John, William and James.

1795 DAWSON, WILLIAM, Ghiskey (wife); William, Mary, Nancy, Agnes, Frances, and Sarah.

1795 DAWSON, WILLIAM, Martha (wife); Sarah McLeroy (daughter).

1799 DUNN, DRURY, Polly, Aaron, William, Ruth, Lucy, Drury, David and Nathaniel; Sally Rhodes and Nancy Love (daughters).

1800 DEEMS NATHANIEL, His children (not named).

1801 DUDLEY, THOMAS, Molly Dudley (sister).

E.

1784 EARP, EDWARD, Susanna (wife); William, Cullen, and Cary Ballinger (stepchildren).

1800 EZELL, JOHN, Asenath (wife); Lucy, Hartwell, Fred, John and Polly (children).

F.

1775 FLYNT, DAVID, Taply, Sanford, Molly, Ann and Elizabeth.

1781 FOWLER, HENRY, Nancy (wife); Martha, Godfry, Sally, William, Burwell. Joseph; Susannah Jacus; Mary Spann and Wilnoth Hopkins, (daughters).

1794 FILGO, DAVID, William, (son); Moses Todd and James Latin (friends).

1794 FOWLER, JOSEPH, Godfry, David, John, and William (brothers); Nancy Vincent (sister); Elizabeth Fowler (sister).

1795 FLEMING, ROBERT, SR. Mary (wife); Robert and Betsy.

1799 FOWLER, WILLIAM, A. Mary (wife); Claiborn, William, Nancy, Lavinia and Delilah.

1802 FITTS, JOHN, Molly (wife); Needham and Molly.

1802 FERRELL, CHRISTIAN, Charity, Archer and James; Sally Allen (daughter).

1801 FREEMAN, JOHN, Martha (wife); Needham, Ramson, John, Francis, Patsy Polly and Cynthia; Clara Cooper and Irany Moore (daughters).

G.

1786 GREEN, WILLIAM, Patience (wife); Needham, Penny, Polly and Gilley.

1788 GILL, DAVID, Isaac, David, John, Jesse and Elizabeth; Susanna Jones (daughter).

1793 GODWIN, JOHN, Penelope (wife); Josiah, (son); Isham (father); and Rachel (mother).

1801 GRADY, ROBERT, Sarah (wife); James, Elizabeth, John, Dennis, Allen, Ruth and Mark.

1803 GILLAM, HARRIS, Mary (wife); Jordan, Herbert, Joshua, William and Amy (children); Susanna Cole, Sarah Ross, Patsy Self, Mary Cooper, Abigail McGehee and Elizabeth Pierce (daughters).

H.

1775 HARDY, BENJAMIN, Mary (wife); William Alston (son-in-law).

1777 HIGH, JOHN, Ruth (wife); John, Michael, Robert, Alsabrook, Sally, Samuel and Mark; Mary Jackson (daughter).

1780 HARRIS, DANIEL, Sarah (wife); Richmond, Jesse, Siree, Giles, Ritta, Oney, Mary and Lucy.

1780 HALL, JOHN, Rebecca (wife); Nathan.

1782 HILL, SION, Sarah (wife); Shadrack, Green, Green, William and Thomas.

1783 HOOD, THOMAS, Mary (wife); Benjamin, Thomas, David, Mary, Dilley and Jesse.

1784 HINTON, JOHN, SR, Grizzel (wife); Kimbrough, David and James; Sarah Bryan, Mary Lane, Alice Jones and Elizabeth Jones (daughters).

1784 HORTON, DAVID, SR. Anne (wife); David, Constant, Sally, Charles, Samuel, Nathan, Wiiliam, Amelia and Matthias; Grace Arendell (daughter).

1786 HUNTER, Jesse, Ann (wife); Elisha and Ruth.

1787 HENDRICK, WILLIAM, SR. Elizabeth (wife); William and Carter.

1789 HAMILTON, WILLIAM, William, Hobbs, James and John; Keziah and Rachel Dorman; Andrew and Elizabeth Stewart.

1789 HUTCHINGS, JOHN, SR., John, Leah; Sarah Duskin (daughter); Anna Atkins (daughter).

1789 HIGH, AMELIA, Abigail (mother); Fanny and Abigail (sisters).

1792 HENDON, JAMES, Hannah (wife); Elijah and Isham; Elizabeth Olive and Sarah Nett (daughters).

1790 HILL, ISAAC, Amy (wife); Jacob, James, Jesse, Isaac and Olive.

1792 HOCUTT, EDWARD, William and Benjamin.

1793 HILL, MARY, John and Nathanial.

1794 HARRIS, SAMUEL, Wife (not named); Thomas, John, Samuel, Tempe, Patsy, Betty and Molly.

1794 HARRIS, JAMES, Nancy (wife); James, William, Tabitha, Nancy, Lucy and Sally.

1795 HILL, NATHANIEL, Wife (not named); Micajah and Peterson.

1790 HOLIFIELD, RALPH, Jemima (wife); Sion H. (grandson).

1798 HOLLAND, JAMES, Sarah (wife); Benjamin, James, Jr., Sampson and Thomas; Nancy Rowland, Mary Lashley, Milly Hood and Sarah Thomas (daughters).

1798 HEAD, ALEX, S. Henry (son).

1798 HUNTER, THEOPHILUS, Jane (wife); Osborn, Theophilus, Henry, Irene and Edith (children); Patsy Lane and Tempe Lane; (granddaughters).

1797 HAYES, DEMPSEY, John Streeter (friend).

1800 HOLDING, SAMUEL, Arthur, Fred and Samuel Jr.; John Streeter (friend).

1789 HOBBS, WILLIAM, Mary (wife); William, James, John, Sarah, Unity, Polly, Betsy, Winnie and Rebecca.

1800 HOLDING, SAMUEL, Martha (wife); Arthur, John, Fred and Samuel.

1801 HAMBLETON, KEZIAH, Louis, William and Asa.

1802 HHTCHINS, JOHN, Martha (wife); Moses and
Isaac; Elizabeth Sugg and Mary Pool (daughters).

1803 HOLLINGSWORTH, THOMAS, Betsy (wife);
Henry, Joel and William; Frances Miller
(daughter).

1803 HENDON, ISHAM, Keziah (wife); James, Isham, William, Thomas and Robinson; Mary
Duskin (daughter); Kerenhappuch Clift
(daughter); Ann Olive (daughter); Ruth
Moore (daughter).

1804 HEFFIN, CHARLES, Mary (wife); Eliase
(daughter).

1804 HEAD, HENRY, Mary (wife); Benjamin and
William.

I.

1794 IVEY, HENRY, Ann (wife); Elizabeth, Nathan,
Susanna, Henry, Mary, Isabella and Boice.

J.

1777 JONES, JAMES, Charity (wife); Thomas,
James, Willis, Mary, Priscilla and Rachel.

1779 JONES, THOMAS, Frances (wife); Thomas,
Willis and Fred.

1779 JONES, WILLIS, Fred and Willis.

1785 JORDAN, JAMES, SR. Elizabeth (wife); Liles,
Reuben, William, Amos, Elias, Elizabeth and
James; Mary Wilder (daughter); Celia
Lewis (daughter); Edie Eddins (daughter).

1787 JONES, ABRIDGETON, Mary (wife); William,
Willis and Jemima; Penny Hardy (daughter).

1796 JORDAN, JAMES, Barbara (wife); His sons
(not named); Polly, Betsy and Cynthia.

1796 JORDAN, AMOS, Sarah (wife); children (not
named).

1790 JONES, WILLIAM, SR. Martha (wife); James,
William, Patsy, Sally, James and Polly; Betsy
Sturdivant, Mourning Franks and Edith
King (daughters).

1797 JENKINS, SAMUEL, Amy (wife); Clarinda,
Irene, Lottie, Jerusha; other children (not
named).

1799 JORDAN, JOHN, John.

1800 JONES, WILLIAM, Anderson, Etheldred and
Young.

1799 JORDAN, JOHN, Sarah (wife); John Jordan
(grandson).

1800 JONES, WILLIAM, Mary (wife); Young, Sy-
thia, Etheldred and Anderson; Winifred,
Matthews (daughter).

K.

1781 KIMBROUGH, NATHANIEL, Mary (wife);
James, John, Gilly, Penny and Charity; Ann
Moore (daughter).

1793 KING, HENRY, Sarah (wife); Betsy, Patsy,
Polly, Rachel and John.

1795 KING, JOHN, Sally (wife); Joel, John W.,
Benjamin, Thomas, William F., and Betsy.

1799   KING, JAMES, Sarah (wife); John, Warren, James, Clara, Betty, Robert and Sukey.

1801   KING, JOHN, Leah Thorne (friend).

L.

1794   LEE, WILLIAM, His children (not named).

1796   LEE, STEPHEN, Betty (wife); Nancy, James, Charity, Rebecca and Sally.

1797   LOWRY, ARTHUR, Ava (wife); Green, Hardy, Anne, Grizzel, Dolly and Elizabeth.

1795   LANE, JOEL, Mary (wife); Henry, James, William, John, Thomas. Joel H., Mary and Martha.

1797   LYNN, JAMES, John, James, Ralph and Joseph; Hannah, Marshal (daughter); Lucy Hartsfield (daughter); Rachel Wilder (daughter); Martha Freeman (daughter).

1798   LANE, JOSEPH, John, Hugh; Sarah McCullers (daughter); Mary Ball (daughter); Penelope Powers (daughter); Tabitha O'Kelly (daughter); Henry A. McCullers (grandson).

1801   LAWRENCE, JOSEPH, Martha (wife); William,. John, Jesse and Mary.

1804   LASSITER, LUKE, Temperance (wife); Polly, Chloe, Henry, Luke, Harrod, Tempe and Matilda.

M.

1778   MOBLY, EDWARD, Mary (wife); Edward, Ezekiel, William, Jeremiah and John; James (grandson)

1777   MAYS, JOHN, Anne (wife); William, John, James and Mary.

1778   MASTEN, JAMES, John Abernathy (friend).

1780   MARK, ELIZABETH, Willis, Silas, Elizabeth and Esther.

1781   MOORE, WILLIAM, Sarah (wife); Lewis, William, John, Rebecca, Susanna, Edward, Mark, Nancy, Patsy and Elizabeth.

1787   MAJOR, WILLIAM, John and Betsy; Hannah, Brassfield.

1787   MANN, JOHN, Elizabeth (wife); Arnold. Judy, Betty, Avy, Anne, Fanny, John, Zaccheus, David, Peter, Joseph, Agnes and Nancy.

1792   MOBLY, MORDICAI, Dorcas (wife); Jesse, Pheraba, Sukey, Edith, Ollep and Betsy; Mary Lawrence, Amelia Shaw, Mavil Shaw and Lydia Jophin.

1794   MOSES, JAMES, Mary, Sarah and James; Mary Irvin and Lucy Smith (daughters).

1794   McBRIDE, JOHN, Dawson, William, Sr. (a friend).

1795   MARTIN, JOHN, Archibald Stokes (a friend).

1795   MITCHELL, GABRIEL, Mary (wife); James (son); Lucy Jones (daughter).

1797   MATTHEWS, REDMOND, Lettice (mother).

1785   McALLISTER, GARLAND, Sally (wife); John, William and Alex (brothers).

1795   MORGAN, JOHN, Shade (brother); Nancy and Lucy (sisters).

1801   MANN, RICHARD, Lucy (wife); children (not named).

1802 MOORE, JOHN, Rachel (wife); Meredith, Lo-
verel, Lewis, John, Henry and Charlotte.
1803 MASSY, RICHARD, Patsy (wife); Dennis, Samuel, Richard, Crissy and Dempsey.
1800 MOORE, JOHN, John and Lewis.

N.

1785 NUTT, ROBERT, John and William.
1795 NICHOLS, WILLIAM, Sarah (wife); John,
Travis, Justice, Elizabeth, James, Patty and
Thomas; Lucy Utley (daughter).
1796 NALLE, RICHARD, Martin (son); Polly Hogan
and Winifred Youngblood (daughters).
1800 NOOE, THOMAS, Mary (wife); Thomas, Bennett and Mary.
1800 NEWBY, THOMAS, Elizabeth (wife); Mary,
Ann and John.
1800 NICHOLS, SARAH, Patsy Ransom and Molly
Bass (daughters).

O.

1780 ORR, ROBERT, Elizabeth (wife); Robert, Daniel, John, Bryan, Samuel, Matthew, Agnes,
and Christopher; Agnes Winfree.
1779 ORR, JOHN, Rebecca (wife); Timothy and
Jesse (sons); Christopher (brother).

P.

1773 POOL, GEORGE, Mary (wife); Lewis, William,
Elizabeth, Hardy and Ede; Hester Stephens
(daughter).
1790 PEEBLES, JOHN, SR., Agnes (wife); John Jr.
and Elisha.
1788 PENDRY, AARON, B., Clement, Elam and
David.
1794 PENDERGRASS, JOHN, Hannah (wife); Moses,
Ann and Jesse.
1794 PRIVITT, WILLIAM, Maria (wife); Jacob, Jordan, Nathan and Haynes.
1795 PRIVITT, JACOB, Sally (wife); Willis, Needham, James, Polly and John.
1795 PARKS, JOHN, Allen (son).
1796 PRIVITT, MARY, John, Willie, Miles, James,
Jarot, John M., Nathan, Gordon and Harris.
1797 PROCTOR, JOHN, Sally (wife); Jenny and
Betsy.
1795 PEEBLES, ELISHA, Temperance (wife); William and other children (not named).
1797 PROCTOR, THOMAS, SR, John, Thomas Jr. Susannah, Sarah and Hannah; Rebecca Moody
(daughter).
1797 PAIN, JOHN, Wife (not named).
1799 POWELL, MOSES, Wife (not named); Ailey,
liam.
1802 PEARSON, SAMUEL, Mary (wife); Simon, Asa,
Preston, Esther, Charity, Patience, Rachel,
Pheraba and Peace.
1803 PENNY, JAMES, Charles, Edward and William
(brothers).

1799 POWELL, MOSES, Wife (not named); Aily, Nancy, Robert, Henry, Moses, William, Martha and Jesse; Prudence Smith, (daughter); Mary Patton (daughter); Susan Matthews (daughter); Sally Tedder and Lucy Gilbert.

1801 PARK, SAMUEL, Sally (wife); Mary and Samuel.

R.

1772 ROGERS, JOB, Mary (wife); Thomas and Peleg; Job Rogers (grandson).

1779 ROGERS, JOHN, James, Josiah, Sarah, John, Priscilla, Rebecca and Penelope; Mary Hillman (daughter).

1783 RAND, JOHN, Elizabeth (wife); Mary Pitt, (sister); Walter and William (brothers).

1776 RUNALDS, SHERARD, Ann (wife); John and Amos; Mary Williams, Nancy Hall, Amy Bledsoe, Rebecca Bledsoe and Susanna Humphries (daughters).

1784 RICH, JEREMIAH, Mary (wife); Charles, John, Jacob and William; Susanna Bridges and Judy Dodd (daughters).

1784 RENCH, JOHN, Rebecca (wife); Charity and Patience.

1788 REED, AARON, Jemima (wife); Clement, Elam, David, Achsa, Rebecca and Sarah; Lewis Barker and Wife Mary.

1788 REAVIS, ISAAC, Hannah (wife); William and John H.

1794 RHODES, RANDOLPH, Elizabeth (wife); Jesse.

1794 RHODES, JOHN, Randolph, Elijah, John Jr., Joseph, Isaac and Nancy.

1803 ROGERS, WILLIE, Celia (mother); Allen, Berry, Willis. Mary, Talitha, Rebecca and Sarah (children).

1802 ROGERS, JOHN, Anne (daughter); Martha T. McCallum (daughter).

1800 ROGERS, SION. Polly (wife); and children (not named)

1797 ROGERS, MICHAEL, Celia (wife); Tabitha, Rebecca, Allen, Bennett, Alice, Willis, Mary and Sarah.

1799 RHODES, JOHN, Frances (wife); Lucy, Dicey, Randolph, Elijah, Jane, Elizabeth, Patsy, Joseph, Isaac and John.

1803 ROBERTON, JOHN, Anne (wife); Lot, Arthur, John, Anne, and Fathey; Winifred Peebles.

S.

1777 SLEMMON, GEORGE, James, Margaret and Mary.

1771 SIMMONS, WILLIS, Dinah Simmons (mother); Elizabeth Simmons (sister); William, James, Adam and Solomon (brothers).

1774 SPEIGHT, WILLIAM, Abigail (wife); William, Winifred and Patience; Sarah Hunter, Lydia Lane, Charity Green, Betty Turner and Mary Mintz (daughters).

1777 SIMMONS, GEORGE, James, Margaret and Mary (brother and sisters).

1783 SPEIGHT, ABIGAIL, William; Mary Myatt, Lydia Lane, Charity Green, Patience Green, Mary Mintz, Sarah Hunter, and Lydia Lane. (daughters); Reuben Hunter (grandson.)

1785 STRICKLAND, LOT, Christiana (mother); Matthew and Brazil (brothers).

1790 SIMMONS, DIANA, Solomon and Mary.

1791 SIMMONS, ISHAM, SR. Mary (wife); Isham Jr. (son); Alethea Upchurch (grand daughter).

1792 STRAIT, DAVID, Priscilla (wife); William, Israel, Lois, David, Wait, Nancy, Dorcas, Sarah and Celia; Amy Riggan (daughter).

1794 SANDY, GERARD, Letitia (wife); Mary, Henry, Francis and Vinson.

1795 STURDIVANT, HOLLEMAN, John, William, Lucy and Franky; Amy Hobbs (daughter).

1795 STRICKLAND, ELISHA, Isaac, Kinchion, Jacob, Priscilla, Charity, Polly and Sally.

1797 STEVENS, MARY, Rebecca Bartlett (daughter).

1798 SPANE, FRED, Mary (wife); Thomas; Polly Robinson, Betsy Robinson and Amelia Terrell (daughters).

1798 SANDERS, BRITAIN, Edith (wife); Alsey, Britain, Theophilus, John and Elizabeth; John (brother).

1804 SCARBOUGH, SAMUEL, Prudence (wife); Meade, Green and Cordy (sons); Lucy Waddell (daughter).

1804 SCARBOUGH, SAMUEL, Prudence (wife); Meade, Green and Cordy (sons; Lucy Waddell (daughter).

T.

1775 TUCKER, EDWARD, Mary (wife); Elizabeth (daughter).

1783 TURNER, SIMON, Anne (wife); John, Simon, David, William, Jonathan, Polly, Anne, Matilda, Edith and Betsy.

1782 TATE, JAMES, Nancy (wife); William S., Mary and Turner; Judith Ferrell and Alse Harrell (daughters).

1782 TATE, JAMES, Samuel and William (brothers).

1792 TUCKER, DANIEL, Joseph, Nancy, Mason, William, Susie, Sally, Daniel, Pascal and Pleasant; Elizabeth Guerrant, Martha Ellington, Lucy Maxcy, Mary Spain and Rebecca Russell (daughters).

1785 THOMAS, JOHN, G. Frances (wife); Giles, Allen, Charles and Betsy, Christian Jones, Charlotte, Patience Rocheslle (daughter). Gaskey Runnels (daughter).

1799 TEMPLE, HENRY, Henry, Martha and Jesse; Lucy Gilbert (daughter).

1801 THOMPSON, SAMUEL, Wife (not named); Nathaniel, Samuel, Ann and John.

1801 THOMPSON, SWAN, Susannah (wife); Solomon, William, James, Mark, Jacob, Drury, Michael and Delilah; Penny Moore and Gilley Grady (daughters).

U.

1794 UTLEY, WILLIAM, Elizabeth (wife); Hezekiah, John, William Jr. Jacob, Isham, David and Littleton; Lucy Sanders and Cynthia Myatt (daughters).

1796 UTLEY, JACOB, Phoebe (wife); William, Littlejohn, Merritt, Jacob, Jr., Gabriel, Phoebe, Elizabeth and Cynthia.

W.

1799 WOODWARD, JOHN, Penelope (wife); Tabitha. Thomas, John, Milly and Sarah.

1785 WOODWARD, CHRISTOPHER, Jordan, Corbell, Pleasant, Richard, James and Elizabeth.

1787 WARD, JOHN, Lydia (wife); Jesse, William, John, Nuett, Fanny, Mary, Letitia and Delilah.

1797 WRIGHT, JOSEPH, Nathan, Claiborne, Jeremiah, Temple and Sion; Patty Perry (daughter).

1797 WARD, WILLIAM, Prudence (wife); William Jr., Thomas, Nathan, Martha, Tabitha, Elizabeth, Mary and Sarah.

1797 WILLIAMS, MARY, Lewis Jones and America Jones.

1783 WIGGINS, DANIEL, Elizabeth (wife); Hannah Cullom, Mary Green, Jennie Hicks and Elizabeth Brewer (daughters).

1803 WATTS, SPENCER, Rachel (wife); John, Samuel, Uel, William and Thomas; Nancy Kirkham, Molly McCoy, Katie Leigh and Rachel Thomas.

1804 WOOD, MOSES, Mary (wife); George, Moses, Mary, Delilah, Patty and James; Pamela Rogers (daughter).

Y.

1785 YARBOROUGH, JOHN, Minerva (wife); John, Mirady, Frankey, Agga, (Agatha); Charles and Jonah.

WARREN—WILLS

A.

1771 ALFORD, JULIUS, John, Isaac, Goodrich, Jacob, Patty, Job, Sarah, Lucy.
1784 ALSTON, PHILIP, Philip G., Samuel.
1785 ALSTON, SOLOMON, James, William; Hunter, Solomon.
1789 AYCOCK, RICHARD, Abner.
1795 ALSTON, WILLIAM, Martha, Medicus, Philip W., Whitmell, Thomas, Samuel.

B.

1771 BUSH, JOHN, Jeremiah, Ann, John.
1775 BALFOUR, JOHN, Sons of James Littlepage; Clark, James Balfour.
1777 BAKER, WILLIAM, James.
1777 BLEDSOE, GEORGE, Jane.
1778 BIRD, JOHN, Jesse, William.
1779 BROWN, WILLIAM J., William B. Sr.
1780 BECKHAM, JOHN, Naomi.
1782 BREWER, JOSEPH, Anne.
1780 BALTHROP, JAMES, John.
1782 BROWN, JOHN, Abigail, John, Jeremiah.
1782 BREWER, ANN, James; Massingale, James Jr.
1782 BELL, THOMAS, wife; William, Munford.
1788 BASKET, JAMES, wife; John, James, Daniel, Peggy.
1791 BABBITT, JOHN, Anne, William, Randall, Stephen.
1792 BEASLEY, JOHN P., Elizabeth; children (not named).
1793 BENNETT, REUBEN, Reuben, Charles, William, Mary.
1795 BURCHETT, JOSEPH, Martha, Elizabeth, Sarah, Ezekiel, Daniel.
1796 BASKET, ELIZABETH, Marcus, William and Thomas.
1797 BARROW, DANIEL, Arabella, Margaret, Mary, Sarah.
1798 BULLOCK, LEN H., Susanna, Richard, Nancy.

C.

1769 CHRISTMAS, THOMAS V., John; Higgason, Katie.
1774 CLANTON, WM., Edward, William.
1774 CARROLL, MILLBROUGH, Charles.
1777 COOPER, BENJAMIN, Martin, Ann.
1777 CHRISTMAS, JOHN JR., Ann, Henry, Mary, Martha.
1777 COLEMAN, DANIEL, Unity, Jacob, Davis, John, Samuel, Eden.
1783 COLDCLOUGH, WILLIAM, Mary, John, Alex, Rue, Frances, Beheathland, Rucy.
1784 CLANTON, EDWARD, Edward Jr.
1782 CHRISTMAS, JOHN, Thomas, Sarah, Rebecca, Middleton.
1785 CHRISTMAS, DREWRY, Jesse, William.
1789 CLANTON, WM., Frances, Dudley, George, Abraham.
1789 CHRISTMAS, HENRY, Mary, Patsy.
1795 POWELL, EDMOND, Ruth.

1794 CAWTHORN, JOHN, Sarah, Polly, John, Thomas.
1794 COOK, THOMAS, Jones, Robert.
1795 CRUTCHFIELD, SAMUEL, Sarah.
1797 CHEATHAM, JAMES, wife; Wyatt, James, Kinchin, Sylvia.

D.

1772 DAWSON, JOSHUA, Bennett, Brittain.
1779 DUKE, JOSEPH, Isham, Sherrod, Hardy, Ransom, Mary.
1787 DUKE, JOHN, Ruth, Benjamin.
1789 DUKE, MARY, Isham, Ransom, Eppy.
1790 DENT, MARY, Susan, Tabitha.
1790 DENT, REBECCA, Susanna, Tabitha.
1793 DURHAM, WM., children (not named).
1794 DINKINS, DIONYSIUS, Susanna, John.
1794 DANIEL, WILLIAM, Joseph, John.

E.

1784 ELLIS, EDMOND, William.
1786 EGERTON, JAMES, Martha, John, G. T., Wilmot, Elizabeth, Ashe, Mary, James.
1788 EMMERSON, JOHN, Catherine, William, James, Betsy, John, Henry, Dicey, Susanna.
1796 ELLIS, BENJAMIN, James, Polly, Benjamin, Edward, Zachariah, Nancy, Stephen.

F.

1768 FOSTER, MARY, Christopher, John.
1775 FOSTER, CHRISTOPHER, John T.
1776 FOOTE, HENRY, William, Henry, Margaret.
1780 FAIN, JOEL, Nancy, John, Joel, William, Daniel, Tyree.
1782 FAIN, WILLOUGHBY, William.
1783 FUSSELL, AARON, William.
1793 FLEMING, JOHN, wife; William, John, Benjamin, Leonard, Daniel, James, Thomas.
1798 FELTS, NATHANIEL, Mary, James, Drury.
1799 FELTS, RANDOLPH, Elizabeth, Drury, Henry, Thomas.

G.

1774 GRAY, THOMAS, Sarah, George.
1795 GREEN, JOSEPH, Josiah, William.
1798 GUFFEY, EPHRAIM, wife; Lucy, Sukey.
1794 GIBBS, WILLIAM, Burt, William.
1799 GREEN, WILLIAM, Henrietta, Solomon, William, John C.

H.

1768 HORTON, JOSEPH, Samuel.
1770 HARRIS, THOMAS, Sarah, West, Elizabeth.
1771 HOWARD, JOHN, Julius, Thomas, John.
1774 HILL, WILLIAM SR., Robert, Amos, Elizabeth.
1785 HARRIS, JOSEPH, Henry, Alsey.
1787 HICKS, JAMES, Susanna.
1786 HOUSE, THOMAS, Daniel, Dudley, Jordan, Thomas.
1786 HAWKINS, JOSEPH, John, Philemon, Benjamin.
1786 HELTON, JOSEPH, Sukey, Dudley, Dyer.
1786 HOLLEMAN, EDWARD, William, Blake.

1788 HAZELWOOD, GEORGE, Mary, David, Joshua,
Rebecca.
1790 HARRIS, JOEL, Katie, David, Jones.
1790 HARRIS, JOHN, Frances, Orren, William,
Moses.
1793 HAYNES, HERBERT, Polly, Elizabeth.
1794 HARRIS, MABEL, Arthur, Edwin, Susanna,
Joel, Michael, Herbert.
1795 HORTON, THOMAS, Thomas, John, Burwell,
Mary, Hardy.
1797 HARRIS, JOSEPH, Jane, Thomas, Robert, Jenny, Lucretia, Tabitha.
1797 HAZELWOOD, RANDAL, Anne.

I.

1772 INGRAM, JOSHUA, Joseph, John, George.

J.

1777 JONES, BENJAMIN, Joanna, William, Samuel.
1780 JENKINS, PATIENCE, Thomas.
1781 JOHNSTON, SARAH, Thornton, Frances.
1794 JAMES, CHARLES, George, Bartliff, Edmund,
Nancy.
1794 JONES, RICHARD, Wright, John.
1794 JONES, JOHN, Henry.
1799 JONES, EDWARD, Thomas, Priscilla, Sarah,
William G.

K.

1777 KENDRICK, WILLIAM, Jones, Ishram.
1779 KIMBALL, PETER, Buckner.
1794 KEARNEY, PHILIP, Thomas, Henry G., William K., Elizabeth, Sarah P., Polly D.
1794 KEARNEY, EDMUND, Sarah, James.
1794 KIMBALL, BENJAMIN, David, James, William,
Ransom.
1796 KEEL, SAMUEL, Betsy, Delia, Nathaniel.
1796 KENDRICK, SARAH, Thornton, Ben.
1797 KEARNEY, THOMAS, Gaston, Philip, Mary, Kinchin, Elizabeth.

L.

1771 LAWTER, HENRY, John, Mary, William, Benjamin.
1778 LONG, DREWRY, Sally, Betsy.
1779 LYNCH, JOHN, Daniel.
1782 LANKFORD, GEORGE, John, George, Jacob,
Kirby.
1792 LANCASTER, LAWRENCE, Lawrence, Patty,
Moses.
1794 LINDSAY, JOSEPH, Caleb, Rachel, Laban.
1796 LONG, JOHN, Lucinda.

M.

1774 MALONE, JOHN, Frederick, Wood.
1774 MALONE, WOOD, William T., Barsheba.
1774 MEADOWS, JOHN, Hannah.
1775 MARTIN, GIBSON, Ann, Thomas.
1777 MYRICK, FRANCIS, Rebecca.
1777 MADDREY, MOSES, William.

1777 MERRIAN, BARTHOLOMEW, Philip, Elizabeth, Milly.
1784 MILLER, THOMAS, Mary, Thomas.
1785 MABRY, FRANCIS, John.
1785 MARTIN, JAMES, Sarah.
1785 MURPHY, WILLIAM, George, Elizabeth, Anne, William, John.
1786 MERRIT, THOMAS, Elender, John, Reuben.
1789 MILAM, ADAM, Lewis, John, Roling, Drury, James.
1790 MOORE, PETER, Martha C.
1791 McLEMORE, ATKINS, Abraham, Young, Robert, Atkins, Sarah.
1791 MABRY, JOSHUA, Lucretia, H. P.
1791 MERRITT, JOSEPH, Major, Joseph, Matthew, Hotenberg, Lenty, Benjamin.
1792 MANNING, SAMUEL, Mary, John, Samuel.
1792 MASSEY, HEZEKIAH, Lucy, Delilah, Griffin, John.
1792 MILLER, THOMAS, Polly, William, Thomas, John.
1794 MOORE, MARK, John, Mary, Owen, David.
1795 MOSELEY, JOHN, Jesse.
1795 MYRICK, WILLIAM, George, Owen, Sarah, Mary, Francis, Betsy, Richard.
1795 MILLER, JAMES, Thomas E.
1795 MILLER, THOMAS, Barrow, Isabella.

N.

1774 NICHOLS, WILLIAM, George.
1790 NICHOLSON, NATHANIEL, Alanson, Urban. Jackey, Mary.
1791 NEWMAN, THOMAS, Thomas, Avery, Daniel, Katy .
1794 NOLES, WILLIAM, Sucky, Butler, Corbin.
1796 NEWELL, JOHN SR., Lucy, William, John, Edward, David H.

P.

1771 PIERSON, WILLIAM, Benjamin, William, Patty, Thomas.
1769 PERDUE, JOHN, John, Joel, Morris, Richard, Sarah.
1772 PERSON, JOSEPH, Henry, Willard, Samuel, Harrison, Peterson, Nancy.
1774 PASCHALL, WILLIAM, Tabitha, Thomas, Richard, Diana, Rachel, Ruth.
1775 PEEBLES, NATHANIEL, Thomas, Nathan.
1776 PIERCY, WILLIAM SR., wife; William, Joshua.
1777 PEGRAM, DANIEL, Daniel, Jr., George, Edward, Gideon, Sally, Patty.
1778 PERSON, WILLIAM, Martha, William, Thomas, Benjamin.
1781 PARK, WILLIAM, Bettie (wife), Bettie, Robert, Ann.
1782 PATTISHALL, JOSHUA, Richard C.
1791 POWERS, WILLIAM, John.
1791 POWELL, WILLIAM, Ruth, Thomas, James, Benjamin, Edmund, Honorias.
1792 PASCHALL, JAMES, Samuel.
1792 PERRY, JOSHUA, Lizzie, Joshua, Priscilla, Rebecca.

1795 PETWAY, JOHN, James, Ann, Elizabeth, John
M., Sarah, Rebecca, Mary, Martha, Rhoda.
Mark H.

R.

1769 RACKLEY, JOHN, wife; Hunt, Henry.
1770 RIGGAN, WILLIAM P., Richard, Charles, Powell,
John, James.
1778 REEVES, WILLIAM, Elender, Frederick, Henry.
1778 ROSE, GEORGE, James, Benjamin, George,
William, Anne.
1780 ROBINS, THOMAS, Sarah, William.
1791 ROBINSON, CHRISTOPHER, John, Thomas,
Isham, Winifred.
1791 RUSSELL, ANN, Richard, John, Burnall, Armistead.
1796 RAY, ANN, Waller, Robert; Rodwell, Nancy;
Prior, Mary.

S.

1773 SAINTSING, JAMES, Peter, James, Charles,
Margaret, Lucretia, Susanna, Mildred.
1773 SIMMONS, JOHN, Susanna; Lee, Mary.
1778 SEAWELL, BENJAMIN, Thomas, Lucy.
1784 SMITH, SARAH, Betty, Sarah; Smith, Ailee.
1785 SUMMER, JETHRO, Thomas E., McKinne H.,
Long, Nicholas Jr.; McCulloch, Benjamin.
1788 SMELLY, MARY, John; Harris, Mary; Reynolds, Ann.
1790 SIMS, SHERWOOD, Matthias, Thomas, Sherwood,
Fanny.
1792 SIMS, EDWARD, Elizabeth.
1792 SMITH, PRISCILLA, Nathan, Pattie, Martin.
1793 SLEDGE, DANIEL, Sherwood, James, Archibald,
Isham, Lucretia.
1795 SHEARIN, JOHN, Thomas, Charles.
1796 SMITH, BETTY, Fleet.

T

1777 TOWNS, DAVID, Richard, Priscilla.
1778 TABB, WILLIAM, Diana, Rebecca N., Mary.
1781 TODD, JOHN, John, Frances.
1788 TURNER, THOMAS, Rebecca, John, James.
1797 THORNTON, FRANCIS, Drusilla.
1799 TURNER, STEPHEN, Susana, Hendley, Tersia,
William, Stephen, Ransom.

W.

1768 WINSTON, JOHN, Mary, George, Sarah.
1771 WYATT, JOHN, Sylvester, William.
1771 WRIGHT, JOHN, Joseph, Sarah, James.
1772 WILLIAMS, ROBERT, Simon, Parmenus, Robert,
Nimrod.
1775 WHITE, RICHARD, John, Mark, Harrison, Richard, Nicholas, Elizabeth.
1776 WHEELER, THOMAS, Mildred, Benjamin, William, John, George, Thomas.
1780 WILLIFORD, NATHAN, Samuel.
1780 WRIGHT, WILLIAM, John, Uell, Tempe, Simon,
Elizabeth, Susanna, Nancy.
1783 WHATLEY, SHIRLEY, Rebecca.

1786 WILLIAMS, ROBERT, John, Ann.
1788 WARD, RICHARD, Benjamin, Richard,   Ann,
      Presley, Martha, Betsy.
1788 WARD, BENJAMIN, John L., Mary, Seth; Mor-
      ris, Mary; Jordan, Martha.
1790 WILLIAMS, NIMROD, Amy, Lewis,   Solomon,
      John.
1791 WILLIAMS, SAMUEL, Thomas, Cressy, Solo-
      mon, Joseph, Samuel, William.
1793 WILLIAMS, FRANCIS, William, Bennett, Leon-
      ard, Zachariah, Margaret,   Fanny,   Betsy,
      Nancy.
1794 WILLIAMS, SOLOMON, William, Henry, Samuel.
1796 WALKER, HARDWICK, Mary, Joe, Ben, Hard-
      ridge.
1799 WILSON, WILLIAM, Richard, Montfort; Blu-
      ford, Sarah; Ragsdale, Judah; Tolson, Eliz-
      abeth.

WAYNE—WILLS

A.

1794 January, ANDERSON, JOHN, wife; Jesse, Thomas, Miles, Nanny, Betty (children).

B.

1788 April, BALLARD, ELIAS, Elizabeth (wife); Joab, Caleb, Levi; Joanno, Rachel, Esther (children).

1785 April, BARDIN, SIMON, Isabel (wife); Simon, Ancilla, Arthur, James, Susanna (children).

1791 January, BARNES, JOHN, Christian (wife); Simon, Benjamin, Elizabeth, Christian, Zilpha, John, Barsheba (children).

1791 April, BASS, ANDREW, Alice (wife); Anna daughter).

1787 July BARDIN, JACOB, Sarah, Fulghum, Drusilla, Hooks, Elizabeth Darden (daughters).

1787 January, BOYET, THOMAS, SR., wife; Thomas, Amos (sons).

1787 January, BRADBURY, THOMAS, wife; Jacob, George, Thomas (children); Hannah Ritter, Rhoda Stanley, Mary Bell.

1790 April, BRIGGS, FREDERICK, Elizabeth Briggs (sister); Matthew Joyner (uncle).

1782 July, BUNDY, MOSES, Jane (wife), Abraham, William, Mark, Gideon, Josiah, Lydia, Miriam, Hannah (children).

1805 Aug., BUNTIN, JAMES, Lydia (wife); James, Jeremiah (sons).

1791 April, BURNS, JESSE, Zilpha (wife); Anna (daughter).

C.

1784 April, CARRAWAY, HENRY, Elizabeth (wife); Zilpha, Mary Ann, Elizabeth, Sibyl, Molly, Eve, Adam, John (children).

1795 October, CATER, GEORGE, Martha (wife); Molly Handley (daughter).

1791 January, COBB, DAVID, Bridget (wife); Mary, Stephen (children).

1761 (Dobbs county), COGDELL, GEORGE, Probated in Wayne July, 1783, Margaret (wife); Francis, Sarah, Charles, David, Richard (children).

1784 April, COGDELL, MARGARET, Richard, Francis, Charles, David, Sarah (children).

1783 April, COOK, JAMES, Martha (wife); Arthur, Stephen, Jacob, Zilpha, William, Thomas, Martha (children).

1794 July, COOR, THOMAS, Rachel (wife); Henry, Fleet, Thomas, William, Mary, Averilly (children).

1795 Oct., COALMAN, ELIAS, Honor (wife); Keziah, Theophilus, Selah (Celia), James, Stephen, Zilpha, and Patience (children).

1785 January, COX, RICHARD, Mary (wife); Micajah, Richard, Thomas, Walter, John (sons).

1795 April, COX, ROBERT, wife; Richard and Smithson Cox (brothers).

1805 Aug., CROOM, RICHARD, Nancy (wife); children (not named).

D.

1796 Oct., DAVIS, HULDAH, Richard, Joshua, John (sons); Sarah, Hall and Rachel Overman (daughters).

1788 April, DAVIS, JOSHUA, Huldah (wife); John, Joshua, Richard, Rachel (children).

1784 April, DAWSON, JOSEPH, Patience (wife); William, Joel, Thomas, Larry (children), Mary Aldridge, Sarah Waterer, Rebekah Smith, Celia Waterer (daughters).

1789 April, DEANS, DAVID, wife; James, Daniel, Bartley, George, John, Dempsey (sons).

1793 April, DICKINSON, JOEL, Mary (wife); Isaac, Matthew, Martha, Charity (children).

E.

1794 July, EDGERTON, THOMAS, Sarah (wife); Joseph, James, John, Thomas, William, Richard (children).

1799 April, EDMUNDSON, JAMES, Penelope (wife); John, Cullen, Bryant, Laney, Wright; Elizabeth Miller; Penelope Pearcey (all children).

F.

FLETCHER, JOSHUA, Sally (wife); James, Joshua, Exum, Ralph, Elizabeth (children); Mary Vick (daughter).

1791 April, FORT, WILLIAM, Benjamin (son); William Sherrard (grandson).

G.

1776 March, GRANTHAM, THOMAS, Mary (wife); Sion (son) and other children (not named).

H.

1791 January, HAMILTON, GUY, Ann (wife); John, Sarah, Darkis (Dorcas); Edith, Barnabas, Barden (children).

1793 January, HARRELL, SAMUEL, Ann (wife); Zilpha, (daughter).

1783 Oct., HAWLEY, ANN., William, Callop, Winnie, Dicey, Milbry (children).

1784 April, HERRING, ANTHONY, wife; Frederick, Solomon, Joel, Zilphia (children); Parthenia Hamm and Pheraba Grantham (daughters).

1789 July, HERRING, FREDERICK, Patty (wife); Jesse, David, Frederick, Elizabeth, Parthenia (children); Alice Stephens (daughter).

1789 July, HERRING, SOLOMON, Jane (wife); Stephen, Solomon, Sally (children).

1794 January, HINES, CHARLES, Nancy (wife); David, Rebekah, Sarah, Esther, Polly (children).

1793 October, HOOKS, ROBERT, Sally (wife); Hilary, Washington (sons).

1798 April, HORN, HENRY, Patience (wife); William, Esther, Isaac, Jeremiah, Henry, Charity, Joel, Damaris, Mourning, Phoebe, Selah (Celia), children; Josiah Horn (grandson).

1795 Dec., HOWELL, JOSHUA, John, Barbara, Edea, Rachel (children).

Admerl, Jasper, Oliff (children).

1793   January, HOWELL, NOEL, Mary (wife); Burwell (son).

1798   January, HOWELL, WILLIAM, Dorcas (wife); John, William, Thomas, Robert, Sally, Exum, Dred, Betsy (children).

J.

1791   January, JERNIGAN, DAVID, Alice (wife); Stephen, David (children); Sally and Stephen Herring (grandchildren); Polly Harrison (granddaughter).

1792   April, JERNIGAN, GEORGE, Lydia (wife); Mary, (son).

1792   Oct., JERNIGAN, GEORGE, Lydia (wife); Mary, George, Arthur, Frederick, Mills, William, Elizabeth (children).

1792   April, JERNIGAN, GEORGE, Lydia (wife); Mary George, Arthur, Frederick, Mills, William, Elizabeth (children).

1783   April, JERNIGAN, ISBELL, Alse Wiggs, Isabel, Hase, Patience Watkins, Priscilla Boyett (daughters).

1797   April, JERNIGAN, LYDIA, George, Zilpah (children); Richard Jernigan (grandson).

1788   Oct., JOHNSTON, MOSES, James, William. Moses, Aaron, Amos, Rebecca, Sarah, Edith,

1783   Oct., JONES, RICHARD, Barshebah (wife); John, Willmouth, Betty, Margaret, Robert (children).

1786   July, JONES, THEOPHILUS, Sarah (wife); James, Honour, Hardy, Willis, Arthur, Betsy, William (children); Jemimah Howell, Grace Tolar, Edith Wise, Patty Holland (daughters).

1782   Oct., JORDAN, JAMES, Elizabeth (wife); Nancy, Silvia, Polly, Elizabeth (daughters), Henry Howell (a friend).

K.

1794   July, KEITHLEY, JOHN, Elizabeth (wife); John, Jonathan, Richard (children).

1785   January, KILLETT, WILLIAM, Sarah (wife); William Fagin (grandson); Elizabeth Fagin (daughter).

L.

1795   April, LAMB, JACOB, Isaac, Reddick, David (children); Phebe, Leney, Cithey (granddaughters); Hardy Watson.

1784   Dec., LANGSTON, JACOB, George, Masey, Absalom, Martha, Lydia (children); Levi Langston (grandson).

1788   April, LEWIS, GRIFFIN, Priscilla Watson (granddaughter), Hopkins Howell (son-in-law).

M.

1789   January, McDANIEL, JAMES, Alice (wife); James, John, Sukey (children).

1793   April, McKINNIE, Barnaby (son); Amy Giles (daughter)

1795 April, MARTIN, AARON, Richard (son), and six younger children (not named).

1793 January, MINSHEW, JOHN, Susanna (wife); Jacob, John, Elizabeth, Absalah (children).

1795 April, MORING, WILLIAM, Celey [Celia] (wife); William, Henry, Nancy, Sally, Betsy (children).

1791 April, MUSGRAVE, CALEB, Elizabeth (wife); Joel, John, Caleb, Richard, Christiana, Elizabeth, Sarah (children).

1794 January, MUSTGRAVE, THOMAS, Christian (wife); Robert, Joshua, Esdras (children).

1789 Oct., PAGE, JACOB, wife; Mary (daughter).

P.

1795 PARKER, JOHN, Isaac, Pheraba, Mary, Martha, Delilah (children), Elizabeth Yelverton (daughter).

1793 January, PACKER, MICAJAH, Keziah (wife); Marmaduke, Dorcas, Levi, John B., Nancy (children).

1791 April, PARKER, SAMUEL, James and Zilpha (children); Mary Lawhorn (daughter).

1787 Oct., PEARSON, PETER, Ann (wife); Benoni, Nathan, Joseph, Jesse, Sarah, Mary, Penina (children).

1789 April, PIPKIN, JOSEPH, Susanna (wife); Elisha (son); Mildred Jernigan (daughter).

1784 May, POWELL, HENRY, Elizabeth (wife); Jacob, Henry (sons).

R.

1798 April, RAIFORD, WILLIAM, wife; John, Jethro, William, Bud, Needham, Isaac.

1793 April, REAVES, WILLIAM, Elizabeth (wife); Stephen, Lovett, Lee, Adam, John, William, Peggy (children).

1784 April, REVELL, JOSEPH JOHN, Elizabeth (wife); Edmond, Manoah, Elizabeth, Penny, John, Matthew (children).

1794 January, RHODES, SARAH, William, Lorohama, John, Alee (children).

1790 April, ROACH, JOHN, Elizabeth (wife).

1783 January, RUFFIN, RICHARD, Avey (wife); children of Purity Deloatch.

S.

1789 April, SANDERS, THOMAS, wife; Wright, John, Benjamin, Elizabeth, Penny, Annie (children).

1782 January, SASSER, JOSIAH, John, William, Susanna, Joseph (children).

1791 April, SIMMS, ROBERT, Mary (wife); Benjamin, Britain, James, Robert, Susanna, Barnes, Abraham (children).

1785 April, SMITH, JOSEPH, Ann (wife); Isaac, Drew, Josiah, Sally (children).

1796 Oct., SMYTH, ARTHUR, Lucretia (wife); James, Polly (children).

1782 January, STEVENS, JAMES, Elizabeth (wife); John (son), and to other children (not named).

T.

1784   January, THOMPSON, JOHN, Rachel (wife); John, William, James, Zadok, Jethro, Sarah, (children).

1783   April, TILTON, JOHN, Elizabeth (wife); William, John, Hannah, Elizabeth, Samuel, Polly, Leonard (children).

1787   January, TOLAR, ROBERT, Robert, John (sons), Delilah Jones, daughter.

1786   July, TOLAR, WILLIAM, Ann (wife); children (not named).

U.

1798   October, UZZELL, ELISHA, Wife; Elisha, Polly, Lucretia. Major, Keziah, James (children).

W.

1794   July, WARWICK, JACOB, Sylvia, Wiot (children).

1795   October, WASDOM, JONATHAN, Sarah (wife); John, David, Avah, Sally (children).

1796   Oct., WATKINS, JOHN, Lydia (wife); John, James, William, Wilson, Matthew, Jesse, Arthur, Ira, Patience, Martha, Lydia, Isabel, Sarah (children).

1794   July, WEST, JOHN, Elizabeth (wife); Charles, Tart, Rachel, Sarah, Alice, Mary (children); Temple and Charles West (grandchildren).

1795   April, WHITFIELD, WILLIAM, Wife; Needham, Lewis, William, Bryan (sons); Elizabeth Campbell, Charity Smith, Rachel Bryan (daughters).

1794   January, WINFIELD, JOSEPH, Sarah and Joseph Winfield (grandchildren).

1784   July, WISE, JAMES, Rebekah (wife); Isaac, Lucy, Thomas, Joseph, Betsy, Mary (children).

1798   April, WOODARD, JOSHUA, Mary (wife); James, Jesse, Elizabeth, Anna (children).

1789   January, WORRELL, DAVID, Wife; James, John, Sarah, Esther (children).

1788   Dec., WORRELL, JOHN, Priscilla (wife).

WILKES COUNTY—WILLS

A.

1786 ALDRIDGE. ELIJAH, Mary (wife); Francis, Edmond and Keziah.

B.

1781 BICKNELL, THOMAS, Rachel (wife); Children (not named).

1784 BISHOP, AVIS, Roger, Francis, and Samuel; Elizabeth Elliott (daughter).

1785 BROWN, JOHN, Elizabeth (wife); John, Reuben, Lydia, Joanna and Rebecca.

C.

1789 COFFEY, JOEL, Martha (wife); James, Joel, Cleveland, Nathan, Katie, Jane and Celia.

1785 COOK. JOHN, Elizabeth (wife); Isaac, Isaiah, Elizabeth and Mary.

1786 CRANE. PHILEMON, Sr. Elizabeth (wife); Philemon, Aaron, Rachel, William, John, James and Mary.

1786 COFFEY, JAMES, Elizabeth (wife); John, James, Reuben, Abious, Eli and Reve; Martha Dunam and Betty Whiteside (daughters).

1796 CARELEY, WILLIAM, Martha (wife); William, Joseph, Larkin, John, Martha, Lucy. Sarah and Wilmuth.

E.

1793 EDMUNDSTON, JAMES, Sarah (wife); Robert and William; Dorothea Duncan and Esther Taylor (daughters); Samuel Edmundston (grandson).

1797 ELLEDGE, JOSEPH, Sarah (wife); Isaac, Jacob and Benjamin.

F.

1786 FUGET, JOHN, Lethea, Ann. Winnie and Patience.

1797 FREEMAN, JAMES, Wife (not named).

G.

1779 GAMBILL, WILLIAM, Mary (wife); Thomas, Henry, James and Sarah.

1782 GRIERSON, JOHN, Nancy (wife); Ann Mitchell and Sarah Demess (daughters); Aquilla, John, Benjamin, John and Jesse Grier; Rachel Mitchell and Sarah Hargrave, (grandchildren).

1796 GREEN, JOSHUA, Sarah (wife); children (not named); Anne Hickerson (daughter).

1799 GORDON, CHARLES, Mary (wife); Nancy B.

1798 GUIN, PETER, Mary and James; Polly Baswell (daughter); Elizabeth and David Hill (grandchildren).

H.

1792 HOOPER, JAMES, Patty (wfe); James and John; Anne Jones, Susanna Parker and Sarah Ann Cooper (daughters).

1793 HIX, DAVID, Samuel and David; John and James Holsclaw (sons-in-law); William, Nancy, Sarah, Thomas and Molly Asher (grandchildren).

1794 HICKSON, MARY, Daniel and Joseph; Jane Miller and Mary Stewart (daughters).

1794 HAMMER, AMBROSE, Ann (Wife); John and Robert; Mary Johnson and Elizabeth Amburge (daughters).

1797 HOLEMAN, THOMAS, Susanna (wife); Absalom, Reuben, Susanna, Rachel. Daniel, Isaac, Thomas, Grace, Elizabeth, Jacob, Margaret and James.

J.

1786 JOHNSON, THOMAS, Rachel (wife); Theophilus, Richard H., John, Benjamin, Rachel, Henry, Philip and Mary.

1789 JOHNSON, JEFFREY, Rachel (wife); Kewis, Jeffrey, George. Samuel, Barbara and Benjamin.

K.

1791 KEELING, OSBURN, Jane (wife); William and Jane.

1799 KING, ROBERT, Mary (wife).

L.

1781 LAWS, WILLIAM, William; Amy Dyer, Mary Cross, Ann Lovelace and Abby Hampton (daughters).

1780 LOW, WILLIAM, Mary (wife); Isaac, Isaiah and David; Stephen Low (grandson).

1795 LEWIS, WILLIAM, Elizabeth (wife); Joseph, Joshua, William, Nathaniel, Benjamin, Sarah, Rachel, Rebecca. and Hannah; Ruth Stinchcombe (daughter).

M.

1779 MALLORY, WILLIAM, Ann, Dorothy, Elizabeth and Mary.

1790 MIZE, JOSHUA, Patty (wife); Isaac, Benjamin. Jeremiah, Lydia and John; Elizabeth Taylor, Edey Chambers, Keziah Chambers, Nancy Brown and Polly Roberts (daughters).

1793 MARTIN, SARAH, Henry, Ann. Thomas and John; Patty Redding (daughter).

1796 MEHAFFEY, THOMAS, Hannah (wife); James, Elizabeth and Thomas; Martha Davis and Isabella Hill (daughters).

1798 MARTIN, ISAAC, Peggy (wife); John; Elizabeth Bagby and Fanny Green (daughters).

N.

1788 NORTHERN, EDMUND, Margaret, John, Rachel, Samuel, Edmund, Mary and Tabitha; Sarah Ferguson and Lucy Ferguson (daughters).

1796 NOLAND, PETER, Sampson, Henry, Pierce and Moses; Martha Carrel, Delilah Davis and Sarah Carrel (daughters).

O.

1788 OWENS, WILLIAM, David, John, William, Thomas and Barnett; Mary Denny, Anne Dudley, and Elizabeth Judd (daughters); Elisha Owen (grandson).

P.

1784 PARKS, JOHN, Wife (not named); Reuben and other children (not named).

1791 PARKS, THOMAS, Priscilla (wife); Peggy, Ambrose, Reuben, Thomas, Aaron and William.

1791 PARKER, JOHN, Mary Ann (wife); James, John, William and Diana.

1793 PARKS, JOHN, John, Samuel, Milly and others (not named); Sarah Sale (daughter).

R.

1792 ROSS, JOHN, Catherine Mehaffey (friend).

1790 RHODES, JOHN, Sarah (wife); John, Nancy and Elizabeth.

1796 ROSE, EMANUEL, Mary (wife); Keziah, Sarah, Elizabeth and Susanna; Mary Holloway (daughter).

S.

1791 STURDIE, WILLIAM, Dorothy Millbanks (daughter).

1781 SMITH, HUGH, Wife (not named); Jonathan, David and Alexander.

1787 SCOTT, HUGH, John, Anna, Nettie, Sarah, Jane, Margaret and William Campbell (all friends); and to his children (not named) "a shilling each."

1788 SALE, WILLIAM, Ann (wife); Cornelius, James, Robert, Leaonard, John, Thomas, Elizabeth, Francis and William; Polly Allen, Sally Robards, Peggy Grant and Molly Martin (daughters).

1791 SLOAN, THOMAS, Sarah (wife); Samuel; Jean Thompson (daughter); Thomas Porterfield (grandson).

1798 SANDERS, WILLIAM, Mary (wife); Cornelius, John, Shadrach and Lucy.

1799 STAMPER, JOHN, SR. Rachel (wife); Jesse and other children (not named).

T.

1793 TERRY, JOHN, Frances (wife); Anne, William, Martha, Joseph, Mary, David, Jesse, Fanny and Hannah.

U.

1787 UPCHURCH, WILLIAM, Sarah (wife); William, Edey, David, Afal, Patty and John; Susanna Pennill (daughter).

W.

1778 WITHERSPOON, JOHN, Wife (not named);
David, Thomas, John, James, Mary, Flora,
Martha, Nancy, Jane and Elizabeth.

1799 WEANT, PETER, Wife (not named); Peter,
Philip and John.

1785 WEBB, JOHN, Ustley (wife); John, Francis,
Culbreth and Hannah.

1790 WITHERSPOON, THOMAS, Joshus, Fitz John,
Daniel, Wesley and Dorcas.

1790 WITHERSPOON, JAMES, John (brother).

1790 WILBANKS, RICHARD, Priscilla (wife); William, Reuben, Nancy, Berryman, John and
Henry; Dolly Sturdie (daughter).

(UNREGISTERED)

A.

1771 ANDERSON, GEORGE T., Mary (wife); Lydia, Elisha, Jerry (children); Kate Harris and Betty Smith (daughters).

1771 ALSTON, SOLOMON, Sarah (wife); Charity, Lemuel, Henry (children); Robert Lewis (friend).

1762 ARENDELL, RICHARD, Eleanor (wife); John, Sarah, Rebekah, Mary, James, Thomas (children).

B.

1770 BRADFORD, PHILIP, Mary (wife); Thomas, Philemon, John, David, Richard (children); Elizabeth Hudspeth and Mary White (daughters).

1753 BLEDSOE, ABRAHAM, Sarah (wife); Isaac, Abraham, Thomas, Jacob, Moses, Aaron (children).

1771 BRASSFIELD, GEORGE, Elizabeth (wife); Caleb, Nancy (children); Abigail Malone, Elizabeth Knott and Fanny Bond (daughters).

1766 BULLOCK, RICHARD, Wife (not named); Zachariah, Leonard, Nathaniel, William, Susanna, John, (children); Sarah Sims, Agatha Nichols and Agnes Williams (daughters).

1772 BOYD, JAMES, Mary (wife); Isabel, Margaret, Samuel (children).

1772 BELL, WILLIAM, Sarah (mother); Joshua (brother); Sarah (sister).

1786 BALL, DAVID, James Johnson (friend).

1757 BRADFORD, RICHARD, Rachel (wife); Richard, John, Sapphira, Elizabeth, (children); Mary Cope, Hannah Poe and Frances Bird, (daughters).

1770 BENTON, SAMUEL, Frances (wife); Samuel Jesse, Penina, Patty, Augustine, (children); Betty Brice (daughter).

1751 BENSON, THOMAS, Sarah (wife); John, Alice, (children).

1762 BRIDGERS, WILLIAMS, Susanna (wife); Joseph (son); Mary Porch, Amy Porch and Susanna Hancock (daughters).

1761 BELL, THOMAS, Mary (wife); Samuel, Thomas, John, Jesse, William, Lucy (children); Ann Riggin and Mary Hartshorn (daughters).

C.

1785 COOK, DOCTOR RICHARD, Richard D, and Rebecca (children).

1761 COOPER, BENJAMIN, Elizabeth (wife); Kenon, Sarah, Grace, William, John, George (children); Mary Jelks and Elizabeth Wiggins (daughters).

D.

1795 DODSON, FRANCIS, William, Charles, Holly, (children); Frances Turner and Polly Fleming (daughters).

1762 DAVIS, RICHARD, Wife (not named); Augustine, Cyrus, Solomon (children); Patience Coyne, Judah Davis and Josephine Berry (daughters); Richard Davis, (grandson).

1768 DRAUGHON, ROBERT, Wife (not named).

1779 DANIEL, JOHN, Celia (wife); Martin (son).

E.

1762 ELWICK, DARWIN, Sarah Willis (niece); children of Benjamin Barton.

F.

1774 FULLILOVE, SUSANNA, Several sisters and cousins.

1771 FOWLER, RICHARD, Grace (wife); William, Richard, Jane, Pharoah (children).

G.

1761 GRIGGS, MINOS, Jane (wife); Minos, John (children).

1766 GOODLOE, JOHN, Susanna (wife); Mary (daughter).

H.

1760 HOWARD, ALEXANDER, Mary (wife); John and Peter Howard (brothers).

1770 HICKS, ABSALOM, Mary (wife).

1749 HOLMES, FREDERICK, Mary (wife); John, Priscilla (children).

1763 HARRIS, SHERWOOD, Jane (wife); Sherwood, Sarah, John, Elizabeth, Anne (children); Mary Hix and Jemima White (daughters).

1781 HIGHTOWER, JOSHUA, Susan (wife); Charnell, Joseph, Robert, Taverner, Epaphroditus (children); Katherine Thorne (daughter).

1760 HUNT, HENRY, Agnes (wife); James, Elizabeth, Henry, William, George, John (children).

1766 HARGRAVE, RICHARD, Richard, John (sons).

L.

1762 LINDSAY, DENNIS, William, Benjamin, Mary, Elizabeth, Katherine, Margaret, Winifred (children).

1766 LAWRENCE, WILLIAM, Deborah (wife); children (not named).

M.

1761 McMILLAN, ALEXANDER, Phoebe (wife); Ammon, Alexander, Henry B., Matthew, James (children); Susanna Beckham and Yourath Basket (daughters).

1762 MACON, GIDEON, Priscilla (wife); Mary, Patty, Martha, John, Nathaniel, Gideon, Harrison, (children); Anne Alston (daughter).

1770 MIARS, MATTHIAS, Mary (wife); Michael (son).

1762 MOSS, WILLIAM, Sarah (wife); children (not named).

1761 MOORE, WILLIAM, Wife (not named); Richard, William, James, John, Holly, Sarah, Edney, Susanna, Anne (children).

1751 MITCHELL, ROBERT, Catherine (wife); Robert, Isaac, Daniel, Mary, Martha, John (children); Susanna Glover and Phoebe Glover (daughters).

1778 MAY, JAMES, Judith, Martha (daughters).

1763 MERSHAW, JOHN, Peter and William Mershaw (brothers).

O.

1762 OLIVER, WILLIAM, Elizabeth (wife); Mary, Latha, Sarah, Polly, Milly (daughters).

P.

1753 PATTERSON, FRANCIS, Mary (wife); unborn child.

1763 PIERCE, JAMES, Elizabeth (wife); Jonas, Philip, Milly, Nancy, Elizabeth, Mary (children).

1759 PRIDDY, ROBERT, Susanna, Patience, Robert, George, William, Thomas (children); Ann Chaven (daughter).

1761 PRIDDY, ROBERT, Eleanor (wife); Robert, Thomas (sons); Eleanor Harlow (daughter).

1764 PARLIC, BENJAMIN, Mary (wife); Charles, Edmond, Benjamin (sons).

1761 PERSON, MARY, Jesse, Lucy, John, Martha (children); Sarah Jones (daughter).

1766 PHIPPS, ISAIAH, Ann (wife); Isaiah (son).

1789 PARRISH, DAVID, Judy (wife); David, Claiborn, Baseker, Sally, Judy, Betty, Anne (children); Sabra Waldrop and Sukey Whichard (daughters); Dicey and Tabby Parrish (granddaughters).

1761 PARKER, ROBERT, Francis (son); Elizabeth Moody (housekeeper).

R.

1772 ROBERTS, RICHARD, David, Willis, Shadrach, Celia, Jesse, Joseph (children); Jane Wharton and Lydia Bridgers (daughters).

1769 ROSE, WILLIAM, Amy (wife); Frederick, William, Elizabeth, Winifred, Patty (children); Sarah Williams (daughter).

1772 RIETHWEIL, LOUIS, Barbara (wife); Louis, Michael, Jacob, John (sons); Margaret Peeler (daughter).

1751 RIEVES, WILLIAM, Margaret (wife); William, James, Benjamin, Burgess, Anne, Malachi, Isaac, Olive (children); Elizabeth Hodges, Mary Carpenter and Sarah Hicks (daughters).

1761 ROBESON, GEORGE, Sarah (mother); children of sons, David, Charles and Israel.

1760 ROBESON, ISRAEL, Matthew, Mary, John, Israel, Sarah, David, Nicholas, Charles, George (children); Susanna Kendrick (daughter).

S.

1752 SHEARON, JOSEPH, Jonathan, John (sons); Jesse Miller (grandson).

1761 SPIVEY, LITTLETON, Ann (wife); Molly, Elizabeth (daughters).

1784 SEARCY, ELIZABETH, William Hargraves, Joseph Moore, Oswald Towns and Martha Tudor (all "natural" children).

1775 SCURRY, GIDEON, Catherine (wife); Thomas, Mary, Elizabeth, Eli, Jesse (children); Sarah Heathone and Lydia Colberdone (daughters).

1770 SMITH, JOHN, Elizabeth Smith (cousin).

1766 SMALLWOOD, WILLIAM, Mary (wife); James, Elisha (sons); Elizabeth Tarvin, Mary Duett, Asenath Foster and Eliza Adcock (daughters).

1766 SIMS, JOHN, Sarah (wife); William, Elisha, Lucretia, Agnes, Sally, Leonard, Cynthia, Susanna, Mary (children); Frances Keeling (daughter).

1789 SMITH, CATHERINE, Catherine McKoy (daughter); William A. McKoy (grandson).

T.

1765 TAYLOR, PHILIP, Mary (wife); Philip, John, James, (children).

V.

1771 VEASEY, EDWARD, Ann (wife); Elizabeth, Ann, Rachel, Elijah (children).

W.

1749 WALSTON, WILLIAM, Wife (not named); Joseph, Mary (children).

1757 WHITE, RICHARD, SR., William, Nicholas, Richard (sons).

1761 WINSTON, ISAAC, Wife (not named); George, John, Mary, Anthony, William (children).

1762 WRIGHT, JOSEPH, John, Joseph, Sarah, William, Jeptha, Ann, Lydia, Elizabeth (children).

1761 WOOD, JOHN, Ann (wife); Britton, Celia, Elizabeth (children).

1767 WILSON, ELEANOR, Lucy Tucker (sister).

1765 WILLIAMS, WILLIAM, Elizabeth (wife); Charles, Stephen (sons); Lucy Pittman (daughter).

1761 WILLIAMS, THOMAS, Wife (not named); Roger, Samuel, William, Thomas (sons).

1772 WHITE, JONATHAN, Sarah (wife); Jonathan, Burgess, William, Philemon (sons).

1760 WOODLIEF, GEORGE, Mary (wife); George, Augustine, Elizabeth, Mary, Martha (children).

1759 WILLIAMS, DANIEL, Wife (not named); Henry, John, James, Joseph, Daniel (children); Mary Mitchell and Maria Goodman (daughters).

1762 WALLACE, JOHN, Isabel (wife); James, Hugh, William, John, Jane, Isabel, Sarah, Elizabeth (children).